The Lost Equilibrium

The Lost Equilibrium

International Relations
in the Post-Soviet Era

Edited by Bettie M. Smolansky
and Oles M. Smolansky

Lehigh
University
Press

Bethlehem: Lehigh University Press
London: Associated University Presses

Associated University Presses
440 Forsgate Drive
Cranbury, NJ 08512

Associated University Presses
16 Barter Street
London WC1A 2AH, England

Associated University Presses
P.O. Box 338, Port Credit
Mississauga, Ontario
Canada L5G 4L8

The paper used in this publication meets the requirements of the American National Standard for Permanence of Paper for Printed Library Materials Z39.48-1984.

Library of Congress Cataloging-in-Publication Data

The lost equilibrium : international relations in the post-Soviet era / edited by Bettie M. Smolansky and Oles M. Smolansky.
    p. cm.
    Includes bibliographical references and index.
    ISBN 0-934223-69-6 (alk. paper)
    1. International relations.   2. Cold War. 3. United States—Foreign relations—Russia (Federation) 4. Russia (Federation)—Foreign relations—United States.   I. Smolansky, Bettie M. (Bettie Moretz), 1940–
II. Smolansky, Oles M.

JZ1242.L67   2001
327.1—dc21   00-066272

For Alvin Z. Rubinstein
scholar, colleague, and friend

Contents

Preface

THIS VOLUME HAS BEEN PRODUCED TO HONOR THE DISTINGUISHED career of our friend and colleague, Dr. Alvin Z. Rubinstein. Dr. Rubinstein, a leading scholar in the field of East-West relations, has been a pioneer in the analysis of the nature of influence relationships between and among nations. He has written extensively on influence and has encouraged others to do so by editing a prestigious series on the topic. Since his career spans much of the cold war, it seemed fitting to focus this volume on its aftermath.

During his long tenure as a member of the Political Science Department at the University of Pennsylvania, Dr. Rubinstein has mentored legions of students, firing their enthusiasm for the understanding of international affairs. He has also encouraged the careers of many junior scholars who did not study with him at Penn through his editorial activities and his work in a number of organizations devoted to the study of international relations. The contributors to this volume were chosen in part because of their various acknowledged intellectual debts to Dr. Rubinstein. They have written their analyses secure in the knowledge that he will respect even those arguments with which he might substantively disagree.

A few words about the practical background and logistics of the volume's preparation also seem appropriate. First, the idea of creating a *Festschrift* to honor Dr. Rubinstein arose a few years ago, and the editors owe special thanks to Dr. George Ginsburgs of Rutgers University Law School for his excellent formative suggestions during the early stages of the project.

Second, it is important for readers to remember that when scholars write about current international affairs there is always the danger that their analyses will be overtaken by events. Thus, it should be kept in mind that the final drafts of the contributed chapters were completed during 1999, some earlier and some later in the year.

Finally, a few words about the division of labor between the co-editors seem in order. While they constructed the theme and structure of the volume in standard collaborative fashion, Oles Smolansky has taken the primary organizing role, soliciting the contributions and dealing with the publisher. He is also the author of the chapter on Ukraine. Bettie Smolansky is the author of the introduction and conclusion, which attempt to create an appropriate context for the understanding of the contributed chapters and to summarize their implications for the shape of the evolving international system after the end of the cold war.

Introduction: Interesting Times

IN 1984, THE POPULAR CARTOONIST JIM BERRY PRODUCED A CARTOON for his syndicated feature "Berry's World" that depicted then Soviet Minister of Defense Marshal Ustinov saying to General Secretary Chernenko,

> Remember, Comrade, people who are willing to destroy an efficient telephone system may not be playing with a full deck.

The reference, of course, was to the breakup of the American Telephone and Telegraph Company (AT&T) underway at the time as a result of the settlement of a protracted antitrust battle between the company and the U.S. Justice Department. The potential for abuse of the kind of untrammeled power represented by monopolies is widely understood, so the breakup of "Ma Bell," then one of the world's largest monopolies, was seen by many as a highly desirable objective.

The accord between the government and AT&T returned competition to the telephone business in the United States (presumably a "socially desirable" end), but it also led to the deconstruction of a system of telecommunications that for many years had been the envy of the world. The irony of this could not have been lost on political leaders in the Soviet Union whose own telephone system was notorious for its unreliability. Thus, Berry's cartoon contains that kernel of truth that is the hallmark of all good political satire.

The analogy to the dissolution of the USSR is equally striking. For almost fifty years following the end of World War II, the emergence of technologies of mass destruction of such power and magnitude as to threaten the very survival of the human race, concomitant with a seemingly irreconcilable conflict between two superpowers who held most of that power, came to be called simply "the cold war." Serious analyses of the international scene almost always contained one or more of the standard innumerable metaphoric references to the potential for nuclear annihilation (e.g., nuclear holocaust, "the nuclear sword of Damocles," the

11

Union of Concerned Scientists' nuclear clock approaching midnight, and so on). However, despite such scares as the U-2 episode, the Cuban Missile crisis, America's Vietnam misadventure, the Kremlin's equally ill-advised foray into Afghanistan, and scores of lesser crises, the superpowers somehow managed to avoid the kind of direct confrontation that led beyond the brink.

Indeed, there evolved in the international arena a kind of system in equilibrium, one which had a certain level of dependability to it from the perspective of actors on the international scene. It came to be seen by many of its participants and analysts as the twentieth century's "great game," and some scholars even tried to formalize the analysis of the metaphor by applying *game theory*.[1]

The game metaphor, as international observers have generally used it, worked fairly well as an organizing tool in a bipolar world. That is, when there were two superpowers and it was widely assumed (both by participants and spectators) that gains for the one constituted losses for the other and vice-versa (i.e., that they were playing a "zero-sum" game), then assessing the state of international affairs or at least "keeping score" was relatively simple. However, even in the dark days of the cold war, some scholars thought that approach oversimplified.[2]

With the collapse of the USSR, it is tempting to turn away from the game metaphor completely, adopting instead a *market model*, especially since the main arena of competition among nations takes place increasingly in the economic realm. That is, the United States now remains the world's only full-scale superpower, but its own democratic-constitutional system constrains the use of its military might in the most crude, coercive form. Thus, the military-strategic factor, having become as it has on the world stage a relatively settled matter, ironically has *declined* in significance. (The opportunities for military mischief by smaller states pursuing regional rivalries, of course, should not be underestimated; if anything, they become even more complex and tempting, especially given the level of the arms trade between/among the First, Second, and Third worlds.)

Thus, the major form of competition among the key players on the international scene now seems to focus primarily on their *economic interests*, and so the use of a market model seems apt. However, a market model is in some ways even more complex than that of the game, for there are actually many "markets" in most developed countries and their interests do not always coincide. Moreover, there are supranational markets and economic coalitions of a sometimes stable and sometimes shifting nature among subgroups of nations. Indeed, the role of huge multinational corporations as quasi-independent actors on the international scene is much discussed but still little understood.

Even more problematic is the fact that a primary assumption of economic markets is that they work best (or at least, predictably) when enacted by rational, well-informed, self-maximizing participants. One can see immediately how unrealistic it is to assume that modern nation-states (especially democracies with their many and conflict-ridden constituencies) will behave in such a fashion. (This omits the further complicating factor of the inclination of politicians, both democratic and authoritarian, to maximize short-run as opposed to long-run advantages.)

It may well be that the "cobweb model" posited by J. W. Burton is the most accurate representation of the reality of international relations.[3] Unfortunately, such a model does little to simplify the task of analysis, for it really suggests that the irreducible variable is *relationships* and that there are separate relationships for various domains of activity (trade, technology, and so on) and each is a separate cobweb overlaid upon others. The cobwebs are not even strictly separate (they are merely depicted as such to facilitate our understanding), so the reality is, once again, much more complex than the model, and the model itself is so intricate as to provide little predictive utility.

Accordingly, while it may seem less satisfying than these neatly constructed models now fashionable among many scholars of international affairs, we believe that any attempt to understand the changing dynamic of international affairs in the post-Soviet world is best served by use of a more loosely constructed framework which examines the distinctive national interests and influence relationships of key players in a representative set of bi- and multilateral relationships.

Our basic premise is that the world stands today at a watershed, and that there is an urgent need to rethink the nature of the international political environment. Clearly, we are experiencing the emergence of small and medium-sized entities that want to further their local ambitions in the new climate which has removed some of the old restraints on their freedom of action but has also erased the balancing opportunities that were a latent effect of the old superpower rivalry. These actors are thus groping for new methods to pursue their interests as they define them. The former rivals, in the meantime, are also busy reassessing and redefining their relationships both with each other and various third parties.

The implicit methodological framework which underlies the

book is that when attempting to understand the complex play of diverse forces which determine the nature of international affairs, the case method undertaken by a scholar who is deeply immersed in the topic is almost always the best approach. Thus, in soliciting scholars (all recognized experts on specific topics/regions of the international scene) to contribute a chapter to this anthology, the editors deliberately provided them not with a narrow, constraining framework into which they had to fit their separate analyses but with loosely focused directions built around a set of general concerns. Most important among the issues raised was the effect of the demise of the USSR and the emergence of Russia as its principal legatee on the various topics under consideration. Our authors were also asked to consider the effect on relations between their focus issue on the one hand and the United States and Russia on the other. Contributors were also asked to speculate, if they felt competent to do so, about how the picture might change under varying circumstances, as well as to offer their professional assessment of the likely future of Russia in the next decade or two. Because the primary focus of the editors' collaborative scholarly work has been on the international affairs of the former Soviet Union, this collection is inevitably organized to emphasize the changing position of its principal heir, Russia, even though American views and interests are also discussed. Thus, the contributed chapters are arranged in five sections. The first provides a salient backdrop to the subsequent case studies by examining one key aspect of the West's failure to anticipate the collapse of the Soviet empire. The next three parts focus in ascending order of their relative importance to Moscow on (1) the Third World[4]; (2) Europe (West and East); and (3) the Commonwealth of Independent States. The last section examines the evolving relationship between the United States and Russia as former superpower rivals now trying to develop a *modus vivendi*.

In chapter 1, Melvin A. Goodman, a former Central Intelligence Agency (CIA) analyst, examines in some detail the period leading up to the demise of the USSR, showing how the ideological mindset of the political leaders of that agency (and most of the rest of the American intelligence community) led them simply to ignore any and all evidence that the old Soviet system was on the brink of collapse. This analysis can be seen as a cautionary tale, for it shows how hard it is to change old patterns of thought and how the failure to do so can lead policymakers to continue "fighting the last war" and to neglect opportunities for improving relations in a variety of international contexts.

One of the grand, diverse arenas of the cold war, especially in the period following the collapse of colonialism, was the array of regions that have come to be called the Third World, and a number of those regions are examined in part 2. Almost everywhere one looked around the globe, throughout the sixties, seventies, and eighties, the rival superpowers competed almost mindlessly for what usually was vaguely called "influence" in scores of less developed nations, searching for "friends" or "clients." Even when the matter seemed a settled issue in a particular country, given the potential and actual levels of political instability in such nations, a change of regime could transform yesterday's enemy into today's ally.

Parenthetically, conspiracy theorists in each bloc almost always cast the blame for the overthrow of a friendly government at the doorstep of subversive activity by the rival superpower, but the true roots of most such upheavals were domestic to the core.

Geopolitics and history, however, combined to give differing relative advantages and disadvantages to East or West in various areas of the world. Thus, the editors have asked a number of scholars to contribute to this anthology intensive analyses of the impact of the end of the cold war and its attendant superpower rivalry on specific regions of the less developed world.

W. Raymond Duncan in chapter 2 looks at the evolution of international affairs in Latin America, long an acknowledged American sphere of influence, despite Washington's fears of subversion in a number of its countries since Castro's rise to power in Cuba. Given this set of circumstances, Duncan examines carefully the issue of whether and to what extent the current situation in Latin America has been a result of ongoing forces already in progress prior to the end of the cold war or has resulted partly from these dramatic changes in the world arena. He also assesses the future prospects of this region.

In chapter 3, Marina Ottaway examines the impact of the cold war and its cessation on the nations of Sub-Saharan Africa. Africa was one of the less important venues of superpower competition even during the heyday of the cold war, despite occasional headline-grabbing events in such areas as the Congo, Eritrea, Ethiopia, Somalia, and others. As Ottaway makes clear, little has changed to enhance the status of most of these states, many of which are among the world's poorest nations; indeed, the prospects for many of them have actually declined.

In chapter 4, Henri J. Barkey probes the changing dynamic of the Middle East that has been evoked by the collapse of the USSR.

He considers a number of broad conceptual and geopolitical changes, as well as the indirect impact of these developments on the domestic political structures of the region.

Since Barkey's analysis focuses most intensively upon the Arab-Israeli sector, Stephen Page in chapter 5 examines in greater depth two distinctive subregions of the Middle East, namely the Red Sea and the Persian Gulf. He looks with special care at the reasons for the quite different levels of interest which these two areas now draw from external great powers.

Shirin Tahir-Kheli assesses the impact of the end of the East-West struggle in South Asia in chapter 6. That struggle has long been intertwined with the rivalry between the region's two major powers—India and Pakistan. Thus, with the end of the cold war, enormous changes in international relations in the subcontinent seemed inevitable. In her case study, Tahir-Kheli carefully analyzes the nature of those changes to date and the prospects for the future.

As Charles E. Ziegler points out in chapter 7, Russia is inevitably interested in the politics of East Asia. After all, great quantities of its territory (if not its population) lie in that region. Thus, the chapter considers the effects of the collapse of the USSR on the regional power balance and on the nature of Russia's identity and ties to other countries within the region. It also evaluates Moscow's participation in the area's developing international organizations.

Less extensive in terms of territory than the Third World, but more significant to Russia and the United States in almost every other aspect of importance to them or any major power, is Europe. Two chapters investigate the emerging international dynamic in Western and Eastern Europe. In chapter 8, Stephen Blank examines the challenges and opportunities presented by the disintegration of the old Eastern bloc for the Western alliance. He contends that the Western powers were initially ill-equipped to deal with the inevitable transformations wrought by the disintegration of the Eastern bloc. However, he sees more recent events, especially the NATO response in the Kosovo crisis, as hopeful signs that Western leaders have begun to see the importance of preserving Europe's indivisibility.

Christopher Jones explains the "logic of NATO expansion" in chapter 9. That logic is based on the evolution of what he labels "the Brussels Syndrome," a self-perpetuating cycle by which the East-West struggle turned the shared defense arrangements that began with NATO into a much more encompassing form of Western cooperation and transformation. He also points out that the

Warsaw Pact has left some residual effects within the countries of the old Eastern bloc which provide significant opportunities for the whole of Europe, if only the will and the way can be found to seize them.

While they differ in their specific focus, both of these chapters implicitly invite the reader to abandon the cold war habit of thinking about Europe exclusively in terms of East and West and realize that, with the collapse of the Warsaw Pact, analysts and policymakers should now start thinking about the prospect of Europe as a single region.

While Europe will inevitably be a major focus of Russia's foreign policy (and vice versa), even more immediately significant to Moscow is the contiguous area known traditionally as "the Near Abroad," now mostly encompassed by the Commonwealth of Independent States (CIS). In chapter 10, Oles M. Smolansky examines the inescapably close but difficult relationship that has emerged in the past decade between Russia and Ukraine. Among all the former Soviet republics, Ukraine has long been the most important to Moscow. The cultures and the economies of Russia and Ukraine have traditionally been intimately interconnected, before, during, and after the Bolshevik era. In the post-Soviet era the two also find themselves interdependent on a level with which neither feels totally comfortable, but which they have had to learn to tolerate.

The chapters in the final section scrutinize the relationship between the two former superpowers, and there are many points of agreement between the two authors, especially as pertains to the causes of the Soviet Union's collapse and the early promise of the new apparently cooperative relationship between the two former rivals. However, they diverge in their views concerning the causes and nature of the subsequent decline in the early spirit of harmony within that evolving relationship.

Henry Trofimenko, chief analyst of the Institute for the U.S. and Canada Studies of the Russian Academy of Sciences, understandably places most of the blame for the lost opportunities of the immediate post–cold war era on the shortcomings of Western leaders. In chapter 11, he acknowledges the souring of relations but cites as the primary cause the West's failure to deliver most of the promised assistance to a Russia struggling to emerge from its long history of totalitarian rule and to become a modern democracy with a market-driven economy. Indeed, the pronounced bitterness of tone in Trofimenko's appraisal, given that he is as well-informed and pro-Western an analyst as one is likely to find among the Russian intelligentsia, should sound as a warning bell for those who simply assume that because the cold war is over and the West has "won," old rivalries have been obliterated and/or they have lost all their significance.

In chapter 12, Harvey Sicherman, an American analyst with the Foreign Policy Research Institute (Philadelphia), places more emphasis on the failures of Yeltsin and the rest of Russia's leaders. He does not, however, spare American leaders (Bush and Clinton) for their vacillating policies, based, in his view, not on reality but on their desires. Moreover, he sees little hope of improvement in the situation under the new Russian leadership until this problem with "blurred vision" is remedied.

The ancient Chinese are said to have used as a subtle and ironic curse, "May you live in interesting times." We do live in interesting times, and whether they prove a blessing or a curse will probably rest upon the ability of Western leaders to make their democratic electorates understand just how interesting (and complex) they really are.

That is, we must resist the temptation to fall into self-congratulatory complacency over the West's "victory" in the cold war, buying into the laughable contention that somehow, therefore, we have achieved "the end of history." These times, like all the interesting eras before them, are full of both promise and challenge. Only those prepared to sift through the surface of events to gain some understanding of their meaning are likely to surmount those challenges and achieve those promises.

NOTES

1. Rarely have analysts of international relations actually used game theory in the formal sense of attempting mathematical estimates of outcomes in competitive and cooperative games, for it makes a number of assumptions about the contest (limited number of players, clear motives, perfect versus imperfect information, and so on) that are patently inapplicable to international affairs, but the metaphor of the game and the conceptual language of strategy analysis has been quite popular in recent years.

2. An earlier work by the editors (Smolansky, O. M., and B. M. Smolansky, *The USSR and Iraq: The Soviet Quest for Influence*. Durham: Duke University Press, 1991) makes this point in a number of ways.

3. The model is explained fully by Burton in his article, "International Relations or World Society?" in *The Study of World Society: A London Perspective*, Pittsburgh: University of Pittsburgh International Studies Association, 1974.

4. The term "Third World" is used here somewhat arbitrarily to indicate a *region* most of whose nations are less developed countries (LDCs). This does not mean that such a region has no developed nations; for example, while we are including East Asia in the analysis of Third World regions, the area contains Japan, which is undoubtedly one of the world's most highly developed countries.

Abbreviations

AIOC: Azerbaijan International Operating Company
ABM: Anti-Ballistic Missile Treaty
ANC: African National Congress
APEC: Asia-Pacific Economic Cooperation
ASEAN: Association of Southeast Asian Nations
BMD: Ballistic Missile Defense
CACM: Central American Common Market
CENTCOM: Central Command (US)
CFA: Communaute Financiere Africaine
CFE: Conventional Forces in Europe
CFSP: Common Foreign and Security Policy
CIA: Central Intelligence Agency
CIS: Commonwealth of Independent States
CMEA: Council for Mutual Economic Assistance
COCOM: Coordinating Committee for Multilateral Export Controls
CSCE: Council for Security and Cooperation in Europe
DIA: Defense Intelligence Agency
DCI: Director of Central Intelligence
DDI: deputy director of intelligence
DRC: Democratic Republic of the Congo
DPRK: Democratic People's Republic of Korea (North Korea)
ECOWAS: Economic Community of West African States
ECOMOG: Economic Community of West African States Monitoring Group
ECSC: European Coal and Steel Community
EEC: European Economic Community

EU: European Union
FMLN: Farabundo Marti National Liberation Front
FIS: Front Islamique de Salut (Islamic Liberation Front)
FRG: Federal Republic of Germany
FTA: Free Trade Area
FTAA: Free Trade Area of the Americas
GCC: Gulf Cooperation Council
GDP: Gross Domestic Product
GDR: German Democratic Republic
GNP: gross national product
GPC: General People's Congress
IAEA: International Atomic Energy Agency
ICBM: Intercontinental Ballistic Missiles
ICTY: International Criminal Tribunal for Yugoslavia
IFOR: Implementation Force
IMEMO: Institute of World Economics and International Relations
IMF: International Monetary Fund
IRA: Irish Republican Army
ISKAN: USA and Canada Institute
KEDO: Korean Energy Development Organization
KLA: Kosovo Liberation Army
LDC: less-developed country
MAD: mutually assured destruction
MBFR: mutual and balanced force reductions
MERCOSUR: Mercado Comun del Sur (South American Common Market)
MIRV: multiple independently targeted re-entry vehicles
MPLA: Movimento Popular de Libertacao de Angola
NACC: North Atlantic Cooperation Council

NAFTA: North American Free Trade Agreement

NAM: nonaligned movement

NATO: North Atlantic Treaty Organization

NJM: New Jewell Movement

NIC: National Intelligence Council

NPT: Nuclear Non-Proliferation Treaty

NCS: National Security Council

OAS: Organization of American States

OPANAL: Organismo para la Proscripcion de las Armas Nucleares en la America Latina y el Caribe (organization that monitors compliance with nuclear non-proliferation treaty in the region)

OPEC: Organization of Petroleum Exporting Countries

OSCE: Organization for Security and Cooperation in Europe

PfP: Partnership for Peace

PKK: Kurdistan Workers' Party

PLO: Palestine Liberation Organization

PRC: People's Republic of China

RFE: Russian Far East

RMA: revolution in military affairs

ROK: Republic of Korea

RPF: Rwandan Patriotic Front

SADC: Southern Africa Development Community

SADF: South African Defense Force

SDI: Strategic Defense Initiative

SEATO: Southeast Asia Treaty Organization

SOE: state-owned enterprise

START I and II: Strategic Arms Reduction Treaty

TMD: theater missile defense

UAE: United Arab Emirates

UNITA: Uniao Nacional para a Independencia Total de Angola

UNSCOM: United Nations Special Commission

VAT: value-added tax

WEU: Western European Union

WMD: weapons of mass destruction

WP: Warsaw Pact

WTO: Warsaw Treaty Organization (same as Warsaw Pact)

YSP: Yemeni Socialist Party

The Lost Equilibrium

I
The Backdrop:
An Intelligence Failure

The CIA and the Soviet Union:
The Politics of Getting It Wrong

MELVIN A. GOODMAN

> "The question is," said Alice, "whether you *can*
>   make words mean so many different things."
>   "The question is," said Humpty Dumpty, "which
> is to be the master—that's all."
> —Lewis Carroll, *Through the Looking Glass*

> "Facts can confuse."
> —CIA Director William J. Casey, 1985

THE QUESTION ABOUT WHO STARTED THE COLD WAR HAS BEEN RE-placed by why the cold war ended the way it did. The answers to the latter question may never be satisfactory to scholars and students of the cold war, but we already know that the collapse of the Warsaw Pact and the Soviet Union totally surprised U.S. policymakers. The Central Intelligence Agency (CIA) had provided no warning. President George Bush stated that he had no idea the Berlin Wall was coming down, and his national security adviser Brent Scowcroft could not recall receiving any CIA warning about the Soviet demise.[1] President Ronald Reagan's last national security adviser and Bush's chairman of the joint chiefs General Colin Powell has written that CIA specialists could not "anticipate events much better than a layman watching television."[2] Former CIA Director Admiral Stansfield Turner charges that the agency's "corporate view missed by a mile" and that it "should not gloss over the enormity of the failure to forecast the magnitude of the Soviet crisis."[3]

The memoirs of former Secretary of State George Shultz offer the best description of the CIA's failure to track the Soviet decline and the revolutionary impact of Gorbachev's leadership. Shultz believed that "CIA analysis was distorted by strong views about policy" and accused CIA Director William Casey of providing "bum dope" to the president. He warned the White House that the agency was "unable to perceive that change was coming in the Soviet Union."[4] He charged that acting CIA Director Robert Gates was trying to "manipulate me" and reminded Gates that the CIA was "usually wrong" about Moscow, having dismissed Gorbachev's policies as "just another Soviet attempt to deceive us."[5] Even "when it became evident that the Soviet Union was in fact changing, the CIA line was that the changes wouldn't really make a difference."[6]

The CIA's failure to recognize the weakness of the Soviet Union and the importance of Gorbachev had serious implications for U.S. national security. The Reagan administration unnecessarily increased defense spending, dragged its feet on arms control, and missed opportunities to resolve regional confrontations. In addition, there were hidden costs. Islamic militants in Afghanistan, funded by the CIA, were responsible for the bombing of the World Trade Center in New York.

THE PROCESS OF POLITICIZATION

Casey and Gates used a variety of methods to politicize intelligence production on the Soviet Union. Occasionally, they forced a particular line of analysis on assessments (as they did on Soviet involvement in international terrorism, Soviet responsibility for the attempted assassination of the Pope, and Soviet policy toward Iran). They rejected papers not compatible with their views. Gates killed a paper that concluded (correctly) that Moscow would not deliver MiG-29s to Nicaragua; he said the CIA should not "go out on a limb" on this issue.[7] Finally, they manipulated the intelligence structure in order to encourage assessments that reinforced their views.

Gates denied his personal role in politicizing intelligence at his confirmation hearings in 1991. Nevertheless, he left little doubt that the intelligence process had been corrupted during the Casey era. Eventually, he acknowledged that he watched Casey "on issue after issue sit in meetings and present intelligence framed in terms of the policy he wanted pursued."[8] Gates did not explain his own failure to correct Casey. In his memoirs, however, he conceded that he had underestimated the dramatic change of course in Soviet policy and had not anticipated Gorbachev's strategic retreat abroad or his destruction of the Soviet system at home.[9] Indeed, Gates and the CIA were wrong on the biggest intelligence issues of the cold war: the strength of the Soviet Union and the intentions of its leaders.

Failure to predict, anticipate, or even imagine the convulsions associated with Moscow's demise followed a forty-five-year period when the CIA's primary focus and 70 percent of its budget were on the USSR and its empire. Instead of conducting a *post mortem* of what went wrong in the 1980s, however, the CIA has tried to exonerate itself. Determined to gloss over the enormity of the agency's analytical failure, Gates proclaimed that the CIA had looked into the matter with great care and found little to fault in its performance.[10] His successors, Jim Woolsey and John Deutch, accepted his verdict.

For the past several years, in fact, the CIA has waged a campaign to demonstrate it anticipated the Soviet collapse. The agency declassified selected documents that suggested it had provided warning of the Soviet demise. Deputy Director of Intelligence (DDI) Douglas MacEachin, who had been the senior office director for the Soviet Union during the 1980s, led this effort. He made sure the documents were given to journalists from the *Los Angeles Times* and the *Baltimore Sun* as background for articles to demonstrate that the CIA "got it right."

The documents also were provided to consultants with close ties to the agency. Former agency consultant Abraham Becker defended the CIA's analysis of the Soviet economy and dismissed the notion that the agency had "cooked the books." Jeffrey Richelson and former agency analyst Bruce Berkowitz cited the CIA documents in a journal article that concluded the agency had been vindicated.

As part of this effort, the CIA entered into a cooperative venture with Harvard University's Kennedy School of Government, financing a case study that concluded the CIA "got it right." The case study was written by a former wire service reporter with no experience in national security policy or Soviet politics. Her methodology consisted of reviewing the declassified documents and interviewing selected CIA officials eager to defend their own analytical views.[11] The author made no attempt to talk to agency critics and made no use of the critical commentary on the CIA offered in the hearings for Gates in 1991, described as "essential reading" on the workings of the intelligence bureaucracy.

Both the CIA and the Kennedy School have benefited from this ethically questionable collaboration. The CIA received high marks from Harvard, and the Kennedy School received millions of dollars in CIA research contracts. MacEachin, now on a sabbatical at the Kennedy School, has completed his own monograph on the CIA's track record; not surprisingly, the agency published it.[12]

Much of the commentary on the Soviet record focused on whether the agency predicted a coup attempt against Gorbachev in 1991, obfuscating more important questions. The CIA must be judged on whether it provided U.S. leaders with accurate assessments of Moscow's weakness and vulnerability and whether it recognized that Gorbachev's stated intentions were genuine. The CIA failed on both counts. It issued only limited warning of Soviet weakness and no warning that the strategic relationship between the United States and the Soviet Union was about to change radically. It therefore could not begin to address the convulsions that accompanied the Soviet decline. Indeed, CIA estimates in the mid-1980s concluded that Gorbachev "endorsed well-established goals for expanded Soviet power and influence" and that Soviet leaders would "run a greater risk of military confrontation with the United States and of actual combat with major powers."[13]

A HISTORY OF PRESSURE

Prior to the Casey-Gates era, the CIA had a good record on sensitive military issues and consistently resisted pressure to slant intelligence to support policy. The CIA demonstrated, for example, that Soviet surface-to-air missiles could not be upgraded to an anti-ballistic missile (ABM) defense, which led to the ABM treaty in 1972. The CIA maintained that because the Soviet SS-9 ICBM was highly inaccurate and did not have multiple, independently targeted reentry vehicles (MIRVs), it could not threaten the U.S. ICBM force. This led to the first strategic arms treaty in 1972. These views repudiated the assessments of President Nixon's national security adviser Henry Kissinger and Secretary of Defense Melvin Laird, who had argued that the Soviets were going for a first-strike nuclear capability in order to justify a U.S. ABM system. Laird and Kissinger selectively leaked sensitive intelligence to buttress their case, but CIA analysts held their ground.

CIA strategic assessments on the Soviet military provided early warning of new Soviet weapon systems. With the exception of Soviet atomic and nuclear testing in the late 1940s and early 1950s, few Soviet military developments surprised U.S. policymakers. While the CIA exaggerated the operational dates and rates of deployment of many Soviet weapon systems, its overall track record was far better than that of any other institution, particularly the

Pentagon's Defense Intelligence Agency (DIA), which resorted to worst case assessments to justify U.S. defense spending.

CIA scientists developed U-2 and SR-71 reconnaissance aircraft and satellite reconnaissance vehicles, which have played a major role in our collection capabilities since the 1950s and have given the United States a decided advantage in all flash point situations involving the Soviet Union since the Cuban missile crisis. Using data from these systems, the CIA provided the Eisenhower administration with evidence that there was no bomber gap and convinced the Kennedy administration that there was no missile gap.

CIA data collection and analysis enabled the United States to verify arms control agreements and supported the Coordinating Committee for Multilateral Export Controls (COCOM), which limited the economic development of Communist states during the cold war. CIA collection currently enables the United Nations and the International Atomic Energy Agency to monitor strategic developments in Iraq and North Korea and contributes to peacekeeping efforts in Bosnia. The Clinton administration, thanks to CIA analysis, was aware of violations of embargo arrangements in the former Yugoslavia and Serbian genocidal crimes in Bosnia. In short, objective intelligence remains essential to our national security.

INTELLIGENCE POLITICIZED

The CIA's objectivity on many critical issues, particularly those concerning the Soviet Union, ended abruptly in 1981 when Bill Casey became director of central intelligence (DCI). For the first time, the DCI became a member of the president's cabinet.[14] Bob Gates became Casey's DDI in 1982 and also chaired the National Intelligence Council. For the first time, one individual had the last word on all national intelligence estimates and all current intelligence. Gates appointed MacEachin (eventually deputy director for intelligence) and then George Kolt (currently national intelligence officer for Russia) to head the office of Soviet analysis from 1983 to 1991; they were in command of Soviet assessments during the period of politicization.

The USSR and International Terrorism

Casey cooked the books in his very first intelligence estimate, which dealt with the Soviet Union and international terrorism.

The day after Reagan's inauguration, Secretary of State Alexander Haig, believing that Moscow had tried to assassinate him in Europe where he served as supreme allied commander, linked the Soviet Union to all acts of international terrorism.[15] There was no evidence to support such a charge but Casey had read the late Claire Sterling's *The Terror Network* and—like Haig—was convinced that a Soviet conspiracy was behind global terrorism. Specialists at the CIA dismissed the book, knowing that much of it was based on CIA "black propaganda," anticommunist allegations planted in the European press. But Casey contemptuously told CIA analysts that he had learned more from Sterling than from all of them.

State Department officials requested a national intelligence estimate on the subject of international terrorism in order to convince Haig that Moscow was not the coordinator of international terrorism. Haig's special consultant at the department was Michael Ledeen, who believed that international terrorism was a "sort of Wurlitzer being played by people in the basement of the Kremlin." Haig also had support from State Department counselor Robert MacFarlane and Director of Policy Planning Paul Wolfowitz, who believed that an intelligence estimate that contradicted the views of the secretary would be embarrassing. Few people in the intelligence community shared Haig's views, and a senior official at the CIA told the author of the estimate that "we will have to let Haig down, but we must do it gently."

The estimate, coordinated by the entire intelligence community, was the first ever on the Soviets and terrorism, and became the most contentious intelligence document produced since the Vietnam War. It asserted that Moscow provided arms and training to groups such as the Palestine Liberation Organization (PLO) that conducted terrorism and that Moscow's East European allies offered safe haven to terrorists from a variety of groups. But it stated there was no evidence that Moscow encouraged or directed these groups to commit terrorist acts and no evidence of Soviet links to such terrorist groups as the Red Brigades in Italy, Baader-Meinhof in West Germany, or the IRA. In fact, there was evidence to the contrary.

The State Department gave this message to Haig, who accused the drafters of "naivete." The CIA gave the same message to Casey, who hit the roof and exercised the first ideological veto of a national intelligence estimate. The drafters did not know that Casey already had told a skeptical Senate Select Committee on Intelligence that Moscow directed all international terrorism; his briefings convinced Senator Barry Goldwater that the director was a loose cannon who should be replaced.

Having rejected the estimate, Casey turned to the DIA, whose director, the late General Eugene Tighe, argued that the lack of evidence of Soviet support for terrorism actually demonstrated how clever the Soviets were. The DIA draft was a worst-case document that even Casey and Gates would not release. A year later, the estimate finally was completed by a visiting scholar on loan from Rutgers University, Professor Richard Mansbach, who had never participated in an intelligence estimate and did not review the voluminous files on Soviet activities for this one. Casey had succeeded in "judge shopping in the courthouse," finding a loyal apparatchik to agree with his verdict that Moscow was "deeply engaged in support for revolutionary violence worldwide."[16]

The estimate on terrorism was widely repudiated in the policy and intelligence communities, contributing to a decline in the CIA's credibility. Secretary Shultz, Haig's successor, completely disagreed with the estimate and shelved it. Judge William Webster, Casey's successor, repudiated it in public. No intelligence service in West Europe supported the CIA view on terrorism and even Israel's Mossad was incredulous. The exercise created an atmosphere of distrust and suspicion at the CIA; the agency created to encourage diversity of views and the search for truth had been unable to protect itself from Casey's political manipulation.

The Papal Canard

Gates used similar techniques four years later to get a Papal plot assessment, citing another Sterling book—*The Time of the Assassins*—which traced the assassination attempt to the KGB. When the CIA produced a specious assessment in 1985, charging the Kremlin with the assassination attempt against Pope John Paul II, its politicization of intelligence on the Soviet Union reached rock bottom. Earlier CIA assessments—and Gates's own testimony to the Senate Select Committee on Intelligence in 1983—had concluded that Moscow had no role in the papal plot; senior officials of the directorate of operations had informed Casey and Gates that Moscow had stopped political assassinations and that neither the Soviets nor the Bulgarians were involved.

But Casey wanted a document that would undermine Shultz's efforts to improve relations with Moscow, and Gates made sure that carefully selected CIA analysts worked *in camera* to prevent proper vetting and coordination of the assessment. An internal

CIA *postmortem* concluded several months after publication of the paper that the assessment had "stacked the deck" and "circumvented" the coordination process; the authors of the *postmortem*—a panel of senior managers at the CIA—described the assessment as "deliberately skewed" and stated that they could find "no one at the working level in the directorates of intelligence or operations—other than the primary authors of the paper—who agreed with the thrust of the assessment."[17]

Indeed, "Agca's Attempt to Kill the Pope: The Case for Soviet Involvement" read like a novelist's fantasy of Communist conspiracy, but Gates's covering note to the president described the report as a "comprehensive examination" that "we feel able to present . . . with some confidence."[18] The character of the still classified report is revealed in its reasoning: "The Soviets were reluctant to invade Poland in 1981 so they decided to demoralize [the Polish] opposition by killing the Polish Pope."[19] The report conceptually tracked an earlier article by a former CIA analyst and then Rand official Harry Gelman, who concluded that, "since the Soviets have not been blamed by world opinion thus far, they are then more inclined than before to undertake adventurous actions."[20] Casey was not going to let the facts stand in his way, and Gates again pandered to the Casey agenda, making sure that the draft document was reviewed in less than twenty-four hours and not seen by senior officials familiar with the issue.

Arms to Iran

CIA also provided an intelligence rationale for arms sales to Iran in 1985. For several years, the CIA and the intelligence community had agreed that Moscow had failed to gain influence in Tehran, that Soviet-Iranian relations were severely strained, and that Moscow was unlikely to consider military intervention. Suddenly, in May 1985, CIA's Graham Fuller collaborated with National Security Council (NSC) officials and prepared an estimate that described Iran as a promising target of opportunity for the Soviet Union and predicted a resumption of Soviet arms sales to Iran. There were no intelligence documents to support any of these judgments.[21] At the same time, Fuller distributed his own memorandum to senior policymakers encouraging Washington to steal a march on Moscow by cultivating so-called moderates in the Khomaini regime, although the consensus of the intelligence community was that there were no such moderates.

THE SOVIET THREAT

Casey and Gates did their greatest damage by influencing the CIA's estimates on the Soviet military. Exaggerated estimates of the military and political power of the Red Army were used to justify increased U.S. defense spending and led to the most significant U.S. intelligence failure since Pearl Harbor—the failure to chart the weakness and collapse of the Soviet Union. The CIA asserted (incorrectly) that the Soviets viewed the 1980s as a "decade of heightened competition in which they will run a greater risk of military confrontation with the United States and of actual combat with major powers."[22]

The CIA's most important series of estimates was entitled *Soviet Capabilities for Strategic Nuclear Conflict*. As late as 1983, six years after Leonid Brezhnev signalled reduced growth in defense spending, the annual estimate in the series concluded that the Soviets sought "superior capabilities to fight and win a nuclear war with the United States, and have been working to improve their chances of prevailing in such a conflict." Ignoring a dissent from the State Department, CIA analysts used language that catered to Western notions of a Communist conspiracy.

> They [The Soviets] have seriously addressed many of the problems of conducting military operations in a nuclear war, thereby improving their ability to deal with the many contingencies of such a conflict, and raising the probability of outcomes favorable to the USSR.[23]

Gates, as acting director and deputy director of the CIA from 1986 to 1988, slanted intelligence estimates on Soviet strategic defense programs to buttress the Reagan administration's case for the Strategic Defense Initiative (SDI). In his 1986 San Francisco speech, Gates claimed that the USSR had spent more than $150 billion on its "Star Wars" programs but never mentioned the fact that most of this money was for air defense, not antimissile defense. He charged incorrectly that the Soviets were preparing an ABM defense of their national territory.

The CIA caricature of a Soviet military octopus with global reach supported the administration's view of the "Evil Empire." Gates used worst case analysis to portray a Soviet Union strong enough to neutralize U.S. strategic forces. Moscow, in fact, had no capability to target dispersed mobile ICBMs and lacked an air defense system that could counter strategic bombers. Moscow had no confidence that its efforts to destroy warheads on land-based missiles would actually find missiles still tethered to their launchers.

The CIA exaggerated both the range of the TU-22 Backfire bomber (which justified U.S. insistence on counting the airplane as a strategic intercontinental bomber) and the accuracy of the SS-19 ICBM (which contributed to the myth of a "window of vulnerability").[24] Some of these errors were acknowledged—in 1989, after Gates left the CIA to join the NSC. Meanwhile, the errors continued to appear in the unclassified DIA publication, *Soviet Military Power*, which served as a propaganda vehicle for the Department of Defense until 1991. The CIA, created as an independent agency, had failed in its role as the "honest broker" between intelligence and policy.

The CIA distorted the military power of Warsaw Pact forces and never anticipated that the Pact would dissolve. As late as 1990, only a few months before the collapse, the CIA concluded that the Warsaw Pact had matched or exceeded NATO's (North Atlantic Treaty Organization) capabilities in all ground force weapons and would keep pace with NATO's modernization programs. CIA assessments ignored Moscow's real concern with U.S. modernization and the presence of U.S. Pershing II and ground-launched cruise missiles in Europe.

CIA errors on military issues delayed important arms control negotiations with the Soviet Union. Estimates of Soviet military manpower in Europe, a key issue in the negotiations for mutual and balanced force reductions (MBFR), assumed 95 percent manning levels when the average was much less. The CIA overestimated Soviet chemical warfare stocks, and Gates delayed release of the excellent work done by CIA analysts demonstrating a change in Soviet thinking about chemical warfare: This assessment would have supported an early decision to seek a chemical weapons ban.[25]

CIA assessments overstated every aspect of the Soviet military and particularly exaggerated Moscow's power projection capability. They downplayed Moscow's lack of sea-based tactical air support, a strong suit of the US navy, which put Moscow at a huge disadvantage beyond Soviet waters. The CIA predicted the production of Soviet nuclear-powered aircraft carriers with attack aircraft, which were never produced, and erroneously described Soviet helicopter carriers that carried short-range, vertical takeoff and landing aircraft as attack carriers.

CIA national intelligence estimates on Soviet policy in the Third World consistently exaggerated Moscow's presence and influence and lacked an appreciation for the problems that the Kremlin faced in its bilateral dealings with key clients. Alvin Z. Rubinstein's *Red Star on the Nile*, which appeared in 1977, had a far more sophisticated understanding of these problems than most CIA assessments and contributed to scholarly debates on the limits on superpower influence in the Third World. The CIA particularly inflated Moscow's capabilities in the Mediterranean and the Indian Ocean and provided no warning of Soviet withdrawal from Afghanistan, Cam Ranh Bay in Vietnam, and the littoral states of Africa. Soviet Foreign Minister Eduard Shevardnadze provided early warning of the withdrawal, but the CIA continued to attribute to Moscow a willingness to assume greater risk of confrontation with the United States.[26] The withdrawal from Afghanistan—Moscow's first major step in its strategic retreat—led to anticommunist revolutions in East Europe and the reunification of Germany, but the CIA was looking elsewhere and missed the greatest triumph of political liberalism in modern history.

THE GORBACHEV FIASCO

Casey and Gates were dead wrong on the most important intelligence question of our time—was Gorbachev serious? They dismissed the stated policies of the new leadership as a sham. As a consequence, the CIA missed virtually every aspect of change during the Gorbachev era, beginning with the significance of his accession to power and the political impact of the shocking appointment of Shevardnadze as foreign minister. Gorbachev and Shevardnadze methodically conducted a revolution in Soviet national security policy but, in 1987, the CIA still argued that the two leaders "give every indication of endorsing well-established Soviet goals for expanded power and influence."[27]

Soviet commentators had been engaged in an active and public debate on the backwardness of the Soviet system since the 1960s but, as late as 1985, a CIA estimate ("Domestic Stresses on the Soviet Union") described a "very stable country" that was a "powerful and *acquisitive* (italics added) actor on the international scene."[28] According to the CIA, the Soviet Union would use:

> assertive diplomacy backed by a combination of military power, propaganda, and subversive tactics to advance its interests. Its ruling elite, now and for the *foreseeable future*, sees its mission in history, its security, and its legitimacy in maximizing its ability to control political life within

and outside Soviet borders. The domestic problems of the USSR are
unlikely to alter this quality of the Soviet system and the *international
appetites* [italics added] that spring from it.

In fact, Moscow's severe domestic problems already had produced
the policies of strategic retreat.

Missing the Revolution in Soviet Security Policy

Shultz's memoirs documented the CIA's failure to track the revolution in Moscow's national security policy and disarmament, particularly Gorbachev's willingness to accept intrusive on-site
inspection (OSI), asymmetric agreements, and unilateral reductions. The CIA distorted the intelligence record and failed to in-
form policymakers that the Kremlin was changing its policies on
virtually all issues. Several months before the summit meeting in
Reykjavik in 1986, Gorbachev had told French President Francois
Mitterrand that Moscow was prepared to accept far-reaching verification measures, including intrusive on-site inspection. The U.S.
negotiators, according to Shultz, were unprepared for Gorbachev's flexibility.

CIA estimates on arms control became highly politicized documents that ignored the sweeping changes in Soviet negotiating positions and missed Moscow's motivation for conciliation. In
January 1977, Brezhnev stated that nuclear war would be suicidal
for both sides and that no meaningful victory was possible. His
speech was followed by immediate cuts in Soviet procurement of
weapons systems and a decline in the growth of military spending.
Brezhnev elaborated on this message at the twenty-sixth party congress in 1981, and Gorbachev expanded it at the twenty-seventh
congress in 1986 but the CIA, as late as 1988, dismissed the Soviet
statements as "self-serving."[29] Gates argued that Moscow was
merely exploiting the disarmament issue in order to weaken the
West. The State Department argued with this view, but the CIA
redacted State's dissent in declassified intelligence estimates.

As a result of the CIA's errors, some due to politicization and
others due to flawed analysis, U.S. policymakers were unprepared
for Gorbachev's concessions. His dramatic announcement of a unilateral reduction of forces at the UN in December 1988, the forty-
seventh anniversary of the attack on Pearl Harbor, was a seminal
statement of Soviet policy. It came as a shock to the Reagan administration, however. The resignation of the chief of the Soviet general staff Marshal Sergei Akhromeyev on the day of Gorbachev's

speech was a clear demonstration of the military's opposition to these cuts, but CIA attributed the resignation to poor health. Declassified documents reveal that the agency's analytical record improved almost immediately after Gates moved to the National Security Council in 1989.

Missing the Soviet Economic Failure

The Soviet economy was in the early stages of collapse from 1976 to 1986 and such economists as Sweden's Anders Aslund, the Soviet Union's Abel Aganbegyan, and Soviet emigre Igor Birman pointed out fissures in the Soviet economy and flaws in the CIA's analysis.[30] In the early 1980s, Birman predicted the Soviet economic collapse before decade's end. Swedish and British analysts had long regarded the Soviet economy as Third World—an Upper Volta with a nuclear arsenal—but CIA economists continued to exaggerate the size of the Soviet economy.

CIA estimates on the Soviet Union were dead wrong on the size and performance of the economy and the military burden. CIA analysts actually believed that the Soviet economy was 60 percent of the U.S. economy and that Soviet per capita consumption was 50 percent of that of the United States. Aslund believed that these figures were too high by one-third.[31] The CIA finally began to chart lower growth rates for the Soviet economy in the mid-1980s, but by then Aslund and Aganbegyan had concluded that there had been zero growth in the Soviet Union between 1980 and 1986, the very years that the Carter and Reagan administrations were using CIA data to justify record defense spending. The agency also failed on the crucial issue of the military burden on the economy, placing the military share of Soviet gross domestic production (GDP) between 15 and 17 percent, while some critics were arguing that it was 25 to 35 percent.

These are not academic arguments. CIA analysis described an economy that could grow and allow military expansion; this had a direct impact on the justification for U.S. defense spending. In the late 1980s, the CIA argued incorrectly that Soviet growth in investment and gross national product (GNP) would allow expansion in military procurement and influence abroad and perceived no "major shifts in military production, at least through 1990." Several months before Gorbachev announced major unilateral cuts in Soviet ground forces in East Europe and along the Sino-Soviet border, the CIA predicted modernization for Soviet forces and argued that Gorbachev would never accept constraints on military programs for economic reasons.[32]

Meanwhile, there were scholars with unclassified information who understood Soviet economic problems far better. The late Ed A. Hewett of the Brookings Institution and Indiana University's Robert Campbell described the backwardness of the Soviet economy. Murray Feshbach of Georgetown University and Nicholas Eberstadt of Harvard University dramatically documented the human and environmental wreckage of Communist mismanagement and charted Moscow's economic and social collapse a full ten years before the CIA. Anecdotal information in U.S. embassy reporting from Moscow documented the impoverished state of the Soviet economy, but this data was rarely used in CIA assessments.

In overestimating the size of the Soviet economy, the CIA completely misread the qualitative and comparative economic picture and provided no warning to policymakers of the dramatic economic decline of the 1980s. Fortunately, Shevardnadze's top economic aides briefed Secretary of State James Baker and others about the plight of the Soviet economy. This allowed the chairman of the Council of Economic Advisors Michael Boskin to tell a congressional hearing in 1990 that "Soviet GNP was . . . about one-third of the GNP of the United States." He ignored CIA estimates that, as late as the 1980s, concluded that the Soviet GNP was three-quarters of the American level.

The CIA also missed the economic collapse in East Europe, which diminished the effectiveness of Warsaw Pact forces and hurt Soviet industrial production. The military-industrial complex in the Soviet Union was dependent on East Europe, particularly for machine tools it was denied in the West. Production and productivity problems in East Europe led to reduced procurement rates of key weapons systems in the Soviet Union, beginning in 1976. But, as late as 1986, the CIA still believed that the East German economy was growing faster than its West German counterpart, and that East Germany had surpassed West Germany in per capita output!

Exaggerated estimates of the size and vigor of the Soviet economy led the CIA to distort the strength of the Soviet military and to ignore Moscow's claim that it needed a "breathing space" in the international arena. The CIA underestimated the increased defense burden in the Soviet Union and never tracked the impact of a declining economy on a bankrupt military-industrial establishment. It continued to spout meaningless and erroneous growth figures throughout the 1980s, failing to show the accelerating gap between the United States and the Soviet Union and the implications of Moscow's isolation from the technological revolution. There were no assessments that examined the military implications of a decline in investment resources or the possibility that Moscow's economic malaise would prevent another vigorous round of defense spending.

The urgency of Gorbachev's efforts to reform the system and capitulate to the United States on arms control matters should have been a clue to agency economists but political and military data were compartmented in the CIA's insular culture, and senior CIA Kremlinologist Kolt refused to permit his analysts to use the term "Soviet economic reform." The agency consistently overstated the value of the ruble, the volume of Soviet investment relative to the United States, and the rate of growth of the Soviet economy. It made major errors in estimating Soviet investment in fixed capital, particularly machinery and equipment, which contributed to overly optimistic accounts of the size and capability of Moscow's military-industrial complex. The CIA analysts totally missed the qualitative disparities between the two nations, arguing that the rate of growth of personal consumption in the Soviet Union from 1951 to 1988 exceeded growth rates in the United States. As a result, they concluded that the "USSR was much less constrained than the United States by domestic considerations."[33] On balance, the overestimation of Soviet consumption and investment contributed to the CIA's failure to anticipate defense burden on the economy, the need for reform, and the imminent economic crisis.

WHAT IS TO BE DONE?

Director of Central Intelligence John Deutch told graduates of the National Defense University in 1995 that the *primary mission* of the intelligence community was to provide the president the best information available.

We have to maintain an *unassailable reputation* for *unvarnished treatment* of the facts, never allowing ourselves to *tailor our analysis* to meet some policy conclusions that may be of convenience to one of our leaders at one time or another. If we do so, it will quickly *destroy the credibility*. . . .

The CIA's credibility was virtually destroyed, however, when Casey and Gates distorted intelligence on Soviet military and economic power and the political intentions of Soviet leaders.

Gates's immediate successors, moreover, have compounded the problem by refusing to face it and deal with it. Rather, they have condoned the efforts of agency officers seeking to obfuscate the record and have recycled those high-level officials who contributed to the politicization of intelligence in the past. Senior officials responsible for corrupting intelligence on the Soviet Union became the national intelligence officer for Russia and the deputy director for intelligence, respectively. The project manager of the papal plot assessment became one of the agency's highest-ranking officers, the deputy director for operations; the co-author of the papal assessment served for years as CIA historian. The senior analyst responsible for the politicization of intelligence on Mexico and Haiti became the director of the Center for the Study of Intelligence, which has major responsibility for contacts with the academic community. The senior analyst responsible for politicization of intelligence on Soviet policy in the Third World became the director of training for all analysts in the directorate of intelligence. Deutch even named Gates to head a panel to determine whether a recent estimate on strategic threats to the United States had been politicized as its critics had charged. Deutch himself was appointed to review security at the nation's weapons laboratories although the former director of central intelligence had placed highly classified information on an unsecured computer, which paralleled the charge again a physicist at the Los Alamos National Laboratory in New Mexico. Certainly it is time for a director of central intelligence to adopt policies that no longer will allow critics of the agency to mock the biblical inscription in the entryway to CIA headquarters: "And ye shall know the truth and the truth shall make you free."

NOTES

1. Jack Matlock, *Autopsy of an Empire* (New York: Random House, 1995), 587–91.

2. Colin Powell, *My American Journal* (New York: Random House, 1995), 375–76.

3. *The National Interest* (winter 1995–96): 111.

4. George P. Shultz, *Turmoil and Triumph* (New York: Charles Scribner's Sons, 1993), 867.

5. Ibid., 864.

6. Ibid., 867.

7. Carolyn Ekedahl, "The Gates Hearings: A Biased Account," *Studies in Intelligence* (fall 1994): 73–78.

8. See *Nomination of Robert M. Gates*, Hearings Before the Select Committee on

Intelligence of the United States Senate (Washington, D.C.: Government Printing Office, 1992), 3 vols.

9. Robert M. Gates, *From the Shadows* (New York: Simon & Schuster, 1996), 563.

10. Robert M. Gates, Speech to Foreign Policy Association, New York, May 1992.

11. Harvard Case Study, "The CIA and the Fall of the Soviet Empire: The Politics of 'Getting it Right'," Cambridge, MA, 1996.

12. Douglas J. MacEachin, "CIA Assessments of the Soviet Union: The Record Versus the Charges," Washington: Central Intelligence Agency, 1996.

13. See CIA Intelligence Assessment, "Soviet National Security Policy: Responses to the Changing Military and Economic Environment," June 1988.

14. U.S. Senate Hearings Before the Select Committee on Intelligence, 102nd Congress, First Session on the "Nomination of Robert M. Gates to be Director of Central Intelligence," 2 vols., Washington, D.C.: U.S. Government Printing Office, 1992.

15. "The 1981 Terrorism Estimate: Bureaucratic Politics Gone Wrong," Wayne Limberg, prepared at the National War College, Washington, D.C., 18 December 1992.

16. See U.S. Senate Hearings, "Nomination of Gates," 1992.

17. James Worthen, "The Gates Hearing: Politicization and Soviet Analysis at CIA," *Studies in Intelligence* (spring 1994): 7–20.

18. See U.S. Senate Hearings, "Nomination of Robert Gates," 1992.

19. Anthony Lewis, "Too Clever By Half," *New York Times*, 7 October 1991, p. 31.

20. *Washington Post*, "Outlook Section," 17 October 1985, p. D-1.

21. U.S. Senate Hearings, "Nomination of Robert Gates," 1992.

22. See Raymond Garthoff's authoritative two-volume study of Soviet-American relations: *Détente and Confrontation* and *The Great Transition*, Washington, D.C.: Brookings Institution, 1985 and 1994.

23. See "Estimates on Soviet Military Power from 1954 to 1984," History Staff, Center for the Study of Intelligence, Central Intelligence Agency, 1994.

24. The General Accounting Office concluded in 1993 that the Department of Defense deliberately exaggerated Soviet capabilities and misrepresented the cost and performance of U.S. weapons systems in order to gain congressional authorization for desired military programs.

25. "Soviet National Security Policy: Responses to the Changing Military and Economic Environment," CIA Intelligence Assessment, June 1988, pp. 5–6.

26. See Carolyn M. Ekedahl and Melvin A. Goodman, *The Wars of Eduard Shevardnadze*, University Park, PA: Penn State Press, 1997.

27. "Gorbachev: Steering the USSR into the 1990s," CIA Intelligence Assessment, July 1987.

28. "Domestic Stresses on the Soviet System," CIA National Intelligence Estimate, November 1985.

29. "Soviet National Security Policy: Responses," CIA Intelligence Assessment, June 1988, pp. 5–6.

30. In the mid-1970s, when asked, "What would you do if you were in [then-premier Alexei] Kosygin's place?" Birman replied that he would "quit immediately."

31. Anders Aslund, "How Small is Soviet National Income," *The Impoverished Economy*, ICI Press, 1990.

32. "Soviet National Security Policy," June 1988.

33. Ibid.

II
The Third World

Latin America and Russia after the Cold War

W. Raymond Duncan

Given the dramatic transformation in world politics during the 1990s, Latin American scholars have been interested in how such changes have impacted on countries south of the Rio Grande.[1] Several global trends affecting Latin America in the 1990s have drawn attention—such as globalization and interdependence, illegal immigration, emerging democratic governments, and the region's turn toward market economies and trade organizations. Of particular interest—and focus of this essay—have been the consequences of the breakup of the former Soviet Union and cold war's end, collapse of Soviet and East European Communist Party rule, and termination of the Moscow-based Warsaw Pact.[2]

Interest in how the collapse of the Soviet Union and cold war politics has impacted Latin America is understandable. For more than three decades—beginning in the early 1960s when Havana aligned itself with Moscow and deposited the cold war just ninety miles from Key West, Florida—Soviet and Soviet-backed Cuban activities in the Western Hemisphere and elsewhere in the Third World fired up a U.S. foreign policy in Latin America almost exclusively preoccupied with Soviet and Cuban activities.[3] Now, decades later, with cold war adversarial relations between Washington, D.C., and Moscow over and Havana no longer backed by the Soviet Union, another chapter in Latin American politics and U.S.–Latin American relations has unfolded.

The era beginning with the USSR's demise in the early 1990s until today finds Russia marginalized on the Latin American scene compared to its cold war years—yet not completely out of the picture. Russian foreign policy analysts continue to tilt toward *geopolitical perceptions* of world affairs and spheres of interest—as they did during the cold war—and today's Russian specialists make the point that Moscow needs to strengthen its position in the Latin American region.[4] This is so, they argue, owing in part to Latin America's geostrategic proximity to the U.S.—a key reason why Moscow was attracted to Cuba after its 1959 revolutionary tensions with the United States. Latin America also is viewed as a region of rising significance in global politics. Russian analysts point to Latin America's big industrializing states like Argentina, Brazil, Chile, and Mexico, which they liken to Russia itself, and note that it boasts huge regional trading blocs like the North American Free Trade Agreement (NAFTA) and the South American Common Market (MERCOSUR). Geopolitical strategic thinking is back in play in Moscow *sans* its earlier Marxist-Leninist ideological trappings.[5]

All this raises a number of key questions as far as Latin America is concerned. What have been the effects of the USSR's collapse and emergence of Russia as its principal legatee on Latin America, on the one hand, and the United States and Russia on the other? Given that Russia is at present the unstable element in the equation, how might this picture change in the future? What might happen, for example, should Russia get its house in order and begin pursuing a vigorous, independent foreign policy emphasizing its own national interest—as it seems to have done in the Kosovo crisis, when it sent its own peace-keeping troops into Kosovo without close coordination with the North Atlantic Treaty Organization (NATO)? What could the future become if Russia succeeded in reestablishing a consortium of the former republics of the USSR under its leadership and began to pursue a foreign agenda on a grander and quasi-imperial scale? Toward exploring these questions, this essay focuses on five issues. They are:

- Soviet policy in Latin America during the cold war years
- Gorbachev's "New Thinking" in Soviet policy
- Russia and Latin America after the Soviet Union's collapse
- Impact of the USSR's collapse on Latin America
- Prospects for the future

To set the scene for this discussion, we first look at two views on the impact of the Soviet collapse on Latin America that have emerged since the cold war ended.

THE SOVIET COLLAPSE AND LATIN AMERICA: TWO VIEWS

The impact of the Soviet Union's demise on Latin America has been the subject of debate—basically over whether Soviet Union's collapse has or has not impacted significantly on the Latin American states. From one perspective, the USSR's collapse arguably has been less than might have been imagined. This view is based on three underlying assumptions.

The Soviet Union's Demise Did Not Impact Latin America Significantly

The first assumption in this perspective is that *Soviet involvement in the Americas after World War II simply was not as extensive as that portrayed by U.S. policymakers.* Some Soviet scholars and former policymakers downplay the scope of Soviet policy in Latin America during the cold war. This perspective is underscored by Sergo A. Mikoyan, former editor-in-chief of the Soviet academic journal, *America Latina*, and a chief researcher at the Institute of Peace at the Russian Academy of Sciences.[6] Mikoyan makes a strong case that Latin America did not receive exceptionally close attention from Moscow before 1991, with the obvious exception of Moscow's tight ties with Cuba. In his words, "the rulers in Moscow were realistic enough not to dream of turning the Caribbean Sea into a Communist lake— having the Socialist island of Cuba there was enough. . . . Grenada and Nicaragua were surprising gifts."[7] Another former high level Soviet official Karen Brutents notes that Soviet policy in Latin America during the cold war years was strictly "defensive." Moscow never intended to establish itself in Latin America as a bridgehead, but rather was taking "diversionary measures" to neutralize or offset activities of the United States in other regions.[8] Brutents, a former foreign policy adviser to President Gorbachev, stresses that the Soviet presence in Latin America "was not very significant."[9]

A second assumption is that *Latin American politics and U.S.–Latin American relations were shaped more by Soviet policy initiatives launched by Mikhail S. Gorbachev during 1985–1991—before the Soviet Union's collapse—than by events after its break-up.* Gorbachev indeed initiated novel foreign policy guidelines, as will be explored later. His "New Thinking" approach to foreign affairs emphasized, among other things, political/diplomatic settlement of Third World regional conflicts—including Latin American cooperative relations with the United States on a wide range of issues. Gorbachev ushered in a period of less adversarial military and ideological competition with the United States, which became pronounced in Russia–U.S. relations after 1991 once Boris Yeltsin came onto the leadership scene. Today's deideologized relations with Latin America, absence of subsidizing Cuba's economy and lowered profile in such places as El Salvador and Nicaragua have their origins in the Gorbachev period.

The third assumption is that *Latin America's post-Soviet and post–cold war political and economic dynamics, apart from Mikhail Gorbachev's influence, were affected by other driving forces at work well before the USSR and cold war ended in 1991.*[10] The idea here is that Latin America already was in a stage of significant transition in politics and economics by the time the Soviet Union collapsed. Widening democratic rule was underway, replacing military-dominated governments—as military rule passed from the scene in Brazil, Chile, Argentina, Uruguay, Paraguay, Bolivia, Guatemala, Honduras, and Haiti. Deepening economic regional interdependence was at work, along with improved diplomatic and trade relations with the United States, increased direct private foreign investment, and widening acceptance of open markets. This latter trend featured downsizing of cumbersome and inefficient public sectors with government ownership of the means of production. Decline of leftist movements and regimes, notably in the Caribbean (Grenada) and Central America (El Salvador and Nicaragua) were central aspects of the late 1980s—before the Soviet Union's collapse.

An Opposing View: The Soviet Collapse Deeply Impacted Latin America

A contrasting view discussed in this chapter is as follows. While accepting the validity of those trends discussed above, it would be misleading to write off the Soviet collapse as insignificant in shaping today's Latin American politics. To begin with, the impact on Cuba's economy and foreign policy, once tied closely to the USSR, has been profound.[11] Cuba's economic system tumbled out of control for a period of time, while Moscow's withdrawal of military forces from Havana undermined Cuba's capacity to back leftist regimes and movements in the Caribbean Basin area and in more far-flung Third World settings. Cuba's leaders have been struggling how to sort out an effective economic policy since then—with less focus on market economic strategies than either China and Vietnam (Moscow's other chief cold war client state), both of which have dropped total command economies and adopted policies of state capitalism.

Second, the demise of a Soviet and Cuban-aided "Communist threat" in Latin America undoubtedly has contributed to the strengthening of democratic regimes—although not responsible for the initiation of democratic processes.[12] Soviet policy in Latin America—notably Moscow's ties with Cuba, coupled with Soviet and Cuban activities in Latin America and other Third World regions—shaped Latin American politics and U.S. policy perceptions in that part of the world during the cold war decades. Moscow's Latin American presence, especially in Cuba, exacerbated tensions between Latin American leftist regimes and movements, on the one hand, and on the other, military rulers and conservative interest groups. Moscow and Havana's presence consequently stimulated conditions for anti-Communist military rule, disdain for democratic government by leftist guerrillas and military dictators alike, and Latin American friction with a United States bent upon fighting, and intervening against, a "Communist threat." Intervention by the United States during the cold war did not endear the United States to many a Latin American government.

Third, without the "Communist threat" in the western hemisphere, the United States has been able to change its foreign policy priorities from "stopping Communism" to more focus on developing market economies, curtailing narcotics trafficking, dealing with refugees, and letting Latin American countries stabilize and govern themselves.[13] Compare the differences in U.S. policy toward Latin America during and after the cold war. Signing NAFTA—linking Mexico economically to the United States and Canada—followed by the $20 billion U.S. loan to support the falling Mexico peso in 1995, stand in sharp contrast to the days of U.S. "anti-Communist" intervention. Cases in point include Guatemala in 1954, a U.S.–backed invasion of Cuba's Bay of Pigs in 1961, and U.S. military intervention in the Dominican Republic in 1965—not to mention the U.S. invasion of Grenada in 1983.[14]

Fourth, socialism's collapse in the Soviet Union, Eastern Europe, and Cuba has encouraged Latin American leaders to off-load gigantic state enterprises with their inefficient bureaucracies in favor of market economic principles, free trade agreements, and foreign investment.[15] Such economic turnarounds are reflected throughout South America—and even once-socialist Nicaragua under Sandinista rule during the 1980s turned toward capitalism, a market economy, foreign investment, and restored relations with the United States in the 1990s.

We now turn to a closer look at our subject, providing a historical perspective in order to appreciate what has happened since Russia replaced the USSR.

SOVIET POLICY IN LATIN AMERICA DURING THE COLD WAR

Soviet policy in Latin America during the cold war years was much akin to its policy goals throughout the Third World. Moscow sought to undercut U.S. power and influence, compete more effectively with the United States, and gain political legitimacy and equality with the United States as a superpower contender in the global arena.[16] Such aims led Moscow to expand its presence and roles in Latin America by backing Cuba and anti-U.S. radical nationalist regimes and leftist guerrilla movements in the Caribbean Basin and Central America, widening diplomatic and trade relations with Latin America's large industrializing states (Argentina, Brazil, and Mexico), and forging close contacts with local Communist parties. This multi-track approach allowed the Soviets elbow room to pursue long-range ideological goals by supporting leftist causes—underscored by ties to Cuba, relations with Nicaragua's Sandinistas, support for Grenada's New Jewell Movement (NJM) during 1979–1983, and links with pro-Soviet Latin American Communist parties—as well as advancing more practical economic and political interests.

By the time Gorbachev came to power in March 1985, the USSR had become a more impressive player in the region than it had been during the 1950s and 1960s. Diplomatic ties had expanded, along with widened commercial contacts, scholarship programs, and technical assistance projects, not to mention Soviet-backed Cuban activities in advancing the interests of leftist groups and leaders.[17] By providing Cuba and Nicaragua with economic and military aid, the Soviets gained a physical presence in the U.S. "strategic backyard," while at the same time helping those and other countries pursue policies that challenged U.S. power and influence. Cuban and Nicaraguan activities helped strengthen Moscow's credentials as an important Third World ally in the Nonaligned Movement and UN General Assembly, while stimulating division within U.S. policymaking elites. Overall, the impact of the growing Soviet presence on Latin America during these cold war years:

- Bolstered leftist regimes (Cuba, Grenada, and Nicaragua)
- Encouraged leftist guerrilla movements (Colombia, El Salvador, and Guatemala)
- Strengthened pro-Soviet Communist parties throughout the area
- Provided military regimes with at least one legitimizing rationale for antidemocratic, tight authoritarian rule [General Augusto Pinochet in Chile is a classic example]
- Drove U.S. policy in the direction of "combating Communism"

in the hemisphere, notably by backing military rule, as opposed to emphasizing economic development.

The U.S. Response

The U.S. reaction to the "Communist threat" was about what one might expect in terms of the Caribbean and Central America's historic geostrategic importance to U.S. security interests—dating back to the nineteenth-century Monroe Doctrine. Washington launched an economic embargo against Cuba, crafted anti-Cuban policies of other types (radio and TV Marti broadcasts), kicked off the Alliance for Progress in 1961 to stimulate Latin American economic development, supported conservative regimes fighting Communism, and—under the leadership of Ronald Reagan—backed anti-Sandinistas *Contras* in Nicaragua. Soviet-Cuban ties sharply escalated cold war tensions between the USSR and U.S., magnified the perceived threat of Soviet and Cuban activities in Latin America, and undermined U.S.–Latin American cooperation on pressing economic and social development problems.

The Downside for Moscow

While Soviet policies in Latin America appeared at first blush to have produced notable successes, a balanced appraisal of Moscow's record suggests numerous costs that were mounting by the time Gorbachev came to power. Soviet activities were escalating tensions with the United States and the West, becoming counterproductive to broader Soviet strategic and economic imperatives. The downside for Moscow was shaped by:

- Bogging Moscow down in costly protracted civil wars on behalf of distinctly weak countries, such as Nicaragua
- Escalating an expensive Soviet–U.S. arms race stimulated by Washington's Strategic Defense Initiative (SDI), a costly defense burden for Moscow
- Hindering commercial and trade ties with the United States and the West
- Embarrassing Moscow by Latin America's debt crisis and need for economic aid, which Moscow could not meet[18]
- Producing a balance of trade deficit with Latin America, owing to insignificant Latin American purchases from the USSR[19]
- Undermining Soviet foreign policy influence by factionalism in the movements backed by Moscow that prohibited unified

party behavior—as in El Salvador's Farabundo Marti National Liberation Front (FMLN)

Soviet-Cuban Relations During the Cold War

The Soviet-Cuban relationship during the cold war essentially was a conversion of interests, with mutual interests served by cooperating with each other. The Soviets gained a location geographically proximate to their cold war adversary—a powerful piece of real estate on the global chessboard, providing the Soviets with influence vis à vis the United States. In addition, Moscow's benefits included intelligence gathering facilities, naval and air deployment assets, and antisubmarine warfare capabilities. The Lourdes intelligence gathering installation, still in place today for Moscow, was the largest facility of its type outside the Soviet Union, monitoring U.S. military activities in and around the Caribbean Basin. In addition, Moscow gained a willing partner in Third World interventions—such as Angola and Ethiopia; Cuba was a country willing to commit ground forces in civil wars to advance Moscow's as well as its own goals.

Cuba, for its part, gained more aid than any other Soviet client state (a little over 50 percent of all extended to Communist and noncommunist countries), aid vital to Cuba's survival. Moscow supplied Soviet oil at well below world market prices, while purchasing Cuban sugar at above world market prices. By the end of the 1980s, Cuba likely owed more than $20 billion to the Soviet Union and more than $5 billion to the Western world. Beyond its extraordinary economic gains, Cuba received free military equipment amounting to more than $13 billion since 1960, which allowed Castro to pursue his quest of "proletariat internationalism" and leadership of the Third World. Soviet ties also provided diplomatic and political support for Cuba's role as a "progressive member" of the world socialist system as opposed to a "capitalist dependent" country as it had been before Castro's revolution in 1959. One can imagine how hard Cuba was hit when Russia ceased to provide such aid after the Soviet Union broke apart.

By the time Gorbachev came to power, however, Soviet and Cuban interests were beginning to diverge, and tensions mounted sharply during Gorbachev's rule. Soviet economic costs were rising owing to annual hard currency losses from subsidizing Cuban oil and sugar trade. This burden was added to other economic problems back in the USSR, notably Moscow's increasing military expenses, and undermined economy owing to cold war competition

with the U.S. and the West.[20] At least one African observer, moreover, had noted that Castro's Cuba was losing influence in that part
of the world as early as 1984–85, where the Soviets and Cubans
were entrenched in Angola's civil war. That "quagmire" was creating a growing impression among Third World leaders that Cuba
had become an "interventionist" foreign power, not exactly what
the Soviets would have planned.[21]

GORBACHEV'S "NEW THINKING" IN FOREIGN POLICY

The Gorbachev era (1985–1991) produced a remarkable shift in
foreign policy emphasis designed to revitalize a sagging economy
and produce an international environment conducive to economic
growth—while maintaining Soviet national security.[22] In pursuit of
such goals, Gorbachev's key foreign policy guidelines, known as his
"New Thinking" in foreign policy, promulgated in 1987, stressed
Russian–U.S. cooperation in managing Third World conflicts, political, as opposed to military settlement of such issues, deideologiz-
ing foreign policy, de-emphasizing military force, and focusing on
global interdependence. This shift away from Soviet–U.S. adversarial relations toward more cooperation led to an era of dramatically close relations with the United States in reducing Third
World conflicts. Cooperation occurred not only in places like Angola and the Horn of Africa, but also in America's Caribbean and
Central American "strategic rear," once considered a prime target
in Soviet–Latin American affairs during the cold war.

Indeed, it would not stretch the point to argue that it was Gorbachev's initiatives that introduced the sea change in Russia's approach to Latin America—not the collapse of the USSR itself. Still,
this is not to say that the Soviet Union's collapse did not have its
own effects as the "Gorbachev momentum" went forward. "New
Thinking" did not lead Moscow to cut back aid to established clients like Cuba and Nicaragua immediately, but it became clear that
the Soviets intended to redefine the nature of Soviet–Latin American ties as well as Moscow's relations with Washington, D.C., south
of the Rio Grande.

As in other Third World arenas, Gorbachev began to downplay
ideological imperatives and stress more pragmatic regional policies—such as improved state-to-state ties—by stepped-up diplomatic contacts in Latin America, nonpolitical forms of competition,
political settlement of ongoing conflicts, and downgraded support
for national liberation movements. Soviet diplomats launched a

diplomatic blitz in high-level meetings with Latin American presidents that underscored the importance of reducing the threat of nuclear war, building zones of peace and cooperation, reducing military spending, and strengthening international control over the environment.[23]

Especially remarkable was the Gorbachev shift toward backing Central American peace initiatives in the late 1980s, previously launched in Esquipulas, Guatemala, in June 1986 by the five Central American presidents. From late 1988 onward, Moscow sponsored a number of initiatives aimed at the complete cessation of arms transfers to Central America, including a cutoff of weapons to Nicaragua's leftist Sandinistas and pressure on that regime to hold elections in February 1990.[24] In working out an election procedure in Nicaragua, a remarkably close collaboration evolved between U.S. Secretary of State James Baker and Soviet Foreign Minister Shevardnadze—and between Assistant Secretary of State for Inter-American Affairs Bernard Aronson and his Soviet counterpart Yuri Pavlov.[25]

The USSR meanwhile joined the United States and other members of the Security Council in November 1989 in supporting unarmed military observers to monitor the commitment by Central American governments to cease aiding insurgents. The Soviets cooperated with the United States in backing UN and the Organization of American States monitoring Nicaragua's February 1990 elections, UN subsequent demobilization of contras in Honduras and enclaves inside Nicaragua, and UN efforts to repatriate the contra rebels. In addition, Moscow leaned on Havana and Angola not to walk away from negotiations during 1988, which led to the Angola/Namibia settlement and the beginning of Cuba's withdrawal of 50,000 troops from Angola. Finally, Moscow continued to support UN mediation of a political agreement on military reform and ceasefire in El Salvador.

A number of other foreign policy trademarks became pronounced during the Gorbachev years. Beyond extensive cooperation with the United States to end East-West confrontations in this part of the world, Moscow endorsed Latin America's democratization process, improved human rights activities, regional economic integration and multilateral diplomacy, interregional cooperation, and moved away from ideological confrontation.[26] These steps reflect Gorbachev's "New Thinking" and his effort to reintegrate the USSR into the world economy based on new cooperative endeavors. Karen Brutents—former deputy director of the International Department of the Central Committee of the Communist Party of the Soviet Union and a subsequent foreign policy adviser to President Gorbachev—summarized all this as an overhaul of Soviet policy to adapt it to the realities of the modern world.[27] Brutents summarized Gorbachev in the following terms:

> We have effectively banished from our political and diplomatic practice those elements that only recently were inseparably linked with the image of a superpower: ideological messianism, global confrontation with the United States and its allies, excessive armaments, and the view that force is central to the conduct of international relations. . . . [W]ith respect to Latin America, this means that we no longer consider it, or the other regions of the world, as the object of confrontation with the United States. . . . The Soviet leadership has declared that it has no strategic interests in Latin America and will resolutely follow this course.[28]

The Soviet Union and Cuba in the Gorbachev Era

Moscow's relations with Havana began to unravel with the coming of Gorbachev in 1985 and his "New Thinking."[29] Under the leadership of Shevardnadze, Gorbachev's foreign secretary, Moscow increasingly asserted Soviet long-term national interests over ideological guidelines. In this context, Shevardnadze pressed steadily forward in helping to negotiate settlements of regional conflicts, as in Angola and Nicaragua, areas in which Castro had exercised considerable influence on Soviet policy and where Havana had its own vested interests at stake. Indeed, Soviet policymakers point out that it was Havana, not Moscow, which took the lead in dragging both countries into Third World conflict—as in Angola.[30] It comes as no surprise that Castro tended to play an obstructionist role in Moscow's efforts to negotiate regional political disputes.

During Gorbachev's rule, Castro's prestige in Moscow eroded significantly, stemming from Moscow's foreign policy reorientation and to Castro's intransigence against easing regional conflicts. The Castro regime did not help itself in Moscow by orchestrating the trial of General Arnaldo Ochoa and others in mid-1989. Charged with criminal conduct allegedly stemming from their involvement in drug smuggling, malfeasance of funds, and insubordination, they were subjected to a "show trial"—reminiscent in Moscow of the notorious Soviet trials of the 1930s—and quickly executed. That the real cause for Ochoa's execution might have been that he posed a threat to the leaders of the Cuban revolution only further undermined the credibility of Cuba as a trusted ally under Gorbachev's "New Thinking" policies.

Soviet-Cuban relations steadily deteriorated during the Gorbachev years, as Moscow moved in one direction to reform the Soviet economic and political systems, and Castro moved in another. As Gorbachev's reforms headed toward more openness, Castro used his dictatorial powers to ban Soviet magazines and newspapers, with the big clampdown coming in 1989. As Gorbachev concentrated on how to jump start the sluggish Soviet economy, Castro focused on battles in Angola rather than trying to solve domestic economic problems.[31] As Yuri Pavlov notes, Castro was "more concerned with the ideological purity of the methods of economic management than with their performance."[32] The end of the 1980s had raised serious doubts in Moscow over the wisdom of large-scale economic aid to Cuba as the Soviet economy deteriorated. After the widely heralded Gorbachev-Castro April 1989 summit in Havana, Gorbachev returned to Moscow likely wondering if Castro would show flexibility in trying to reform Cuba's economic and political system "from above." After the Gorbachev visit, Moscow began to review all matters relating to Cuba in an effort to put its trade and economic cooperation with Havana "on a more equitable basis." This meant that the old subsidized arrangement was in for a major overhaul.[33]

RUSSIA AND LATIN AMERICA AFTER THE SOVIET COLLAPSE

Geopolitical strategic thinking—noted above—was back in play in Moscow by the end of the decade of the 1990s absent earlier Marxist-Leninist ideological trappings. Such end-of-the decade Russian perceptions, however, contrast sharply with the period immediately following the Soviet collapse at the beginning of the 1990s when Boris Yeltsin replaced Gorbachev as head of state. At that point in time Latin America and Cuba seemed to slip off the radarscope of Russian policymakers. When the Soviet Union began to fall apart in 1991, it was as if Moscow was uncertain how to treat Latin America, especially given its desire to work cooperatively with the United States—which meant, among other things, distancing itself from Communist Cuba and Fidel Castro. After all, before the Cuban Revolution, the Soviets had tended to give little attention to Latin America, perceiving the region through the lenses of "Geographic Fatalism." Translated, that meant Latin America lay in the U.S. "Sphere of Interest"—at least until the headlines-grabbing Cuban Revolution came along. Before Cuba's revolution, Latin America was an arena little studied by Soviet specialists. It was viewed as home to only weak Communist parties, a region steeped in Hispano-Catholic culture and traditional religious sentiments incompatible with Communism where strong-arm authoritarian leaders backed by conservative land-holding elites ran its governments. Russian policymakers seemed to believe at the time, why establish extensive diplomatic contacts in this part of the world?

So it would seem that Russian policymakers, reeling with the collapse of the Soviet empire—and already cooperating with the United States in negotiating conflict resolution in Third World arenas like El Salvador and Nicaragua—returned temporarily to this pre-Cuban Revolution geopolitical approach to the region. Such a broad brushstroke view of Latin America in the early 1990s was mirrored in Moscow's key foreign policy journal, *International Affairs*, when it published articles on "Russia's Spheres of Interest" in 1992–93 (Europe, Africa, Middle East, South Asia, and the Far East) that simply ignored Latin America.[34] Indeed, Russian scholars make quite clear that the Soviet Union's collapse left Latin America on the back burner. By the time the last issue of *International Affairs* came out in 1991, Soviet scholars were stating that "the prospects of relations between Latin America and the Soviet Union . . . had ceased to exist."[35]

Let us look more closely at why Russia relegated Latin America so low in policy priority. **First**, according to Russian analysts, the situation was based on "*geopolitics*." Owing to the nature of the post-Soviet epoch, following the USSR's breakup, Russia was placed in a situation of "shrinking opportunities for communication," which at the time pushed Russia toward increased "isolationism."[36] This was a time of Russia's orientating itself with the highly developed countries rather than poor developing states.

Second, Russia's downscaling Latin America stemmed from *its separation and withdrawal from Cuba*. As one Soviet analyst put it, "for three decades running, all events in Latin America were assessed from the standpoint of our relations with revolutionary Cuba."[37] Cuba as a driving force in Soviet views of Latin America during the cold war clearly had been a huge factor in shaping its diplomacy.

Third, *amicable relations with the United States and cold war's end* changed everything. The cold war Soviet leadership tended to view "the vast diversity of developments in Latin American countries with the Soviet Union through the prism of confrontation

with the United States. The extent to which it favored this or that
regime was directly proportional to its dislike for Washington, and
vice versa."[38] In withdrawing hastily from Cuba and ending the
cold war with the United States, therefore, it would follow that
overall relations with Latin America would be dramatically downs-
caled. The bottom line was that the Russian foreign ministry,
which largely determined Russia's presence in Latin America, experienced cut appropriations, which directly affected relations
with "remote developing countries."[39]

Renewed Interest in Latin America From the Mid-1990s Onwards

By 1996, however, Russia had begun to give Latin America more
attention with renewed realism and power politics that recognized
the geopolitical role this part of the world might play to promote
Russian national interests as we noted above. Vladimir Sudarev,
deputy director of the Institute of Latin America, Russian Academy of Sciences, writing in 1997, puts it this way:

> After a difficult and contradictory process of establishing relations be-
> tween Russia and Latin America during the preceding five years
> (1992–97, author's note), when the state of these relations was inter-
> preted among the public as the loss of interest in Latin America on
> Russia's part, the policy in regard to it seems to have received a boost
> in recent months.[40]

Russia indeed became more active from the mid-1990s onwards.
Russian Minister of Foreign Affairs Yevgeny Primakov made a historic visit to Latin America (Mexico, Cuba, Venezuela) during May
1996—the first visit by a Russian head of a foreign policy department. Until then, it was back in 1987 that a minister of foreign affairs of the USSR (Shevardnadze) had visited the region
(Argentina, Brazil, and Uruguay). Primakov's mission represented
a turning point in Russia's relations with Latin America, a hurried
up effort to pull Latin America back from the extreme periphery of
foreign policy to which it had been relegated.[41] This trip produced
agreements on trade and scientific-technical cooperation with
Mexico and Venezuela and underscored Russia's renewed interest
in Cuba, having fallen off dramatically when the Soviet Union collapsed. Such interest included the "oil for sugar" one-way trade
deal—agreed on in October 1995—which provides for the delivery
of 10.5 million tons of oil to Cuba from 1996–1998 in exchange for
four million tons of sugar.

Primakov returned to Latin America in November 1997, this time visiting Brazil, Argentina, Colombia, and Costa Rica—in what has been described as a kind of "rediscovery of the southern part of the new world."[42] His Brazil trip produced agreements on cooperation in culture, education, and space research, with Russia agreeing to assist Brazil in producing satellites and their launch from the Alcantara space center. The Argentina visit led to a joint Russian-Argentinean declaration and agreements on cultural and scientific-technical cooperation; similar agreements, including cooperation in fighting drug trafficking, were signed in Colombia. In Costa Rica agreements on cooperation in the sphere of science and culture were signed.

Following Primakov's swing through South America and Costa Rica, First Vice Premier Boris Nemtsov visited Chile, Mexico, and Venezuela. Nemtsov stressed in his visits the geopolitical importance for Russia to "establish firm positions south of the Rio Grande as a basis on which to conduct an equal dialogue with other countries, including the United States, and actively build up our influence in the former Soviet republics."[43] Nemtsov's trip highlighted a brand of diplomacy that envisioned the importance of Russia's presence in Latin America as a geopolitical counterpart to the American presence in the Caspian, Central Asian, and the Commonwealth of Independent States (CIS) countries.[44] In assessing the impact of these visits, *International Affairs* noted that Latin American leaders expressed the view that with the breakup of the Soviet Union, "the checks and balances, capable of effectively curbing the extreme manifestations of the imperial ambitions of the great northern neighbor have disappeared."[45] Moscow's new links in Latin America apparently have been viewed as moving in the direction of addressing this situation from a joint perspective of both Russia and the Latin American countries on which it was now focused.

In assessing the shift in Russia's relations with Latin America from the mid-1990s onwards, it should be noted that Latin American states by then had begun to show interest in Russia as the successor to the USSR. The foreign minister of Brazil visited Russia in October 1994, followed by a trip to Moscow by President Fernando Henrique Cardoso of Brazil—his first unofficial trip abroad. During that year the Argentine Minister of Foreign Affairs Guido di Tella also traveled to Russia, as did Colombian Foreign Minister Noemi Sanin. Such visits led to new trade agreements and bilateral military-technical cooperation, with Russia selling Mi-17 helicopters to Colombia and Igla anti-aircraft missiles to Brazil.[46] The military agreement with Colombia was renewed in 1966 and three years later, August 1999, found Boris Yeltsin telling Colombia's government that Russia was prepared to supply more helicopters to its army and air force.

As for Cuba, Moscow's old cold war partner in Latin America, it appears that Russia's revived interest in Latin America as an arena to play checks and balances great power politics vis à vis the United States included a sharpened focus on Cuba. When then Cuban Foreign Minister Roberto Robaina met with Russian Foreign Minister Igor Ivanov in January 1999, both officials emphasized that relations between the two countries were becoming a "top priority" in their foreign policies. Of course Cuba's imposing debt to Russia remained a sticking point, but Russia continued to rank its radio-electronic station at Lourdes—a key intelligence-gathering installation—as a high priority for Moscow. Meanwhile, tens of thousands of Cubans speak Russian and might be used to develop economic and trade ties with other Latin American countries. As one Russian analyst states it, Cuba in many respects remains "Russia's gateway to Latin America."[47] With Russia disillusioned with the amount of U.S. aid flowing in its direction, the movement of NATO toward the East, and opposing interests in such places as Southeast Europe—notably Kosovo—a renewed interest in Cuba as a strategic position vis à vis the United States makes sense from Moscow's perspective.

To summarize, by the end of the decade of the 1990s, Moscow was back to a brand of *realism* in its approach to Latin America. It had adopted a power politics and strategic *geopolitical analysis* that reminds old students of Soviet–Third World relations (1960–90) of the type of thinking that prevailed during the cold war *without Marxist-Leninist ideological trappings*. Toward the end of the decade Russia once again was in pursuit of great power *realist* ambitions and strategic national interests in Latin America. These included the pursuit of policies and exploiting opportunities designed to achieve:

- Access to raw materials, markets, and capital
- Competitive influence with the United States on the world stage
- Enhanced political equality for Russia vis à vis the United States
- Acceptance of Russia as a legitimate player south of the Rio Grande
- Strategic objectives and interests shared by Russia and the

leading states of Latin America—notably preventing a one-pole world order led by the United States

In contrast to the beginning of the decade Russia had come to perceive Latin America as a region of growing geopolitical significance.[48] Russian scholars and policymakers saw Latin America on the same transition phase of development and modernization (developing civic institutions and market economies) as Russia, equally interested in preventing a U.S.-dominated one-pole world order, and open to multilateral trade, scientific, and cultural contacts. As to multilateral links, Moscow had received observer status in the Organization of American States (OAS) and became a member—with Mexico, Chile, and Peru—of the Council for Pacific Economic Cooperation. Russian analysts indicate that Moscow would like to expand multilateral links between the CIS and NAFTA as well as with MERCOSUR. So the building of a "Pacific Bridge" between Russia/CIS and the stronger Latin American states was distinctly in focus as the new millennium approached.

IMPACT OF THE SOVIET COLLAPSE ON LATIN AMERICA

How did the end of the cold war and breakup of the Soviet Union alter regional economic, political, and social dynamics south of the Rio Grande? At least five broad trends were set in motion by the USSR's demise as the 1990s unfolded. They are as follows:

- U.S.–Latin American relations shifted from military and strategic issues to a more complex multidimensional agenda
- Latin American governments were strengthened in their previous redirection from authoritarian military regimes to democratic political systems
- Latin America's momentum toward open markets, ending of statist development models and interregional trade moved forward briskly
- Cuba became devalued as a socialist model, and placed on the sidelines of regional and global affairs
- Latin American militaries began to seek new roles apart from fighting Communism and left-wing movements

1. U.S.–LATIN AMERICAN RELATIONS SHIFTED FROM MILITARY AND STRATEGIC ISSUES TO A MORE COMPLEX MULTIDIMENSIONAL AGENDA

Whereas the cold war years emphasized military and strategic issues in western hemispheric relations, the post-Soviet era has seen a shift toward advancing a more multidimensional agenda. As discussed earlier, U.S. perceptions of Latin America and the Caribbean during the three-decade 1960–90 period were driven by cold war policies oriented to an East-West struggle for power with security interests placed on the front burner. Although the United States paid lip service to promoting democracy, most U.S. programs were geared to stopping Communism, combating leftist regimes and movements, and blocking Soviet and Cuban inroads, especially in the Caribbean Basin. This cold war perspective led the United States to support authoritarian dictatorial (frequently military) regimes over democratic governments—especially when an authoritarian government postured itself as "anti-Communist" and friendly to the United States.[49]

With the passing of a perceived cold war extrahemispheric security threat to the Western hemisphere, defense issues have waned as key driving forces in U.S.–Latin American relations. In contrast to cold war problems of security, the Soviet Union's collapse—and with it Moscow's huge support to Havana—has opened the door to a wide range of new issues that began to define U.S.–Latin American ties.[50] The new cooperative agenda includes how to promote regional democratic development and market economies, control of immigration and drugs, and moderating environmental deterioration.[51] While such a shift in the U.S.–Latin American agenda has not led to the United States getting deeply involved across the board in Latin American domestic politics and economics, the United States has engaged in cooperative inter-American activities where United States interests were served. Passage of NAFTA (and the U.S. financial bailout of Mexico), work with Colombia (and other Andean countries) and Mexico on narcotics trafficking, and cooperative policies with Mexico, the Caribbean, and Central America on illegal immigration illustrate the point.

The new U.S.–Latin America post–cold war agenda has forged a closer identity of interests between the United States and Latin America than in decades—perhaps a closer identity than any time in history.[52] Democracy in the region is no longer defined by the United States in strictly anti-Communist tones. The United States and Latin America both favor free trade and market economies. Cooperation on "intermestic" issues (issues that span the domestic and international realms) such as drugs, immigration, and the environment occurs frequently. That the end of the cold war and demise of the Soviet Union has produced a new political atmosphere south of the Rio Grande that favors U.S.–Latin American cooperation on a multidimensional agenda has been expressed by more than one Latin American observer. As Juan Gabriel Valdes, former Chilean ambassador to Spain has observed,

> Certain elements of tension in our relations with the United States very quickly disappeared . . . Nothing, or almost nothing, and no one, or almost no one, could today be challenged by Washington as being pro-Soviet. The charge of being soft on Communism, which for decades faced so many Latin American projects and so many of its leaders, has vanished. The cold war, in fact, had promoted throughout the region a perverse tension between continental security and social and economic crisis. The significance that certain elements of Latin America's ruling elite drew from North America's overriding interest in security was that any attempt at social change (matters as central and as various as public education, the fight against poverty, the role of the state in the economy, and the alignment of foreign trade), was open to accusations of undermining the continent's security.[53]

2. LATIN AMERICAN GOVERNMENTS WERE STRENGTHENED IN THEIR PREVIOUS REDIRECTION FROM AUTHORITARIAN MILITARY REGIMES TO DEMOCRATIC POLITICAL SYSTEMS

One huge effect of the end of the cold war was a weakening of the forces of the far left and far right—between leftist movements on the one hand, and on the other, military bureaucratic authoritarian elites. Whereas the cold war tended to polarize the left and right, the post–cold war era reduced such polarization in domestic political systems, strengthened centrist groups, promoted the political liberalization that had begun in the 1980s, and thus widened the possibilities for more democratic systems.[54] The region's revolutionary ferment lost steam, guerrilla movements faded (albeit not completely), and Cuba, of course, became quickly marginalized, as discussed below. As for the far right, its posturing as "anti-Communist" to curry U.S. favor lost its legitimacy.

The collapse of the Soviet Union and former Communist countries of Eastern Europe—coupled with glittering political and economic problems in Cuba—discredited leftist alternative political models in Latin America. While the end of the Soviet Union did not lead to the death of Latin American Communism or radicalism, as a brief look at Colombia and Mexico indicates, it eliminated Soviet and Cuban support for such ideologies and movements. Guerrillas in Colombia, Peru, Mexico, and elsewhere continued to advocate old line thinking and positions, but, in the words of one observer, "their rhetoric seemed intended more to justify their cause than to convert others."[55] The Soviet Union's demise and downgraded Communism have ended Latin American Communist party-to-party relations with the USSR, hemispheric meetings of leftist leaders with Soviet and Cuban leaders in attendance, leftist-backed cultural events, scholarships for study in Cuba and the USSR, and other types of programs.

Cuba, moreover, no longer plays its once large role in backing leftist regimes and movements around the world—including the Caribbean Basin. Nor is Havana any longer a driving force in the Third World nonaligned movement, using its position to throw Third World leaders behind the Soviets. Some observers remain convinced, however, that despite the loss of Soviet and Cuban-inspired revolutionary ideals, collapse of socialism in Europe, obsolescence of the Cuban model, and democratic changes sweeping the western hemisphere, the left still might rise again to play a key role in post–cold war Latin America.[56]

As for the far right, anti-Communism has been undermined in Latin America with the fall of Soviet Communism and Cuba's lowered profile, owing to the collapse of a discernible enemy that could be used by political elites resisting reform in the region. Right-wing regimes—such as those that operated in Argentina, Brazil, Chile, Uruguay, and throughout Central America during the cold war years—could no longer point the finger at Soviet and Cuban-backed leftist guerrillas, political parties, and interest groups to legitimize repressive rule. This does not mean, however, that groups resisting reform will simply go away, for they have long been more powerful than the revolutionaries.[57] Still, an undermined anti-Communism has relieved some countries like El Salvador and Guatemala of a central source of violence, despite the probability that the extreme right will continue to try to avoid power sharing with the lower and middle classes.[58]

3. LATIN AMERICA'S MOMENTUM TOWARD OPEN MARKET SYSTEMS AND ENDING OF STATIST DEVELOPMENT MODELS MOVED FORWARD BRISKLY

With the statist economic models dead in the former Soviet Union and East Europe—and Cuba's version of a state-controlled economy languishing—the idea that statist models work drifted away like a soap bubble. Country after country in Latin America began to trim the role of government in private sector economic activities, reduced trade barriers, and opened their arms to direct private foreign investors. Privatization of state-owned industries became pronounced, as leaders began to concentrate on export-led growth models followed in the United States and western countries as well as the hard-charging economies of Asia. Such models of development went hand in hand with the region's new interest in democratic political systems. As a consequence of new market economy initiatives, Latin American and Caribbean trade growth demonstrated remarkable vigor, increasing from 4 to 5 percent of world trade between 1990 and 1996.[59]

The fall of the Soviet Union, by ending cold war tensions, facilitated interregional trade and strengthened regional intergovernmental economic organizations in Latin America—in some respects with U.S. cooperation and in other respects apart from U.S. participation. In June 1990, President Bush announced his Enterprise for the Americas Initiative, with its focus on investment promotion, reducing debts, and eliminating trade barriers. The Enterprise for the Americas Initiative produced new bilateral trade agreements between a number of Latin American countries and the United States and was followed in 1994 by NAFTA linking Canada and the United States with Mexico. With NAFTA up and running, the next step was the summit agreement in Miami at the end of 1994, that by 2005 a hemisphere-wide Free Trade Area (FTA) would be up and running. Meanwhile, Brazil, Argentina, Uruguay, and Paraguay had signed a common market treaty in 1991 to create a single trade area called MERCOSUR—with a common external tariff by 1995. The Central American Common Market (CACM), for its part, took steps to reduce internal trade barriers and move to a common external tariff. All in all, such trends can be described as a new global agenda for Latin America that emphasizes liberalized trade and export-led economic development.

4. CUBA BECAME DEVALUED AS A SOCIALIST MODEL AND PLACED ON THE SIDELINES OF REGIONAL AND GLOBAL AFFAIRS

Cuba, once the Soviet Union's premier Third World client state, took the biggest hit with the USSR's collapse and ended cold war competition. Moscow's relations with Cuba deteriorated rapidly from 1991 onwards, ending Havana's preferential trade relations that had been in place since the 1960s and putting the two countries on a more normal, but from Cuba's perspective horrendous, trading basis. Oil imports from Russia, for example, fell from an estimated 13.3 million tons in 1989 to between five and six million tons in 1992.[60] While a ton of Cuba's sugar brought in 4.5 tons of Soviet oil in 1989, by 1992 a ton of sugar brought only 1.4 tons of oil.[61] Food imports from the former Soviet Union correspondingly dropped, owing to deceased purchasing capability. It should be noted that at one time Cuba was able to sell surplus subsidized Soviet oil on the open market for hard currency. Such days have long ago passed.

On the military front, post-Soviet relations became limited to maintenance, training, and spare parts—on a commercial basis—as Cuba stopped receiving Russian weapons in 1990. A U.S. delegation visiting Cuba in July 1993 was informed that no Russian naval ships had visited Cuba in the previous three years and that Russia was "not sending military ships or planes on systematic visits as a matter of policy."[62] Nevertheless, Russian military personnel remained in Cuba despite Gorbachev's unilateral announcement in September 1991 that he intended to withdraw the Soviet military brigade in the near future. By March 1993, nearly 1,500 Soviet soldiers, 200 military advisers, and 1,200 intelligence personnel were still in Cuba. In June 1993, however, the soldiers pulled out.[63] The Lourdes intelligence gathering installation remained under Russian control, for which Russia agreed to pay Cuba $200 million (in oil and other materials).[64]

Russia's diplomats, in the face of Havana's shock of losing its lucrative links with Moscow, attempted to ease the strain on Havana's economy from its changed relationship. Moscow signed agreements with Havana to establish rules for creating joint ventures, granted Cuba credit worth $380 million to help complete 12 of the 600 projects left unfinished by the former Soviet Union (including nuclear plant construction), and arranged for Cuba to import Soviet oil to be paid for by sugar.[65] Such oil supplies—whereby Russia delivered two million tons per year to Venezuela-owned refineries in Europe, with Venezuela shipping an equivalent amount of its own oil to Cuba—amounted to only a third of that supplied previously. In contrast to its once prime economic position in Cuba, Russia by early 1994 ranked ninth in terms of number of foreign companies operating in Cuba, with Spain in first place with seventy-eight companies.[66]

Despite face-saving activities, the Soviet Union's collapse and loss of Soviet subsidies in effect devastated Cuba's economy, once a showcase of socialist development. Cuba entered what its leaders described as a "Special Period" during which imports dried up and industry sunk to new lows, with factories producing at 30 percent capacity and shortages mounting in all goods—from pots and pans to clothing and cosmetics.[67] The 1995 sugar crop amounted to less than four million tons—low compared to the past and significant in that sugar represents more than 60 percent of the country's exports. With Soviet aid and subsidies virtually gone—and with them the loss of Cuba's economic lifeline and political protection from Moscow—Cuba became almost overnight a devalued socialist model. Placed on the sidelines of global politics, Havana no longer was an inspiration to other would-be leftist leaders in Latin America. In Robert Pastor's words, "Castro insisted that Cuba would remain socialist, but (after the Soviet collapse) his words no longer carried weight outside the island."[68] For his part, the fiery Cuban leader frankly acknowledges that Cuba no longer is in support of revolutions in Latin America. "Cuba," he has stated, is "not going to (support revolutions) anymore."[69]

At the end of the decade Cuba remained on the sidelines of regional and world politics—in sharp contrast to the role it once played in Latin American, Caribbean, and world affairs during the 1970s and 1980s. A papal visit to Cuba in 1998 produced a flurry of activity which indicated that Cuba might be moving toward more open relations with the world with potentially improved living conditions on the island. Yet by 1999, a year after Pope John Paul II's visit and message to Cuba to "open herself to the world, and the world needs to draw closer to Cuba," much remained the same in Havana.[70] Austere living conditions—resulting in large part from the Soviet Union's collapse—were locked in place, Cuba's human rights record remained dismal, and the gap between rich and poor had widened as a shortage in all kinds of goods mounted and a black market thrived. The average Cuban made about 200 pesos a month, approximately ten dollars.[71]

Still, as noted above, by 1996 it appeared that Moscow and Havana were elevating their relationship—nowhere near what it had been during the cold war days, but yet consistent with Russia's revived interest in playing a stronger Latin American role than in the immediate years after its collapse. In addition to his visit to Mexico and Venezuela in May 1996, then Foreign Minister Primakov paid his respects to Cuba—which Russian analysts described as signaling "a thaw" in relations between Moscow and Havana.[72] Among all Russia's contacts in Latin America, Cuba has been described as one of special and separate value—a point underscored by Primakov's sharp criticism of the Helms-Burton Act (U.S. embargo of Cuba) and support of Cuba as "candidate number one" for joining NAFTA.[73] And in his analysis of an emerging power center in Latin America, K. Khachaturov, chairman of the Russian Committee for Cooperation with Latin America and professor of the Diplomatic Academy of the Foreign Ministry of Russia, has stressed that "Cuba holds a special place in world politics" and by implication for Russia.[74] Then Cuban Foreign Minister Roberto Robaina echoed this view in his visit to Russia in January 1999.[75]

5. LATIN AMERICAN MILITARIES BEGAN TO SEEK NEW ROLES APART FROM FIGHTING COMMUNISM AND LEFT-WING MOVEMENTS

With Soviet and Cuban extrahemispheric activities curtailed, Latin American militaries began to seek new roles. After the collapse of the Soviet Union and cold war's end, the region as a whole became one of the lowest defense spenders in the world as governments attempted to reduce the size of their military establishments and defense budgets.[76] New missions for the Latin American militaries have included fighting drug traffickers and engaging in United Nations "Blue Helmet" peacekeeping operations abroad. Military involvement in antidrug operations, to be sure, date back to the 1970s and 1980s in some countries, as in Mexico. But with the end of the cold war has come a broader antidrug offensive in several countries. As to peacekeeping efforts, Argentina has played the largest role among the Latin American countries, while Brazil has lagged behind. Indeed in identifying this trend of new roles for the military, Argentina stands out with its cut in defense spending by 35%, reduction of military personnel by 32%, and abolishing conscription.

Seeking a new agenda, however, has not necessarily gone smoothly south of the Rio Grande, because a smaller establishment has not always accompanied less military funding. This means less pay for disgruntled soldiers and an open door to corruption. Involving the military heavily in antidrug operations, moreover, can render soldiers vulnerable to corruption—as the case of Mexico vividly illustrates. Finally, a new agenda for the military may be ill-defined, because the end of the cold war has not ended guerrilla insurgencies nor territorial border disputes that fall in the domain of old security threats that require defense spending. So the role of the military in the post–cold war Latin America varies greatly from country to country, and its place in politics and economics by no means has disappeared as democratic and market economies are pursued.

WHAT REMAINED UNCHANGED IN LATIN AMERICA AFTER THE SOVIET COLLAPSE?

In discussing this overall impact of the collapse of the Soviet Union on Latin America, one important caveat is in order. Underscoring the significance of the collapse of the Soviet Union on Latin America should not be overdrawn. The cold war's end is but one factor in assessing Latin American economics and politics as the twentieth century came to a close. A more complete assessment would take into account older conditioning cultural and political forces still at work—as they have been long before the cold war. An authoritarian political culture still percolates beneath the surface of democratic institution-building—as we see so vividly in today's Venezuela. Democratic politics are far from consolidated in Latin America.[77] Personalities and personal influence tend to make executive branches of government more powerful than check and balancing judiciaries and legislatures. Income maldistribution still plagues Latin America as in the past—as does rampant crime and corruption—both of which make institutionalizing democracy difficult.[78] Latin America continues to be one of the most unequal regions in the world, with insufficient investments that stifle the people's education and social progress. Human rights are still abused, journalists still murdered, and narcotic trafficking still counts for much in countries like Bolivia, Colombia, and Mexico. Insurgencies constantly plague parts of the region, notably in Colombia and Mexico, many territorial border disputes remain unsolved, and a brain drain continues as in the past.

An inconsistent U.S. policy toward Latin America is still a major issue—as it was before the cold war came along.[79] Central America, which once dominated U.S. attention when the Soviets and Cubans and leftists seemed to threaten, has faded dramatically as a U.S. policy priority—probably owning to the lack of vital security interests. The U.S. pursuit of a Free Trade Area of the Americas (FTAA) has languished since its launching in the Miami Declaration in December 1994, largely due to lack of presidential fast-track negotiating authority provided by Congress. Such policy drift does not augur well for the future. Despite the glaring problems in Latin America, the region remains on the periphery of U.S. policymaking—owing in part to the fragmented bureaucratic nature of policymaking in Washington, D.C.[80] With no immediate extrahemispheric challenges in Latin America, the United States has in many respects returned to a pattern of neglect (with notable exceptions like Mexico and NAFTA or interregional cooperation on narcotics trafficking) as pursued in pre–cold war eras.

PROGNOSIS FOR THE FUTURE

Russia is unlikely to have a major impact on Latin American relations in the foreseeable future. This prognosis seems logical, given the scope of post–cold war change in Latin America, Latin America's distance from Russia, and Russia's notorious economic and political problems. To argue that Russia will not have a major impact on Latin America does not mean that Russia will be inactive south of the Rio Grande. Russia remains focused on major geopolitical threats to its security and national sovereignty.[81] These include an expanded NATO into Russia's former "buffer state" East European arena, a western presence in southeastern Europe (Bosnia, Kosovo), and other perceived national security threats arising from the loss of empire. In a classic game of global chessboard power politics, Russian policymakers are likely to use Latin America (for reasons described above) as part of the broader Asia-Pacific region worthy of its own expanded presence. Cuba is a natural pawn in this strategy, which would explain Moscow's increased attention to Havana as Moscow's problems with the United States and NATO have expanded.

If Russia were to get its house in order and begin pursuing a vigorous, independent foreign policy emphasizing its own national interests—the foreshadowing of which is visible in Moscow's approach to Kosovo—its activities in Latin America and Cuba presumably would be stepped up. But would expanded Soviet activities in Latin America be of the type to cause friction with the United States as during the cold war? Probably not, so long as Russia perceives its national interests as lying with the United States—which is likely to be the case for some time to come, even as Russia gets back on its feet. Despite all its talk of cooperating with fellow Slavs in Kosovo, for example, it was Moscow that informed Milosevic that the game was up in Kosovo, in the end abandoning the Milosevic regime. Nor did Russia supply Milosevic with its latest military technology as he tried to defend against NATO bombing. All this because Russia–U.S. cooperation still counts in Moscow.

Should Russia succeed in reestablishing a consortium of the former republics of the USSR under its leadership and begin to pursue a foreign policy agenda on a grander and quasi-imperial scale, Latin America conceivably might come more into play—depending on the type of government and its ideology in Moscow. If Castro or a Castro look-alike were in power, still Communist and still anti-American in posture, today's closer Moscow-Havana relations could presage expanded Russian-Cuban ties—through Lourdes, nuclear energy cooperation, or more favorable trade relations for Cuba. But given that the margins for Soviet–Latin American cooperation outside Cuba have been historically quite narrow, albeit highly significant during the cold war, the region probably would not suddenly jump into high priority compared to areas like Eastern Europe, Southeastern Europe, Central Asia, and the Middle and Far East.

We are left with a post–cold war setting in Latin America where unique political cultures will continue to create complex political settings and challenges to democratic institution-building, where commercial and trade interdependence should grow, and where U.S.–Latin American relations have the potential to improve significantly. Such a post–cold war Latin America does not mean an end to leftists and guerrilla wars, border disputes, an immediate thaw in U.S.–Cuban relations, nor absence of strains in U.S.–Latin American relations. Such issues as drug trafficking, illegal immigration, environmental deterioration, and trade and aid issues, moreover, will affect U.S.–Latin and inter-American cooperation. Still, the new era promises a more viable setting for progress in U.S.–Latin American cooperation and for regional economic development, political stability, and democracy. Given the region's huge disparity in income distribution and widespread economic difficulties, such progress would be welcome. Russia will be there, but not as a major threat to U.S. interests.

NOTES

1. See Abraham F. Lowenthal and Gregory F. Treverton, eds., *Latin America in a New World* (Boulder: Westview Press, 1994); Michael J. Kryzanek, *Latin America: Change and Challenge* (Harper Collins College Publisher, 1995); Peter H. Smith, *Talons of the Eagle: Dynamics of Latin American Relations* (New York: Oxford University Press, 1996); and Yuri Pavlov, *The Soviet Union and Cuba* (Coral Gables: University of Miami Press, 1993).

2. See Wayne Smith, ed., *The Russians Aren't Coming* (New York: Lynne Rienner Publishers, 1992); Vladimir P. Sudarev, "Russia and Latin America," *Hemisphere* 5, no. 2 (winter/spring 1993): 12–15; Pavlov, *The Soviet Union and Cuba*; and earlier works, such as Eusebio Mujal-Leon, *The USSR and Latin America: A Developing Relationship* (Boston: Unwin Hyman, 1989).

3. This point is underscored by the series of congressional hearings from the early 1960s onward that centered on the "Communist Threat in the Western Hemisphere." See also Pavlov, *The Soviet Union and Cuba*; Sergo A. Mikoyan, "Russia and Latin America in the 1990s," in Lowenthal and Treverton, *Latin America in a New World*, chap. 6; and Robert A. Pastor, *Whirlpool: U.S. Foreign Policy Toward Latin America and the Caribbean* (Princeton: Princeton University Press, 1992).

4. K. Khachaturov, "An Emerging Power Center in Latin America," *International Affairs* 45, no. 1 (1999): 49–56; K. Khachaturov, "To the South of the Rio Grande," *International Affairs* 44, no. 2 (1988): 63–70; V. Sudarev, "Russian Diplomacy Towards Latin America," *International Affairs* 43, no. 2 (1997): 50–61;

and K. Khachaturov, "Ye. Primakov in Latin America," *International Affairs* 42, no. 4 (1996): 51–56.

5. Khachaturov, "An Emerging Power Center in Latin America," 49–56.

6. See Mikoyan, "Russia and Latin America in the 1990s," in Lowenthal and Treverton, *Latin America in a New World*, 108.

7. Ibid., 107.

8. Karen Brutents, "A New Soviet Perspective," in Smith, ed., *The Russians Aren't Coming*, 72.

9. Ibid., 73.

10. This perspective is from Lowenthal and Treverton, *Latin America in a New World*, 2.

11. Jaime Suchlicki, "Cuba Without Soviet Subsidies," A Freedom House Publications, 3/1997, 3–7.

12. Smith, *Talons of the Eagle*, chap. 12; see also Joseph S. Tulchin, ed., *Consolidation of Democracy in Latin America* (Washington, D.C.: Woodrow Wilson Center, 1995), chap. 8.

13. *Ibid.*

14. See Michael J. Kryzanek, *Latin America: Change and Challenge* (Harper Collins College Publishers, 1995), 61, 89, 95.

15. On these and other activities in U.S.–Latin American relations, see Walter LaFeber, *Inevitable Revolutions: The United States and Central America* (New York: W.W. Norton & Co., 1984).

16. See Cole Blasier, *The Giant's Rival: The USSR and Latin America* (Pittsburgh: University of Pittsburgh Press, 1987).

17. *Ibid.*

18. Ibid., 64.

19. Ibid., chap. 3.

20. By 1990 Soviet analysts were arguing that Third World "economic burdens . . . have not helped the Soviet Union . . . this is the cost of imperial overreach." Author's interviews with members of the Institute for the Study of the USA and Canada, Moscow, January and May 1990.

21. Interview with Goshu Wolde, Foreign Minister of Ethiopia, 1983–86, 16 December 1990, Washington, D.C.

22. W. Raymond Duncan and Carolyn McGiffert Ekedahl, *Moscow and the Third World Under Gorbachev* (Boulder, CO: Westview Press, 1990), chap. 3.

23. *Federal Broadcast Information Reports (FBIS)-Latin America* cover Foreign Minister Shevardnadze's trip to Mexico in October 1986, the first visit by a Soviet foreign minister to a Latin American country other than Cuba. See FBIS for Deputy Foreign Minister Viktor Komplektov's visits to Brazil, Uruguay, and Mexico shortly thereafter; Boris Yeltsin's travels to Nicaragua in March 1987 and Shevardnadze's return trip to Latin America in the fall of 1987. Shevardnadze met with top officials in Brazil, Argentina, Uruguay, and Cuba. Gorbachev made a historic visit to Cuba in April 1989 and Shevardnadze returned to Nicaragua in October 1989. Various Latin American presidents were visiting Gorbachev and Shevardnadze in the Soviet Union during this period. Soviet trips to Latin America averaged around thirteen per year during 1976–1984. They jumped to around twenty per year after 1985 when Gorbachev came to power.

24. Valery Nikolayenko, " An Official Statement of the New Soviet Policy in Latin America," in Smith, ed., *The Russians Aren't Coming*, 58.

25. Michael Kramer, "Anger, Bluff-and Cooperation," *Time* (4 June 1990): 38–45;

and *Washington Post*, 30 May 1990, 1.

26. Nikolayenko, "An Official Statement of the New Soviet Policy in Latin America," 57–65.

27. Brutents, "A New Soviet Perspective," in Smith, ed., *The Russians Aren't Coming*," 66.

28. Ibid., p. 74.

29. See the superb study of Soviet-Cuban relations, Yuri Pavlov, *Soviet-Cuban Alliance: 1959–1991* (New Brunswick and London: Transaction Publishers, 1994), produced by the North-South Center, University of Florida. Pavlov is a veteran Soviet foreign service officer with extensive experience in international affairs.

30. Anatoly Dobrynin, Moscow's ambassador to America's six cold war presidents, notes that the "myth" of Cuba as a Soviet proxy "was especially damaging for us in America, where the Cuban Crisis of 1962 had fixed the idea firmly. But it was the Cubans and not us who had initially interfered (in Angola) by sending their own military forces to back the MPLA, on their own initiative and without consulting us." Dobrynin goes on to write that "The Soviet leadership never contemplated using the Cuban troops in any third country, but the Cubans quickly managed to involve us there in the pretext of international solidarity." See Dobrynin's memoirs, *In Confidence*, (New York: Random House, Times Books, 1995), 362–63.

31. Pavlov, *Soviet-Cuban Alliance*, 116.

32. Ibid., 117.

33. Ibid., 138.

34. See *International Affairs* 1 (January 1993).

35. Karen Khachaturov, "Latin America and We," *International Affairs* (October 1992): 32.

36. Vladimir Razuvayev, "Russia and the Post-Soviet Geopolitical Area," *International Affairs* (August 1993): 111.

37. See Khachaturov, "Latin America and We," 36

38. Ibid.

39. Ibid., 39.

40. "Russia's Diplomacy Towards Latin America," *International Affairs* 43, no. 2 (1997): 50.

41. See K. Khachaturov, "Ye. Primakov in Latin America," *International Affairs* 42, no. 4 (1996): 51–56.

42. Khachaturov, "To the South of the Rio Grande," *International Affairs* 44, no. 2 (1998): 61–70.

43. Ibid., 64.

44. Ibid. In discussing the Primakov and Nemtsov trips to Latin America, *International Affairs* analyst, Khachaturov reminded his audience that the United States has long been sensitive about Russia's presence in its "backyard," while Washington had little difficulty in declaring some of the former USSR zones as in its "vital interests." So Russia diplomacy by the mid-1990s was geared to countering the U.S. presence in Russia's strategic arena with a renewed Russian presence in the U.S. "backyard."

45. Ibid., 70.

46. Ibid., 66.

47. Khachaturov, "Ye Primakov in Latin America," 54.

48. Sudarev, "Russian Diplomacy Towards Latin America," 50–61.

49. See Jorge I. Domínguez and Susan Kaufman Purcell, "Political Evolution in the Hemisphere," in Albert Fishlow and James Jones, eds., *The United States*

and the Americas: A Twenty-First Century View, The American Assembly, Columbia University (New York: W. W. Norton, 1998), chap. 6.

50. Tulchin, *The Consolidation of Democracy in Latin America,* 136.

51. Abraham F. Lowenthal, "United States–Latin American Relations at the Century's Turn: Managing the 'Intermestic' Agenda, in Albert Fishlow and James Jones, *The United States and the Americas.* The American Assembly, Columbia University (New York: W.W. Norton & Company, 1998).

52. Mario Baeza and Sidney Weinraub, "Economic and Political Constants/ Changes in Latin America," in Fishlow and Jones, *United States,* 52.

53. Juan Gabriel Valdes, "Changing Paradigms in Latin America: From Dependency to Neoliberalism in the International Context," in Tulchin, *Consolidation,* 136.

54. Smith, *Talons of the Eagle,* 292.

55. Pastor, *Whirlpool,* 222.

56. Jorge G. Castañeda. *Utopia Unarmed: The Latin American Left After the Cold War* (New York: Alfred A. Knopf, 1994).

57. Mark Falcoff in "Latin America After the Cold War," in *Latin America: U.S. Policy After the Cold War* (New York: American Society, 1991), 33.

58. Pastor, *Whirlpool,* 222.

59. Baeza and Weinraub, "Economic and Political Constants," in Fishlow and Jones, *United States,* 46.

60. Jack Mendelsonn, "Huddling with the Honchos in Havana," *Bulletin of the Atomic Scientists* 49, issue 7 (September 1993): 14–19.

61. *Strategic Survey, 1992–1993,* The Institute for Strategic Studies (London, 1993), 61.

62. *Latin America Weekly Report,* 11 March 1993, 118.

63. Ibid.

64. *Latin America Weekly Report,* 24 November 1994.

65. *Latin America Weekly Report,* 9 December 1993; 22 July 1993; and 25 March 1993.

66. *Latin America Weekly Report,* 31 March 1994.

67. *Time* 145, no. 7 (20 February 1995): 51.

68. Pastor, *Whirlpool,* p. 222.

69. Ibid., 224.

70. *New York Times,* 17 January 1999.

71. *Cuba: A Year After the Pope—Return of the Iron Curtain?* PAX Christi, Netherlands, February 1999, pp. 8–10.

72. Sudarev, "Russian Diplomacy Toward Latin America," 58.

73. Ibid.

74. Khachaturov, "An Emerging Power Center in Latin America," 52.

75. *The Current Digest of the Post-Soviet Press* 51, no. 3 (17 February 1999): 21.

76. *Latin America Special Reports,* December 1998, p. 1.

77. Tulchin, *Consolidation,* 136. See also William A. Barnes, "Incomplete Democracy in Central America: Polarization and Voter Turnout in Nicaragua and El Salvador," *Journal of Interamerican Studies and World Affairs* 40, no. 3 (fall 1998): 63–101.

78. Domínguez and Purcell, "Political Evolution in the Hemisphere," 159 ff.

79. Tulchin, *Consolidation,* 136; Baeza and Weintraub, "Economic and Political Constants," 54 ff.

80. Peter H. Smith, "Trouble Ahead? Prospects for U.S. Relations with Latin America," in *The United States and the Americas,* chap. 7.

81. L. Klepatskii, "Russia's Foreign Policy Landmarks," *International Affairs* 45, no. 2 (1999): 18–22.

Sub-Saharan Africa after the Cold War

Marina Ottaway

Ten years after the end of the cold war, Africa is buffeted by contradictory trends. Largely ignored by the major powers, African countries are nonetheless deeply influenced by the forces of globalization. Overlooked by foreign investors worried about political instability and poor communications, they are under pressure to open up their markets to foreign competition; unable to take full advantage of the opportunities offered by the information revolution, they are affected by the unfettered spread of information technological change has fostered; still dominated by largely authoritarian governments fearful of losing their grip on power, they feel compelled to at least speak the language of democracy, transparency, and accountability and to open up their political systems enough to satisfy aid donors.

Abandoned to their own devices on the one hand and deeply influenced by worldwide trends on the other, African countries are struggling to find their place in the international economy and the international order, as well as to establish a new order in the region. Ten years after the end of the cold war, Africa is a continent in turmoil, facing a serious crisis but also new opportunities.

AFRICA MARGINALIZED

The end of the cold war was greeted in Africa with relief at first, because the confrontation between the superpowers had some obvious negative repercussions for the continent. Although the confrontation did not create conflicts that would otherwise not have existed, it caused them to become more costly, prolonged, and internationalized. The first Ethio-Somali War in 1963, for example, was an obscure, purely bilateral conflict over borders and range land which lasted a few days and to which the world paid no attention. The second Ethio-Somali War in 1977 continued for more than a year, and was fought with tanks and planes, with the Soviet

Union and the United States each supporting one of the combatants and Cuban troops deployed on the battlefield.

The relief that Africa was no longer a battleground for outside interests soon turned into dismay. Although it had led to the internationalization and thus intensification of many conflicts, the cold war had at least kept Africa on the international map and had provided benefits for a variety of actors. Furthermore, numerous African leaders who had been kept in power by the United States, the Soviet Union, or France suddenly found their position precarious. Many governments had become dependent on international assistance—including those preaching self-reliance—and feared the flow of money would dry up if it no longer served the donors' strategic interests.[1] Indeed, many African governments during the cold war deliberately tried to increase foreign assistance by playing one superpower against the other, and some had even succeeded. While it is true that many African conflicts were exacerbated by foreign intervention, African governments and liberation movements usually pleaded for even more help and more weapons than they received, not for less.[2]

The earlier experiences of many Third World countries suggested that détente between the major powers was dangerous. In the early 1970s, Egypt blamed the perpetuation of the "no war, no peace" situation that followed the 1967 war with Israel on détente and the resulting decrease of U.S. interest in the Middle East. This led Anwar Sadat to go to war in October 1973, forcing the United States and the Soviet Union to reengage in the Middle East peace process.[3] African countries felt they had suffered a similar fate of marginalization from the mid-1960s to the mid-1970s, when the Soviet Union had lost interest in the continent following the demise of several radical African leaders and the beginning of détente.[4] The rise of a new generation of African Marxist-Leninist regimes in the mid-1970s had been good for Africa, rekindling superpower interest. If détente had been dangerous, the end of the cold war was much worse. Soon, Africans were bemoaning the marginalization of their continent and pointing out that African countries could no longer rely on outside help to straighten out their problems.[5] Selim Selim, the Organization of African Unity's general secretary, warned repeatedly of that danger. In retrospect, the cold war period did not appear so bad for Africa.

The new epoch was very uncertain. During a brief period of optimism engendered by the successful transition from apartheid in South Africa, there was some heady talk of an African renaissance under the guidance of a new generation of dynamic, democratic leaders. It was enough to convince both U.S. Secretary of State Madeleine Albright and President Bill Clinton to visit the continent in quick succession in 1997 and 1998, but the enthusiasm could not be sustained. Africa's problems were too deep, and progress would be too slow and costly, for foreign powers without major interests at stake to sustain their involvement. Even at its peak, enthusiasm about the African renaissance never went beyond rhetoric: assistance programs remained modest.

By the end of the 1990s, international optimism was replaced by renewed pessimism as conflict broke out all over Central Africa, and U.S. and European interest in Africa plummeted. Theoretically, this gave African countries greater autonomy to shape their future, but most were not ready to take advantage of it. The continent had not recovered yet from the profound economic crisis of the 1980s. While some countries were showing signs of an economic turnaround, in most economic growth rates still remained low, below those for population growth.[6] Even more threatening, the number of failed or collapsed states mired in conflict was increasing steadily. Somalia was no longer a state, but simply a space on the map of Africa. In Sudan, civil war had become permanent. Sierra Leone was approaching the same condition, moving from crisis to crisis with little evidence that a lasting accommodation could be reached. By the end of the decade Rwanda, Burundi, and Liberia had stabilized somewhat after earlier upheavals, but the possibility of a new outbreak of conflict loomed large in all of them. Ethiopia and Eritrea, which had emerged from decades of civil conflict in 1991, were at war with each other by 1998. In Angola, prospects for peace appeared more distant than ever. In the Democratic Republic of the Congo (formerly Zaire), the collapse of the state appeared imminent; the power vacuum left by the weakness of the central government allowed domestic conflicts to proliferate and invited the intervention of neighboring countries.

In the cold war era, such conflicts would not have been ignored by the outside world, but in the 1990s Africa was no longer seen as a region whose quarrels affected the national interests of the major powers. Long gone were the days when National Security Advisor Zbigniew Brzezinski could declare "SALT lies buried in the sands of the Ogaden." [7] In the 1990s, the entire state of Somalia was allowed to wither away. Even the new humanitarian and human rights concerns that dominated the political rhetoric of the 1990s were not sufficient to cause intervention in Africa. The 1994 massacre of some 800,000 civilians in Rwanda was greeted with horror but not with action. Watching NATO (North Atlantic Treaty Orga-

nization) intervention in Kosovo and the generous assistance provided to refugees there five years later, Africans expressed growing
resentment at what they perceived as race-based neglect of their
region.

LOOKING TO THE FUTURE

Ten years after the end of the cold war, Sub-Saharan Africa faces
two major challenges. The first is to overcome its political and economic marginalization. The second is to devise a regional order
that can be enforced from within Africa, to replace the imperial
order enforced first by the colonial powers and later by the superpowers; it is the demise of this order after the end of the cold war
that led to the unprecedented outbreak of conflict in Africa in the
late 1990s. It is only by meeting these challenges that African countries can emerge as truly independent international actors in the
post–cold war world, overcoming the subordinate position in
which they have remained even after the end of the colonial period.

Overcoming Marginalization

The post–cold war international order is still very fluid, and African countries are not in a position to influence its characteristics.
They can, however, position themselves in the emerging order. Africa will be able to overcome its marginalization if it either reac-
quires some importance to the security of the United States and
other major actors or realizes its potential as a significant new market and supplier of economic goods.

SECURITY CONCERNS

It is unlikely that most African countries will be able to make
themselves relevant to the security of any major power. Only a few,
such as Ethiopia and Uganda, may be able to play the security
card, and even these countries can succeed only if they remain politically stable.

Africa always occupied a marginal position in the international
order. The last of the continents to be absorbed into international
society, Africa remained a preserve of the colonial powers until the
1960s.[8] As African countries moved toward independence, the superpowers increased their involvement, while Britain allowed its

ties to the former possessions to slacken greatly. France, on the other hand, maintained a high profile on the continent. It pursued an extremely interventionist policy in its former colonies in order to maintain in power leaders willing to protect French interests, going as far as sending troops on several occasions to restore the order it wanted. It also kept strong economic linkages to its former possessions and largely controlled their monetary policies through the CFA franc, the common currency of these countries, which was pegged to the French franc at a fixed rate. France's decision to stop propping up the CFA franc in January 1994, causing it to be devalued by 50 percent, signaled the decreasing commitment to Africa even on the part of the country that had maintained the strongest presence in its former colonies.

The United States, which had no significant historical ties to Africa, quickly emerged as a major player in postcolonial Africa. Although the United States never deemed Africa to be crucial to the protection of its interests, it was unwilling to allow the spread of Soviet influence, either. The same was true of the Soviet Union. Its interests in Africa were limited, but in order to retain its superpower image it could not leave a part of the world in the hands of the West without challenge. In addition, a decision to increase the Soviet navy's ability to operate in the Indian Ocean during the 1970s heightened Soviet interest in acquiring access to naval facilities in the Horn of Africa.

Soviet involvement in Africa was highly opportunistic, waxing and waning depending on the circumstances. Involvement was considerable in the early 1960s, when many radical nationalist leaders, buoyed by their success in achieving independence, were eager to establish ties to the socialist countries and to decrease their dependence on the West. But Soviet interest waned when a wave of coups d'état in the mid-1960s led to the demise of many of the early radical leaders. It revived again in the mid-1970s, when the self-proclaimed Marxist-Leninist regimes that seized power in Ethiopia as well as in newly independent Angola and Mozambique offered new, easy opportunities to establish a strong presence in Africa.[9] But the Soviet Union became disillusioned with Africa once again during the 1980s. Ethiopia, Angola, and Mozambique were all entangled in costly and unwinnable wars, demanding weapons and economic assistance, but offering no countervailing political or economic returns. Coupled with the pressure resulting from domestic turmoil, the seemingly intractable problems of its African allies led the Soviet Union to push Mozambique toward the West, to cooperate with the United States in finding a solution to the conflict in Angola, and to abandon Ethiopia to its fate. Indeed, the late 1980s saw a considerable flourishing of U.S.–Soviet cooperation in Africa.[10]

The superpowers' competition in Africa was particularly intense from the mid-1970s to the mid-1980s, concentrating in two areas, the Horn and southern Africa. The presence of radical, self-proclaimed Marxist-Leninist regimes—Somalia after 1971, Ethiopia after 1974, Mozambique and Angola after 1975—heightened U.S. fears that the Soviet Union would establish military bases or facilities in these areas—as indeed Moscow tried to do. The Soviet Union obtained access to the port of Berbera in Somalia around 1974, developing it into an important facility including a petroleum storage depot, a naval missile-handling facility, a dry dock, and an airfield used for reconnaissance flights.[11] When the reversal of alliances during the 1977–78 Ethio-Somali war caused the Soviets to be expelled from Berbera, they obtained a new facility from Ethiopia, in the Dahlak Islands off the coast of Eritrea. The Soviet Union never obtained a base in southern Africa. However, it had access to airfields in Angola, and from there it was able to conduct surveillance flights over the southern Atlantic.

Military bases were less important to the United States, which had much greater access to Africa to begin with. Until 1975, Angola and Mozambique were controlled by Portugal, a member of NATO. Beginning in 1969, following a policy review ordered by then National Security Advisor Henry Kissinger, the United States also supported the white regimes in Rhodesia and South Africa, counting on them to keep the Soviet Union at a distance.[12] But the United States also maintained some facilities of its own in Africa. It developed a base in Asmara, then in Ethiopia, from 1952 to 1977, which served as an important link in ship-to-shore communications with the Indian Ocean fleet. When the Soviet Union was expelled from Berbera, the United States took over the installations there. Finally, it helped the Zairian government develop military facilities in Kamina, in southern Zaire, thereby acquiring easier access to potential conflict areas in Shaba province and in Angola.

The involvement of the superpowers was based almost entirely on security considerations during the cold war. Economic interests of the United States were minor and concentrated on a few mineral or oil rich countries—Zaire, South Africa, Nigeria, Rhodesia (later Zimbabwe), and Angola. The Soviet Union's economic involvement was mostly limited to a small amount of barter trade and, in the late 1970s, fishing agreements with several countries, which caused considerable friction between the USSR and the African partners, but were certainly not vital to the USSR.

Since the disappearance of the Soviet Union, Africa has lost its relevance to the security of the United States or of any other major power. Regional conflicts, once seen as potential proxy wars between superpowers, are now considered to have little or no international importance. During the 1970s and 1980s, the struggle for power in Angola between the MPLA and UNITA brought in the United States and South Africa on the side of the União Nacional para a Independencia Total de Angola (UNITA), the Soviet Union and Cuba on that of the Movimento Popular de Libertação de Angola (MPLA), delayed the independence of Namibia, and was at the center of intense diplomatic maneuvering to find a solution.[13] When the confrontation resumed after the failed elections of 1992 and then again after the failure to implement the 1994 Lusaka Protocol, the world largely ignored it. Indeed, all African civil wars are now seen as purely internal conflicts, of interest only to the participants. Without the Soviet Union ready to arm one side, conflicts in Somalia, Rwanda, Sierra Leone, or the Democratic Republic of the Congo can be safely ignored by the United States. The United States is generous with exhortations to negotiate and with offers of mediation. However, even humanitarian assistance is becoming increasingly niggardly in African countries, such as Sudan and Angola, where war has become a chronic condition.

African countries today would enter the security considerations of the United States only in two ways: either if they themselves controlled nuclear, biological, or chemical weapons that could pose an international rather than domestic threat; or if there was a possibility of their becoming allied with countries hostile to the United States—thus recreating the situation that existed during the cold war. While the former scenario is highly unlikely, the latter is emerging in the Horn of Africa.

In themselves, African countries do not pose a threat to the United States or any other major power, just as they never did in the past. African militaries are not equipped with weapons of mass destruction. Far from being capable of projecting power outside their countries' borders, many have trouble controlling their own territory. Indeed, the weakness of African militaries is proving to be an obstacle to plans by the Organization of African Unity to take on a more important role in conflict resolution in Africa, with African peacekeepers replacing United Nations troops. Most African armies do not have the organization, equipment, or training to operate successfully in such a role. The intervention in Liberia by

ECOMOG (Economic Community of West African States' Monitoring Group) provided clear evidence both of the technical shortcomings of African armies and of the difficulty peacekeepers
encounter in maintaining neutrality when they come from neighboring countries with a direct interest in the outcome of the conflict. Nigeria, the country with the greatest military capability, also
had the highest degree of political involvement.[14] Initiatives by
both the United States and France to train African troops for
peacekeeping operations had only reached a few thousand soldiers
in a small number of countries by the end of the 1990s. Furthermore, there was still no agreement on when and under whose
command such troops might be deployed.[15]

Only one country in Africa has ever had nuclear weapons—
South Africa under the apartheid regime. During the 1970s and
1980s, the National Party government—convinced that the Soviet
Union was planning "total onslaught" against South Africa to put
in power its puppet, the African National Congress (ANC)—
developed a "total response" strategy that included the building
up of the South African Defense Force (SADF), the creation of an
arms industry, and the development of nuclear capacity, in addition to giving the military a role in maintaining domestic security.[16]
The development of nuclear weapons was carried out in secret—
formally, South Africa's nuclear capability was limited to the generation of electricity. But there were repeated indications that South
Africa was working on the development of nuclear weapons, probably in collaboration with Israel. In March 1993, in the waning
days of apartheid, President F. W. de Klerk admitted that South
Africa had developed nuclear bombs in the past but that the program had been scrapped and the bombs deactivated.[17] As a result,
South Africa in the late 1990s is not a nuclear power, although it
must be assumed to still have the capacity to resume a nuclear
weapons program.

In the days of the cold war, an ANC-governed South Africa having nuclear weapons or capable of producing them would have
been considered a security threat to the United States. Without the
Soviet Union, and with South Africa more concerned with attracting aid and investment from the industrialized countries than with
defying the United States, South Africa's nuclear potential is not
seen as a significant threat. Additional guarantees were provided
in 1995, when South Africa signed the indefinite extension of the
nuclear non-proliferation treaty.

In the immediate post–cold war period, thus, no African country
is or is likely to become a threat to U.S. security in its own right.

Any threat coming from Africa will be indirect in the future as it was in the past, the result of an alliance between African governments and a country or countries hostile to the United States. With the disappearance of the Soviet Union, the greatest danger for the United States is the possibility that African states will form alliances with radical governments or Islamist organizations in the Middle East. Movements with links to international terrorist organizations supported by Iran and Iraq are indeed operating in African countries. This is the major potential security threat coming from Africa in the late 1990s.

The area most affected is the Horn of Africa. As a result, the United States has pursued policies and entered into alliances very similar to those of the cold war period. Several factors make the Horn into a sensitive area, some constant and some new. Location, between Africa and the Middle East, and between North Africa and Sub-Saharan Africa, is obviously a constant. The mixed religious affiliation of the population is another: Sudan is divided between a Moslem north and a Christian or animist south; Ethiopia and Eritrea are divided between Christian highlands and Moslem lowlands; Uganda and Kenya also have mixed populations—only Somalia is homogeneously Moslem. The Horn has also been an extremely unstable area for the last twenty years at least, divided by power conflicts, ethnic conflicts, class conflicts, and the meddling of the superpowers.[18] To this dangerous mixture, a new element was added in the late 1980s, when the ousting of President Jafaar Nimeiri eventually led to the rise of an Islamist military government in Sudan. The Islamic militancy of this government heightened the southern populations' fear of Moslem domination, leading to an escalation of the chronic conflict between north and south. The brutal policies of the Sudanese government led the Western aid donors to withdraw their support. A bankrupt Sudan has turned increasingly to Iran, Iraq, and to extremist Islamist organizations for help. As a result, it has become a staging area from which money and support flow to Islamist groups in neighboring countries.

The United States has responded with a policy of containment, supporting the countries bordering on Sudan, as it had bolstered in the past the pro-Western countries bordering a Soviet ally. Ethiopia, Eritrea, and Uganda in particular have received much support from the United States as well as Israel. As in the past, this strategy of containment has a downside. The Horn has again become polarized. Countries enjoying close relations with the United States and Israel automatically have bad relations with Sudan and

Islamist movements, just as in the past they had bad relations with
the Soviet Union and its African allies. This exacerbates regional
conflicts and lends them, as in the days of the cold war, an international dimension. Diplomatic relations between Eritrea and Sudan
were severed in December 1994, after Eritrea accused Sudan of
fomenting resistance among Eritrean Moslems. Relations between
Uganda and Sudan also deteriorated rapidly, culminating in a
break in April 1995. In this case, too, Khartoum was accused of
supporting Islamist groups and fomenting unrest.

The specific pattern of alliances caused by the policies of the Sudanese regime will probably not last. The outbreak of a border
conflict between Eritrea and Ethiopia in mid-1998 led both countries to seek to improve their relations with Sudan, while at the
same time causing the United States to revise its earlier optimistic
appraisal of the two regimes. But while the specific alignment will
continue to change, the lesson of the Horn remains: in the post–
cold war period, the threat posed by political Islam has emerged as
the major security issue that causes the United States to pay some
attention to Africa—a new cold war of sorts. The threat posed by
politicized Islam, however, will not rekindle U.S. interest in Africa
on a large scale. The old cold war affected not only the Horn, but
the entire continent, particularly southern Africa and Zaire. The
new "cold war" is much more contained. There is no perception,
at this point, that Islamist movements could take advantage of any
African conflict, as the Soviet Union could.

DEALING WITH THE MARKET

Competition for markets is likely to remain a major concern of
all countries in the post–cold war period. In this global competition, Africa is truly marginal in the 1990s. Overcoming that marginal status is the most important challenge for the next decade.
Africa is not competing actively for a share of the international
market; the composition and direction of African exports has
changed remarkably little during thirty years of independence; in
general, the level of exports is stagnating and even decreasing. Exporting countries elsewhere in the world, furthermore, are not
competing with each other for a share of the African market. In
1990, African exports only amounted to 1.10 percent of global exports, its imports to 1.24 percent.[19] At the end of the decade, the
figures were unchanged. The reason for this marginality is simple:
Africa remains extremely poor, and the realization of its economic

potential is stymied by political instability and by the uncertain macroeconomic policies of most governments.

Many African countries should be attractive to investors and sellers alike. Because of their population size, Nigeria and the Democratic Republic of the Congo (DRC) could become important markets, with Nigeria's oil and the Congo's copper, cobalt, and diamonds providing the foreign exchange needed to import goods. The political situation prevents that potential from being realized. Both countries are perceived as crisis areas, not as promising new markets. The restoration of civilian rule in Nigeria following the 1999 elections may eventually alter the international perception of Nigeria as an unstable, troubled state, but it is unlikely to have an immediate effect. Even South Africa, which attracted considerable foreign investment as long as the white regime appeared firmly in control, is finding it difficult to convince investors that it had stabilized again under majority rule and that it is a safe place for business.

Another factor that keeps Africa on the margins of the world's economic activity is the high cost of doing business there. Transport, communications, and energy costs are much higher than in other parts of the world. Corruption, government hostility to the private sector, and simple incompetence of public bureaucracies compound the problem.[20] So does the poor level of education of the work force, a situation worsened by the brain drain that deprives African countries of much needed managerial and technical skills.

The economic policies pursued by most African governments since independence have contributed to economic stagnation and remain a deterrent to foreign investment. Well into the 1980s, most African countries pursued development through state intervention, the creation of parastatal enterprises, and the maintaining of high tariff barriers, all steps that aimed at promoting import substitution rather than export promotion. Overvalued exchange rates and heavy taxation discouraged exporters. As a result, exports stagnated and Africa remained a supplier of raw materials and an importer of manufactured goods. African countries also became importers of food, as low producer prices discouraged domestic production.[21] Many countries started reforming their policies during the 1990s, mostly as the result of the conditionality imposed by the International Monetary Fund, the World Bank, and the bilateral donors. But, studies show, the process has been slow, the commitments of most governments uncertain, and the results very modest, if not outright disappointing. Africa does not appear on the verge of an economic revolution yet.[22]

Nevertheless, there is now a growing conviction that even African countries at some point will join the process of development. When that happens, Africa will represent a last frontier, the last potentially large, untapped market in the world. At present, South Africa is being watched as the country most likely to experience rapid growth, and also as a potential gateway to the rest of the continent; doubts about the country's political stability, however, have prevented this interest from being translated into substantial investment. There is not yet enough confidence in the future to stave off the prospects of the continued economic marginalization of Africa in the short run.

Establishing An African Order

Increasing marginalization puts much greater responsibility on Africans for reestablishing order and good government in their respective countries and also for creating a regional order that can be maintained without outside intervention. Given the difficult economic conditions that prevail in much of Africa, the weakness of most governments and their institutions, and the problems that plague the Organization of African Unity and subregional groupings such as the Economic Community of West African States (ECOWAS) and the Southern Africa Development Community (SADC), it will be a considerable burden for African countries to find viable solutions to the continent's multiple problems in the near future. However, the present neglect of Africa by outside powers also provides opportunities: for the first time since the beginning of the colonial period, Africans are allowed to forge an order, within and among their countries, that they can accept and sustain. The prize for success is the real decolonization of Africa. The cost of failure is the perpetuation and spreading of the conflicts that already affect a large swath of Africa extending from the Horn in the northeast to Angola in the southwest.

African states have been troubled entities since the early days of decolonization in the 1960s. At the root of the problem was the imbalance between the effective capacity of the new states—which had weak administrative structures, scant economic resources, and a shortage of trained personnel, and the ambitious models of economic development and political control they chose to pursue. The model of economic development adopted by most African countries put an enormous burden on the state, which was expected to become the most important agent of development. The idea was not controversial at the time. European countries had reconstructed their infrastructure and their industries after World War II under state control. In addition, in both the United States and Europe the state had become responsible for providing a vast array of services to its citizens. Development economists—including those at the World Bank and the U.S. Agency for International Development—fully accepted the view that the state had to become the major agent of development, particularly in African countries where there was no well-established entrepreneurial class. African leaders embraced these ideas with enthusiasm, but the African state did not have the administrative or financial capacity to discharge such onerous responsibilities. The attempt to take on responsibilities they could not possibly discharge started most African countries on a path of economic decline.

African governments, furthermore, sought to impose strict political controls on their countries. Here, too, their capacity did not match their ambitions. They quickly dismantled the democratic institutions the colonial powers hastily tried to put in place before independence and drifted toward single-party systems and military regimes with the tacit acceptance of the Western powers convinced that authoritarian governments would maintain stability better than democratic ones. In reality, many of the new regimes became extremely repressive, but few managed to govern their countries effectively. African states thus became authoritarian and at the same time "soft"—that is, incapable of exercising authority.

Relations among African states were also governed by principles that were widely accepted at the time, but proved extremely difficult to implement in Africa. After the experience of the interwar period and World War II, nationalism was discredited and rejected around the world, except in the form of anticolonial nationalism. The United Nations recognized the right to self-determination, but this was interpreted narrowly as a right for colonized peoples to independence, not a right for all groups claiming a distinctive national or ethnic identity to have their own states, or even a degree of autonomy.[23] Borders were assumed to be immutable. In the African context, these ideas led the Organization of African Unity to proclaim the inviolability of colonial borders and to adopt the principle of noninterference in the internal affairs of other countries.

The impact of these ideas was mixed. Noninterference led African governments to accept all incumbent leaders without asking questions, no matter how illegitimate their path to power or un-

conscionable their policies—Idi Amin in Uganda or Emperor Bo-
kassa in the Central African Republic were never officially
criticized by the Organization of African Unity. Recognition of colonial borders proved a mixed blessing. While it helped avoid
some border disputes and wars, it also provided a justification for
the maintenance of the status quo, no matter the specific circumstances or the cost. Eritrean nationalists fought for thirty years
without any support or recognition by African countries, although
their bid for independence was based on the fact that a colonial
border had separated Eritrea from Ethiopia for half a century.
Compounding the problem, many African states came to rely
heavily on foreign powers to safeguard their territorial integrity
and independence, rather than on their own administrative capacity, the allegiance of their populations, and the capacity of their
armed forces to maintain security. Many countries thus became
quasi-states, entities the international community recognizes as
sovereign de jure, but that have little effective capacity to exercise
that sovereignty de facto.[24]

In the late 1980s, the dominant ideas that had influenced the
internal political and economic development of African states as
well as their relations to each other were suddenly challenged by
events abroad and at home. Internationally, the Soviet Union,
faced with a growing economic crisis, essentially withdrew from the
continent, leaving African countries with no choice but to turn to
the West for assistance. The evidence of the economic failure of
the socialist countries, coupled with the direct pressure to institute
market-oriented economic reforms exercised by the International
Monetary Fund, the World Bank, and even bilateral donors, led
most African countries to rethink their economic policies. The fall
of the socialist regimes, which led to the emergence of strong pro-
democracy movements throughout Central Europe and the former Soviet Union, encouraged similar trends in African countries.
At the same time, the explosion of ethnic nationalism and the con-
sequent fragmentation of the Soviet Union, Yugoslavia, and
Czechoslovakia shook Africa's illusions that its borders were immutable and that ethnic nationalism was a thing of the past.

With all the ideas that had influenced Africa economically and
politically being challenged, African countries were confronted
with the task of defining new directions domestically and of forging a new system to maintain stability on the continent. At the beginning of the new millennium, the old order has been shattered,
but a new one has not emerged yet. As a result, Africa is rife with
possibilities but also torn by conflicts.

DOMESTIC TRENDS

The fall of socialist regimes in Eastern Europe and the Soviet Union encouraged the growth of pro-democracy movements in Africa as it did in the rest of the world. To be sure, there were strong pressures for change in Africa even before the demise of socialist regimes, but until then demands for change were not necessarily demands for democracy.

Although pro-democracy movements in Africa were initially weak, they were significant enough to undermine the ruling regimes' claim that single party rule suited the needs of Africa better than multiparty democracy. But together with the reappearance of political movements and organizations of civil society independent of the state there also came an upsurge of ethnic consciousness and ethnic political movements. As countries turned away from single-party rule and organized multiparty elections, the new political parties organized mostly along ethnic lines. Ethnic nationalism, once dismissed as "tribalism" by African leaders and intellectuals, gained a new respectability because of events in the rest of the world. The international community accepted, in some cases even welcomed, the fall of the Soviet empire and its division into its ethnic republics. What right did it have, then, to condemn attempts to restore the independence of the nations trapped within the arbitrary African state borders?[25]

At the turn of the decade, it remains difficult to judge how much progress toward democracy African countries have made. Superficially, the change has been considerable, with only a handful of countries still refusing to hold multiparty elections. But multiparty elections are only a first step in a long and difficult process. Democratic institutions remain weak in Africa, and the organizations of civil society that have multiplied rapidly thanks to donor funding are mostly artificial creations unlikely to survive without outside support. Furthermore, the number of elected governments overthrown by military movements is increasing—Niger, Sierra Leone, and Congo-Brazzaville are some of the examples.

Although it is premature to talk about democracy, trends toward greater political openness are evident everywhere.[26] By and large, political parties and all forms of voluntary associations operate more openly in most countries. The number of independent newspapers and magazines has increased, although it remains quite modest and most publications still struggle with government harassment and lack of funds. All political openings have a downside, however. To some extent, they may complicate the implementa-

tion of structural adjustment programs, because many governments hesitate to impose unpopular though needed reforms when
they have to stand for elections, and even take economically counterproductive populist measures in order to win support.[27]

TRENDS IN INTERSTATE RELATIONS

Ten years after the end of the cold war, the collapse of the old
order in Africa is much more evident than the emergence of a new
one. From the Horn of Africa in the northeast to Angola in the
southwest Africa is rent apart by multiple conflicts, many of them
linked to each other in intricate ways. There is little reason to believe that stability will return to the area in the near future. The
most worrisome situation is a cluster of conflicts involving the
Democratic Republic of the Congo, Rwanda, Uganda, Angola, and
Congo-Brazzaville as main actors, plus Zimbabwe, Zambia, Namibia, and the Central African Republic in secondary roles. It is
worthwhile discussing these conflicts at some length, because they
illustrate both the collapse of the old order and the difficulties of
creating a new one.

The crisis can be traced back to 1994, when a series of relatively
unconnected political threads started becoming entangled into
one major snarl. The first thread was ethnic conflict in Rwanda.
With ethnicity highly politicized since colonial times, the demographic composition of Rwanda—14 percent Tutsi and 86 percent
Hutu—was a dangerous mix. Hutus dominated the politics of the
independent country, after a showdown in 1959 sent several hundred thousand Tutsis fleeing across the border into Uganda. Tutsi
exiles supported Ugandan President Yoweri Museveni in his fight
for power in the early 1980s, gaining both political and military
support. This support facilitated the formation of the Rwandan Patriotic Front (RPF), which first launched attacks into Rwanda in
1990. With the help of other countries in the region, the conflict
was halted, and a promising agreement to form a government of
national reconciliation and an integrated national army was
reached in Arusha, Tanzania, in 1993. However, the implementation of the agreement was opposed by Hutu extremists in the military and a semiautonomous militia known as the Interahamwe.
When the Rwandan president, a Hutu, was killed in a still unexplained plane crash in 1994, Hutu extremists launched a mass
slaughter of Tutsis and moderate Hutus. In turn, the RPF
launched an all-out attack on Rwanda. When the country settled
after several months of horror, probably 800,000 people were

dead, the RPF was in power in Kigali, and two million people, including both refugees from the massacre and its perpetrators, were living in camps in Eastern Zaire.

There, the thread of ethnic conflict in Rwanda became entangled with that of the domestic politics of Zaire in the waning days of the regime of President Mobutu Sese Seko. In the 1990s, Zaire was in practice a country without a government. In Kinshasa, an ailing Mobutu still manipulated allies and foes effectively enough to prevent the formation of another government, but he had little or no control over the rest of the country and little hope of reestablishing it.

For Rwanda and also for Uganda, the weakness of the Zairian state was a problem. Opponents of the Ugandan government operated from eastern Zaire with the support of Sudan. In the refugee camps, members of the old Rwandan army defeated by the RPF and of the Interahamwe militia were reorganizing and rearming, under the eyes of humanitarian organizations that saw what was happening but did not have the means to separate refugees and armed men and could not stop housing and feeding the latter without starving the former. The international community was unwilling to intervene with the force necessary to do the job.

Seeking to protect itself against the threat posed by Hutu extremists rearming in the camps, the new Rwandan government, with the help of Uganda, chose a radical solution: it destroyed the camps from which the attacks were being mounted, and also sought to replace the Mobutu regime with one it hoped would be friendlier and more capable of controlling Zairian territory. So advanced was the disintegration of the Zairian state, compounded by the waning political skills of a dying Mobutu, that a weak guerrilla force, supported by Rwanda and Uganda and headed by a virtually unknown local warlord, Laurent Kabila, marched across the country and seized power in a few months.

But President Kabila proved to be an incompetent leader. He quickly alienated most domestic groups, from aspiring politicians in Kinshasa to provincial elites and organizations of civil society. He never gained the confidence of the international donor community, whose help the country badly needed. He also soon lost the support of the Ugandan and Rwandan governments, which were disillusioned by his lack of political acumen and even more by his incapacity to control the eastern region of the renamed DRC. With their enemies once again reorganizing and rearming in the Congo, Rwanda and Uganda abandoned Kabila in 1998 and threw their support behind his enemies. The new round of fighting gathered more threads into the growing tangle.

One of these threads was the struggle between the MPLA government and UNITA in Angola. The enmity between UNITA and the MPLA dated back to the 1960s, when both were fighting against the Portuguese government for the independence of Angola. The first round was won by the MPLA, which assumed power when Angola became independent in 1975. But UNITA did not desist and with the assistance of South Africa and the United States went to war against the MPLA, which had been receiving Soviet and Cuban support for years. The war in Angola thus turned into a proxy war between the superpowers. That phase came to an end in late 1988, when an agreement provided for the withdrawal of the Cubans and South Africans from Angola, as well as for the independence of Namibia. With this settlement, the United States and the Soviet Union were transformed from participants in the conflict to mediators of the continuing rivalry between the MPLA and UNITA. A peace agreement was signed by the two rivals in 1991 but did not hold. After losing elections in 1992, UNITA returned to war. A new agreement negotiated in 1994 was never implemented completely. As a result, the war in Angola resumed as the new conflict in the DRC was flaring up and the two became linked. The MPLA, fearful that UNITA would turn to the Congo for help, as it had done in the past, decided to back the Congolese government. Inevitably, UNITA supported the anti-Kabila insurgents.

Other foreign components added to the growing imbroglio. Zimbabwe, whose president Robert Mugabe has mining interests in the Congo, sent planes and troops to Kabila's defense with the financial support of Libya. Congo-Brazzaville, whose government was supported by the Angolan government and had ties to Kabila, nevertheless allowed—or at least was incapable of preventing—Congolese insurgents from using its territory to launch attacks.

The international community, as indicated earlier, remained aloof from these conflicts, offering little more than mediation and humanitarian assistance—the latter with increasing reluctance. A positive result of this neglect was that African governments and organizations were forced to step up and take charge of the conflict resolution efforts. A comprehensive agreement, mediated by President Frederick Chiluba of Zambia, was signed by all parties in September 1999. Given the intricacy of the Central African situation, the agreement will probably not be implemented entirely. Nevertheless, the negotiations and signing of this agreement were a major event, marking a shifting of the responsibility for stability in Africa away from foreign powers and into the hands of African leaders.

This shifting of responsibility marked the true end of the imposed colonial order in Africa. The implications are far reaching. A new order emerging from within Africa, rather than imposed from the outside, will probably cause some African states to disappear or to be fundamentally altered. Anxious to maintain stability, external powers propped up all the postcolonial states, regardless of their capacity to develop the internal cohesion, effective government, administrative capacity and fiscal solvency to become independent states not only in name, but also in reality. They protected Zaire (the Democratic Republic of the Congo) long after its government had ceased to control the country; they recognized Angola as a state even if no government ever administered the entire territory in a quarter century of independence. African states and institutions on their own are probably not going to be able to continue supporting nonviable entities in their midst. Somalia in the second half of the 1990s offered an interesting example of the implications of international withdrawal. Abandoned by the United States and the UN after an unsuccessful attempt to impose peace on the warring clans, Somalia became a relatively peaceful area, but it also reverted to a conglomerate of small semiindependent entities which bore little resemblance to the state the colonial powers had left behind.

One of the consequences of the marginalization of Africa is thus the likely modification of the postindependence state system, with its immutable colonial borders delimiting states, many of which were purely fictional by the late 1990s. Like the rest of the world, Africa is not immune to the realignment and redefinition of boundaries that has accompanied the end of the cold war in Eastern Europe, the former Soviet Union, and the Balkans.

CONCLUSIONS

Ten years after the end of the cold war, Africa is a marginal region. Internal developments will determine whether this marginalization will persist or Africa will become better integrated into the rest of the world. If the negative scenario of intensified ethnic conflict and state disintegration prevails, the marginalization of Africa will continue. Without the rivalry between superpowers, there is no incentive for the United States or any other country to become mired in the quagmire of African conflicts. The international community's escape from Somalia in 1995 and the failure to intervene at all in Liberia, Rwanda, or Burundi suggest that the likely consequence of increased turmoil will not be decisive foreign intervention, but increasing neglect. The difficulty humanitarian agencies encounter in raising funds for relief work in countries like Angola and Sudan is a reminder of what could happen.

If the positive domestic trends toward economic restructuring and political liberalization prevail in at least some countries, Africa will eventually become part of an economic rather than a security calculus not only for the United States and the European countries, but for the rapidly growing Asian countries as well. Despite its present poverty, Africa has resources and economic potential. Political stability and a degree of macroeconomic order would remove the most immediate obstacles to investment, and allow over time the elimination of the infrastructural weaknesses that make doing business in Africa a costly proposition at present. The high degree of international economic competition of the postwar world makes it highly unlikely that a potential market of over half a billion people will be neglected for long if the political situation and government economic policies stabilize.

Which scenario prevails, marginalization or integration into an increasingly internationalized economy, will be the result of what happens in African countries, rather than what happens elsewhere. With the end of the cold war, the age of imperialism has truly come to an end in Africa. The future is not the scramble for Africa, but the scramble by Africa to find its place in a changing world.

NOTES

1. The flow of U.S. economic and military aid to Africa shows clearly that the cold war was the major determinant of U.S. interest. It remained fairly constant from the mid-1960s to the mid-1970s, a period during which the Soviet Union appeared to disengage from Africa, increased sharply from the mid-1970s to the mid-1980s, when the Soviet Union, buoyed by the appearance of self-proclaimed Marxist-Leninist regimes pursued a more active role, and decreased again sharply thereafter, as U.S.–Soviet relations improved under Gorbachev and the Soviet Union sought to disengage from Africa. See Michael Clough, *U.S. Policy Toward Africa and the End of the Cold War* (New York: Council on Foreign Relations Press, 1992), esp. 8–13.

2. For an example of how African countries used the superpowers for their own purposes, rather than being manipulated by them, see Marina Ottaway, *So-*

viet and American Influence in the Horn of Africa (New York: Praeger Publisher, 1982).

3. Ismail Fahmi, *Negotiating for Peace in the Middle East* (Baltimore: The Johns Hopkins University Press, 1983).

4. Zaki Laidi, *The Superpowers and Africa, 1960–1990* (Chicago: University of Chicago Press, 1990), chap. 2, "Africa Marginalized?" (1965–1974).

5. For example, see Philip Ndegwa, "Africa and the World: Africa on Its Own," in Olusegun Obasanjo and Felix Mosha, eds., *Africa: Rise to Challenge* (Africa Leadership Forum, 1993), 13–25; and Michael Chege, "Remembering Africa," *Foreign Affairs* 7, no. 1 (1992): 146–63.

6. In the 1990–97 period, the average population growth rate for Sub-Saharan Africa was 2.7% a year. In the same period, GDP growth rate for the region was only 2.1%. World Bank Development Report 1998/99, tables 3 and 11.

7. "Brzezinski calls Democrats Soft Toward Moscow," *New York Times*, 30 November 1980. The Ogaden is the region of Ethiopia bordered by Somalia and contested by the latter as its own.

8. See Hedley Bull, "European States and African Political Communities," in Hedley Bull and Adam Watson, *The Expansion of International Society* (Oxford: Clarendon Press, 1984), 99–114.

9. For an overview of Soviet involvement, see David Albright, "Moscow's Africa Policy in the 1970s" in David Albright, ed., *Communism in Africa* (Bloomington: Indiana University Press, 1980), 35–66.

10. Kurt M. Campbell "Superpower Politics in Southern Africa: Rapprochement, Realignment and Retrenchment;" and Marina Ottaway, "Soviet-American Conflict Resolution in the Horn of Africa," in Mark Katz, ed., *Soviet-American Conflict Resolution in the Third World* (Washington, D.C.: United States Institute for Peace, 1991).

11. U.S. Central Intelligence Agency, *Communist Aid to the Less Developed Countries*, 1977, p. 19; and London Institute for International Studies, *Strategic Survey, 1976*, p. 60.

12. For a discussion of U.S. policy in southern Africa, see Anthony Lake, *The "Tar Baby" Option: American Policy Toward Southern Rhodesia* (New York: Columbia University Press, 1976).

13. See Chester A. Crocker, *High Noon in Southern Africa: Making Peace in a Rough Neighborhood* (New York: W.W. Norton & Co., 1992).

14. For an overview of the Liberian conflict and the role of ECOMOG in Liberia, see Karl P. Magyar and Earl Conteh-Morgan, eds., *Peacekeeping in Africa: ECOMOG in Liberia* (New York: St. Martin's Press, 1998).

15. The American project, the African Crisis Response Initiative (ACRI), launched in 1966, aimed at training a total of 10–12,000 soldiers from the militaries of a number of countries for peacekeeping operations. By 1999 only a few thousand had been trained. The French program, Reinforcement of Capabilities of African Peace Keeping Missions (RECAMP), was very similar in scope.

16. See Kenneth Grundy, *The Militarization of South African Politics* (Bloomington: Indiana University Press, 1986).

17. See *Africa Confidential* 35, no. 3,4 (February 1994).

18. John Markakis, *National and Class Conflict in the Horn of Africa* (Cambridge: Cambridge University Press, 1987).

19. United Nations Development Program/World Bank, *African Development Indicators*, 1992, tables 5.45 and 5.48.

20. The World Bank, *Adjustment in Africa: Reforms, Results and the Road Ahead*

(Oxford: Oxford University Press, 1994), 90; and The World Bank, *From Crisis to Sustainable Growth* (Washington, D.C.: The World Bank, 1989), 27.

21. On the economic crisis in Africa, see Richard Sandbrook, *The Politics of Africa's Economic Stagnation* (Cambridge: Cambridge University Press, 1985); and Thomas Callaghy and John Ravenhill, eds., *Hemmed In: Responses to Africa's Economic Decline* (New York: Columbia University Press, 1993).

22. The World Bank's own assessment of structural adjustment in Africa, probably the most optimistic to date, admits that very little progress has been made. See The World Bank, *Adjustment in Africa: Reforms, Results and the Road Ahead* (Oxford: Oxford University Press, 1994).

23. See Morton H. Halperin and David J. Scheffer, *Self-Determination in the New World Order* (Washington, D.C.: Carnegie Endowment for International Peace, 1992).

24. The term "quasi-state" is taken from Robert Jackson, *Quasi States: Sovereignty, International Relations and the Third World* (Cambridge: Cambridge University Press, 1990).

25. See Crawford Young, ed., *The Rising Tide of Cultural Pluralism* (University of Wisconsin Press, 1993); and Marina Ottaway, *Democratization and Ethnic Nationalism: African and Eastern European Experiences* (Washington, D.C.: Overseas Development Council, 1994).

26. See John W. Harbeson, Donald Rothchild, and Naomi Chazan, eds., *Civil Society and the State in Africa* (Boulder: Lynne Rienner, 1994).

27. The relationship between democratization and economic reform has been much better studied in Eastern Europe and Latin America than in Africa, but the same issues appear on that continent. See Joan Nelson, ed., *Intricate Links: Democratization and Market Reforms in Latin America and Western Europe* (Washington, D.C.: Overseas Development Council, 1994); and Stephan Haggard and Steven B. Webb, eds., *Voting for Reform: Democracy, Political Liberalization, and Economic Adjustment* (Oxford University Press, 1994). On Africa, see Thomas Callaghy, "Africa: Back to the Future?" *Journal of Democracy* 5, no. 4 (October 1994): 133–45.

The Middle East after the Soviet Union

Henri J. Barkey

One of the less memorable international events of the Christmas season was a Euro-Arab conference held in Paris. Twelve foreign ministers from the European Community sat facing 20 or so of their counterparts from the League of Arab States. Advisers sitting behind them passed forward freshly deciphered telegrams from Bucharest, which traveled from hand to eager hand along the European side of the table. Finally the French foreign minister, who was in the chair, interrupted the proceedings to announce that Ceausescu had been overthrown. At this news the Europeans burst into a spontaneous round of applause. The Arab ministers, on their side, stayed silent and stony-faced.[1]

THE STONY SILENCE WITH WHICH ARAB FOREIGN MINISTERS RE-ceived the news of Ceausescu's fall was a reflection of the general ambivalence with which many Middle Eastern states and their leaders welcomed the demise of the Soviet bloc. For many the Soviet Union was a patron of primary importance. It could be relied upon to supply them with weapons, provide political support, and act as a buffer against U.S. interests or intentions. For others, including even those who despised the USSR and what it stood for, the USSR was a necessary evil that challenged the U.S. and, thereby, ensured continued U.S. interest in them and in their regional affairs.

As far as the states of the Middle East were concerned, immediately preceding and following the collapse of the Soviet Union, Moscow was an ally of the United States and of Western interests. Starved for funds and preoccupied with its transitional problems, the new Russia acted, at least for a while, more as a client of the West than a superpower. Although Moscow has decided to reassert itself in the region and is no longer as amenable to U.S. solicitations as before, it must achieve this from a weakened position; it has definitely lost its superpower status. Russia cannot afford to be generous, either with economic or military aid, toward the countries of the region. Perhaps more importantly, it also confronts a

99

different geography in its relations with the Middle East. The emergence of the new nations in both the Caucasus and Central Asia has distanced Russia from the Middle East politically and physically.

The disappearance of the ideological rivalry and the competition between East and West and of Russian resources made available to most who wished to stand up to the West and its allies profoundly shook the Middle East. Some of the impact has been psychological: it has increased the vulnerability of certain regimes and has weakened those forces in Middle Eastern societies which looked up to the Soviet Union, however imperfect, as a model, or partial model, of societal and state organization. The Soviet Union's demise fundamentally altered the region's relationship with the West with which Middle Eastern states have had the strongest bonds. These bonds, the result of a colonial past, modern trade links, cultural diffusion, alliance and conflict patterns, have not always been constructed of trust.

Not all the changes in the region were due to the end of the cold war. The Arab-Israeli peace process, which has its roots in the *intifada* and the respective regimes' inability to construct legitimate forms of rule, has contributed to the rise of Islamic movements challenging them. What the end of the cold war has done is to accelerate certain regional trends and add an additional dynamic to domestic and regional change.

THREE WAYS IN WHICH THE USSR's DEMISE CHANGED THE MIDDLE EAST

The Soviet Union's demise has had three sets of implications for the Middle East. The first is broad and conceptual: it deals with what the Soviet Union represented from the point of view of societal organization, democracy, and economic systems. The second is geopolitical: the creation of new states in Central Asia and the Caucasus has distanced Moscow from the Middle East both politically and geographically. The end of the East-West rivalry has also transformed interregional relationships with direct implications for alliance patterns and military and economic relationships. The third is the indirect impact on the domestic political structures of the region. Because of crisscrossing influences at work, these categories must not be interpreted as being completely distinct from each other. This essay will start with the broadest category and progress toward the more specific issues.

Conceptual Changes

The conceptual changes to be discussed in this section are global and not necessarily specific to the Middle East. However, in many ways, the Middle East is one of the regions most affected by them. The conceptual changes can be viewed from three different perspectives.

1. The demise of the Soviet Union represented the failure of an economic ideology and practice. In the absence of intense superpower competition, economic issues, seemingly depoliticized, have assumed a more prominent profile for the individual citizen of the Middle East.
2. The Soviet Union was also a powerful ideological beacon for many Third World elites intent on maintaining power at the expense of their respective citizenry. The demise of the Soviet Union does not, of course, imply that the urge to democratize in the Third World has assumed an overwhelming momentum. But it is a force to be reckoned with, and there is a distinct likelihood of it gathering further momentum with time.
3. The rise of ethnic politics was the direct consequence of the demise of the Soviet Union, an event that removed some of the artificial limitations on the expression of ethnic identity.

THE RELEVANCE OF ECONOMICS AND THE NECESSITY TO REFORM

The collapse of the Soviet Union exposed not only the basic failure of its economic policies, which had been applied for decades but, with the environmental devastation left in its aftermath, also the myth of the socially responsible superpower. This Soviets' demise has severely undermined the basis of state-managed attempts at industrialization and development. It has given a considerable intellectual boost to advocates of privatization and other types of economic reform in the Third World. To be sure, in a few countries of the Middle East the winds of change had started to blow even before the dissolution of the USSR. In other parts of the world, in Latin America and the Far East in particular, integration with the international market and the beginnings of economic reform preceded the fall of the Berlin Wall and the disintegration of the Soviet bloc. In contrast, the Middle East has been slow to adapt to the exigencies of the new international market place and the globalization of trade and financial networks.

The Middle Eastern countries, not unlike their counterparts in Latin America and the Far East, embarked on their economic development strategy by emphasizing, to varying degrees, the role of the state in investment and actual management of day-to-day economic affairs. In the 1950s and 1960s, a strategy that put excessive reliance on autarky and inward-oriented development schemes did pay off. Incomes rose, the state became a major source of employment and, by and large, there was a perception that standards of living were improving. In the Arab world, Arab socialism became an attractive model: it was sufficiently distinct from the total state control system that Soviet bloc countries followed to allow some level of private activity, but the state was the undisputed economic agent and engine of change. In Turkey and Iran, while the state was an important agent for investment and infrastructure development, the private sector enjoyed greater latitude than in the Arab world. In Israel, the state and its close relation, the Histradut, the labor union confederation, owned large segments of industry coexisting all the while with an increasingly dynamic private sector.

The advent of the oil crises of the seventies dramatically altered the economic picture of the Middle East. States fortunate enough to be sitting on large reserves of oil procured windfall profits. In turn, oil revenues underwrote a massive consumption boom throughout the region. Within the Arab world, oil revenues also created a two-tier ordering of states: those that enjoyed the full benefits of oil rents and those that were the indirect recipients of these rents through interregional transfers of aid, capital, and especially workers' remittances. Egypt was, and continues to this day to be, a major recipient of workers' remittances whereas Syria benefited from its front-line position vis à vis Israel to acquire direct aid from Saudi Arabia and other Gulf countries. Among the recipients of the oil rents, two types of states emerged. Nationalist populist ones, such as Algeria and Iraq, embarked upon, with varying degrees of success, massive state-led industrialization drives. Iraq, with its military focus, appears to have been considerably more successful than others in developing an industrial edifice. By contrast, Saudi Arabia, Kuwait, and the Gulf Emirates were content to create substantial welfare states for their small populations. For both the direct and indirect beneficiaries of the rush of petrodollars into the region, the resulting abundance of foreign exchange delayed the need to seek alternative economic strategies. Instead, bureaucratic structures expanded and little was done to construct productive and competitive enterprises.

The opposite can be said of Turkey and to a lesser extent of Israel. These, with almost no oil of their own and some remittances, were the countries most negatively affected by the oil price hikes. By the end of the decade Turkey was bankrupt, and in 1980 it was forced to dramatically restructure its economic strategy: it replaced the inward-looking strategy with an export-oriented one. The results, helped initially by the advent of the Iran-Iraq war which made both belligerents Turkey's principal trading partners for a while, were dramatic. In Israel, the oil price hikes, economic mismanagement together with the costs of the 1973 war, and the 1982 invasion of Lebanon spurred runaway inflation, which was finally brought under control in 1985. Although both Turkey and Israel have a great deal more left to accomplish in the realm of economic reform, they have each succeeded in integrating themselves into the new dynamism of the international market.

By contrast, declining oil prices in the 1980s did not trigger a similar urge in the Arab world to seek alternative economic responses. As a result, at the onset of the post–cold war era, many of the Arab economies found themselves with large, inefficient, and cumbersome public sectors that drained their national treasuries. Years of economic mismanagement had had a debilitating impact not just on the public but also their private sectors, rendering these economies uncompetitive and unfit to partake in an international market where the competition, especially from the new tigers of East Asia, has been fierce. The Middle Eastern states have also been in the unenviable position of having to compete internationally with Latin American countries, which after a debilitating debt crisis, are in the process of putting their economic houses in order.

With the end of the cold war, strategic rents, another source of foreign exchange for many of the Middle Eastern states, disappeared. These rents were derived from the intense superpower competition where location and natural resources or proximity to them could be parlayed into superpower support. The promise of Soviet aid or interest would often mobilize Washington or other Western capitals to deliver aid packages of their own. The reverse was also true, though to a lesser extent in view of the Soviets' general financial difficulties. Military agreements and arms transfers were additional vehicles through which superpowers transferred resources to their client states. Although the Middle East, as the primary source of oil, will continue to be important to the well-being of Western democracies and others, the end of the superpower competition removes the premium local regimes could charge for their allegiance to one or the other of the superpowers.

There remain some exceptions. While Egypt may continue to retain its strategic importance to the United States because of the peace process and thus remain a major beneficiary of U.S. largesse, it is also unlikely that aid at this level will be maintained for long.

The end of the cold war has made economic concerns more salient. This change in priorities is also due to the fact that unlike the conclusion to World War II when a bitter ideological rivalry emerged, the end of the cold war has been accompanied by a general agreement on broad economic policies and beliefs. Unlike the post-World War II period, the United States, despite its sole superpower status, has no longer the resources, capacity, or even the will to exercise the role of hegemon. After 1945, it had provided the international system with liquidity and tolerated protectionist policies instituted by noncommunist states, all because it feared that economic problems in these societies could lead to the installation of Communist regimes. The United States started the decade indebted and facing domestic problems of enormous magnitude. Despite the intensity of the debate on the "proper" role for the United States, no real consensus has emerged.[2] By the end of the decade, the budget deficits had been transformed into surpluses, but the trade deficits continued to mushroom. The largesse of the United States essentially stops here: Washington will sustain large trade deficits, vital to the continued health of the world economy, so long as its economy continues along its path of growth with low inflation. Already, the United States has demonstrated that it is much less tolerant of protectionism and more aggressive about opening markets for exports, preferably, for its own products. The United States has devoted considerable energy not only to forcing open some markets, such as the Japanese, but also to creating new ones. Among the Middle Eastern countries, only Turkey has figured in the Commerce Department's list of the big emerging markets (Israel has a free trade agreement with the United States) which have been designated as future core markets for trade and investments.

This does not mean that economic concerns will always be paramount; political principles and interests will continue to figure prominently. In the Middle East, the United States presently maintains unilateral sanctions on Iran and is the most forceful supporter of continued UN-sponsored sanctions on Libya (until recently) and Iraq. By contrast, the Clinton administration threatened to impose sanctions on China not when that country trampled on human rights of its citizens but rather when the pirating of U.S. software and movie industry products assumed a massive dimension. Clearly, the relative size of China's market and the economic costs of sanctions have deterred the U.S. from emphasizing political differences. The reverse is true for Iraq and Iran, despite the fact that some of Washington's Western allies are eager to have the sanctions lifted on Iraq and have refused to go along with U.S. policy on Iran precisely because of the two countries' potential economic benefits.

The Asian financial crisis, which left the Middle East largely untouched except in so far as it pushed oil prices down, may have demonstrated a temporary weakness in that region's economic growth trajectory. All indications, however, are that the Asian tigers are making a comeback and will once again prove to be a formidable source of competition worldwide. The former Soviet-bloc countries are also vying for a piece of the international pie, particularly with regard to exports or capital. In addition to the East Asian economies and the Latin American states such as Brazil, Chile, and Argentina which have made painful transitions to more competitive market economies, Hungary, the Czech Republic, and Poland are also new forces to contend with. For risk-averse investors, these countries are far more attractive locations to invest their capital than the Middle East with its slow pace of market reforms.

In spite of the massive transfers of wealth that occurred following the oil price hikes, the Middle East remains an economically underdeveloped part of the world. Oil and gas revenues, if not properly managed, will not make a country developed or rich. The case of Algeria is a perfect example as billions were squandered in the pursuit of economic policies and projects that were ill-suited for it. The regime has had to fight for its life against its disaffected population that had turned to a violent Islamist underground. Moreover, significant resources in the Middle East have been wasted not just on the purchasing of military hardware but also in the wars fought between Arabs and Israelis, Iraqis and Iranians, and most recently in the Gulf conflict. Capital that flowed out of the Arab world into the West in the form of equity investments or numbered bank accounts still exists but is unlikely to return to the region unless profitable opportunities are created for it.

The challenge ahead for many Middle Eastern states is to forge strategies which will open up their economies while minimizing the dislocations that generally accompany such measures. The state, in these societies, has failed not because it got involved in micromanaging the country's development in the first place but because it did not know how to extract itself and make room for the burgeoning of a private sector. Failure to pick up the challenge will

mean that the Middle East will remain backward and the gap between it and other Third World societies will increase. Some Middle Eastern states, in addition to Israel and Turkey, have begun to
implement reforms: Tunisia, Morocco, and Jordan are among the
more prominent ones. In Egypt the pace of reform was slowed by
the vastness of the project at hand, the lack of resources, and the
strength of entrenched vested interests that have often succeeded
in blocking the path to reform. It, too, in recent years has tried to
step up the pace of change.

The primary roadblock in the path of reform in the Middle East
is the regimes themselves. Even in democratic societies, such as Israel and Turkey, resistance to privatization is strong. Nowhere,
however, is the resistance stronger than in those states where individual regimes have staked so much of their own well-being on the
continued maintenance of patronage networks that bind society to
the regime through intricate arrays of contractual relationships,
kinship, and sectarian ties. It is this interconnection between political power and patronage networks that sustain the regimes which
is at the core of their inability to institute necessary reforms that
could allow them to produce more efficiently and compete more
effectively. Ironically, the regimes, because they have constrained
the development of a civil society, face limited pressure from inside
to speed up economic reforms.

Hence the present-day pressure to reform is externally derived:
it is the product of the new international economic order which
threatens to leave behind all those that do not reform. Among the
sources of pressure is the European Union, which, worried by the
potential instability to its south, has begun a close cooperative project, dubbed the Euro-Med Dialogue or the Barcelona Process, to
influence its neighbors to undertake economic reforms. Nonexis-
tent or mediocre rates of economic development in an age of in-
stant communications will ultimately convert the external pressure
into a domestic one although the domestic variant will not necessarily assume a form that is in line with the exigencies of the new
economic order. Instead, it could assume an Islamist or even an
autarchic-nationalist character further severing the links with the
outside.[3]

The regimes, therefore, are confronted with a series of dilemmas: they could try to institute reforms so as to keep up with others, but there is no guarantee that they will succeed: undoing years
of learned behavior in favor of policies that require a significant
degree of finesse and vigilance necessitate time and patience. If reforms are successful, they will almost certainly entail a correspond-

ing decrease in the state's control over the economy and the regime's ability to manipulate groups in society thereby undermining some of the foundations of the existing political order. On the other hand, the cost of not trying assures falling behind others. Hence, the risks of action and inaction are politically consequential and it is to this issue of political reform that we turn next.

THE PLURALISTIC IMPERATIVE

The imperfections of the "democratic" systems that swept through Soviet bloc countries following the collapse of the Berlin Wall have been on display for all to see. These imperfections notwithstanding, the failure of the Soviet Union as a totalitarian state, the revelations regarding its past domestic practices, and the lack of enthusiasm in the West for supporting authoritarian governments will increase the indigenous pressures within many Third World countries to politically liberalize. Just as with dirigiste economic policies, the failure of the Soviet Union eliminates the ideological underpinnings of one-party states and other forms of authoritarian rule. It would be unrealistic to assume that a wave of democratic regimes will sweep through the Middle East. Democracy requires the building of institutions, the creation of groups and associations independent and often in opposition to the state. In short, meaningful democracy needs a rigorous civil society. This has yet to materialize in most of the Middle East. There are, however, signs of increasing pluralism and growing demands for increased pluralism. In part, this is a response to the failure of the state in these societies to provide for some of the essential necessities of life. As Rami Khouri argues, the inability of modern Arab governments to deal with economic and political challenges has forced them to become more open, but as he also accurately points out, this is not enough. They also have to become more accountable.[4]

The demand for greater pluralism is also a response to the increasing sense that authoritarianism may have run its course. This, of course, does not ignore the existence of groups and interests, such as the Islamists, who have a radically different conceptualization of societal organization. Their agitation, however, is another indication of the push for increased diversity of interests.

Two other consequences of the demise of the Soviet Union will encourage the trend toward pluralism. The first is the beginning of the end of the Arab-Israeli conflict that would not have happened, at least now, had the Soviet Union continued to exist. For many years the conflict with Israel allowed Arab regimes to sustain national-security states that stifled political dissent and mobilized capital and human resources for the ever present and future combat with Israel. These states received the active encouragement of Moscow, which had helped them build the various security apparatuses in the first place. In fact, the national security argument masked not only the stark failures of these regimes but also provided their raison d'etre. With the advent of peace, these regimes will have to confront the same difficult problems all governments around the world have: how to manage complex societies and a multiplicity of demands with limited resources. It is not clear that these regimes are ready for the task at hand. The elimination of the state of belligerency will liberate resources devoted to military expenditures, although there will be a corresponding increase in the citizenry's expectation of the "peace dividend."

The other pluralist impulse comes from the economic changes discussed above. Because economic liberalization rests on two pillars, the gradual retreat of the state from productive functions in society in favor of private interests and the opening of the economy to domestic and international competition, the function and role of the state has to change. In the Middle East, this would undermine the basis of many regimes that have exploited the inefficiency of their private sector to co-opt it politically and bind it to them. The more resources are transferred to the private sector or the more it is allowed to develop and flourish the greater will be the constraints on regime behavior. Economic liberalization will entail a degree of pluralism without which businesses cannot make reliable decisions, unions cannot engage in collective bargaining, and individuals cannot become rational consumers.

There is no guarantee that the chain reaction started by the Soviet collapse will result in pluralistic politics. What seems clear is that Arab regimes, in particular, facing resource constraints, inefficient and bloated bureaucracies, and high birth rates risk severe internal turmoil.[5] In the Arab world, the emergence of the Qatari-based satellite television channel al-Jazzira is perhaps one of the more surprising developments of recent times. The quick rise in the popularity of the station together with its managers' willingness to explore subjects hitherto rarely discussed is another sign of the changing political environment of the region.[6] In addition, the large numbers of expatriates living in the West, who routinely travel back to their countries of origin or keep in close contact through the internet and other forms of communication, will have a gradual but determined impact on the politics of the region. The expatriate community, especially Arab and Iranian, has given rise to an independent press, whether in London or Los Angeles, which is difficult to control.

THE RISE OF ETHNIC POLITICS

The breakup of the Soviet Union and the awakening of long-dormant ethnic differences, not just within the former superpower's boundaries but in Europe as well, have underscored many states' multiethnic character. In the Middle East, the single largest minority without a state has been the Kurds. Kurdish activism in pursuit of a separate state or autonomy is not new to Iraq. However, in the mid-1980s a similar movement emerged in Turkey. It gained prominence with the Iraqi invasion of Kuwait and the subsequent Iraqi Kurdish debacle that led to hundreds of thousands taking refuge across the border in southeastern Turkey. This event mobilized Turkish Kurds and focused worldwide attention on the plight of the Kurds not just in Iraq but in all the surrounding countries, but especially in Turkey.

The Kurds are just one such fissure in the Middle East. Sunni-Shiite, Berber-Arab, Arab-Christian, Arab-black African, Persian-Azerbaijani, Turkmen-Persian, and Israeli Jews-Palestinian are just some of the many divisions that run through the states of the region. Nationalism is not a new idea. The desire of many minorities to rule themselves and benefit from the trappings of being an independent state in not new either. Although nationalist movements among minorities may emerge even when the "minority is happy," the current upsurge has a direct connection to the fact that states facing revolts have throughout their modern history attempted to forcibly construct modern monoethnic units and engage in state-led economic development. What is also different about this recent upsurge in nationalism is that for the first time since Wilsonianism there is again a general recognition that the third- and second-world variants of the modern nation state have failed their minorities: the nation state has brought them neither freedom nor prosperity.

Preferring democratic solutions to problems of ethnicity, the United States and the West in general have, even in the most egregious cases of discrimination, discouraged secessionist movements. For the West, one of the main impediments to the breakup of states in the past was their geopolitical impact on the cold war balance of power. Hence, at the peak of the superpower rivalry it would have been almost unimaginable that either side would have consented to the independence of Eritrea, yet this has occurred. Therefore, resistance to self-determination has diminished somewhat, and it is difficult to imagine active opposition by the United States or its Western allies to a peaceful separation of ethnic and religious groups in a post-Saddam Iraq. There are instances when, as Michael Lind observes, the goals of promoting democracy and preserving a multiethnic entity cannot be reconciled.[7] As a result, pressure within the democratic countries to minimize dealings with those who oppress their minorities will continue to build.

This is not to say that there will be an upsurge of support for ethnic movements seeking autonomy, devolution, or even independence. What is suggested, however, is that unless multiethnic states do a better job of caring for their minorities, rebellions and civil disobedience movements will have a greater chance of attracting international support than ever before. The Middle East, already the cauldron of many such conflicts, will not be an exception to this trend.

The Geopolitical Transformation

Not surprisingly, the Middle East, because of its integral part in the cold war conflict, was profoundly jolted by the demise of the Soviet Union. First and foremost, the withdrawal of the Soviet Union together with its revisionist jargon and foreign policy pulled the rug from under some of the regimes in the region. The Soviet Union had been, for better or for worse, their primary source of armaments and political support. It could always be relied upon to raise its banner in their defense at the numerous international forums.

The withdrawal did not manifest itself simply in the form of a superpower no longer able to assist its friends but also in a change in geography. With the sudden appearance of new Muslim states, such as Azerbaijan, Turkmenistan, Kazakhstan, Kyrgyzstan, and Tajikistan, the borders of the Middle East have moved eastward. Or so it seemed in the early 1990s. The vacuum created in Central Asia and the Caucasus by the chaotic politics in Moscow attracted the likes of Turkey, Iran, and Saudi Arabia. These three, in part to sell their own domestic ideology and in part to deny the others this fertile terrain, quickly moved in, only to find themselves stymied by Soviet era rulers who were initially anxious not to overtly break ranks with the former colonial master and also uninterested in replacing one overlord with another.

In this section we will take up three separate issues relating to the geopolitical transformation. The first is the changing map of the region and the entry of new actors onto the scene. These include both the new states of the Caucasus and Central Asia as well as Russia. The second is the impact of the Arab-Israeli peace process, which despite its ups and downs has proven to be resilient as witnessed by the beginning of the Israeli-Syrian peace talks in December 1999. Finally, the Middle East's relationship with the West in general will be explored especially in light of the conceptual changes outlined above.

THE NEW MAP OF THE MIDDLE EAST

Where does the Middle East begin and end? Some believe that the sudden appearance of new Muslim states—such as Azerbaijan, Turkmenistan, Kazakhstan, Uzbekistan, Tajikistan and Kyrgyzstan—which share many of the characteristics of Middle Eastern states including rich deposits of oil and gas, has expanded the boundaries of the region further eastward.[8] Despite their strong resemblance to Middle Eastern societies, these formerly Soviet republics have strong colonial-type bonds that attach them to Russia. For the latter, these are part of its "Near Abroad," areas that are integral to Russia's sphere of influence. Until their political and economic fates are disentangled from that of Russia's, these new republics will remain on the sidelines of the Middle East, unable to make a significant mark on this region's economic and political life. Still, their presence has had an indirect impact on the region as exemplified by Turkey and Saudi Arabia's mobilization of resources to abate Iranian influence following their independence. In other words, the new Muslim states will gain in importance as Middle Eastern dynamics get exported to them.

On the other hand, the vast oil and gas deposits believed to be under the Caspian Sea and the adjoining Central Asian states will have a direct impact on the oil exporting states of the Middle East. Once its transportation problems were resolved, the Caspian Sea area was expected to "become the West's second largest supplier of oil and natural gas, reducing reliance on the Persian Gulf."[9] However, notwithstanding the rush of Western companies into the region, the great boom in oil and gas production has yet to materialize. A combination of factors, ranging from the lack of adequate exploration facilities in the form of platforms to low oil prices in the early 1990s and political disagreements on the best possible route for the transportation of these hydrocarbon resources have caused a delay in the expected bonanza for the region. Should

Central Asian oil and gas resources come on to the market in substantial quantities, there is no question that their first impact would be on the price of oil.

The delay in the realization of the Caspian Sea riches has also diminished the urgency given by both Ankara and Tehran to their competition in Central Asia as a whole. What was initially a furious foray into the Central Asian heartland by these ideological (and to a lesser extent economic) competitors has been replaced by a more pragmatic approach. The one area which remains potentially an explosive one for Iran and Turkey is Azerbaijan. Given that a sizable segment of Azerbaijan is formally part of Iran, Tehran has been vigilant in its monitoring of ties between Ankara and Baku. It is possible that in the uncertainties that underlie the transition from Azeri leader Aliyev, the tension between Ankara and Tehran will once again heat up.

On the new map of the Middle East, Russia is geographically farther away from the Middle East. It no longer borders Turkey and Iran. This sheer physical distance from the Middle East has been buttressed by the difficulties at home and the need to remain engaged in the Near Abroad. Therefore, its role has changed significantly. Russia, especially in the early 1990s, was put on the defensive by Turkey's (supported by the West) and other countries' efforts at penetrating its former territories. The Central Asian republics have not drifted westward, as some in Russia had feared. This is in large part due to the style of the leaders: they maintained almost all the practices of their authoritarian past, including sham elections, human rights violations, and abuses of power. Even Turkey, with all its willingness to help these countries, has found the going rough, especially with Uzbekistan. On the other hand, Turkey's role in the Caucasus has expanded dramatically. For one thing, this involves the yet to be realized Baku-Ceyhan oil pipeline. Moreover, perhaps more importantly, as a result of the efforts expanded for that pipeline, Georgia in addition to Azerbaijan has become dependent on Ankara for its security. Russia's involvement in the Middle East in general has been limited: a cosponsor of the 1991 Madrid Peace Talks, it has been largely absent from this endeavor. It is only in Iraq that Russia, both as an old patron of the Baathi regime and as a UN Security Council permanent member, has managed to play an active role.

The nature of the Russian role in the Middle East has undergone a transformation in line with its change of status. Although Russia's interests reflect the fact that it no longer is a revisionist superpower, it nonetheless remains a great power with diversified interests. Instead of constantly interfering with U.S. objectives, Russia has sought to carve a niche for itself based on past clients, which will continue to procure Russian armaments, and on new markets where it can peddle its military wares. The current U.S.– Iranian discord, therefore, serves Russia's interests well because it effectively detaches Iran from Western arms markets. Moscow's decision to sell three Kilo-class submarines to Tehran, followed by the announcement that it would help build two nuclear reactors, led to friction with the United States.[10]

Moscow's divergent approach to Baghdad is fueled by commercial and strategic concerns. Iraq owes Russia an estimated $7 billion, which Iraq can start paying back only after it is allowed to freely resume pumping oil. Under the food-for-oil provisions of the UN Security Council Resolution 986 and its successors, Baghdad has not been allowed to pay its creditors back. A rehabilitated Baathi Iraq is a vast potential market for Russian arms. Iraq's past reliance on Soviet arms, Russian efforts to have the UN eliminate the sanctions regime, and its influence on the present Iraqi leadership (as when it convinced the latter to recognize Kuwait's borders and, thereby, comply with one of the UN's demands) are both indicators and expectations of a significant future Russian role in Iraq. Some have gone as far as to suggest that Iraq represents "Russia's road back to greatness" because it could provide it with a say in the oil market since combined Russian and Iraqi oil production surpasses that of the Gulf countries.[11] Continued U.S. opposition to the regime in Baghdad as long as the latter does not fully comply with UN resolutions has not deterred Russia from whittling away at the sanctions regime; in fact, as Daniel Byman argues, Russia's aggressive advocacy of Iraq has helped erode the international consensus which was behind UNSCOM's (United Nations Special Commission) earlier disarmament success.[12]

Does Moscow still have strategic interests in the region? It no longer is a country with hegemonic ambitions capable of playing even the role of a spoiler. Its reverses in the region go back to the Soviet days. In his 1977 seminal work, *Red Star on the Nile*, Alvin Rubinstein looking at the Soviet-Egyptian relationship argued, "[t]he Egyptian connection has been Moscow's costliest in the Third World—and its most valuable. . . . Involvement begat commitments. The frequent difficulties, irregular dividends, and occasional losses notwithstanding, Moscow persisted, drawn by the prospect of strategic gains."[13] What would be the equivalent of those strategic gains in the twenty-first century? Beyond obvious commercial ties, does Russia have genuine interests in such areas

as the Persian Gulf or the eastern Mediterranean?[14] Russia has concrete concerns regarding Turkish, Iranian, and even Western attempts at penetrating Central Asian markets and accessing their
resources. In the mid-1990s, there remained an element of superpower temptation, which was more the result of a peculiar domestic political constellation linking the extreme right wing with
Communist nostalgists that has succeeded in putting the Yeltsin regime on the defensive. Moscow did find out that the exercise of
raw power in pursuit of more influence would not alleviate the
pain of transition to a market economy. In the longer run, Russian
interest in the Persian Gulf may become the function of its own
dwindling energy supplies. Lukoil, the state-owned oil company,
has aggressively pursued opportunities not only in its own backyard composed of the Caucasus and Central Asia but also in Iraq.

Ironically, it is the Arab and other Middle Eastern countries'
conviction that Russia is a much diminished and, perhaps, inconse-
quential power compared to the United States that is the most
damaging to Russia's future aspirations. Lamenting the fact that
Arab leaders constantly harped on Russia's subservience to the
United States, Russian Deputy Foreign Minister, Viktor Posuva-
lyuk, argued in an article in the pan-Arab-daily, *al-Hayat*, that
Arabs did not appreciate the extent to which Moscow's policy was
indifferent and even in opposition to that of the United States.
From his perspective the problem lies in the fact that the Arab
media and leaders perceive the world through a "Western" prism,
which, in turn, leads to the neglect of Russia by Arab commercial
and investment interests. This also explains why Russia's commercial and other relations with the West and Israel have grown so
much faster.[15]

Russian protestations to the contrary, the fact remains that in the
post-cold war environment in the Middle East, Moscow has become largely irrelevant to the calculations of the regional actors. In
the discussions on the future of Iraq, for instance, there is almost
no mention in the Arab press of Russian preferences and possible
influence. Similarly, with respect to the peace process, the Russian
role is ceremonial at best. In effect, the regional actors behave as if
there is only one relevant external power: the United States. All
dialogue, irrespective of its friendly or hostile content, is with the
United States. If, in the eyes of primarily Arab powers, there is a
constellation of powers looming on the horizon that can challenge
the United States, it is located in Europe and not in Russia. All
these point to a Russian foreign policy in the region that is likely
to be opportunistic in nature; it will seek to attract Western, espe-

cially U.S., attention mostly as a reminder to all of its existence and ultimately for commercial reasons.

Russia has also discovered that it has a new interest in the Middle East. Unlike other ambitions, be they commercial or hegemonic, this one is not Moscow driven: it is as the Chechen wars demonstrated a piece of the Middle East which has come to Russia proper.[16] Although a majority of the Soviet Union's Muslim populations no longer live within Russia's borders, there are still significant Muslim minorities in Chechnya, Dagestan, and Tatarstan, to name a few areas. The conflict in Chechnya has demonstrated the tenuousness of the links between the Russians and these populations. Moscow has succeeded in blunting criticism from Muslim countries for its support for the Serbs in Bosnia and Kosovo and, more poignantly, over its conduct in Chechnya the first time around. Even if there was more criticism during the opening phases of the assault on Grozny in 1999, the fact that Iran, potentially the most vocal of the critics, kept its silence represented a significant victory for Moscow.[17]

But clearly everyone has been watching with some amazement the ability of the Chechen irregulars to punish the Russian army. While the long-term impact of this development on Russian influence is not certain, there is no question that more irregulars claiming to fight the good war against the Russian infidel are likely to join the fray the longer the conflict continues and especially if it spreads to any other regions. In the end, the Middle Eastern countries, despite their uneasiness regarding interference in the domestic affairs of another country, will be forced to take sides. Already moneys are collected for "Chechen refugees" in many Middle Eastern countries without much supervision on their disposition. As a result, Moscow may be in greater need of Muslim states' quiescence in the future since its domestic problems with its Muslim minorities may accelerate rather than abate.

There is perhaps one further irony to Russia's Middle East engagement. With the outflow of many Russians, Jews and non-Jews alike, following the collapse of the Soviet Union, Israel today has a very large Russian minority which keeps active links, some unsavory, with the old country. As a result, trade and investment between Israel and Russia have expanded significantly as have other types of relations. The former refusnik and minister in both the Netanyahu and Barak cabinets, Nathan Sharansky, has visited Moscow in his official capacity attempting to further enhance ties between these two countries. Nowhere else in the region does Russia have a potentially sympathetic and loyal community it can, to a limited extent, rely on.

THE GULF WAR AND ARAB-ISRAELI RAPPROCHEMENT

A far more significant result of the collapse of the Soviet Union is the arduous peace process between Israelis and Arabs. The process was put into motion by the Gulf War because "with Iraq's defeat the regional military trend toward any viable Arab 'peace through strength' strategy was smashed"[18] and with it any illusion of Arab unity was put to rest. The Gulf War underscored the importance of individual state and regime interests in the Middle East as opposed to the more amorphous notion of a larger community. Michael Barnett argues that this "new realism" has allowed individual states to identify security threats directed at them and show greater interest in subregional blocs, such as the Arab Mahgreb Union or the Gulf Cooperation Council.[19]

The Madrid Conference convened by the United States and the Soviet Union designed to start the process of reconciliation between Arabs and Israelis proved to be the last joint accomplishment of the superpowers in this region as they both delivered their client states and groups to the negotiating table. Although it floundered at the beginning, the United States assumed the leadership from that point onwards and helped the process along. Even if the Oslo talks that culminated in the Israeli-Palestinian breakthrough occurred without direct U.S. involvement, it is the "new realism" hastened by the end of the cold war that made this development possible.

The Palestinians inadvertently provided an important impetus to the peace process by publicly backing Saddam Hussein. Because so much of the belief in Arab solidarity had been constructed around their cause, Palestinian support for Iraq drove home the reality that states in the region were alone to fend for themselves. As a result, Palestinians found themselves exposed and abandoned at the end the Gulf War by many of the states that had championed their causes over the years. The weakening of the Palestinian position both within and outside the Arab world provided a strategic window of opportunity to Israelis who had elected a more pragmatic leadership to replace the ideological one represented by the Likud. The regional realignment that characterized the period during and following the Gulf War would perhaps have been possible without the beginning of the collapse of the Soviet Union.

Nonetheless it was certainly helped by the fact that the Soviet leadership was far too distracted by the rapid internal developments to adequately focus on the longer term consequences of the crisis in the Gulf. Gorbachev's last minute brinkmanship to find Saddam a face-saving formula for exiting Kuwait failed.

The Arab-Israeli peace process weathered enormous challenges in the period since Oslo: Rabin's assassination, bombs in Tel Aviv and Jerusalem, a massacre in Hebron, Netanyahu's election and the temporary collapse of the process, and the passing away of two monarchs in Jordan and Morocco who had actively taken risks to push the process along. This is not an insubstantial list. Yet, Israelis and Palestinians and now Syrians have managed to return to the table and make further progress.

Both the Gulf War and peace process have allowed the United States to implant itself concretely and become the predominant power in the Middle East and the Gulf. Ironically, the United States succeeded in doing so not because it wanted to but rather because it beat a hasty retreat after the end of the war. The fact that 500,000 troops were withdrawn so fast convinced the Gulf Arab countries that the United States was not interested in a long-term and substantial presence in the region. Yet, no one in 1991 could have predicted that sanctions on Iraq would have lasted as long as they have. The United States and Britain actively patrol the skies over much of Iraqi territory, occasionally getting into firefights with Iraqi antiaircraft batteries. Although Gulf countries initially appeared to be comfortable with the U.S. presence there, the prolongation of the sanctions regime against Iraq has begun to reveal fault lines. The resilience of Saddam Hussein and his regime has unnerved many; it has also cast a shadow over Washington's capabilities. Few in the region understand Washington's self-imposed constraints in dealing with Saddam, thus creating a dangerous illusion: either Washington is truly an incapable power or is deliberately propping up Saddam with the aim of extending American domination of the region.

INTRA-REGIONAL POLITICS

The end of the cold war has also transformed intra-regional relations. In tandem with the peace process, the change in the geopolitical make-up of the world has made Israel an integral part of the region—not just as an adversary but also an economic and strategic partner. More time is needed for the residual hostility to Israel in the region to disappear and, thus, achieve a degree of normalcy. Some changes in regional alliances are already evident. Turkish attempts at improving relations with Israel after years of neglect by Ankara, the emergence of a Jerusalem-Amman axis with its possible extension to the Palestinians and even beyond, and the intensification of economic ties between Morocco, Tunisia, Israel, and other more reform-minded states are all representative of an emerging new regional order.

It is Egypt which has had the greatest difficulty in adapting to the changes in its environment. By virtue of its peace treaty with Israel, it had played a critical role in U.S. calculations in the region. Long accustomed to being the center of the Arab world even when it was at odds with it, Egypt has perceived a decline in its regional position with the advent of peace in the Middle East and the absence of the menacing Soviet colossus. The resulting possible loss of U.S. political and economic support, which had hitherto provided an infusion of much needed aid, culminated in an odd spectacle in the fall and winter 1994–1995. In part responding to genuine and long-held security concerns and positions, Egypt took a strong public stand against the extension of the Non-Proliferation Treaty (NPT) at the United Nations, which ignored Israel's nuclear program not under NPT supervision. By rallying other Arab countries behind it, Cairo sought to demonstrate to those in and outside the region the critical role it could still play. The problem for the regime in Egypt was that it chose an issue that it could not parlay beyond the immediate region. The other occurrence that underscored the underlying insecurity with which the Egyptian leadership approaches relations with the United States was the almost hysterical reaction generated in the Cairo press by a few articles critical of Egypt that appeared in the U.S. press. Interpreting these articles as part of an orchestrated attack on Egypt's importance and, therefore, the beginning of a cutback in assistance, the Egyptian press managed to temporarily create the appearance of a veritable crisis in the Egyptian–U.S. relationship.

Despite Egyptian doubts, the U.S. relationship with Egypt is unlikely to experience a change in intensity but perhaps will in its direction. Stability in the Middle East is still a critical U.S. concern and goal. In this respect, Egypt's own domestic stability, because of this country's historical role in the Arab world and the fact that it is its most populous one, is linked to the overall stability of the region.[20]

Although it is difficult to discern any meaningful signs of unity among Arab states, the same cannot be said of pan-Arabism. On the one hand, as much as the end of this movement has been heralded, it would be wrong to assume that the "new realism" of the Arab states has obviated the appeal of pan-Arab causes. Whether it can exist as a constructive force—in the context of a democratic revolution within the Arab world—devoted to region-wide cooperation on issues of economic, social, and environmental concerns as Rami Khouri envisages it remains to be seen.[21] On the other hand, as the early days of the Gulf crisis and Egypt's stance on the NPT demonstrated for brief periods of time, pan-Arabism is still capable of reemerging in its "anti-Western and reactionary" formulation although its security implications would be severely diminished. More importantly, there is a better chance that pan-Arabism will metamorphose under the influence and tutelage of the new Islamist movements. Ghassan Salamé suggests that the defeat of pan-Arabism and the de-Christianization of the Arab world have, in effect, pushed the new intellectuals away from secularism toward a more Islamicized vision of nationalism.[22]

But clearly, pan-Arabism could not stage a comeback when the peace process between Arabs and Israelis faltered. Neither did the much heralded (in the Arab press at least) Turkish-Israeli alliance or Ankara's bullying of Syria in 1998 to expel PKK (Kurdistan Workers' Party) leader Abdullah Ocalan. If Syria and Israel are able to conclude a deal, which will remove Israeli troops from southern Lebanon, it is Iran's reach and potentially its relations with Syria which are bound to suffer the most.

Impact on Domestic Politics

It is the traditional rejectionist front that has suffered the most from the demise of the Soviet Union. The decline of regimes and groups associated with the Soviet Union has created an ideological vacuum. With previously anti-American regimes collaborating with the West, the Palestine Liberation Organization (PLO) engaging in peace talks with Israel, it is Islamic extremists who have attempted to fill the ideological vacuum as the new revisionists. The stage had been previously set by the 1979 Iranian revolution. The strongest opposition to status quo regimes such as those of Egypt and Tunisia or radical ones such as Algeria and even the PLO comes from Islamists.

The Islamist challenge is primarily one directed at the regimes themselves. They criticize not only the regimes' lack of religiosity but also their corruption. These radical Islamist movements are fundamentally the products of dire economic circumstances that are unlikely to change for the better in the short term. The exigencies of the new economic reforms and changes conditioned by the need to participate in international markets will disproportionately fall on those who can least afford to. It is primarily the regimes, both status quo oriented and radical ones, that are to blame for the economic hardships that fuel the discontent. For Islamists, therefore, the primary aim is not the West, but rather the ruling regimes themselves. The Islamists' anger will not turn against the West until they perceive the latter as directly implicated in what they perceive to be an attempt at blocking their political progress.

The future struggle in the Middle East will be internally generated. In effect, with the end of the cold war the source of instability has shifted inwards from outside the state boundaries. Anti-regime Islamist groups are not new to the region. After all, the Muslim Brotherhood in Egypt has been in existence for the better part of this century. What is new is the fact that the Islamist groups have de facto inherited the mantle of the real and genuine opposition. It is unlikely that the traditional methods of repression that have served Middle East rulers will ensure political stability.

The rise of what, in the West, is perceived to be an "undemocratic" Islamist opposition creates a quandary for the outside powers willing to foster the development of pluralist institutions. While the cold war provided the fig leaf necessary to support undemocratic and sometimes brutal regimes in the name of combating Communism, the demise of the Soviets has blown this cover away. Hence, Western states face an unsavory choice: to push for political liberalization in states where regimes have little legitimacy and increase the likelihood of Islamic opposition groups gaining ground, or even power. The sensitivity of the regimes to criticism can be seen in the Egyptian interior minister's accusations that Western governments and human rights organizations are supporting "terrorists" in both Egypt and Algeria.[23] The quandary is accentuated for countries such as France that harbor so many residents of Middle Eastern origin because of the potential for the spread of such opposition on their own soil.

In this respect Algeria may prove to be the critical arena where the future course of Western-Islamic relations is defined. French and, to a lesser extent, other Western support for the Algerian state was predicated on the belief that the Islamist party, the Front Islamique de Salut ([Islamic Liberation Front], FIS), would have undermined not just Western interests had it been allowed to assume power following a second, but canceled, round of elections but that the demonstration effect from such a victory could have spread all along North Africa and beyond. The French were also concerned by the potential influx of refugees fleeing an Islamic Algeria. As Salamé argues, the panicky European reaction to events in Algeria is not only driven by the fear of terrorism on their soil—not an unreasonable fear in view of the wave of bombings that hit France in late summer 1995—but also by a political culture less accommodating of religious politics.[24] In the end the regime did not succumb to the FIS; President Bouteflika's efforts at shepherding a reconciliation of sorts despite the opposition of extremists among the ranks of the opposition and the state itself remain the best hope for not unleashing Samuel Huntington's much-feared "clash of civilizations." [25]

From the perspective of domestic politics, the demise of the Soviet Union had the most direct and immediate impact on Israel. Israeli society had to absorb hundreds of thousands of Soviet Jews in a record amount of time. This influx not only provided a dose of self-confidence, but the newcomers with their more secular and less ideological perspective may have provided the Labor Party of Yitzhak Rabin with the necessary margin of victory in the 1992 elections. This political alliance between Labor and the Russians may yet prove illusory, as the debate over the Golan Heights will show.

CONCLUSION

The demise of the Soviet bloc ushered in changes in many places around the globe: but no other region experienced as profound a transformation as the Middle East with the exception of the places where Moscow exercised a direct and everyday control, such as Eastern Europe. Most of these post–cold war changes have been beneficial: the beginning and maturing of the Arab-Israeli peace process is at the heart of them. When the process is completed, as most observers expect it to be, the pace of change in the region, especially within the Arab societies, is also expected to quicken. With few exceptions, most of the regimes are poorly equipped to confront this new challenge.

One by-product of the end of Soviet-American competition and especially of the Gulf War has been the unparalleled supremacy in the region by the United States. For better or for worse, Washington is the dominant player, and this is a role which comes with a heavy burden. Perhaps more importantly, it is not clear that the United States can shoulder this burden or is willing to do it over

the long term. Hence, for the regimes in the region which are dependent on the U.S. security umbrella, it is one thing to worry
about a resurgent Iraq or a hegemonic Iran, but it is another to
face potential trouble at home brewing from developing civil society and demands for greater accountability. These are ideas that
are dear to the United States. Moreover, Kuwaiti parliament's refusal to "grant" women the right to vote in the closing days of the
twentieth century was deeply embarrassing even to Washington
which liberated it from the tyrant Saddam Hussein.

While the Arab-Israeli peace process will undoubtedly provide a
general sense of relief, it is the mounting pressures from domestic
economic and political interests as well as the burgeoning populations that will drive the region's agenda. Unlike their counterparts
in other regions of the world, many Middle Eastern regimes have
yet to formulate a mission or vision for themselves. In East Asia
and Latin America the focus has for some time been on economic
development. Western Europe's determination to build an economic and political union has not been distracted by the collapse
of the Soviet Union: on the contrary, it has made the challenge
simply more complex. In the southern cone of Latin America, Argentina, Brazil, Paraguay, and Uruguay have formed Mercado
Comun del Sur (MERCOSUR), a common market, while Chile has
set its sight on joining NAFTA. With the exception of Turkey
which, following the decision of the December 1999 Helsinki Summit, will strive to do its outmost to get closer to the European
Union and Israel which has fashioned free trade agreements with
both the EU and the United States, few Middle Eastern states have
sought to conceptualize their role in the post-cold war world.

There is the distinct possibility that faced with a challenge of integration with the rest of the world and saddled with a cumulative
set of past failures, many Middle Eastern states will revert back to,
as Rami Khouri has argued, "older, traditional social structures
that are patriarchal and even authoritarian."[26] Will Islam then, not
in its fundamentalist but in its "civilizational" form, become the alternative to the failed secular regimes? The answer lies in the present regimes' ability to usher in change while offering a new vision
for their societies.

NOTES

1. Edward Mortimer, "Romanian goose, Iraqi gander," *Financial Times*, 9 January 1990, 17.

2. Charles William Maynes, "America's Fading Commitments," *World Policy Journal* 16, no. 2 (summer 1999): 11–22.

3. Perhaps one of the more interesting dilemmas regards the liberalization of such new technologies as the internet. The speed at which the internet is evolving in regions other than the Middle East (here again Israel and Turkey continue to buck the trend in this region) is creating another gulf between the countries of the region and the rest of the world. Regimes, such as the Syrian one, remain suspicious of the power of the internet. They are in some ways right. For dissident groups, ranging from Islamists to ethnic separatists, the internet is a relatively cheap and certainly very rapid means to communicate.

4. Rami Khouri, "The rhetoric and reality of democratic accountability," *Jordan Times*, 5 January 2000.

5. Augustus Richard Norton and Robin Wright, "The Post-Peace Crisis in the Middle East," *Survival* 36, no. 4 (winter 1994–95): 8.

6. For a discussion of the impact of new technologies on the Arab world, see Jon B. Alterman, *New Media, New Politics?* (Washington, D.C.: Washington Institute for Near East Policy, 1998).

7. Michael Lind, "In Defense of Liberal Nationalism," *Foreign Affairs* 73, no. 3 (May/June 1994): 96.

8. For a redefinition of the Middle East, see Bernard Lewis, "Rethinking the Middle East," *Foreign Affairs* 71, no. 4 (fall 1992).

9. Steve LeVine, "Way Sought for Pipeline to Bypass Russia," *New York Times* 9 September 1995. By one estimate alone, the Kazakh portion of the Caspian Sea may contain as much as 3.55 billion tons of oil and 2.53 trillion cubic meters of gas, see Paul Thomas, "Kazakhstan sells its silver," *The Financial Times Energy Economist*, June 1995. For an alternative view, see Amy Myers Jaffe and Robert Manning, "The Myth of the Caspian 'Great Game': The Real Geopolitics of Energy," *Survival* 40, no. 4 (winter 1998–99): 112–31.

10. Repeated U.S. attempts to get Moscow to cancel the nuclear reactor deal have come to naught. The Russians, however, conceded to U.S. concerns by "canceling" the sale of gas centrifuges to Iran. It is not clear whether the Russians ever intended to sell the centrifuges in the first place.

11. See, for instance, Ragheda Dergham in *al-Hayat*, reprinted in *Mideast Mirror*, 16 December 1994, 21–22.

12. Daniel Byman, "A Farewell to Arms Inspections," *Foreign Affairs* 79, no. 1 (January/February 2000): 130.

13. Alvin Z. Rubinstein, *Red Star on the Nile* (Princeton: Princeton University Press, 1977), 330.

14. Moscow signed military cooperation agreements with both the UAE and Kuwait in 1993 with the expectation that these will generate purchases of Russian military equipment. Alvin Z. Rubinstein, "Moscow and the Gulf War: Decisions and Consequences," *International Journal* 49 (spring 1994): 320.

15. *Mideast Mirror*, 13 June 1995, 15–17.

16. Rajan Menon, "The Middle East in Russian and Chinese Strategic Thinking," *Proceedings of the Washington Institute for Near East Policy, 1997 Policy Conference*, Wye Plantation, Queenstown, MD (19–21 September 1997): 11–13.

17. Turkey, which has a small Chechen and a significantly larger and politically relevant Bosnian minority, was sidelined by Russia which used the Kurdish card with great effectiveness. Moscow's political skillfulness can be evidenced by the fact that two Turkish firms, ENKA and GAMA, were awarded a sizable contract to rebuild Grozny, *Hurriyet*, 7 September 1995. Iran may have been silenced

the first time around through the sale of nuclear reactors and Russian resistance to U.S. pressure to forgo the deal.

18. Richard K. Herrmann, "The Middle East and the New World Order," *International Security* 16, no. 2 (fall 1991): 56.

19. Michael Barnett, "From Community to the New Realism: The Elusive Search for Regional Order in the Middle East," in *Arab-American Relations: A New Beginning?* (Washington, D.C.: Foundation on Democratization and Political Change in the Middle East, 1995): 27–28.

20. In the atmosphere of hysteria unleashed in Cairo, few noticed the importance of this aspect of the relationship. For an exception please see Osama Saraya, "The Future of the American Aid to Egypt," *al-Ahram*, 28 November 1994, reprinted in *Mideast Mirror*, same date, 14–16.

21. Rami Khouri, "Pan-Arab Nationalism: Is it Dying or Being Born?" in *Jordan Times*, reprinted in *Mideast Mirror*, 14 December 1993, 23–25.

22. Ghassan Salamé, "Le Nationalisme Arabe: Mort ou Mutation?"in Jacques Rupnik, ed., *Le Déchirement des Nations* (Paris: Seuil, 1995), 205–7.

23. Interview with Hassan al-Alfi, *al-Hayat*, reprinted in *Mideast Mirror*, 10 February 1995, 17–18.

24. Ghassan Salamé, "Torn between the Atlantic and the Mediterranean: Europe and the Middle East in the Post-Cold War Era," *Middle East Journal* 48, no. 2 (spring 1994): 239.

25. Samuel Huntington, "The Clash of Civilizations?" *Foreign Affairs* 72:3 (summer 1993). To some Islamists, such as the Egyptian writer, Fahmi Howeidi, Western support for the 1992 coup in Algeria is a continuation of the West's historical animosity toward Islam that dates back to the Crusades. In fact, he does see this conflict as a civilizational one, in *al-Majalla*, reprinted in *Mideast Mirror*, 8 April 1994.

26. Rami Khouri, "The Middle East, Russia and dreams of chocolate ducks," *Jordan Times*, 21 December 1993, reprinted in *Mideast Mirror*, 21 December 1993, 22. Khouri sees a parallel between the changes in the Middle East and those in the former Soviet-bloc countries and argues that the politics of ethnicity, religion, and tribalism serve as a substitute for the state that has failed people in the past.

After the Cold War:
Relationships in the Red Sea and
Persian Gulf Regions

Stephen Page

THE END OF THE COLD WAR AND THE COLLAPSE OF THE USSR HAD A dynamic effect on domestic and international relationships in the Third World. In countries and regions around the globe, the end of the competition between superpowers for friends and influence forced a new awareness and calculation of regional and internal political and security balances, of national interests, and of intrinsic strengths and weaknesses.

The new calculations led to radically different outcomes in different regions, and nowhere was this truer than in the contrast between developments in the Red Sea and Persian Gulf regions after the mid-1980s. In the Red Sea region, it was demonstrated that the Soviet competition for presence and influence in the 1970s and 1980s had had more to do with cold war zero-sum assumptions, worst-case scenarios, ideologically driven quests for Third World allies, and habitual behavior of strategic denial than with actual geopolitical importance. It is not surprising, then, that when the cold war ended, and particularly when the USSR collapsed, Russia lost interest in the region, and (except for humanitarian spasms) its member-states were left to their own devices.

The Persian Gulf countries, by contrast, have not been left to their own devices. Their reserves of oil and their ability to make major purchases of arms and other high-technology commodities have ensured their status as a region of continuing global importance. There was never any question that the United States would continue to see the Gulf in zero-sum terms; and the experience of the 1980s indicated that Washington would expend considerable efforts to defend American interests there. By the end of the 1980s, the USSR was only a marginal player in the region, although it continued to aspire to a role that was more than nominal. After the collapse, geopolitical position alone dictated that Russia would pick up this banner as soon as possible.

*   *   *

Before the collapse of the USSR, the Red Sea region was one of the casualties of Gorbachev's new political thinking, which dictated retrenchment from the costs of an activist policy toward the Third World. With the Soviet retreat, Washington could relinquish its professed fear of Moscow astride the Bab al-Mandeb chokepoint at the south end of the Red Sea—just as the Red Sea was gaining increased importance to the international oil trade, while retaining its significance for the security and trade of both Saudi Arabia and Israel.

The construction of additional oil pipeline capacity in the 1980s from Gulf oilfields to Saudi Red Sea ports allowed all Saudi exports, and much of Iraqi and Kuwaiti exports, to bypass the troublesome Strait of Hormuz. Potentially, this route also bypassed the Bab al-Mandeb; however, bottlenecks at the Suez Canal meant that in fact much of the oil had to be shipped through those straits.[1] Furthermore, the development of North and South Yemeni oilfields, with export points on the Red Sea and the Gulf of Aden, apparently added a new factor to the region's importance.

In the early 1980s, the Soviet Union had what appeared to be solid positions in the southern end of the Red Sea. For its part, the United States was solidly entrenched in the north; outside the southern end of the Red Sea, in return for small amounts of military and economic aid, it had as much access to Somalia as it deemed necessary. However, its interest in each was mainly geared not to the Red Sea but to other issues, namely the Arab-Israeli conflict and the Gulf.

The Soviet positions were expensive to maintain; by the end of the decade, the USSR was owed $2.8 billion by Ethiopia, $1.8 billion by South Yemen, and almost $1 billion by North Yemen.[2] The two Yemens had oil reserves (which in the south were being developed by Soviet technicians), and might be expected someday to begin repaying their debts. However, they also had huge development needs, and were not in any hurry to begin paying the debts down. Ethiopia was one of the poorest countries in the world, and could not realistically be expected to repay its debts. Furthermore, neither the South Yemeni nor the Ethiopian regimes had ever achieved stability. In the Red Sea region, as elsewhere, the USSR was tied to basket cases.

The Gorbachev leadership recognized the impasse and rejected its continuation. Gradually over five years, Mengistu's military supplies were curtailed and then completely halted. By May 1991, the Ethiopian army had collapsed, and Mengistu fled; the new ruling group (assisted in a remarkably peaceful transition by American diplomacy) had accepted the idea of Eritrean independence. By then, South Yemen itself had disappeared. Faced with the drastic curtailment of Soviet aid (by 1990, $400 million annually)[3] and deteriorating economic and social conditions, the South Yemeni leaders in November 1989 had accepted the proposal of North Yemeni President Ali Abdullah Saleh for a merger on an equal basis, in a republic which nevertheless abandoned the "socialism" of the south and adopted the "democracy" and capitalism of the north. Moscow accepted these transformations with equanimity and reduced its presence and activities to those of a "normal" friendly state.

The United States did not treat these events as an opportunity to expand its presence and influence in the region; there was no global enemy to supplant, and as it turned out, there were no paramount strategic interests to ensure. Aid programs to Ethiopia and Eritrea that might have promoted pro-U.S. sentiments were not forthcoming, largely because there seemed no pressing American interest. The Gulf crisis, during which there was no need of the Somali facilities at Berbera, demonstrated the geopolitical marginality of the Horn. In the case of Yemen, U.S. policy had long been the hostage of its more important interests in Saudi Arabia and of Saudi fear of and hostility toward Yemen.

For Yemen, this situation was compounded by its policy toward Iraq's invasion of Kuwait; then a member of the UN Security Council, Yemen condemned the invasion and called for an immediate Iraqi withdrawal, but refused to support the United States in its demands for a forceful UN response or the military action which followed. For this stance, Yemen received severe punishment. Not only did it lose virtually all its economic aid; its already shaky economy had as well to cope with absorbing one million Yemenis forced to return from Kuwait and from Saudi Arabia when it abruptly changed its residence permit requirements; approximately $500 million in annual remittances were lost.[4] Eight years later, despite promising increases in proven oil reserves, the economic situation has not improved.

There are, of course, problems other than these. Much of the economy's weakness is also due to structural problems common to underdeveloped countries and to the shortcomings of the unity arrangement of May 1990.[5] It was concluded only because the ruling group in the dominant north (the General People's Congress [GPC] run by President Saleh) accepted equity with the ruling group in the south (the Yemeni Socialist Party, YSP). Thus both groups, and the bureaucracies and the militaries they represented and depended on, were combined *in toto* in the new Yemeni state. While this made good political sense at the time, it could not be sustained by the economy, especially after the shocks of 1990.

In addition, the new openness of the united political system prompted the appearance of political forces which resented the monopoly of the old leaderships. In particular, northern (and in some instances southern) conservative tribal elements and their natural Islamist allies were hostile to the continued share in power of the secular "socialists" of the south. Together they formed *Islah* (Reform), a political party dedicated to restoring the old Yemeni values and Islam as the most basic of those values. (Militant Islamists have to date been in a small minority of the party.)[6] *Islah*, a natural ally of the GPC, grew to challenge the YSP as the second largest party after the general elections held in April 1993. Saleh, in the Middle East tradition of seeking consensus (and probably in another Middle East tradition of playing off one's opponents against each other) constructed a Presidential Council and a government containing all three parties, thereby further diluting the YSP's status.

This arrangement never sat easily, and by spring 1994, it had broken down. The YSP were under threat politically from *Islah* even on their home ground, and physically from apparently unknown gunmen. Now realizing, after several years of Western oil company exploration, that the south contained larger reserves than the north (as well as the only oil refinery in the country), the YSP pressed for a disproportionately large share in oil revenues for their region, and even began to talk about the desirability of a federal system. In society as a whole, tensions and frustrations were growing at the deteriorating economy, pervasive corruption, and political deadlock. Independent political figures met to suggest initiatives, and a new national pact seemed to have been agreed on in a meeting of government leaders in Jordan in February 1994. However, that, too, broke down, and Saleh (perhaps fearing outside attempts to interfere—Saudi Arabia had for some time been applying overt pressure over their frontier, which is disputed along its entirety, and in particular over the section in which Yemen had granted oil exploration contracts) apparently decided to take the initiative to impose unity in the country by force.[7]

Northern units began attacking southern units in May, initiating a civil war which ended in July after a brutal siege of Aden.

In all of these events, the role of the USSR and Russia was negligible, except in the negative sense that they did not oppose unification, and their cessation of arms supplies to Aden made its defeat inevitable when war broke out. Their only visible concern during these years was to try to persuade Yemen to begin repaying its accumulated debt, and even to invest in Russia. However, the outbreak of the civil war gave Russia another opportunity to demonstrate the less pro-West foreign policy stance it had adopted by then. As the fighting seemed to be stalemated, both sides sent representatives to Moscow, and the ceasefire that had eluded Arab mediators was signed on 30 June (although in the end not implemented for long, as the northern forces regained their momentum). There were possibly other motives for the initiative, other than gaining international status or simply ending the fighting. The southern forces' aim was to reestablish an independent country; an effective ceasefire at that moment would have given them, perhaps, the breathing space to mobilize outside political support. It seems certain that Saudi Arabia and Kuwait were supporting this aim, to the extent of helping to pay for southern weapons (including MiG-29s purchased from Bulgaria).[8] One might speculate that Moscow had many reasons to want to be on the side of Saudi Arabia and Kuwait, and would not be averse to being a supporter of old friends in charge of what might become a relatively wealthy oil state. At the same time, none of these considerations was important enough for Moscow to want to be seen to be taking sides, and it did not. With a northern victory, it lost little; Yemen needed friends.

In the aftermath of the conflict, the promise of the early 1990s for Yemen has been badly tarnished. Independent and party newspapers have continued to publish, but there are occasional reports of papers' being charged with antigovernment bias and closed temporarily, and of journalists' and intellectuals' being harassed. The freely elected parliament continues to sit (without YSP members, as the party boycotted the April 1997 elections) but is ineffectual; the president runs the show. The economy continues to deteriorate. Gulf Cooperation Council (GCC) aid has not resumed. Southern grievances do not appear to have been addressed. On a brighter note, Saudi Arabia's vendetta against Saleh seems to be relaxing, after he was forced to agree to Saudi terms on the border.

On the African side of the Red Sea, Russia has had little role to play. Civil strife abounds in Somalia, Ethiopia, Djibouti, and Sudan, but there is little if anything to be gained from encouraging it even though none of these governments are particularly well-disposed to Russia; Moscow is not in the game any more. It has reestablished good relations with Egypt, for reasons of debt repayment and an interest in the Middle East peace process.

There is little reason to think that most of the rest of the African side will prosper or excite the interest of outsiders (although it should be noted that Iraq was active on both sides of the region in the 1980s).[9] Somalia is effectively divided into north and south and has fragmented further; the two states barely exist as political and economic entities. Eritrea has the best chance of developing, if it were to get substantial assistance; this seems unlikely. Ethiopia has embarked on an ambitious political and economic restructuring which intends to give much more power (including the right to secede) to its ethnic regions;[10] even with substantial aid, it would be difficult to see a prosperous Ethiopia.

Sudan, mired in a long-running civil war over ethnicity, religion, territory, and oil, is also unlikely to prosper. However, it appears that it will attract interest. Sudan is now considered to be one of the founts of Islamic militancy and a supporter of terrorism. With financial support from abroad, including from Iran (which provided at least $300 million for the purchase of Chinese arms, and with which it has been reported to have signed a "security pact")[11], it may be developing a capacity to meddle seriously in key Middle East states such as Egypt (with which it has long had an ambivalent relationship) and Saudi Arabia. This certainly is a matter for concern in Washington, given its interests in those countries, and also its fears about Islamic militancy in general. Russia is no less susceptible to those fears, but must focus on regions closer to home.

Nothing could better demonstrate the impact of the end of the cold war and the lack of strategic value of the Red Sea than the two crises of the 1990s involving Eritrea—the conflict with Yemen over the Hanish Islands, and the border war with Ethiopia.

The first was precipitated when Eritrean forces invaded one of the tiny group of islands in the Red Sea on 15 December 1995, dislodging a small Yemeni force. The motive for the attack has never been clear, with speculation ranging from fear of competition for proposed Eritrean tourist facilities on the Dahlak Islands, to an Israeli plot, to a preemptive move to establish Eritrean ownership of the seabed in an area thought to be promising for oil.[12] The short conflict provoked an outcry in the Arab press. Media voices in Yemen demanded a military response. A number of Arab countries offered to mediate. However, it received almost no notice in the Russian media or in official pronouncements, and virtually no notice in the American media. Despite the palpable interest of the two parties in involving the United States in some form of dispute resolution, Washington passed. Eritrea withdrew its forces and both sides accepted a French proposal for international mediation. As of August 1999, the issue had yet to be resolved. Should the result of mediation cause a rise in military tension between the parties, Lefebvre suggests that it will be left to France to take action;[13] the United States might involve itself by diplomatic means, but not militarily except in an extreme case. There is no prospect of Russia's being involved, nor wanting to be.

Similarly, the dispute between Eritrea and Ethiopia over a 15-kilometer section of their border has been allowed to fester and blossom into armed conflict. Russia, having no close ties with either government, has barely commented. The United States, seeing no interest at stake, has devoted few resources to seeking a solution.

*   *   *

In contrast to the Red Sea region, the end of the cold war and the collapse of the USSR did not reduce the strategic importance of the Persian Gulf region. In fact, these events may well have increased the threat to Western interests; the putative threat of Soviet military and ideological expansionism has been replaced by regional powers' demonstrated expansionist ambitions and by the prospect of domestic unrest. The end of the cold war contributed to the easing of restrictions on the actions of regional powers (although this process had begun earlier, with the Iranian Revolution in 1979 and the Iraqi attack on Iran in 1980), while democratization in the former Soviet Union and Eastern Europe unleashed political and social expectations which have yet to work themselves out in the Gulf.

The Gulf Arab states (excluding Iraq) are alike in that they are traditional, family-based monarchies resistant to political transformation, with small, mostly Sunni Muslim populations in wealthy (in some cases immensely so) oil-based economies. Despite the pace of modernization over the past fifty years, their rulers have managed to blunt its effects by playing on Islamic conservatism, by co-opting or repressing dissident forces, and by spreading the oil wealth, which they personally control, judiciously. The forces of modernization, however, are constantly working to subvert this political and social order, as they do elsewhere. Supplementing them in the Gulf Arab states are four specific factors: ideological

subversion, the need for outsiders for defense, changes in the
global oil picture, and regional countries' ambitions.

Ideological subversion is a much greater danger to Gulf Arab
rulers now than it ever was during the cold war, because Communism was atheist and alien, and the rulers could use it to legitimize
their rule and to some extent to justify their ties to the West. The
ideological threat now comes from two sources. The least dangerous thus far is democracy. This is partly for reasons of history and
culture. It is also because there are no attractive examples of working Arab democracies. It appeared for a few years that Yemen
could provide such an example; this may provide at least a partial
explanation of Riyadh's continued meddling in Yemeni tribal politics, its renewed pressures on Yemen's borders, and its support for
secessionist forces in the 1994 civil war. The example of Iran's (im-
perfectly functioning) electoral system is also noted, particularly in
the southern Gulf, and perhaps Bahrain.[14]

In spite of the imperfections, it is evident that the desire for
democratic institutions exists in these states as elsewhere, and is
probably growing as it is elsewhere. In the aftermath of the expul-
sion of the Iraqi military from Kuwait, the al-Sabah (Kuwait's ruling family) were forced to reactivate the Constitution suspended in
1976 and hold elections in 1992. The voting returned a legislature
reasonably representative of Kuwait's male citizenry, but the al-
Sabah have kept control of the government.[15] Saudi Arabia is the
key to change in this region, and even its ruling family, the al-
Sa'ud, has had to bend slightly to the wind. On 30 December 1993,
King Fahd convened the long-promised *Majlis al-Shura*, a Consultative Council appointed from some of the major social and economic groups in the kingdom. On paper, the *Majlis* is to have
considerable powers of legislative initiative and review, including
over the budget; however, the king retains the final decision-making power, and Fahd has stated unequivocally that this will not become an elected body, and, indeed, that Western-style democracy
has no place in the region.[16] In July 1997, perhaps in recognition
of the shifting demographic and educational profile of the population, Fahd appointed a new Consultative Council, whose enlarged
membership was more representative of the Saudi nonroyal elite;
however, its powers were not expanded.[17] There the matter
stands, for the moment. Nevertheless, the al-Sa'ud have been sur-
vivors, and a generational change is imminent within the royal
family. It is possible that democratization will come out of this, but
it is important to recognize that the main opposition today is from
conservative religious forces, not from aspirants for Western-style

democracy. The ruling family appears to have more than sufficient security forces to maintain stability. However, this means that if pressures for change build up (in any of the Gulf Arab states), the only outlet will be violent social upheaval.

At the moment, the more dangerous forces of ideological subversion in those states are religious. In the recent past, the danger was thought to come from the militant Islam of revolutionary Iran; however, Shi'a Islam tied to Iranian nationalism has proved not to be palatable to the Sunni Arabs (nor indeed even to Shi'i Arabs). In Saudi Arabia, religious opposition has arisen from within. The strongest challenge has been spearheaded by young, conservative clergy, angered by the corruption of the royal family and its perceived departures from Islamic law and custom. Even members of the clerical establishment joined the criticism in October 1992;[18] Fahd reacted by replacing them with a new Supreme Council of Religious Affairs dominated by members of the royal family, by arresting militants and claiming that they were the tools of foreign governments (probably meaning Sudan),[19] and by establishing the *Majlis* to dilute their support in the country. This has not silenced the criticism from some mosques and religious universities, that on rare occasions even question the legitimacy of the al-Sa'ud to rule.[20] Nevertheless, there is as yet no real threat to the royal family; nor is there likely to be, for at the sign of a real threat they will move to accommodate these forces by adopting stricter implementation of Islamic laws.

One of the strongest points of complaint by all the Islamic opposition has been the al-Sa'ud's alliance with the United States as evidenced by the presence of U.S. and coalition forces on Saudi territory during the Kuwait crisis, and Riyadh's subsequent acceptance of the Middle East peace process. It is not clear how widespread this feeling is; presumably most of the population would prefer not to be left at the tender mercies of Iraq. Nevertheless, it is likely to be a festering sore that may increase in seriousness as popular memories of the threat recede and other domestic complaints surface. The royal family has moved to reduce the impact of this Saudi dependence. Whereas in the spring of 1991 it rejected the idea (embodied in the Damascus Declaration) of extraregional but Arab countries (mainly Egypt and Syria) providing military security in the Gulf in favor of a visible tie with the United States, it quickly reduced that visibility. Instead of bases and regular joint exercises, it opted for some prepositioning of equipment, and approval of U.S. military presence elsewhere in the region. More recently, it has also distanced itself from the United States on some issues (e.g., joining the boycott of the Middle East and North Africa Economic Conference in Doha in November 1997 because of Israeli footdragging in the peace process, and establishing somewhat closer relations with Iran).[21] It also adopted a policy of further massive arms purchases of Western weapons, the high-tech variety which had proved their capabilities in the 1991 Gulf War. This policy has complicated its economic situation, and it is not certain that the over-the-horizon arrangement with the United States will defuse the political ramifications of dependence.

In the rest of the Gulf Arab states, there is a visible U.S. military presence, particularly in Bahrain and Kuwait. In Bahrain the small Central Command (U.S., CENTCOM) headquarters has grown to a major establishment reportedly occupying the southern fifth of the island.[22] With Bahrain not under military threat, this could easily become the focus of the existing discontent among the majority Shi'i, and will certainly be kept under the spotlight of Iranian and Iraqi propaganda in future. Kuwait is under obvious military threat and will remain so for the foreseeable future, despite Iraq's formal acceptance of its sovereignty in November 1994. Foreign military commitments to Kuwait's defense are thus as welcome to its citizens as to the al-Sabah; agreements have been signed with the United States, Britain, and France, as well as with Russia.[22] Enough U.S. equipment for a mechanized infantry brigade has been prepositioned, and joint rapid reaction exercises have taken place with United States and British units, and joint naval exercises with Russian units. Regular exercises have occurred without domestic discontent. However, they are and will continue to be the cause of considerable Iranian and Iraqi unhappiness, in ever-increasing volume. The impact of foreign propaganda on domestic stability is by no means certain, but it is likely to keep the region unsettled. The danger to stability, however, continues to emanate mostly from within. In Bahrein unrest stems from the declining economy, the corruption of the ruling family, and its refusal to restore the Constitution and reconvene the representative assembly suspended in 1975.[23] Moreover, everywhere the United States' military presence and activities remind people that decades of military spending by their rulers have not provided the ability to defend themselves. In time of direct threat this may not be a problem; however, when Gulf Arab goals diverge from American goals, difficult choices have to be made. In 1998, Saudi Arabia, Bahrain, and the United Arab Emirates (UAE) refused permission for the United States to fly missions directly over Iraq;[24] and U.S.

administration officials are reported to believe that wealthy Gulf Arabs are hedging their bets by supporting Usama bin Laden.[25]

The third factor working to weaken the existing social and political order in the region is the global oil picture, which seems set for a lengthy period of low prices. Iraq presumably will have to be reincorporated into the supply picture eventually, and Iran is unhappy with its production quota. Saudi Arabia, burdened with social subsidies, recent bills for the coalition defense efforts, and current and future bills for its arms purchases, has been running budget deficits for years; it is unwilling (and indeed unable) to play its old swing producer role. The addition of Iraq and other producers like Kazakhstan and Azerbaijan would make it difficult for OPEC to sustain even the current level of prices. The Saudi government, already forced into austerity measures, will have to make further spending cuts which are bound to increase unemployment and inflation, and further unsettle society. The same is likely to be true of Kuwait and Bahrain; the others may be able to contain the impact of continued low prices for some time.

The final factor is the ambition of regional countries, which brings into play all the other three factors to a greater or lesser extent. Iraq merely provides the most serious example. Its invasion of Kuwait exacerbated (although it did not create) the social, economic, and political factors already mentioned. Even in defeat, it continues to unsettle the region. A change in leadership is unlikely to alter this. Only a radical change of its entire political system could begin to reassure its neighbors, and even then the resentments engendered by its defeat and the long and onerous blockade, not to mention the difficulty of reincorporating it into the oil market, will make Iraq a difficult member of the region for years to come.

Iran after the revolution demonstrated ideologically expansionist ambitions which kept the region in an unsettled state until 1990. The emergence of a less militant regime since the death of Ayatollah Khomaini in 1989, Iran's neutral behavior during the Kuwait crisis, and the landslide election victory of moderate cleric Mohamed Khatami as president in May 1997 have begun to alleviate regional concerns. However, Iran can at best be considered a state in a transitional phase; it is not clear that it has decided to base its regional policy on good-neighborly relations, or rejected a desire for regional hegemony. It has embarked on a significant arms purchase program, although this is by no means as large in dollar terms as Saudi Arabia's; Iran has large equipment losses from the Iran-Iraq War of 1980–87 still to remedy, and it can certainly point to enemies both real and potential.[26] Its purchase and development of missiles is disturbing now that Iraq's missile capability has (at least for the moment) been dismantled. Finally, there are unanswered questions about its intention to develop nuclear weapons. President Khatami was able to end Iran's regional isolation to a large extent when Teheran hosted the December 1997 meeting of the Islamic Conference Organization, to which Saudi Arabia and the other Gulf states sent high-level delegations. Saudi Arabia and Iran have continued to put their relations on a more normal footing, and in other parts of the lower Gulf Iran is once again being seen as a balancer for Iraq. However, it must be noted that the internal power struggle in Teheran between moderates and hardliners is by no means over.

Saudi Arabia itself has contributed to uncertainty on the Arab side of the Gulf and in the peninsula generally. Its border dispute with Qatar has continued; this was likely one of the reasons behind the overthrow in June 1995 of the ruler by the crown prince, who favors a foreign policy more independent of Saudi Arabia. Qatar's new ruler is not the only one to resent Saudi dominance of the GCC, a situation that has contributed to the weakness of that organization. Saudi meddling in Yemen's internal affairs and its border pressure have caused serious instability in that country.

*   *   *

For Washington, instability in the Gulf is both a bigger and a smaller issue than it was in the 1970s. It is bigger because the United States is now much more dependent on the oil and markets (especially the arms markets) of the Gulf Arab monarchies, and because the causes of instability are indigenous and therefore more intractable. It is smaller because there is no longer a superpower competing for influence in the region, actively (though carefully) seeking domestic weaknesses in pro-Western Gulf states. The Soviet Union's abandonment of subversive intent in the Gulf dates from two events: the Iranian revolution, which threatened a result (the spread of Islamic militancy) which Moscow feared; and its invasion of Afghanistan and the near universal condemnation with which that act was greeted in the region. Moscow's reaction to the Iran-Iraq War of 1980–87 underlined its decision to opt for regional stability.

The Kuwait crisis enhanced the USSR's status in the Gulf. The Bush administration's invitation to involve the USSR in the Gulf was justified by the active role Moscow played in the initial response to the attack and in the UN Security Council. The relationship with Iraq was cut, despite its being very lucrative. Shevardnadze helped to pave the way for the UN's eventual military response; the Soviet refusal to participate in the coalition military force was accepted (possibly even with relief by Washington and Riyadh). The Saudi government rewarded the USSR with the resumption of diplomatic relations (suspended in 1938) and $1 billion in economic assistance; Kuwait provided $1 billion in credit on the most favorable terms, and the UAE contributed a loan of $500 million.[27]

Moscow's responses to the crisis appeared to enhance its position in the Gulf. The Gulf Arab states were grateful for its abandonment of Iraq and reassured by the precipitous decline in Soviet power, which made the USSR an aid supplicant. The Iraqis had little to thank Moscow for, but had no other friends. Iran was worried by the immense U.S. military presence in the Gulf, and its apparent intention to remain there in some strength. Since it was clear that American and Iranian interests would clash, Tehran saw that Moscow could be useful, should it develop a foreign policy less attentive to American concerns.

After the collapse of the USSR, the initial Yeltsin-Kozyrev foreign policy line brought no comfort to Baghdad or Tehran. Firmly Atlanticist, it stressed the advantages and the need (both economic and moral) of a partnership with the Western democracies; among the many "common values" it espoused were adherence to UN sanctions and restrictions on arms sales to potential conflict zones like the Gulf. On a whole range of issues, the emphasis was put on cooperation with, even concession to, Western, and particularly American, policies.

This did not last, nor should it have been expected to. From the start, political forces arose to oppose the Yeltsin-Kozyrev policy.[28] Some of these were on the radical fringes, apparently marginalized. However, a significant and constantly growing segment of the political elite resented Russia's humiliations and concessions to Washington, and advocated tougher policies which would defend Russia's interests by (among other things) pursuing independent policies in the Third World, particularly in the Middle East. Western reluctance (either real or in Russian perception) to accept Russia as an equal partner, to accept a "balance of interests," increased elite and societal dissatisfaction with the liberals' leadership. In addition, the failure of Western economic aid to meet exaggerated expectations to prevent or alleviate economic disaster further discredited the pro-West foreign policy line.

Kozyrev was forced on the defensive, despite his protestations as early as April 1992 that he was pursuing policies which demonstrated that Russia was a great power. Over the next eighteen months, he was compelled to cede ground to more nationalist forces. By the end of 1993, a consensus on Russian national interest appeared to have been reached (in documents on a foreign policy concept[29] and a new military doctrine)[30] which recognized that Russia has interests as a nuclear superpower, as a great power in the world, and as a regional power, and that some of those interests would have to be pursued in competition with its Western partners.

One of those interests was an economic one, based on the expectation that the weapons industry was one of the very few internationally competitive sectors of the economy, one whose sales could help to bridge the economic transition to the market of the rest of the economy. This was never realistic. Although Soviet arms transfers may have been valued at as much as $20 billion per year in their heyday,[31] in fact the bulk of these were to Soviet client states that were unlikely to pay for them, even in local currency. However, arms sales quickly became a symbol of Russia's status in the world. Barely two months after Russian independence, Yeltsin called for an increase in arms exports, and a year later delivered a bitter rebuke to his senior economic ministers for failing to accomplish this.[32] Arms sales around the world declined noticeably in the early 1990s, except in the Persian Gulf region. Soviet and Russian arms sales, however, declined precipitously, reportedly from $11 billion in 1988 to $4 billion in 1992, to $1.7 billion in 1994,[33] in part because two of Russia's best customers under those conditions, Libya and Iraq, were under international arms embargoes to which Russia was faithfully adhering, at a cost often quoted in the Russian media of $16–18 billion in sales.[34]

Under these circumstances, it was particularly galling to Russian elites of all political stripes to see the United States building its market share of conventional weapons orders to more than 50%[35] by aggressively pursuing arms orders in the Gulf. In the aftermath of the coalition victory over Iraq, Saudi Arabia, Kuwait, and the UAE placed orders for major weapons systems; Saudi Arabia (the largest arms purchaser in the world) ordered $27 billion worth of military hardware and support systems.[36] Backed by Presidents Bush and Clinton and senior members of their administrations, U.S. arms producers picked up the bulk of the orders. Russia was left scratching for crumbs at the margin. High-level delegations visited the Gulf in April 1992 (led by Foreign Minister Andrei Kozyrev) and in November 1994 (led by Prime Minister Viktor Chernomyrdin, with Defense Minister Pavel Grachev and other defense ministry officials accompanying him); Russian manufacturers were a major presence at the arms exhibitions in Abu Dhabi in February 1993 and March 1995. Russia and the UAE signed a military agreement in January 1993; Russia and Kuwait signed one in December 1993, and held joint naval exercises that same month. Gulf rulers stressed the importance of Russia to Gulf security, and signed general agreements on economic cooperation. However, despite official optimism, there were few orders. The deals were not insubstantial, but paled in comparison to U.S. and Western sales. Russian liberal commentators have speculated that the orders were placed simply as sops to weaken hard-line domestic criticism of Yeltsin, and to stiffen perceived Russian wavering on Iraq, despite doubts about Russia's long-term ability to service these systems, and indeed about the reliability of its friendship;[37] Moscow's arms sales to Iran are of great concern to the Gulf Arabs.

Whatever the reasons for Russia's failure to break into new arms markets, it quickly became received wisdom that it was being deliberately excluded by the West, either out of pure greed or a desire to destroy Russia's potential for economic recovery to great-power status.[38] Early in 1993, Kozyrev seemed to be subscribing to this theory when he proposed that Western countries open up some of their established arms markets to Russian competition. Not surprisingly, this did not happen. Equally not surprisingly, Russia has tried to develop the markets in which it is welcome, in particular Iran. The bases for Russian involvement were the contracts signed in the Gorbachev period, in 1989 for $3.2 billion in aircraft (including state-of-the-art MiG-29s), tanks, armored infantry vehicles, artillery, SAMs, and 3 Kilo-class diesel-powered submarines.[39] One submarine was delivered in November 1992, and a second in August 1993; in 1994, Washington launched a concerted campaign to prevent the sale of the third submarine (variously described by a "top Russian diplomat" as one of "three old diesel submarines," and by "the Western military" as "a black hole at sea"[40]). The United States saw these as offensive weapons arrayed against shipping in the Strait of Hormuz; Iran, pointing to Western naval activities in the Persian Gulf and attacks on Iran during the Iran-Iraq war, saw them as defensive and deterrent. A source in the Russian foreign ministry saw their use as "none of our business,"[41] while others pointed to the hypocrisy of the Americans' complaining while at the same time selling billions of dollars worth of equipment to the Gulf Arabs. Clearly what was important was the $500

million price tag. American pressure, which included Congress'
threat to suspend aid to Russia, and Clinton's threat to exclude
Russia from the new COCOM, was much resented, despite Yeltsin's eventual refusal to cancel the third sale. The issue was defused
by an agreement in 1995 between Vice-President Al Gore and
Prime Minister Viktor Chernomyrdin that Russia would fulfill its
existing arms sales agreements with Iran, but would not sign new
deals. However, indications that Moscow is seeking ways of getting
around this agreement have been reported.[42]

It is not surprising, therefore, that Russia was not averse to a $1
billion contract to complete two German-built nuclear energy reactors in Iran, nor that American pressure in 1995 to kill the deal
was received with great resentment. Not only has a less cooperative
foreign policy line been in place in Moscow since mid-1993, buttressed by the success of hard-line parties in the elections to the
State Duma in December 1993 and again in December 1995. In
addition, bureaucratic politics has played a role. Russia's political
and economic troubles have had the effect of weakening executive
control over policy generally; it appears that in this case, the Ministry of Nuclear Energy was able to conclude this agreement without
input from other interested ministries, and present the Ministry of
Foreign Affairs with a *fait accompli*.

The United States has put tremendous pressure on Russia to ab-
rogate the deal. It believes that Iran is engaged in a crash program
to develop nuclear weapons,[43] which as a "rogue state" it will use
to establish a malevolent regional hegemony. The extent to which
this is true is unclear. Certainly Iran has vast reserves of natural
gas which could be used to generate electricity; it is also the case
that electricity is in short supply in Iran, and the reactors were relatively close to completion when construction was abandoned, and
the work was well preserved. In the debate, there has been considerable heat generated over the ability of Iran to use the spent fuel
for the construction of nuclear weapons; Russian government officials have consistently argued that this cannot be accomplished
with this type of reactor, which is a "water-cooled, water-moder-
ated" reactor of the type the United States has agreed to supply to
North Korea.[44] Besides, the Russians argue, Iran is a signatory of
the Nuclear Non-Proliferation Treaty, and has agreed to rigorous
International Atomic Energy Agency (IAEA) inspections, none of
which has turned up evidence of a nuclear weapons development
program. As a member of the NPT, they say, Iran has the right to
acquire peaceful nuclear technology.[45] Recently it has been reported that, despite Washington's continuing lobbying and

threats, Russia intends to speed up the work of technicians at the plant, and even to undertake additional nuclear projects in Iran, including possibly a second reactor at Bushehr.[46] The *Wall Street Journal* on 15 December 1998 quoted U.S. intelligence officials that Russian research institutes were negotiating to sell technology that would enhance Iran's ability to develop nuclear weapons.

What is clear from this dispute is that Russia is determined to establish itself in Iran even if this policy has a detrimental effect on Russian-American relations. Its motive is certainly economic in part. It is also nationalist in part, an assertion of great-power status, and a reaction to Russia's difficulty in breaking into European and Western councils. With the appointment of Yevgeny Primakov as foreign minister in January 1996, and then as prime minister in September 1998, geopolitics apparently became the motivating theory behind Russian foreign policy, no longer just the preoccupation of academics and opposition forces.[47] The 'Primakov Doctrine' mandates that Russia will pursue an active and independent foreign policy where it can, undermining the unipolar tendencies of U.S. foreign policy without, however, seriously harming relations with the United States and the West.[48] However, it is also a recognition of regional realities. Iran will be a major economic, political, and military player in the Gulf and southwest Asia regions, which are contiguous with the borders of the Commonwealth of Independent States, regarded by Russia as its own borders. Tehran is making a determined bid for at least a strong economic role in Central Asia; if it continues on its move away from Islamic radicalism, it will become more acceptable politically as well. Russia is and will be in no position to prevent this. It is already having to deal with Tehran on an equal basis on economic issues (such as its dispute over Azerbaijan's use of offshore Caspian Sea oil) and security issues (such as its attempts to resolve the civil war in Tajikistan and prevent the spread of Islamic radicalism via Afghanistan). For this reason alone, it is necessary for Russia to be on good terms with Iran. In the words of Viktor Vishnyakov, chairman of the Russian Duma's Subcommittee for Issues of International Law, Russia sees Iran as "a potential ally in many of the most important areas" of Russian foreign and economic policy.[49]

There are, of course, other reasons. There are lucrative military and economic contracts to be won in Iran, and Western countries are not well-positioned to win them. Iran is determined to rebuild its military, and at the moment Russia can provide the best equipment at the lowest cost. The same is less true of infrastructure and other industrial technology, but for political reasons Russia is still

well-placed. From a broader regional perspective, Moscow's policies will cause some anxieties on the Arab side of the Gulf; however, it is not realistic to think that Russia will displace U.S. or even
Western European economic, military, or political positions in
those countries to any extent. In these circumstances, Russia's
focus on Iran is realistic. Moscow might even hope that it can build
influence in Tehran and sell itself to the Gulf Arabs as a security
partner on that basis; however, the history of superpower influ-
ence-building in the Third World should not give it cause for optimism.

One of the difficulties Russia will have in the longer-term is its
relationship with Iraq once that country is allowed back into the
community of nations. Events from 1990 to the present have not
changed the geopolitical reality of Iraq's position in the region; it
will eventually again become Iran's competitor, and it will continue
to concern the Gulf Arabs. Russia has very strong interests in the
recovery of Iraq, not least the approximately $6 billion in accumu-
lated debt owed to the USSR.[50] Ties go back more than twenty-five
years, and Russia should be well-placed to win a significant portion
of economic and military contracts (if its own economy has recovered sufficiently). Moreover, Russian politicians, especially from
the Liberal-Democratic Party, and economic bureaucrats have continually given hope to Baghdad that the UN embargo was shaky.

Given the large rewards to be garnered from Iraq for breaking
the embargo, it says a great deal about the current international
system and about Yeltsin's commitment to a modified version of
Atlanticism, that Russia has not broken ranks. However, it has actively positioned itself for the day when the embargo is lifted. Since
late 1993, discussions have taken place between Russian and Iraqi
economic bureaucrats about debt repayment and Russian participation in the rehabilitation and development of Iraqi oilfields once
that happens.[51] Moreover Russia, apparently out of conviction that
Iraq has come close to fulfilling the terms of the embargo, and
should be encouraged to complete that process, has since mid-
1994 advocated gradually lifting it.

The first real light at the end of the tunnel in Kozyrev's eyes
came in the midst of the October 1994 crisis when Saddam Hussein moved troops to Kuwait's borders, and the United States responded with an airlift of troops to Kuwait. Iraq's troops were only
partially withdrawn, and it appeared another battle was imminent.
Kozyrev flew to Baghdad, and after what he described as "a very
strong move by Russia,"[52] the troops were withdrawn to their original positions, and a joint statement intimated that Iraq was willing

to recognize Kuwait's sovereignty and borders. Kozyrev then went to the UN where he called for a six-month trial period after which the embargo would be gradually lifted.[53] Two weeks later, Kozyrev was in Baghdad attending a session of Iraq's National Council in which it ratified acceptance of Kuwait's sovereignty.[54] Despite U.S. anger at his claims of defusing the crisis, Kozyrev continued his advocacy in the UN, reportedly receiving support from France and China. As Russian foreign policy continued to distance itself from the United States, the debate in the Security Council over continuing sanctions against Iraq proved to be a useful substitute for more radical Russian action. In the face of Washington's insistence that sanctions must not be lifted until Iraq complies fully with UN resolutions and UNSCOM's reports (or the removal of Saddam Hussein), Russia has looked for ways to lift sanctions partially to respond to what Moscow (and Paris and Beijing) have seen as Iraqi steps in that direction. When Saddam Hussein created crises by refusing to cooperate with UNSCOM in its attempts to identify Iraq's Weapons of Mass Destruction programs, Moscow actively attempted to mediate. When these crises resulted in U.S. and British bombing campaigns, Russia reacted angrily, claiming that they were not authorized by Security Council resolutions. Russia has led the attack on UNSCOM in the Security Council, and the search for a new type of arms monitoring agency.[55]

While this more independent policy toward Iraq played well at home, it is not clear how the Gulf Arab governments reacted to it. They are skeptical, to a greater or lesser degree, about the efficacy of military solutions to Iraqi intransigence. However, they also have no desire to bring Iraqi production back into a soft oil market. They have hard evidence that the United States is committed for the long term to their military security; economic security cannot be so easily assured.

Russia's policy toward Iran and its clear intent to restore good relations with Iraq as soon as possible is significantly at odds with U.S. policy. The Clinton administration has declared both to be "backlash" states, toward which the United States has "a special responsibility for developing a strategy to neutralize, contain and, through selective pressure, perhaps eventually transform them into constructive members of the international community."[56] Thus far, the strategy is to isolate both to the maximum extent possible. In spring 1995, the United States applied a complete economic embargo on Iran, including sanctions against any foreign firm that invests more than $40 million per year in the development of Iran's energy resources. The strategy also envisages a long-term U.S. military presence and rapid response capability in order to preserve a power balance in favor of the Gulf Arab states.

Dual containment can only be effective if all countries which could be major economic and military partners of the target states subscribe to it. Thus far, isolation of Iraq has been effective, but a number of states besides Russia are beginning to ask if it is not time to begin the process of easing up. With regard to Iran, the United States has had no success in its call for boycott; Japan and Western Europe have rejected it, as has Russia; even the Gulf Arab states are unconvinced. One of the problems is historical experience: states that have been powerful, but are being kept artificially weak, have not meekly accepted their "fate," but have aggressively expanded their strength as soon as that was feasible. Enhanced security does not follow. Outside the United States, the urge to try inclusion rather than exclusion is strong, at least in the case of Iran. Another major problem is not so noble; there are great profits to be made in the reconstruction of the Iranian economy and military, and the rebuilding of Iraq. (To be fair to others, this fact has not been lost on American companies, and it has been suggested, in the Russian media for example, that dual containment is a device aimed at changing those governments to allow the re-entry of U.S. business.)[57]

A third problem is the fear that dual containment will be judged as not simply anti-Iraq or anti-Iran under their present regimes, or even as anti-Islamic militancy, but as anti-Islam;[58] this would have particularly serious repercussions for the Gulf Arab governments, which are susceptible to the charge of being propped up by the U.S. military. It is also something which could damage Russian interests in Central Asia as well as the Gulf if Moscow subscribed. Muslim perception that Russia was participating in an anti-Islamic "crusade" would also jeopardize its chances of loans and investment from the Gulf Arabs; furthermore, the money which is said to be funnelling into "virtually every mosque" in Central Asia from "Saudi shaikhs" and "Iranian Revolutionary Guards"[59] might be put to anti-Russian causes. Finally, such a perception might awaken dormant reactions to its activities in its own Muslim territories, like Chechnya.[60]

Nor are other U.S. interests in the Gulf necessarily parallel to Russia's. There is no likelihood that Washington will deliberately make space for Russian companies to win contracts, particularly major military contracts. Although the Soviet Union was invited to participate in Gulf security in 1990, it became clear that it was on U.S. terms. There has been no evidence of American concessions to Moscow (in either economic or status terms) to bring it onside in the dual containment strategy.

*   *   *

The foregoing examination of the developments in the Red Sea and Persian Gulf regions in the 1990s, and of Russian foreign policy in regards to them, makes clear Moscow's progression to more nationalist policies, based on a return to some of the old national interests: economic gain and regional influence where the region retains its geopolitical importance. What is missing is the ideological component; not all regions are of geopolitical importance, and resources (even if they existed) do not have to be expended in blind competition with the West and the U.S. in particular.

Nevertheless, it is clear that Russian and American interests in the Gulf do differ (as they do elsewhere), and that a more competitive Russian stance was to be expected. Even Kozyrev and other advocates of the Atlanticist end of the foreign policy spectrum accepted this; they did not merely react to a more critical domestic political situation, nor only to strengthened pressure groups, although these have been factors as well. It took some time for the Russian leadership to discover that taking one's place among the "civilized" states did not mean having one's interests accommodated in a friendly and cooperative fashion; a "balance of interests" has to be earned, often in disputes. Compromises may have to be forced; concessions need not always be given. This is not to argue that a more conciliatory or cooperative set of U.S. policies would have changed the direction of Russian foreign policy; Russia is determined to be a great power again, and its aspirations now outreach its capabilities. A nationalist reaction to its condition in the world of the 1990s was inevitable.

What of the future? Turmoil seems the most likely state of affairs in both regions. In the Red Sea, this is unlikely to attract reaction from Russia, or from the United States, unless it affects Egypt or Saudi Arabia; witness the lack of a robust reaction to the border war between Eritrea and Ethiopia. In the Persian Gulf, it will attract the attentions of both. If it is externally generated turmoil, in the form of an attack by Iraq or Iran, the United States seems committed to intervene on the side of the Gulf Arabs; Russia will support this, although probably from the sidelines.

However, it is domestic turmoil that is more likely in all the Gulf countries. The shocks of the early 1990s have by no means worked themselves out. Iraq and Iran are unstable politically and economically. Turmoil there will not be amenable to outside intervention. In the small Gulf Arab states, regime-threatening turmoil would probably generate a Saudi response, with U.S. backing; the more overt that backing, the more chance there will be of a backlash dangerous to U.S. interests. It is instability in Saudi Arabia which is of greatest danger to U.S. interests. If the rule of the al-Sa'ud were to be threatened, the temptation to intervene would be powerful, but an unsuccessful (and even a successful) intervention would shake U.S. interests to the core. It would also benefit Russia; by remaining aloof, it could find itself with more economic opportunities.

For Russia, remaining aloof from U.S.-driven policies in the Gulf will probably be easier in the future. While the results of Boris Yeltsin's disappearance from the political scene are not entirely clear, it is likely that Russia's attempts to promote its interests will become more pronounced, particularly in its relationship with Iran. Nevertheless, the consequences of a radical break with its erstwhile partners both in the Gulf and the broader world (withdrawing from the Iraq blockade, for example) are still too painful to bear.

NOTES

1. P. McDonald, "Red Sea: the Middle East's next troublespot?" *The World Today* 44, no. 5 (May 1988): 76–77; A. George, "The new Red Sea oil route," *The Middle East* 182 (February 1990): 48.

2. *Izvestiia*, 1 March 1990.

3. *Izvestiia*, 28 July 1990.

4. The UN has estimated that Yemen lost $2 billion as a result of the Gulf crisis. S. Edge, "Yemen copes in adversity," *MEED*, 28 August 1992: 2–3.

5. M. C. Dunn, "The Wrong Place, the Wrong Time: Why Yemen Unity Failed," *Middle East Policy* 3, no. 2(1994): 148–56.

6. M. C. Dunn, "Islamist Parties in Democratic States: A Look at Jordan and Yemen," *Middle East Policy* 2(1993): 24.

7. S. Carapico, "From Ballot Box to Battlefield: the War of the Two Alis," *Middle East Report* 190 (September–October 1994): 27.

8. *Izvestiia*, 24 August 1994.

9. J. A. Lefebvre, "The Geopolitics of the Horn of Africa," *Middle East Policy* 1, no. 3(1992): 21.

10. *New York Times*, 7 May 1995.

11. Lefebvre, "The Geopolitics of the Horn of Africa," 19.

12. J. A. Lefebvre, "Red Sea Security and the Geopolitical Economy of the Hanish Islands Dispute," *Middle East Journal* 52, no. 3(Summer 1998): 373–75. For years during the cold war the Dahlaks, which contain no source of fresh water, were said to house a Soviet submarine resupply base.

13. *Ibid.*, 382–83.

14. E. Hooglund, "Iranian Populism and Political Change in the Gulf," *Middle East Report* 174 (January–February 1992): 20.

15. Rabat radio, 6 October 1992, in U.S., Foreign Broadcast Information Service, *Daily Report: Near East and South Asia* (hereinafter cited as *FBIS/NESA*), 7 October 1992, 17; *Al Quds al-'Arabi* (London), 19 October 1992, in *FBIS/NESA*, 21 October 1992, 14.

16. *New York Times*, 2 May 1992; 30 March 1992; and 30 December 1993; *MEED*, 10 April 1992, 22.

17. R. H. Dekmejian, "Saudi Arabia's Consultative Council," *Middle East Journal* 52, no. 2(September 1998): 204.

18. *New York Times*, 31 December 1991 and 8 October 1992; R. H. Dekmejian, "Political Islamism in Saudi Arabia," *Middle East Journal* 48, no. 4(autumn 1994): 634.

19. *New York Times*, 22 December 1992; 22 September 1994; 28 September 1994; and 6 October 1994.

20. M. Al-Rasheed, "Saudi Arabia's Islamic Opposition," *Current History* (January 1996): 17–18.

21. J. A. Kechichian, "Trends in Saudi National Security," *Middle East Journal* 53, no. 2(spring 1999): 237.

22. S. Zunes, "The U.S.–GCC Relationship: its Rise and Potential Fall," *Middle East Policy* 2, no. 1 (1993): 108.

23. *Strategic Survey 1995/6*, London: IISS, p. 168; D. L. Byman and J. D. Green, "The Enigma of Political Stability in the Persian Gulf Monarchies," *MERIA Journal* 3, no. 3(September 1999): 5.

24. *The Military Balance 1998/9*, 115.

25. *New York Times*, 8 July 1999.

26. J. Bill, "The United States and Iran: Mutual Mythologies," *Middle East Policy* 2, no. 3(1993): 103–4; J. W. Moore, "An Assessment of the Iranian Military Rearmament Program," *Comparative Strategy* 13, no. 4(1994): 372–73.

27. *MEED*, 10 April 1992, p. 20; A. Z. Rubinstein, "Moscow and the Gulf War: decisions and consequences," *International Journal* 49, no. 2 (spring 1994): 318.

28. For a summary of the various positions in the Russian debate over foreign policy direction, see H. Adomeit, "Russia as a 'great power' in world affairs: images and reality," *International Affairs* (London) 71, no. 1 (January 1995): 35–68; O. Alexandrova, "Divergent Russian Foreign Policy Concepts," *Aussenpolitik* 44, no. 4 (1993): 363–72.

29. The text of the Foreign Policy Concept can be found in Foreign Broadcast Information Service, *FBIS Report: Central Eurasia* (hereinafter cited as FBIS/CE) 25 March 1993, 1–20.

30. A. Arbatov, "Russian National Interest," in R. D. Blackwill and S. A. Karaganov (eds.), *Damage Limitation or Crisis? Russia and the Outside World*, Washington: Brassey's, 1994 (Harvard University: CSIA Studies in International Security no. 5, 58.)

31. S. Foye, "Russian Arms Exports After the Cold War," *RFE/RL Research Report* 2, no. 13 (26 March 1993): 62.

32. *Ibid.*, 63, 60.

33. U.S., Department of Defense, *Worldwide Conventional Arms Trade 1994–2000: A Forecast and Analysis*, Washington, December 1994, 1; U.S., Library of Congress, Congressional Research Service, *Conventional Arms Transfers to the Third World 1986–1993*, Washington, July 1994, 5. Russian arms sales remained at this level in 1998. *RFE/RL Newsline* 3, no. 154, part 1 (11 August 1999).

34. R. Dannreuther, "Russia, Central Asia, and the Persian Gulf," *Survival* 35, no. 4(winter 1993–94): 108.

35. D. Mussington, "Understanding Contemporary International Arms Transfers,"*Adelphi Papers* 291(September 1994): 8.

36. S. Simon, "U.S. Strategy in the Persian Gulf," *Survival* 34, no. 3 (autumn 1992): 35–6; S. Zunes, "The U.S.–GCC Relationship," 105; *Strategic Survey 1991–92*, 101; *MEED*, 15 May 1992, 16.

37. *Moscow News*, 10–16 June 1994; *Moscow News*, 26 August–1 September 1994.

38. This belief is said to be firmly embedded in the military-industrial elite. S. A. Karaganov, "Russia's Elites," in Blackwill and Karaganov (eds.), *Damage Limitation or Crisis?*, 49.

39. Rubinstein, "Moscow and the Gulf War," 321.

40. A. K. Pushkov, "Letter from Eurasia: Russia and America: the Honeymoon's Over," *Foreign Policy* 93(winter 1993–94): 87; *Komsomolskaia pravda*, 29 April 1995, in *FBIS/CE*, 1 May 1995, 2.

41. *Izvestiia*, 22 July 1994.

42. *Segodnia*, 26 January 1999.

43. *New York Times*, 5 January 1995.

44. *Izvestiia*, 15 February 1995.

45. Interfax in English, 28 September 1994, in *FBIS/CE*, 29 September 1994, 19; *Izvestiia*, 15 February 1995. For an analysis which argues that Iran is seeking nuclear weapons, see S. Chubin, "Does Iran Want Nuclear Weapons?" *Survival* 37, no. 1 (spring 1995): 86–104.

46. *Monitor* 5, no. 8(13 January 1999).

47. C. Clover, "Dreams of the Eurasian Heartland," *Foreign Affairs* 78, no. 2 (March/April 1999): 11–13.

48. A. Pushkov, "The 'Primakov Doctrine' and a New European Order," *International Affairs* (Moscow) 44, no. 2 (1998): 12; Ye. Primakov, "Russia in World Politics: A Lecture in Honor of Chancellor Gorchakov," *International Affairs* (Moscow) 44, no. 3 (1998): 7–12.

49. V. Vishniakov, "Russian-Iranian Relations and Regional Stability," *International Affairs* (Moscow) 45, no. 1(1999): 144.

50. *Kommersant* (Moscow), 23 August 1993. The deputy director of the Russian Academy of Sciences' Institute of Oriental Studies claims that sanctions against Iraq have cost Russia $40–$50 billion in lost business. ITAR-TASS in English, 13 March 1995, in *FBIS/CE*, 14 March 1995, 14.

51. *Kommersant* (Moscow), 23 August 1993, in *FBIS/CE*, 8 September 1993, 40–1; *Kommersant Daily*, 23 October 1993, in *FBIS/CE*, 11 November 1993, 71; INTERFAX in English, 1 February 1995, in *FBIS/CE*, 2 February 1995, 3; *The Independent*, 23 October 1993 reported that Russia and Iraq had signed an arms deal to take effect when the sanctions are lifted. Iraq appears to believe that Russia needs participation in its oil fields badly enough that it might be pushed to break the sanctions. In July 1999, Baghdad told LUKoil to follow through on its oil development agreements or face cancellation of the contracts. LUKoil reportedly did request that Russia press the United Nations Security Council to allow some kinds of works to proceed, *Monitor* 5, no. 127 (1 July 1999), but aside from continuing its criticism of American and British military actions in the 'no-fly zone', Russia has not acted. *Monitor* 5, no. 132 (9 July 1999).

52. ITAR-TASS World Service in Russian, 17 October 1994, in *FBIS/CE*, 18 October 1994, 4.

53. Interfax in English, 17 October in *FBIS/CE*, 18 October 1994, 4.

54. ITAR-TASS World Service in Russian, 10 November 1994, in *FBIS/CE*, 10

November 1994, 4. Kozyrev, somewhat infelicitously, praised Saddam's "political wisdom" in coming to this decision.

55. *Monitor* 5, no. 146 (29 July 1999).

56. A. Lake, "Confronting Backlash States," *Foreign Affairs* 73, no. 2(March–April 1994): 46.

57. *Izvestiia*, 7 December 1994; *Krasnaia zvezda*, 21 February 1995; *Trud*, 6 April 1995, in *FBIS/CE*, 6 April 1995, 9–10 claimed that the United States is trying to prevent Russia from selling on the nuclear technology market.

58. B. Lewis, "License to Kill," *Foreign Affairs* 77, no. 6 (November/December 1998): 14–19.

59. Unnamed source in the Russian foreign ministry, quoted in INTERFAX in English, 22 May 1995, in Open Media Research Institute, *Daily Digest*, 22 May 1995.

60. The Organization of the Islamic Conference, meeting in February 1995, chose to regard the Chechen conflict as an internal affair of Russia, and issue only a mild call for a peaceful settlement. *Moscow News*, 10–16 February 1995.

In the Shadow of Soviet Collapse:
South Asia Without Superpower Competition

SHIRIN TAHIR-KHELI

WITHDRAWAL OF BRITAIN FROM THE INDIAN SUBCONTINENT OC-
curred in 1947 just as the Iron Curtain came down between the
USSR and the United States. The relationships between the South
Asian neighbors were influenced by the East-West rivalry that was
a salient feature of the cold war era. Located at the edge of the
Communist world, India and Pakistan were drawn into the vortex
almost as soon as they became independent. Throughout the cold
war, the interactions between these two states and the rest of the
world were conditioned by their rivalry with each other. India and
Pakistan fought two and a half wars, in 1948, 1965, and 1971, respectively. There were several alarms that brought one or both superpowers into defusing tensions (e.g., in May 1990 and July
1999).

South Asia served as the proving ground for the Reagan Doctrine that the Soviet Empire need not last and could be reduced.
The defeat of the USSR in Afghanistan and its subsequent withdrawal had major consequences for the Soviet state and the future
of Communism. The demise of the Soviet Union caused serious
reappraisals in India and Pakistan. This paper examines the salient features of the cold war as they affected the subcontinent; it
looks at the direct and indirect consequences of the collapse of the
USSR for India and Pakistan; it speculates on the future of South
Asia—without superpower competition.

BACKGROUND

Had the history of British India's partition into two new successor states been different, perhaps there would not have been any
need for outside patrons for India and Pakistan.[1] The hasty British
withdrawal and the lack of care in the drawing of the boundaries

left a bitter legacy which continues to this day. Kashmir was the first flash point. There, once Pathan fighters crossed over into Kashmir from Pakistan in 1948, Indian forces arrived as the ruler signed onto the Indian state. New Delhi's previously declared promise of a referendum to decide the future of Kashmir was thus overtaken by events. From that point on, Pakistani leaders saw themselves as being at the total mercy of a larger and hostile India, one which did not accept partition.

India inherited the bulk of the territory and the resources from colonial rule. But its leaders who fought hard to rid the nation of the Raj nursed a vision of a vast, populous, and dynamic state that would be thoroughly secular and democratic. For these leaders, Pakistan, as a Muslim state whose existence was a direct consequence of its religion, was too much of a disappointment. Things were said in public that resulted in unfriendly relations between the two states.

India was the star on the postwar anticolonial stage. Pakistan had to scramble to put itself on the map. Expectations that there would be an automatic cache—with other Islamic states, such as Egypt—failed to materialize. The net for much needed support had to be more widely cast. In the early 1950s, Washington was already on the lookout for states that could be counted on as friends in the escalating cold war with the Soviet Union. The victory of the Chinese communists added further impetus to the search. Strategic location offered India and Pakistan an early chance to get outside assistance for their development plans as well as for the modern armies that each saw as a prerequisite for national defense.

For a while, Moscow and Washington competed to befriend each of the two major subcontinental powers, each offering economic aid and military sales. By 1955, U.S. and Soviet policy diverged as India became a key player in the nonaligned movement and Pakistan was cementing relations with the United States. The result was a Mutual Defense Agreement and membership in two alliances: the Baghdad Pact in the west and the Southeast Asia Treaty Organization (SEATO) in the east.

Membership brought rewards in the form of assistance as well as a psychological element of support even beyond its actual material worth. For nearly a decade thereafter, Pakistani policy assumed a firm relationship with the United States that it saw as compensating for the disapproval of its policy by the Nonaligned Movement (NAM) where India remained an important player. India was open to support from the Soviet Union and the United States. The former provided economic assistance for the public sector and hardware for Indian defense needs at concessional terms. Denial of India to the United States was an important goal, and Moscow exercised great care in its relationship so that Indian leaders were not tempted to move closer to Washington. During the fifties, on diplomatic matters, even those as serious as the Soviet move into Hungary, Indian support for the USSR seemed a given.

From the Soviet perspective, Pakistan's support for American spy planes flying over Soviet territory was serious business. When one such plane, a U-2, took off from Peshawar and crashed inside Soviet airspace, there was not even the fig leaf of evenhandedness in Pakistani policy, leading Soviet leaders to threaten retaliation. Pakistani leaders felt that they were simply fulfilling their promise of a close collaborative policy with the United States. However, the utility of such collaboration declined as spy satellites replaced the aircraft for which Pakistan provided a critical launching pad. Satellites were launched from the continental United States and required no base near the Soviet Union.

The Sino-Indian border war in October 1962 came largely as a surprise to Delhi, as demonstrated by the lack of general preparedness. For a while, it seemed that China would prevail and that the Indian plains were open once the Chinese forces made a conclusive thrust into the mountainous terrain on two fronts. In Washington, the Kennedy administration moved quickly with material support for India. Pakistani leaders chafed at the lack of prior consultation between the United States and Pakistan before the latter offered assistance to India to cope with the war with China. The only nod toward Pakistan came as Kennedy put pressure on Pakistan not to take advantage of Indian vulnerability, so glaringly demonstrated at Chinese hands.[2]

With the dawning of the Sino-Soviet rivalry,[3] further options became available to Pakistan as the Soviets seemed willing to be somewhat neutral in their support of India, having become quite nervous about friendly relations between China and Pakistan. From the outset, Pakistan tried to cultivate good relations with China. Pakistan's close relations with the United States cast a shadow as the Korean War became the first major test of Communist China's resolve against the United States. The spirit of Bandung that was prevalent in the mid-fifties meant that there was a great deal of talk of friendly ties, bordering on "brotherhood" between China and India. However, the Chinese were more solicitous than their Soviet counterparts in cultivating cordial relations with Pakistan. That policy came in handy as the northern Chinese border with the Soviet Union began to bristle with arms and the diplomatic war of words to define the superior model of Communism heated up.

While there was a different set of relationships that the United States and the USSR each had with India and Pakistan, neither was pleased with the 1965 war and the danger of its widening beyond the border areas. Both superpowers called on the participants to end the fighting and move toward negotiations for resolving their differences over Kashmir. The Soviets offered to mediate the end of the war and invited the leaders of India and Pakistan to Tashkent, the first and only real attempt by Moscow to play honest broker in subcontinental matters. Having committed its prestige to the enterprise, Moscow persevered until there was an agreement to end the war, disengage the armies, and return the combatants to a more normal relationship. The "spirit of Tashkent" that was meant to launch a new era between Pakistan and the USSR vanished after it became clear that Moscow would always prefer Delhi over Islamabad.

Throughout the 1970s, Soviet support for India was important to the policies of both. Geopolitics dictated a close relationship, and the desire of the United States for opening relations with China in the Nixon administration and its use of Pakistan as the conduit for that opening in July 1971 made Moscow and Delhi doubly suspicious. Coming as Sino-American normalization did in the midst of another mounting crisis in South Asia, namely, the separation of the eastern wing of Pakistan into the independent nation of Bangladesh, India felt stymied. Delhi saw the events unfolding in East Pakistan and the resultant flow of refugees into India to escape persecution at the hands of the Pakistani Army as requiring a response which could not be denied because of the China-Pakistan-U.S. triangle.

The response came in the form of an announcement that a twenty-year "friendship" treaty had been signed between the USSR and India in August 1971, and it jolted Islamabad. Signed at the end of Soviet Foreign Minister Gromyko's visit to India, the joint communiqué stated that both sides believed the treaty to be a historic event and that it was a logical culmination of a long history of "sincere friendship, respect, mutual trust, and comprehensive relations which have been established between the Soviet Union and India over many years and which have stood the test of time."[4] The immediate effect of the treaty was to prevent any Soviet assistance to Pakistan or Indian help for China. Such aid was specifically precluded by the operative articles contained in the treaty.

India immediately began to receive military hardware on a massive scale prior to its 1971 war with Pakistan. A number of advantages accrued to the Soviet Union as well: successful alignment of India in a legal and binding manner, a guaranteed future Soviet role in South Asian matters, as well as countering fear of China and the incipient Sino-American rapprochement.

The remaining part of the decade nearly passed without any further dramatic shifts. The United States was less and less focused on the subcontinent except in bringing negative pressures that the Carter administration began to apply through its nuclear non-proliferation efforts against India and Pakistan. Carter journeyed to India and Iran in late 1979, carefully bypassing Pakistan. There were other signals regarding the declining relationship with Islamabad and an astonishing lack of U.S. interest in the unfolding events in Afghanistan after the Communist coup in Kabul in 1978. Even the 1979 assassination of the American ambassador in Kabul did not seriously alter Washington's attitude. Carter was seeking a serious opening to the Soviet Union, and American foreign policy initiatives were not to be deterred by events in distant and unimportant places.

CRISIS AND ROLLING BACK THE SOVIET EMPIRE

The decade of the eighties began with the Soviet invasion of Afghanistan and ended in humiliating retreat for the former Soviet Union.[5] As 100,000 Soviet soldiers marched into Afghanistan in December 1979, the United States was forced into action. Beyond the shock evoked in the Carter statement that the president had discovered the "true nature of the Soviet Union," there was the need for action. Suddenly, Pakistan began to look useful from the American perspective. For India with its close ties to Moscow, the invasion by the Soviet Union of a small nonaligned neighbor was hard to brush off. Nearly universal condemnation of the invasion made it especially important that India react carefully. New reality indicated that Pakistan had become the new buffer state between the Soviet Union's sphere of influence and vital American interests in the Persian Gulf.

For nearly a decade after the 1979 invasion, Soviet policy in South Asia reflected loss of ground in terms of respectability. Years of cultivation of a carefully crafted image as a friend of the nonaligned world was lost in the aftermath of the brutal move into Afghanistan. Soviet activism in poor Third World states in the 1970s and 1980s was meant to showcase socialism and to build influence. All that was disastrously set aside as Marxism-Leninism failed to deliver economic development.

The Soviet action came in the last days of the Carter administration. As the number two in the State Department, Warren Christopher was put in charge of the American response. Beyond words of censure, a positive response necessitated Pakistani help. Christopher tried to get the Pakistanis to be forthcoming, but the United States was not willing to put sufficient resources into the endeavor even though there was no possibility of victory on the cheap.

The equation between the United States and Pakistan changed as Ronald Reagan was inaugurated president. Reflected in the sizable assistance package that was forthcoming, Pakistani leaders felt that the new American administration understood the magnitude of the task and the urgency with which it had to be addressed. Washington signed an agreement in September 1981 that committed $3.2 billion over a five-year period equally divided between economic and military assistance. A critical assumption in American policy was the belief that Soviet withdrawal from Afghanistan was essential and possible. The arms package was designed to help Pakistan withstand Soviet pressure. Continuity was important to Pakistan and the package covered a multiyear effort. The economic component aimed at assisting Pakistan cope with economic pressures, including the flow of nearly 3 million Afghan refugees fleeing Soviet occupation.

The U.S. strategy focused on the importance of improved Indo-Pakistani links so that Islamabad would not be distracted from the Afghan effort. Additionally, it was in the American interest to build a productive relationship with India, a major democracy and a country that still had a standing treaty of friendship with the Soviet Union. Washington assumed that it was possible to establish better relations with India even as relations with Pakistan were upgraded. Further, the United States hoped to use enhanced relations with both India and Pakistan to help improve Indo-Pakistani relations.

By 1984, Indian Prime Minister Indira Gandhi had begun the dialogue that moved Indo–U.S. relations forward. Despite her assassination in October of that year, the assumption of that office by Rajiv Gandhi continued the process. The younger Gandhi was of a new generation of Indian leaders, with only faint memories of the early days of the cold war. He was willing to look at alternate sources for Indian development. By the middle of the decade, the patina of the Soviet economic model was fast fading and the Soviet fighting machine got increasingly bogged down in Afghanistan.

As Rajiv Gandhi prepared for his first official visit to the United States in May 1985, Soviet leader Mikhail Gorbachev announced a set of Moscow's long-term goals for a collective security concept in Asia. Gorbachev pronounced his proposal similar to that offered by Council for Security and Cooperation in Europe (CSCE), the European collective security accord reached at Helsinki in 1975. The overture was contained in Gorbachev's first speech on Asia when he was welcoming Rajiv Gandhi to Moscow. Recycling the old Leonid Brezhnev concept, Gorbachev admitted that progress toward the Asian collective security would be complicated but reiterated the need for an Asian security conference.

Gandhi was cautious in responding to the Gorbachev speech, calling the proposal "an old concept." He linked the idea to several initiatives put forward by Delhi, including that of a nuclear free zone in the Indian Ocean.[6] The proposal had little impact as many Asian states viewed the Soviet march into Afghanistan as the critical threat in Asia in the 1990s. Furthermore, the Soviet proposal seemed to be an attempt to distract attention from the mounting losses inside Afghanistan where the Mujahidin were beginning to inflict humiliating losses on the much larger force of a superpower.

Gorbachev reminded Gandhi that Indo-Soviet cooperation continued in various dimensions, was free of pressure, and was based on mutual respect. Expressing satisfaction, Gorbachev noted that economic ties between the USSR and India had "helped solve major problems" at various levels of Indian development. He hoped that the Soviet Union would make "a worthy contribution to the development of India's economy and strengthen its defenses on the threshold of a new century."

Gandhi's June 1985 U.S. visit went well. He was in search of a new relationship with the United States, one in which access to American technology figured prominently. He found Washington responsive, agreeing to the export of the Cray XMP 14 supercomputer and the General Electric 404 engine for the Indian Light Combat Aircraft. Indian assurances aimed at safeguarding American technology were critical to the release of that technology. These and other sales demonstrated that Indian needs could be met by sources other than the Soviet Union, thereby reinforcing the message that Moscow's utility was declining for India. By 1987, the United States became India's largest trading partner with two-way trade in excess of $6 billion, up from the $4 billion mark for the previous four years combined.

The USSR lowered its profile in the subcontinent, especially as the tide of world opinion turned against the Soviet Union with strong annual condemnation of Soviet policies in general and of its military occupation of Afghanistan in particular. Moscow was particularly disappointed with the cool Indian reaction to its diplomatic proposal for collective security in Asia. Even with the 1971 friendship treaty still in place, Delhi was unwilling to draw closer on the Asian security proposal. In the end, Afghanistan cost Moscow the diplomatic offensive. On the military front, the Kremlin continued to offer generous terms for Indian purchases and for manufacture in India of Soviet military hardware.

In November 1987, Gennady Gerasimov, the official Soviet spokesman, held out the possibility of Soviet withdrawal from Afghanistan within a seven- to twelve-month period. Gorbachev followed up the offer at the December 1987 summit meeting in Washington predicating the withdrawal on the cessation of financial and military assistance for the Mujahidin. Discussions of a Soviet pullout from Afghanistan were conducted through proximity talks among the UN, Pakistan, the Kabul regime, the Soviet Union, and the United States. One of the key areas of difficulty over the several years that the talks covered was the timetable for withdrawal. The 1987 proposal plus the earlier Gorbachev statement that the Soviets had made a "mistake" by invading Afghanistan opened up the possibility of Soviet withdrawal. Even earlier, in March 1986, President Zia ul-Haq of Pakistan reported that Pakistan was in direct contact with Moscow and that the Soviets wished to withdraw their forces from Afghanistan. Washington had not shared in that optimistic assessment, worrying instead that perhaps it was wishful thinking on the part of the Pakistanis and that Zia was losing his resolve due to increased Soviet bombings inside Pakistan despite mounting Soviet casualties.

The Geneva Agreement was signed on 14 April 1988. It provided for mutual nonintervention and noninterference; withdrawal of all Soviet troops within nine months (with half leaving in the first three months); return of Afghan refugees to their homes; and respect for Afghanistan's neutrality and nonaligned status. The government of the Communist leader, Najibullah, fell soon after the agreement. Soviet withdrawal demonstrated that Brezhnev was wrong in postulating that Communist gains are irreversible. As 115,000 Soviet soldiers left the country by 15 February 1988, the situation in Afghanistan demonstrated that Soviet military adventures were not tolerable.

The most articulate view of Indian policy throughout the Soviet occupation of Afghanistan was offered by a former Indian foreign secretary stating that India's inability to participate in the search for a democratic, moderate, and nonaligned Afghanistan resulted in "side-lining" India. Such a policy was based on the fact that the Soviet Union was a tried and tested friend of India. By giving support in the early stages of the Soviet occupation, India did not help "rescue the Soviet Union from a no-win situation" in Afghanistan. Indian standing at the time was also hurt as India voted differently from all of its smaller neighbors in the annual UN vote on Afghanistan, implying justification for the intervention by a large country in total disregard for the sovereignty of a small neighbor.[7]

THE USSR COLLAPSES

Indian policy remained geared to a special relationship with the Soviet Union even as difficulties mounted in Moscow. The short-lived coup against Gorbachev in August 1991 was watched warily from Delhi. The fabric of Indo-Soviet relations was complex, and there was no easy substitute for the central Soviet state with all of its constituent parts. For one thing, there were a myriad different economic agreements covering the import of raw materials at very favorable terms from throughout the territory of the former USSR. The collapse of central authority and the breakup of the Soviet Union into a number of Central Asian republics meant that each of those agreements would have to be renegotiated, probably at competitive terms with a host of different governments. Loss of time and production would be costly as these governments got their bearings. Indian policymakers would have to renegotiate their contracts with new leaders, some of whom might not be sympathetic to Indian needs.

After the withdrawal of the Soviet Union from Afghanistan, American involvement in the subcontinent declined. Pakistan sought a continued relationship, but U.S. legislation required an end to assistance because of the Pakistani nuclear program. India and Pakistan looked for alternate scenarios for their foreign policy as the USSR underwent fundamental changes and the cold war ended. Living in the shadow of the cold war, South Asia was conditioned by the East-West struggle and benefited handsomely in the process. Without the challenge of Soviet competition, it was far from clear whether the United States would at all engage in the region and what the alternate sources of support were likely to be.

Collapse of the Soviet Union changed China's relationship with

India as well. Sino-Soviet rivalry had shaped Chinese policy toward the subcontinent. As Moscow's relations with Delhi changed in the mid-1980s, Rajiv Gandhi signaled in October 1987 that he was willing to take a fresh look at Sino-Indian relations. Putting the border dispute to the side, India and China could increase their trade and cultural contacts. While China remained friendly with Pakistan, Beijing was not averse to better ties with Delhi.

For twenty years, the Soviet Union took advantage of perceived Indian security needs to build one of its most important relationships with a non-Marxist state. In return, India carefully cultivated its special relationship with Moscow even in the face of difficult decisions, such as recognition of the Heng Samrin regime in Cambodia and avoidance of public criticism of Soviet policy in Afghanistan, even though Delhi privately expressed its unhappiness with continued Soviet occupation. Close Indo-Soviet ties were a valuable asset for Delhi's relations with Islamabad. Yet Moscow continued to have a separate relationship with Pakistan somewhat independent of its ties to India. The invasion of Afghanistan hurt because it made Pakistan more important and increased support from the West, especially the United States and from the Muslim world.[8]

Soviet leaders' statements in the aftermath of the retreat from Afghanistan to the effect that military means were no longer sufficient guarantors of national security were meant to signal a rearrangement in national priorities. Gorbachev indicated that less time was to be devoted to East-West competition. Foreign relations were to be managed through a "balance of interests" approach, meaning that some traditional Soviet interests could be sacrificed. Under these conditions, commitments to allies were no longer sacrosanct. Soviet Foreign Minister Eduard Shevardnadze went as far as to say that the Soviet Union wanted a world in which peace was ensured "exclusively" by the UN and the Security Council.[9]

The Soviet position in the international community declined steadily after 1988. Economic difficulties were apparent even earlier as energy prices fell during the mid-1980s reducing its income and the ability to project Soviet policy in the Third World states. Relations with countries in the eastern bloc became difficult as Gorbachev simultaneously urged perestroika-style reform while proclaiming the right of all socialist states to make their own choices.[10]

With the collapse of the former Soviet Union into a collection of independent republics, the rules of engagement in South Asia also changed. As Russia itself needed U.S. help, there was no question of competing elsewhere for access or influence. A pliant Moscow agreed to a variety of American initiatives inside the UN. Within the Security Council, venue for some of the most spectacular battles of the cold war era, Russian diplomats signed on in haste to U.S. policy priorities. The Gulf War precipitated by the occupation of Kuwait by a former Soviet client state, Iraq, dramatically demonstrated how pliant Moscow had become. Even as Washington worried about vetoes from China, few believed that Moscow would find it hard to sign on to the punitive measures enacted in the Security Council to punish Iraq for its aggression. India, in the midst of a two-year term on the Security Council, was an eyewitness to the fall of its friend and former superpower. It must have been a sad experience for the Rao government which soon thereafter concluded that India's future lay elsewhere.

CHANGING COURSE

The economic collapse of the former Soviet Union caused immediate difficulties for India. Overnight, the special arrangements that had existed between the two economies had to be renegotiated. Trade and aid were brought to a virtual standstill as Delhi tried to figure out the new players. The process became more complicated as Pakistan sought openings in the Central Asian republics, citing historical links and the ties of Islam.

Prime Minister Narasimha Rao boldly decided to change the very nature of the Indian economic system through fundamental reforms. His aim was to open up India and to bring it into the world economy. There was no longer any alternative and the notoriously inefficient public sector, the hallmark of the halcyon days of Soviet influence on India, was in dire need of change. As articulated by the Rao government, the 1991 reforms aimed at far-reaching and sustained changes. Their goal included a reduction in the number of absolute poor in India within a generation. For such an effort, support from the private sector was important. India also needed to tap into the vast investment pool available in the West for emerging markets.

The 1991 package provided for incentives for the private sector in the following ways: the elimination of import licensing requirements and lower tariff for capital and intermediate goods, trade account convertibility of the rupee, and removal of the require-

ment for government approval of domestic investment applications for all except fifteen industries defined as sensitive.

International response to the Indian move was extremely positive. The speed with which Rao moved meant seriousness and a
willingness to take bold action. The liberalization of the capital
markets, including its opening, to foreign institutional investors
paid handsome dividends. Portfolio investment increased from
$200 million in 1991 to $3 billion for 1993–94. Revitalized economic performance led to an increase in exports by 20 percent in
1992–93 and another 18 percent in 1994–95. That sum was above
the $4 billion mark in 1998–99. India actively sought foreign part-
ners and provided attractive terms and was helped by the U.S.
Commerce Department's 1995 classification of India as one of the
top ten "big emerging markets" which gave India a special priority.

Opposition to the reforms came from a variety of areas. In terms
of this paper, the most significant was that from India's labor which
had been cushioned by strong unions and a large public sector
which had been set up with Soviet help. Emphasis on profitability
meant closing down some public sector enterprises. However, Rao
had to put political considerations ahead of purely economic ones
given the human costs of massive layoffs in a society such as India,
where each earning member of the family supports more than a
dozen dependents. Facing elections in 1996, Rao was careful in
dealing with the charge that the reforms were increasing the gap
between the rich and the poor. The left in Indian politics has substantial support and the government felt vulnerable. While politicians of different hues all endorsed the reforms and declared that
they were here to stay, the Congress Party suffered heavily in state
elections in March 1995. The final verdict laid blame for the poor
election results for the Congress on the reforms and their slow
pace.

Starting with Rajiv Gandhi, continuing with Narasimha Rao,
through to the current government of Prime Minister A. B. Vaj-
payee, the Indian government emphasized its relations with the
United States. The economic component was to become the driving force. As the two-way trade reached beyond $10 billion and as
the United States became India's largest trading partner, it seemed
as if indeed Indo–U.S. ties were strong and developing quickly.
India adjusted to international economic changes and found alternatives to its past reliance on the former Soviet Union and the eastern bloc countries for a special status for its large public sector.
While the American connection was not problem-free, it clearly

was a path carefully chosen by India as the vehicle for economic progress.

India also focused on military relations with the United States subsequent to the collapse of the Soviet Union. The U.S. Secretary of Defense, William Perry, went to South Asia in January 1995. He signed a military agreement with India aimed at launching "a new era" in security relations between the two states. His Indian counterpart stated that the accord was an attempt to forget the past in defense matters and make a new beginning. Military-to-military relations moved forward until sanctions imposed by the May 1998 nuclear tests cut them off.

BROADENING OPTIONS

Pakistani policy turned northward as the Nawaz Sharif and Benazir Bhutto governments respectively sought closer links with former Soviet republics. Using historical connections between the two geographical areas, Pakistani leaders were among the first to visit neighboring republics with promises of trade and assistance. A much publicized convoy carrying goods transited Afghanistan with much difficulty on its journey to Turkmenistan. Pakistan hoped for great access to Central Asia and wanted to serve as a bridge to that region. However, continuing strife in Afghanistan made these goals unrealistic.

Energy became one of the top priorities of the Bhutto government. A number of Memoranda of Understanding (MOU's) were signed with a variety of western companies. Regionally, Pakistan signed agreements with Qatar and with Iran for future pipelines carrying natural gas to Pakistan. In addition, the Bhutto government and its successor, the Nawaz Sharif government, remained keen on developing a pipeline from Turkmenistan for natural gas for use in Pakistan and beyond. Here again, conditions inside Afghanistan acted as a deterrent in the early execution of the proposal.

Pakistan's search for closer links with fellow Islamic states once a part of the Soviet empire led to Indian discomfort with the "Islamic Arc" so close to India. Delhi alerted western nations to the potential of future Islamic fundamentalism in the area and expressed an interest in containing these forces. Such fears found resonance in Washington, complicating the relationship with Pakistan.

The euphoria in Pakistan surrounding Soviet withdrawal from

Afghanistan vanished even before the collapse of the USSR. As a front-line state that had cooperated fully with the United States in the successful struggle to roll back the Soviet Empire, Islamabad had expected some dividends. At a minimum, U.S.–Pakistan relations were expected to remain on a smooth footing. As the only remaining superpower, the United States had been a beneficiary and a benefactor in the joint Afghan strategy. The future looked bright. Pakistani leaders were wrong in their assessment. The end of the cold war took away the very raison d'etre of the American interest in the first place. There were other interests, such as Pakistan's proximity to the Persian Gulf and its potential as a moderate Islamic state, but they were more distant and less obvious to a Washington more focused on economic relations and less engaged with foreign policy. Another complication was Pakistan's nuclear program and Islamabad's unwillingness to make the program more transparent as was requested by the United States. Washington's unhappiness with Pakistan in its pursuit of nuclear weapons finally led to the cutoff of American assistance in September 1990. Thereafter, institutional links built up in the course of a decade were lost as all assistance and most forms of interaction came to a halt.

In the course of ten years of fighting the Soviet occupation of Afghanistan, Pakistan served as the conduit for assistance to the Mujahidin. The influx of weapons changed Pakistan forever. The "Kalashnikov" culture that became a permanent aspect of politics and life inside Pakistan was a direct product of the Afghan war. Along with the guns came the growth of Pakistan as a conduit for Afghan drugs destined for the West. Together these two elements played havoc with civilian life. They also isolated Pakistan from the international community.

The diplomatic front was affected in other ways as well. The demise of the USSR gave greater impetus to Sino-Indian normalization. That process was already launched by 1988, but India's treaty of friendship with the Soviet Union remained operable and there was some hesitation as the Chinese were accused by Washington of supplying Pakistan with sensitive nuclear technology. With the threat from the north reduced, Beijing was willing to move faster toward exchanges and trade with India. While Pakistan's relations with China were built on a solid foundation, Islamabad worried about the potential for a rapprochement between India and China and its consequences for Indo-Pakistan relations.

That worry was realized rather rapidly in terms of Pakistani policy in Kashmir. After the kidnapping of the daughter of the Indian

home minister, Kashmiri militants sought and obtained the release
of some of their jailed compatriots from the government of India.
The level of Kashmiri dissatisfaction with India grew into a full-
fledged revolt, and Delhi dispatched half a million troops and par-
amilitary forces to keep order in the state. The promise of fresh
elections and representative government to reflect the views of the
Kashmiri Muslim population did little to assuage concerns.

While India increasingly saw the revolt as a reflection of Pakistani mischief-making, outside agencies reported large-scale and
frequent Indian violations of human rights against Muslims, including women.[11] At the same time, the American government
found Pakistani support of Kashmiri militants as a factor in the escalating violence inside Indian Kashmir and nearly declared Pakistan as a state supporting terrorism. As then Pakistani Prime
Minister Benazir Bhutto raised the political rhetoric favoring the
uprising in Kashmir, Indo-Pakistani relations took a decidedly
downward turn.

The United States worried that tensions and the respective nuclear capabilities of India and Pakistan were a volatile mix with a
real potential for war. Deputy National Security Advisor Robert
Gates visited the subcontinent in May 1990. His special mission
aimed at lowering tensions. He also called for some movement on
the nuclear issue and warned Pakistan to back off from its open
support of the Kashmiri insurgency across the border. According
to the account of the American ambassador then serving in Islamabad, Gates gave a very sobering account of the consequences for
Pakistan of a war with India over Kashmir. He warned the Pakistanis that the results could well be Indian naval action against
Karachi and Indian air force raids deep inside Pakistani territory.
Gates made it plain that Pakistan could not count on American
help in the case of war. Gates added that the United States was
not saying that Pakistan wanted war, but that by supporting the
Kashmiris in a way analogous to Pakistan's earlier support for the
fight in Afghanistan, a basic change in the equation between India
and Pakistan was possible.[12]

Gates stopped in Delhi after Islamabad. There the Indian Prime
Minister V. P. Singh told him that there could be no dialogue with
Pakistan until the latter stopped all support for terrorism and subversion in Jammu and Kashmir. Asking both sides to de-escalate
the crisis, the American spokesman said that concern was not tantamount to a desire on the part of the United States to seek a role
for itself as a mediator between India and Pakistan. Rather, as a
friend of both states, the United States wished to contribute to the

lowering of tensions through a dialogue and offered a list of confidence-building measures designed to do just that.

Gates also went to Moscow on his way to the subcontinent for consultations. But times had changed. The Soviet leadership was not happy at the prospect of another Indo-Pakistan war so soon after extricating itself from Afghanistan while in the midst of its own troubles. Beyond words of general encouragement about the need for conflict avoidance, little was possible. Moscow declined to undertake joint action with the United States in seeking the lowering of tensions. This was a definitely different Soviet response than that of 1965, when Soviet diplomacy was central to the end of the Indo-Pakistan war. Under internal pressure and spent overseas, the Kremlin showed no desire to seriously reengage with the quarrelsome neighbors of the subcontinent.

Pakistan continued to rely on support from China for confrontations with India. However, increasingly, the silence from Beijing was deafening. Once touted as the backbone of the Pakistani foreign policy, the relationship with China had changed after 1987. Without the prospect of a Soviet response, caring about its own efforts to improve trade and economic relations with the United States, China was in no mood to give the sort of guarantees against India on Kashmir that it had in earlier wars. Pakistan's relief at the demise of the USSR was thus accompanied by the worry of seeing erstwhile friends slip away one by one. It seemed that the major powers who had underwritten South Asian security for four decades were either preoccupied or had other interests that bypassed the subcontinent.

THE FUTURE

It is always dangerous to make predictions about the course of future events, and South Asia with its own turbulent history makes guessing even more difficult. However, a look at current Russian policy leads one to speculate tentatively about the road ahead.

Because the position and the foreign policy of the former Soviet Union were deeply influenced by the collapse of the former Soviet state, the dislocations were tremendous. South Asia, which was an area of special interest for the USSR throughout the cold war, immediately suffered in its aftermath. Indifference replaced involvement. While the subcontinent slowly adjusted to the new security environment, the problems that followed in Russia with massive economic dislocation, the separation of the former republics, and the leadership problems all cast a shadow. Indians and Pakistanis worried that the rise of a more nationalist Russia could lead to a different set of perceptions regarding the country's national interests. Having given virtual autonomy to the former republics of the USSR, there may be future attempts to bring these back more closely into the Russian fold.

Unsettled conditions inside Afghanistan also make the future difficult. The ongoing civil war, the Taliban regime's backing of fundamentalism in the surrounding areas, including former Soviet Central Asian republics creates issues where Russia and India are on the side of the opposition in Afghanistan and Pakistan supports the Taliban regime.[13] There is the danger that the Afghan issue can further worsen the poor state of the India-Pakistan relationship.

South Asia has learned to live without a very active Russia. Throughout the cold war period, this area benefited from rivalry between the two superpowers. The focus remains on the two largest countries of the region, India and Pakistan. Both have understood the new realities and the need for their focus to shift to the international economic scene. While each maintains a formidable defense establishment, each recognizes that the preferential terms offered by Russia in previous years cannot be duplicated in the new century just unfolding. Even as Russia remains a crucial source of military sales to India, the focus of Indian foreign policy is the United States. The visit of President Clinton to India and Pakistan in March 2000 was a poignant reminder of the central role of the United States in the subcontinent. Despite difficulties related to non-proliferation policies, India and Pakistan now focus on Washington as the primary foreign policy actor and the world's only superpower.

NOTES

1. British India was divided into India and Pakistan on the basis of a referendum offering the Muslims of India a choice of remaining in India or joining the new state of Pakistan. That choice was not offered in Kashmir, a Muslim majority state now claimed by both India and Pakistan.

2. Herbert Feldman, *From Crisis to Crisis: Pakistan 1962–1969* (London: Oxford University Press, 1979).

3. Donald S. Zagoria, *The Sino-Soviet Conflict: 1956–61* (New York: Anthenum, 1964), 350–51.

4. "Joint Soviet-Indian Statement," *Pravda*, 12 August 1971, CDSP, 23, no. 32.

5. Francis Fukuyama, "Discord or Cooperation in the Third World: Coping

with Gorbachev's Soviet Union," The Center for Strategic and International Studies, Washington D.C., 1988.

6. Congressional Research Service, *Policy Alert*, Washington, D.C., 28 May 1985.

7. Jagat Mehta, *Indian Express*, 29 March 1989.

8. U.S. Department of State, *The Soviet Role in Asia*, Washington, D.C., 19 October 1983.

9. Statement to the General Assembly, 23 September 1987.

10. Stephen Sestanovich, "Gorbachev's Foreign Policy: A Diplomacy of Decline," *Problems of Communism* (January–February 1988).

11. Paula Newberg, *Double Betrayal: Repression and Insurgency in Kashmir* (Washington, D.C., Carnegie Endowment, 1995).

12. Remarks by Robert Oakley, The Stimson Center, Washington, D.C., *Conflict Prevention and Confidence—Building in South Asia: The 1990 Crisis* (1996): 8–9.

13. Ahmed Rashid, "The Taliban: Exporting Extremism," *Foreign Affairs* (November/December 1999): 22–35.

Russia and Northeast Asia

CHARLES E. ZIEGLER

RUSSIA AND THE COUNTRIES OF NORTHEAST ASIA ARE EXPERIENCING internal transformations and shifting international alignments that make the future of the Asia-Pacific region highly uncertain. Moscow's approaches to Northeast Asia have been influenced by domestic political infighting, economic crisis, regional separatism, and the severe deterioration of the military. The Asian economic crisis of 1997–98, North Korea's continued development of ballistic missile capabilities, China-Taiwan tensions, plans by the United States and its allies to deploy a theater missile defense in the region, Japan's persistent economic troubles, and the collapse of the Suharto regime in Indonesia have altered the region's strategic calculus.

This paper analyzes the impact of the Soviet breakup on the regional power balance in the Asia-Pacific and on Russia's foreign policy identity; discusses Moscow's political, economic, and security ties with the major Northeast Asian nations; and makes some general observations on the implications of changes in Asia for Russian and American security interests.

Three themes emerge from this analysis. First, a more nationalist Russia is seeking to reestablish its influence as a respected great power in the Asia-Pacific. This process began under Boris Yeltsin and has been reaffirmed by Vladimir Putin. Russia's limited economic and military capabilities, and its ongoing political crisis, make it very unlikely that the Russian Federation will acquire the great power status it seeks. Second, policies formulated in Moscow toward Northeast Asia are increasingly at odds with eastern Russia's regional interests and priorities. Russia's peculiar form of federalism has introduced a new dynamic into regional politics. Third, while the United States and Russia have similar interests in stabilizing the region, the two differ substantially over China, East Asia's ascendant power. While both have sought a strategic partnership with Beijing, neither has managed to craft a successful long-term China policy.

The Soviet Collapse and Northeast Asia

Late-era Soviet policy toward Northeast Asia was governed by a triangular relationship dominated by cold war competition with the United States, and complicated by a longstanding conflict with China. From Moscow's perspective, the huge expanses of sparsely populated territory in Siberia and the Russian Far East were vulnerable to Chinese encroachment (Beijing contested regions bordering Heilongjiang and Xinjiang provinces) and to U.S. naval assault in the event of a superpower conflict.[1] To contain the USSR in Asia, the United States maintained a series of bilateral alliances with Japan, South Korea, the Philippines, Australia, and Thailand. Moscow and Beijing competed for influence with North Korea, and Vietnam, India, and Pakistan were all drawn into this triangular rivalry in various permutations.

Cold war considerations led Moscow into several unproductive and expensive relationships in Asia—the disastrous conflict in Afghanistan, frigid political ties with Japan, a rather brittle and costly alliance with North Korea. The USSR was a military superpower in Asia, but its economic influence and political presence were very weak. As Japan and the economically vibrant smaller countries of the region developed international reputations far out of proportion to their military capabilities, it became clear that the Soviet Union would be increasingly marginalized in Asia unless major reforms were enacted.

Mikhail Gorbachev's reform program elevated domestic issues to the top of the policy agenda, reversing years of Soviet imperial power politics. Gorbachev's Asia-Pacific initiatives centered around resolving the extraordinarily expensive conflict with China, which he did between 1987 and 1989. During the same period, U.S.–Soviet relations improved dramatically through a series of treaties and agreements, lowering tensions in the Pacific. As ties with China and the United States improved, the North Korean, Vietnamese, and Indian alliances lost much of their importance for Soviet policy.

In East Asia the Soviet collapse transformed the cold war era balance of power.[2] The region is no longer dominated by a bilateral superpower confrontation: Russia is extremely weak, and the United States, with its stated commitment to maintaining a military presence in the western Pacific, has become the sole superpower in the region. China, with its rapidly developing economy, increased military spending, and growing international confidence is an ascendant regional power. China's future role, however, is complicated by the daunting problems of reforming its state-owned enterprises and the banking system; addressing corruption, unemployment, and the floating population problem; and managing pressures for change from below.[3] Japan still dominates the region economically, notwithstanding the recession of the 1990s, but this is changing as China, South Korea, and the other Asian dynamos produce an increasing share of Asia's gross domestic product (GDP). In any case, Japan's internal political difficulties and disagreements over its proper role in world politics continue to limit its potential as a regional leader.

There are other forces at work that are transforming East Asia's power balance. Regional organizations, most notably Asia Pacific Economic Cooperation (APEC) and the Association of Southeast Asian Nations (ASEAN, with its ASEAN Regional Forum), are providing the basis for an institutional framework, however weak, in a region long noted for lacking such structures. A number of territorial disputes have the potential to erupt into violent conflict, particularly on the divided Korean peninsula, between Taiwan and the People's Republic of China (PRC), and between China and five Southeast Asian nations over the contested Spratly and Paracel islands. India is engaged in nuclear competition with Pakistan and, given its long history of conflict with China, is a potentially significant factor in East Asian politics. Central Asia also has the potential to affect the Russian-Chinese dynamic; however, an extended discussion of South and Central Asia in Russia's East Asian policy is beyond the scope of this paper.[4]

FINDING A NEW RUSSIAN IDENTITY

Boris Yeltsin's administration initially accepted the fundamental premises of Gorbachev's East Asian policy, albeit with some modifications. During the first year following the collapse of the Soviet Union, Russian foreign policy virtually ignored East Asia, focusing instead on close cooperation with the industrial democracies of Western Europe and the United States. However, the backlash from nationalists, conservatives, and even moderates who accused President Boris Yeltsin of kowtowing to Western interests, led to a reorientation of Russian foreign policy by early 1993. Defense of Russia's national interests on its new borders, and protection of the 25 million Russian expatriots living in the "Near Abroad," moved to the fore in Russian foreign policy.

The "Eurasianist" movement in Russia has emphasized the

country's cultural links to Central and East Asia. Karen Brutents, for example, argues that Russians have lived together with Tatars, Bashkirs, Kazakhs, Yakuts, Uzbeks, and other Asian nationalities for so long that their cultural perspectives are closely intertwined, linking Russia's fate with that of Asia.[5] Other Eurasianists claim that Russians and Asians are more warm-hearted and spiritually inclined than the cold, rational, and materialistic Americans and Europeans. Members of the Eurasian group were highly critical of what they perceive as a misguided orientation toward the West, reflected in the reliance on Western multilateral institutions and slavish imitation of Western developmental models. Even moderates have criticized the Yeltsin administration for accepting the role of a "junior partner" to America in foreign affairs.[6]

Setting aside considerations of political expediency, Moscow's foreign policy makers have had difficulty articulating a Russian foreign policy identity to replace the Soviet vision. A poll conducted by the journal *Mirovaia ekonomika i mezhdunarodnye otnosheniia (MEiMO)* in 1993 found 52 percent of foreign policy elites identified themselves as "Westernizers," preferring a foreign policy linked closely to the West and based on the values of Western civilization. An additional 45 percent considered themselves "Slavophiles," who preferred Russia to follow a distinctly Slavic path based on equidistance between Europe and Asia.[7] Tensions between those who preferred cooperative ties with the West and the great-power restorationists who favored a more Eastern-oriented foreign policy continued through the 1990s. Yevgeny Primakov's tenure as minister of foreign affairs (1996–98) and as prime minister (1998–99) symbolized the rise of a more conservative strain in Russian foreign policy, although few specific changes were realized during this period.

In the early to mid-1990s, conservatives and moderates forced the Yeltsin administration to elevate the "Near Abroad" countries (the former Soviet republics) to a leading position in Russian foreign policy, pushed the reformers to adopt a more confrontational stance in their dealings with the United States and Western Europe, and encouraged Moscow to seek closer ties with authoritarian China and the restoration of links with Moscow's former client states. Conservatives and nationalists perceived Asian developmental strategies more favorably than they did the American neoliberal economic model. The Chinese and South Korean cases, at least prior to the collapse of 1997, provided examples of how high economic growth rates could be achieved under the guidance of a strong, activist state.

By 1994–95, the outlines of a more assertive East Asia policy were emerging in Moscow. In the second half of the decade Russia's foreign policy makers would seek a strategic partnership with China, approach Japan with plans to conclude a peace treaty by the year 2000, and attempt to mend fences with North Korea while preserving close ties to Seoul. The Yeltsin administration declared its intention to develop good relations with all Asian-Pacific nations, and to participate constructively in major regional organizations. China ranked at the top of Moscow's Asia policy.

China

China is easily the most important country in Asia for Russia, and will undoubtedly dominate Russia's Asian policy well into the 21st century. Over the past decade China has absorbed Hong Kong, effected a smooth transition from the Deng era, maintained economic growth rates of 8 to 10 percent, and undertaken a program of military modernization. China's successes have generated a deep-seated nationalism, as was evident in the aftermath of the U.S. bombing of Beijing's Yugoslav embassy. Rapid change has also generated new domestic problems, which include difficult reforms of the state-owned enterprises (SOEs), restructuring the financial sectors, securing adequate energy supplies, coping with pollution and shrinking agricultural land, balancing national and regional interests, fighting corruption, and responding to the demands of an incipient civil society.

As Russia seeks to restore its great-power status in the world, China has become an important partner and foil against the West. Beijing and Moscow have found common ground in their antipathy toward American pressures on human rights, arms sales, and trade issues. Russia and China refuse to accept a unipolar world dominated by the United States. Although both sides have ruled out a return to the alliance system of the 1950s, there has been significant progress in military and economic forms of cooperation.

The virtual collapse of Russia's Far East and Pacific military forces has generated interest in collective security within Moscow's defense establishment. Former defense minister Pavel Grachev proposed the formation of a six-power regional security system for Northeast Asia, consisting of Russia, China, Japan, the two Koreas, and the United States, during his May 1995 visit to Beijing.[8] More recently, former prime minister Yevgeny Primakov proposed a security triangle among Russia, China, and India to balance U.S.

hegemony in the Asia-Pacific region. China, however, seems reluctant to enter into multilateral arrangements that might restrict its freedom of maneuver, and is less than enthusiastic about forming a cooperative arrangement with India.

America's international behavior in the 1990s has strengthened ties between Russia and China. Beijing and Moscow share an antipathy to U.S. interference in their domestic affairs. China, mindful of the implications for maintaining control of Tibet and Xinjiang, supported Moscow in its 1994–96 military action against Chechnya, and again in its 1999–2000 campaign. Russia in turn has avoided criticizing China over repression in these minority provinces, vocally supports the one-China concept, and like Beijing resists Washington's attempts to exert economic leverage through the IMF and World Bank. Both China and Russia opposed NATO attacks on Yugoslavia as unwarranted interference in that country's internal affairs. At their August 1999 summit meeting in Bishkek, Kyrgyzstan, President Jiang Zemin and President Boris Yeltsin called for a strategic cooperative partnership and expressed their intention to work toward a more multipolar world order.[9]

One development that is changing the strategic balance in the Asia-Pacific is China's efforts to modernize its armed forces. China is currently adding newer weaponry to its inventories, as part of a strategy to downsize its military and shift to a more mobile, rapid-response force, replacing the Maoist commitment to large infantry divisions. China's modernization program has been made possible by impressive economic growth rates achieved over the last decade. However, China's military expansion does not pose a significant threat to Russian security, at least in the immediate future.[10] China reduced its army by approximately 25 percent in the 1980s, and has withdrawn much of its forces formerly deployed along the Sino-Russian border. China's growing military might is directed primarily toward altering the strategic balance vis-à-vis Taiwan in Beijing's favor, defending Beijing's claims to the disputed Spratly and Paracel islands in the South China Sea, and maintaining order within the PRC.

A major security concern for Russia emanating from China is the possibility of widespread immigration into Siberia and the Far East. China's impending political transition raises uncertainties about the future of Chinese reform and about the possibility of fragmentation along China's western boundaries. Beijing's hold over the provinces in increasingly tenuous, and centrifugal forces are gaining strength.[11] Officials in Russia and China alike are concerned about the possibility of Muslim nationalist movements—in China's Xinjiang-Uighur autonomous province, in inner Mongolia, and in Afghanistan—destabilizing the Central Asian region.[12] China's minorities—the Mongols, Tibetans, Kazakhs, and Uighurs—suffered greatly during the cultural revolution, and Beijing's largely symbolic efforts to improve the status of China's minorities, together with a deliberate government policy of flooding minority regions with Han Chinese settlers, failed to dampen nationalist aspirations.[13]

Should China's border regions acquire greater autonomy from Beijing, the situation in Central Asia could deteriorate rapidly. Increased movement across the Kazakh-Xinjiang border, for example, would intensify the insecurities of Kazakhstan's Russians, who fear losing their identity and privileges to Asians. Moscow is committed to protect the ten million Russian speakers residing in Central Asia. Islamic fundamentalist movements such as Afghanistan's Taliban threaten stability in the region and are a vital security concern for both Moscow and Beijing.

Economic cooperation is important for both Moscow and Beijing, but expectations for bilateral trade have not been borne out. Russian-Chinese trade increased from $3.96 billion in 1991 to $6.5 billion in 1992. In 1993, trade expanded to $7.7 billion, with Moscow enjoying a $2 billion surplus, and about 80 percent of this trade consisted of border exchanges between China's northeastern provinces and the Russian Far East. Most of the shuttle trade is unreported, and may account for an additional 20 to 25 percent. The limitations of shuttle trade, a Chinese tendency to dump low-quality goods on Russian consumers, and tighter Russian visa restrictions on Chinese entrepreneurs led to a 30 percent decline in Russian-Chinese trade during 1994, to $5.1 billion.[14] Trade rebounded in 1996 largely due to arms purchases, which constituted $1.4 billion of total trade turnover worth $6.8 billion. However, trade stagnated in the late 1990s. Although Moscow and Beijing declared their intention to expand trade to the $20 billion mark by 2000, in 1998 it reached only $5.5 billion.[15]

A significant proportion of Russia's exports to China in the 1990s has consisted of weapons. Valued at roughly $6 billion from 1992 to 1997, Russian deliveries to China have consisted of Su-27 fighters, S-300 surface-to-air missiles, four Kilo-class submarines, and other equipment. In 1999, Russia and China signed a contract for the delivery of more than 40 Su-30MKK jet fighter aircraft valued at $2 billion.[16] Chinese exports to Russia consist largely of food, textiles, and other consumer goods. Russia's nonmilitary exports to China consist largely of fertilizer, aluminum, petroleum products, and other primary and intermediate goods.[17] Arms sales provide a short-term solution to the problems facing Russian defense industries, but arming China contributes to apprehensions in East Asia and fuels the region's arms race, which may over time work against Russia's interests. China's military modernization also complicates Washington's support for Taiwan's security.

Political relations between Russia and China in the 1990s have been good, as indicated by the frequent visits of dignitaries and pledges to work toward a strategic partnership. President Yeltsin first visited Beijing in December 1992, and Chinese President Jiang Zemin made two trips to Moscow, in September 1994 and May 1995. Frequent summit meetings occurred in the late 1990s, and visits of foreign and defense ministers became routine. Russian President Vladimir Putin and China's Jiang Zemin scheduled an extraordinary four meetings in 2000. These dialogues have led to new agreements on Sino-Russian economic cooperation and military exchanges and resulted in the conclusion of a border accord. National leaders of both countries criticize the United States for acting unilaterally around the world. Russia and China are both concerned with the destabilizing effects of Muslim fundamentalism in Central Asia, and expressed their determination to combat terrorism at the Bishkek summit in August 1999 and the July 2000 summit in Dushanbe.[18]

While Sino-Russian relations are amicable at the national level, there is considerable suspicion and hostility directed toward China by locals in Siberia and the Russian Far East (RFE). The inhabitants of these sparsely populated territories fear a possible influx of millions of Chinese. Russia's population in the RFE declined to about 7 million by 2000, while the four provinces in China's northeast region, just across the border from Primorskii krai and Khabarovsk, are home to a population of 130 million, nineteen times that of Russia's Far East. However, the most knowledgeable specialists such as Sergei Pushkarev, Head of the Federal Migration Service for Primorskii krai, place the number of Chinese visitors to the RFE, including illegal immigrants, at no more than a few tens of thousands per year, with most returning to China when their visas expire. Russian resentment is directed toward Chinese migrants who reportedly are buying up land illegally and who have flooded the Far East with poor quality merchandise. Chinese tend to have a stronger work ethic than the local Russian population, and so are popular with Russian businesses. And Russian locals blame the Chinese for high crime rates in Vladivostok, Khabarovsk, and other Far Eastern cities.[19]

Regional interests in the RFE often clash with those of the national government in Moscow. Areas of dispute have included investment incentives for foreign businesses, how to divide tax receipts, and environmental regulations. Territorial issues also enter into the equation. Officials in the RFE felt betrayed by the central government's decision to return 1,500 hectares of territory, comprised of three parcels near Lake Khanka and north of the North Korean border, to China. Primorskii krai governor Evgeny Nazdratenko rejected the agreement ratified by the Russian Federation Supreme Soviet in 1992 as illegitimate, and confronted the Ministry of Foreign Affairs over changing the existing boundaries. Nazdratenko encouraged militant Cossack groups to settle in the disputed areas, while other local officials called for a referendum on the issue.[20] Ultimately Beijing compromised, allowing Russia to retain control over some 140 hectares surrounding a Russian cemetary, considered sacred ground by Russian nationalists.

Japan

Russo-Japanese relations at the national level have been cool through the first half of the 1990s, while cooperation at the local level developed steadily. The legacy of distrust and suspicion stemming from repeated conflicts in this century, and maintained by the territorial dispute over the Kurile islands (Northern Territories), poisoned postwar relations. In the first years after the collapse of Communism Japan's policymakers maintained a jaundiced view of Russia's new democracy. Moscow's attack on Chechnya in 1994–96 provided further cause for suspicion. Japanese officials were reluctant to discount Russia's military potential and intentions in the western Pacific until late in the 1990s, despite its clearly weakened position.[21]

The territorial question, of course, is the single greatest obstacle to better relations between Russia and Japan. Gorbachev was reportedly considering a deal during his April 1991 visit to Tokyo, but public opinion and conservative pressure apparently quashed a settlement. Yeltsin faced strident criticism from the national-patriotic opposition early in the postcommunist era for his alleged willingness to compromise with Japan. Yeltsin's twice-postponed visit to Tokyo, cavalier treatment by former Foreign Minister Andrei Kozyrev, and hostile remarks by Duma members have perpetuated the hostility. Russia's Pacific Fleet angered Tokyo by dumping radioactive waste and obsolete ammunition in the Sea of Japan in late 1993, immediately after Yeltsin's October trip to Tokyo.[22] Russian border patrols have periodically fired on Japanese fishing vessels operating near the Kuriles, and in early 1995 Moscow froze the bank accounts of Japanese airlines because of tax irregularities.[23]

By the mid-1990s, some marginal improvements in Russo-Japanese relations were evident. Japan, the United States, and Russia agreed to a series of three low-key security meetings called the "Trilateral Forum," with the first meeting held in Tokyo in February 1994. Over the next five years a series of summit meetings and other diplomatic exchanges, new economic and security agreements, and cultural visits gave the impression that momentum was building toward a territorial solution and peace treaty. At the "noneckties" summit between President Yeltsin and Japanese Prime Minster Ryutaro Hashimoto in Krasnoiarsk in November 1997, the two sides signed a joint agreement to work toward a peace treaty by the year 2000. Bilateral relations were supposed to evolve based on the principles of the 1993 Tokyo Declaration mandating serious negotiations on the territorial issue predicated on "historical and legal facts" and "principles of law and justice." From Tokyo's perspective, Russian adherence to these provisions commits that country to abide by nineteenth- and twentieth-century treaties, none of which recognize Russian sovereignty over the Northern Territories.

Japanese and Russian leaders reiterated their intentions to seek a comprehensive peace treaty and to continue high-level dialogue at the Kawana summit in April 1998, and during Prime Minister Keizo Obuchi's visit to Moscow in November 1998. During the latter summit two subcommissions were created, on border demarcation and joint economic activities on the disputed islands. Tokyo viewed this agreement as a stage in the eventual transfer of the islands to Japanese control. Moscow's goal, by contrast, was to secure a declarative treaty on peace, friendship, and cooperation, a type of intermediate agreement separate from the former peace treaty.[24] The wide gap in interpretations of this document indicates how far apart the two sides remain in their efforts to conclude a peace treaty. President Putin continued to pursue economic and cultural cooperation with Japan, while pushing the territorial issue aside, in his September 2000 visit to Tokyo.

Russo-Japanese relations at the local level, in contrast to national relations, have been quietly evolving toward mutual respect and cooperation. For Russia's Far Easterners, Moscow is distant, poor, and neglectful of their needs. Japan is close, rich, and appears ready to be of assistance. Sea links established between Vladivostok and Niigata after the Soviet collapse resulted in a flood of used Toyotas and Hondas into the Far East auto markets. Tourist packages were designed for Russians who wanted to visit Hokkaido, and hotels catering to Japanese businessmen opened in Vladivostok and Iuzhno-Sakhalinsk. At times Russian locals appealed to Japan to help ease fuel shortages and sought Japanese assistance in the wake of the Kurile and Neftegorsk earthquakes.

Expectations for Japanese trade, investment, and other forms of assistance, however, have not been fully realized. Japanese investment in all of Russia for 1995 was a paltry $30 million; in 1996 this figure dropped to only $18 million.[25] Total investment as of 1999 was only $181 million in direct foreign investment, with Japan ranking in eighth place among foreign investors.[26] Inefficiencies in transportation, organized crime and corruption, and general political and social instability make doing business in Russia very risky, and Japanese businessmen are generally cautious. Bilateral trade declined from a high of 732 billion yen ($6 billion) in 1991, to 441 billion yen in 1992 and 424 billion in 1993 (approximately $3.9 billion). Trade declined further in 1994, to $3.25 billion, as Russian imports dropped below one billion dollars for that year.[27] Trade peaked in 1995 at $5.9 billion, slipped to $5.38 billion in 1996 and declined significantly to $3.92 billion in 1997. Russo-Japanese trade continued to decline in 1998, hitting a decade low at $2.97 billion. This was just over 4 percent of Russia's total trade, but only three-fourths of one percent of Japan's total trade turnover.[28]

Over the long term, Russo-Japanese economics will likely be dominated by energy.[29] The demand for new energy sources, especially oil and natural gas, will continue to rise in the Asia-Pacific region. Former energy exporting countries such as China and Indonesia are now importing energy. China's oil consumption is projected to increase at an average annual rate of 3.6 percent, while domestic production will remain static over the next decade. The Middle East market, which supplies close to 90 percent of the region's crude oil, is potentially unstable.[30] Russia's supplies of oil and natural gas present opportunities for joint development using Japanese investment capital and technical capability. Japan, which now imports four-fifths of its oil from the Middle East, could benefit by diversifying its energy supply. In addition, to the extent that Russia supplies energy to a resource-hungry China, the prospects of an international clash over oil in the South China Sea are mitigated. This clearly serves Japan's foreign policy interests, as well as its economic goals. Still, Russia will not have the capability of supplying more than a fraction of Japan's energy needs.

From Moscow's perspective, Japanese assistance in developing various regional oil and gas projects is vital to Russia's economic future. Two natural gas pipelines are planned from Sakha to Japan, one via Sakhalin to northern Hokkaido and the second through Vladivostok and Pusan to Kitakyushu, near Fukuoka. Total cost of the first line is estimated at $10 billion; the second will run approximately $15.5 billion.[31] The Japanese companies Mitsui and Mitsubishi are also participating in the Sakhalin I and II oil development projects, capitalized at an initial $10 billion. Japan has also expressed interest in developing the Irkutsk natural gas field, which is primarily being developed for export to China. A survey of Japanese and Korean trade industry representatives found a strong preference for natural gas over other energy forms such as oil, coal, or nuclear power.[32] However, energy cooperation in Northeast Asia faces serious obstacles. Pipelines must be laid over long distances through the extraordinarily harsh environments of Eastern Siberia and the RFE. Fluctuations in international prices for oil make long-term investments less attractive. In addition, political disputes between Moscow and the regions have delayed progress on these projects and have raised costs.

The Yeltsin-Hashimoto summits of 1997–98 emphasized the two countries' commitment to expand economic cooperation. At Kawana an agreement was reached to form a joint company to promote Japanese investment in the form of joint ventures in Russia. Former Prime Minister Sergei Kiriyenko's visit to Tokyo in July 1998 resulted in a Memorandum on Protecting Mutual Investments, designed to reduce the risk for Japanese businesses considering investing in Russia. Japan also agreed to provide Russia $1.5 billion in credit in 1998–99 for servicing Soviet-era debt through the Export-Import Bank of Japan. Russia received $400 million of this credit in July, but with the abrupt devaluation of the ruble and the collapse of the Russian stock market in August 1998 Japan conditioned disbursal of the remaining funds on International Monetary Fund (IMF) negotiations with Moscow.[33] Plans to construct a large auto plant in Moscow oblast, with participation by Toyota and Mitsui, were also mentioned at the Kawana summit.[34] These are promising developments, but few Japanese firms can be expected to invest substantially in Russia unless the Putin government succeeds in developing a more effective market economy.

As noted above, the RFE is heavily dependent on trade and investment from Asia. However, Japan's economic crisis has slowed imports from Primorskii and Khabarovskii krais, and Sakhalin oblast, hurting the region's timber, fishing, and coal industries. For example, Japan's trade with Sakhalin decreased by $40.5 million in 1997, and is now in second place behind South Korea at $152 million. Japan has 121 firms active in Sakhalin, compared with 67 American and 54 Korean firms, but the Japanese businesses are small-scale.[35] The territorial impasse, and Russia's uncertain economic climate, discourage more substantial investment from Japan.

Japan committed approximately $4.5 billion in assistance to the Russian Federation from 1991 to 1997, making it third in the world behind Germany and the United States. Of this, export credits accounted for $1.2 billion, trade insurance for $2.9 billion, and technical and humanitarian assistance another $435 million.[36] The Japanese government's emphasis on assisting the RFE economically can help improve stability in a potentially volatile region. The presence of Japanese consulates in Vladivostok, Khabarovsk, and Iuzhno-Sakhalinsk, and Japanese financing for reconstruction of the port at Zarubino, illustrate this regional focus. Given Moscow's extremely limited capability to funnel investment into Siberia and the Far East, Japan's economic assistance is greatly needed.

Politics interferes in Russo-Japanese economic cooperation far less than it did during the Communist era, but politics still intrudes occasionally. For example, the Sakhalin oil projects have been hindered by nationalist deputies in the Russian Duma opposed to foreign exploitation of the country's natural resources.[37] Local environmentalists resent foreign firms' insensitivity to ecological issues. And some nationalists resent Japanese economic assistance to the RFE, charging it is aimed at weaning the region away from Moscow's authority. Considering the extent to which the RFE has been neglected by Moscow in recent years, Japanese assistance may well encourage greater regional autonomy.

Political turmoil in Moscow and Tokyo suggests that neither will be strong enough in the near future to surmount the territorial question. Vladimir Putin's government will likely continue to resist Japanese demands for returning the islands. At the same time, Moscow will follow Japan's search for a new foreign policy role in the Pacific with great interest. While the Japanese constitution and public opinion will constrain Tokyo's international behavior, nationalism and distance from past aggression may encourage a more assertive foreign policy in the twenty-first century. Japan's regional position, however, will be greatly influenced by the actions of its East Asian neighbors, China and the Koreas.

Korea

After a slow start, Russian policy in the 1990s has aimed to restore Russian influence in Korean peninsular affairs. Moscow seeks to prevent North Korea from deploying or using nuclear weapons, to avoid the chaos that would result from the sudden collapse of the North, to secure the denuclearization of the entire peninsula, to maintain and expand economic relations with the Republic of Korea, and to position Russia as a respected great power included in all major peninsular issues.[38] Russia's interests coincide more closely with those of South Korea than with the North. To accomplish these goals, Moscow is pursuing a strategy of trying to maintain and strengthen links to the South. At the same time, since the mid-1990s the Russian government has reoriented its Korea policy toward rebuilding the relationship with North Korea.

Relations between the former Soviet Union and North Korea had deteriorated markedly in the late Gorbachev era, bottoming out with the September 1990 diplomatic recognition of South Korea and Moscow's stipulation that Pyongyang pay for oil and other goods in hard currency starting in January 1991. Relations between Russia and North Korea did not improve with the collapse of the Soviet Union; in fact, they suffered further deterioration during the early years of Russia's independence. During his November 1992 visit to Seoul, President Yeltsin praised the progress in Russian-South Korean ties, promising that Russia intended to renegotiate the terms of the 1961 Soviet Democratic People's Republic of Korea (DPRK) mutual assistance treaty. Yeltsin made it clear that Russia would not support North Korea militarily in the event of a conflict.

President Kim Young Sam visited Moscow in June 1994 for talks on bilateral cooperation and security issues on the Korean peninsula. Kim expressed support for Russian participation in APEC, and Yeltsin provided the Korean delegation with documents from the Korean War. The two leaders were optimistic about the potential complementarity of Korean technology and Russian natural resources for developing the Far East. Yeltsin also pledged Russia's support for the denuclearization of the Korean peninsula. Russia has also sought recently to enlist South Korean support for a multipolar world order. During President Kim Dae Jung's May 1999 visit to Moscow the two sides adopted a joint statement acknowledging the United Nations as the central element of the international system. Yeltsin and Kim expressed their joint opposition to nuclear proliferation and expressed support for strengthening a "pluralistic" world.[39]

One remarkable development in Russian-South Korean relations is the emerging military cooperation between these two former enemies. A memorandum of understanding was signed during Yeltsin's visit, providing for exchange of military personnel, joint observation of military exercises, and port visits by naval vessels. Defense Minister Grachev led a military delegation to Seoul in May 1995, where agreements were signed for the protection of military secrets and cooperation in the research and development, and possible joint production, of military equipment.[40] Moscow and Seoul also concluded an agreement in spring 1995 allowing Russia to repay part of the debt incurred during the late Soviet era through deliveries of modern weaponry.[41] However, Moscow has been unable to pay off the Korean loans, and with interest the debt has mounted to $1.47 billion. By mid-1999 Korean banks were pressing their government, guarantor for 90 percent of the loans, to pay Russia's debts, and the administration was contemplating accepting payment from Moscow in the form of three Amur class diesel submarines.[42]

Moscow's perception that it has been unfairly excluded from peninsular affairs has rankled. For example, the 1994 Geneva Agreement between the United States and DPRK, under which Pyongyang agreed to phase out its nuclear program in exchange for 500,000 tons of crude oil and assistance in constructing two light-water reactors (through the Korean Energy Development Organization, or KEDO), appeared to slight Russian interests. Moscow had contracted in 1991 to provide three light-water reactors to North Korea, but Yeltsin cancelled the deal in 1993 when Pyongyang threatened to withdraw from the Nuclear Non-Proliferation Treaty (NPT).[43] During the U.S.–DPRK negotiations, Moscow repeatedly offered to supply the reactors, in the hope of recouping some of the lost revenue, but Seoul was adamant the reactors should be of South Korean manufacture.

For Russia, denuclearization of the Korean peninsula is a top foreign policy goal. The presence of nuclear weapons in Korea could influence neighboring states—Japan is the primary candidate—to develop nuclear weapons. A number of states in the southern arc already either possess nuclear weapons or could readily develop them, including Pakistan, India, and China. Moreover, the presence of nuclear weapons in North Korea, and in particular the August 1998 launch of a ballistic missile across Japanese territory, has strengthened Washington's determination to erect a theater missile defense (TMD) shield, which Russia opposes. From Moscow's perspective a non-nuclear, unified, and stable Korea could provide an important counterweight to Chinese or Japanese expansionism.[44] It would also negate the potentially destabilizing effects of TMD deployment.

Korea is also important for Russia economically. Russian-South Korean economic ties expanded following the breakup of the USSR. In the first tumultuous year of Russian independence, bilateral trade dropped from $1.2 billion in 1991 to $860 million for 1992. However, trade rebounded to $1.57 billion in 1993, grew to $2.2 billion in 1994 and then reached $3.2 billion in 1997.[45] However, with the 1997 crisis in Asia's economies and Russia's 1998 stock market collapse, bilateral trade declined to $2.4 billion in 1998.[46] Russian-Korean trade has been constrained by the relative unattractiveness of Russian goods and Moscow's inability to repay its debts to Seoul.

Korean firms, particularly the large chaebol, Samsung and Daewoo, have been more willing to take a chance in the Russian market than have the cautious Japanese firms. Korean direct investment in Russia remains low, however, totaling only $161 million as of 1999, or 0.5 percent of total investment in the Russian economy. There are now roughly 200 Russian-Korean joint ventures operating in the Russian Federation. Nearly two-thirds are engaged in trade and brokerage, with the remainder involved in oil and gas production, electronics, automobile manufacturing, and fish processing.[47] Russian and South Korean businesses have been planning several huge projects for years, including the construction of a natural gas pipeline from the Sakha Republic and the development of an industrial complex in Nakhodka's free economic zone. However, economic circumstances led the Korean government to scale back the Nahkodka project to one-sixth its original planned size.[48] Other possible avenues for Russian-South Korean economic cooperation—the Sakha pipeline and the much-studied Tumangan river area development zone—can only be fully realized following reunification.

Under pressure from conservatives and nationalists in the Russian parliament, and after a concerted lobbying campaign by Pyongyang, the Yeltsin administration tried to reinvigorate its ties with North Korea. Moscow's goal is to enjoy good relations with both Koreas and to enhance Russia's position as a respected and influential world power (and incidentally to recoup the estimated $3.6

billion Pyongyang owes from the Soviet era).[49] But Russian influence in the DPRK, never very strong, eroded dramatically from 1990–1993. Pyongyang's machinations over the NPT and KEDO were a desperate bid to secure international recognition (*de facto* if not *de jure*) from the United States. Moscow submitted a draft revised treaty to Pyongyang in August 1995 that would eliminate the military assistance provisions of the 1961 pact and place Russian-DPRK and Russian Republic of Korea (ROK) ties on an equal footing.[50] North Korean officials, who vehemently reject attempts to equate North and South as sovereign states, were studiously cool toward the proposal. The Treaty on Friendship, Good Neighborliness, and Cooperation signed in February 2000 deleted the provision for automatic military intervention included in the 1961 treaty. Moscow praised the June 2000 summit between Kim Dae Jung and Kim Jong Il, and the South Korean government welcomed Putin's plans to visit North Korea en route to the G-8 meeting on Okinawa.

Russian–South Korean relations are good in the areas of political and military cooperation, but commercial ties are circumscribed by Russia's economic crisis. Should the Russian economy take off, economic cooperation could improve significantly, particularly in the area of energy exports to Korea. South Korea and Russia agree on the goal of containing the North's nuclear program, although Seoul realizes Moscow still has minimal leverage with Pyongyang. The Putin administration is attempting to rebuild ties to the North but, like its predecessor, shows no intention of reverting to Soviet-era policies. Moscow intends to exercise Russia's rightful role as a world power in peninsular affairs by developing friendly relations with both Koreas.

SECURITY AND THEATER MISSILE DEFENSE

Northeast Asia is a potentially volatile region, with unresolved territorial disputes, the world's highest concentration of armed forces, and a history of military conflict. Rapid economic growth has enhanced regional stability, but economic crises such as that in 1997–98 may increase tensions. China is becoming more nationalistic and increasingly confident of its position in the region. China's military modernization is directed first toward ensuring Taiwan does not opt for formal independence, and toward raising the costs of any U.S. defense of Taipei. It is also designed to position China for a possible confrontation over the Spratly Islands. The United

States, according to the latest (1998) East Asian Security Initiative, is committed to maintaining the status quo of some 100,000 troops in Korea, Japan, and the Western Pacific for the immediate future. In 1997, the United States and Japan renewed their security agreement, with Washington calling Japan the lynchpin of U.S. security strategy in the Asia-Pacific.

One issue with the potential to transform the Northeast Asian security environment is the American proposed deployment of TMD in South Korea, Japan, and Taiwan, as one component of a broader National Missile Defense (NMD) shield for the United States. President Clinton's defense budget for 2000 requested an additional $6.6 billion from Congress for general ballistic missile defense. Beijing is adamantly opposed to the plan, viewing it as an attempt to negate China's nuclear deterrent capability. Washington, Tokyo, and Seoul envision a regional TMD as a shield against the North Korean ballistic missile threat. Taiwanese deployment of such a shield would negate much of China's ballistic missile build-up on the eastern coast, which is to be used against the island in the event of a declaration of independence. Beijing also opposes TMD deployment in Japan as a possible spur to Japanese militarism. Russia and China are in accord in their opposition to TMD in the Pacific. Russian officials claim this would violate the 1972 Anti-Ballistic Missile Treaty, which Washington has proposed re-negotiating, and would provoke a regional arms race.[51]

CONCLUSIONS

Three themes have emerged from this survey of Russian relations with East Asia. First, after relative neglect in the first half of the 1990s, Russia is now pursuing an active diplomacy designed to maintain good political and economic relations with all Asian countries. Also, Russian foreign policy has evolved in a distinctly more nationalistic direction. Politicians and commentators of all persuasions frequently advocate a foreign policy based on Russia's "national interests," although the precise nature of those interests in East Asia is still nebulous. However, Russia's political efforts to be accorded great power status in Asia have been undermined by deteriorating military power, the weakness of Russia's economy, and internal political battles. The economic factor is particularly important in Northeast Asia, where economic might is respected more than military muscle. Russia may some day play the role of a respected major power in the Asia-Pacific, but that day is at least a decade off.

Second, Russia's decentralization, the opening up of previously closed areas in the Russian Far East and Siberia, and Moscow's neglect of its eastern periphery, have changed Russia's relations with East Asia, most notably with respect to China, Japan, and South Korea. The center's interests and goals often clash with local priorities. The emergence of subnational foreign policies has been noted in Western democracies, but it is a significant departure from Soviet-era practice.[52] Russian Far Easterners historically followed their own path—they enjoyed close ties with their Asian neighbors and rather weak links to the capital.[53] It appears that the collapse of Soviet central control set into motion new dynamics for regional interaction, creating new challenges for Russian foreign policy. Vladimir Putin's decree creating seven federal regions headed by appointed representatives will likely restrict the governors' independence in foreign relations.[54]

Third, Russia and the United States no longer confront each other in Northeast Asia, but a range of new issues poses problems for regional stability. China's high economic growth rates, nationalism, and growing confidence as an Asian power have led to frequent confrontations with Washington, from which Russia has benefited marginally. Japan's recession may be ending, and a reinvigorated Japan can be expected to continue its search for a more appropriate post–cold war foreign policy, one less dependent on the United States. Washington's lecturing on economic issues provokes Japanese resentment, as does its continued military presence there. In addition, American public opinion appears to be increasingly isolationist, and calls for withdrawing U.S. forces from Japan and from Korea could mount. Russia, China, Japan, and the United States share a commitment to stability on the Korean peninsula, but Pyongyang's ballistic missile program and Washington's proposed missile defense system radically change the regional security calculus. In short, trends in the region, within Russia and within America, suggest a volatile Northeast Asia in the early twenty-first century.

Notes

1. U.S warfighting strategy during the Reagan era called for utilizing America's naval superiority against the Soviet Union's vulnerable east coast in the event of a conflict in Europe, thus forcing Moscow to fight on two fronts.

2. For an excellent discussion, see Paul Dibb, *Towards a New Balance of Power in Asia*, Adelphi Paper #295 (London: IISS, May 1995).

3. On China's domestic problems, see Elizabeth Economy, "Reforming China," *Survival* 41 (autumn 1999): 21–42.

4. See Rajan Menon, "In the Shadow of the Bear: Security in Post-Soviet Central Asia," *International Security* 20 (summer 1995): 149–81; and Charles E. Ziegler, "Russia and East Asia After the Cold War," in *East Asia in Transition: Toward a New Regional Order*, ed. Robert S. Ross (Armonk, NY: M. E. Sharpe, 1995).

5. Brutents is advisor to the president of the Foundation for Political Studies. Karen Brutents, "Russia and the East," *International Affairs* (Moscow) no. 1–2 (January 1994): 40–44.

6. Commentator Pavel Felgengauer presents a strong defense of Russia's more assertive stance in foreign policy in *Segodnia* (26 May 1995), in *Current Digest of the Post-Soviet Press* 47, no. 21 (21 June 1995): 1–4.

7. N. Popov, "Vneshniaia politika Rossii," *Mirovaia ekonomika i mezhdunarodnye otnosheniia*, no. 3 (1994): 58.

8. Aleksandr Isayev and Natalya Gorodetskaya, "Pavel Grachev Creating Security System in Northeast Asia," *Segodnia*, in *Current Digest of the Post-Soviet Press* (hereafter *CDPSP*) 47, no. 20 (14 June 1995): 21–22.

9. *The Straits Times* (Singapore), 1 September 1999.

10. Michael G. Forsythe, "China's Navy Stirs," *Naval Institute Proceedings*, 120 (August 1994): 39–45.

11. Specialists disagree on whether China will fragment in the post-Deng era. See, for example, Jack A. Goldstone, "The Coming Chinese Collapse," *Foreign Policy*, no. 99 (summer 1995): 35–53; and Yasheng Huang, "Why China Will Not Collapse," *Foreign Policy*, no. 99 (summer 1995): 54–68.

12. Aleksei Voskresenskii, "Vyzov KNR i rossiiskie interesy," *Nezavisimaia gazeta*, 16 September 1994.

13. Uighur separatist movements in western China, for example, are attempting to recreate historic Eastern Turkestan, with support from inside the newly independent Central Asian states. Interviews conducted in Almaty, Kazakhstan, May 1995. Also, see Igor' Rotar', "Etnicheskaia bomba na severno-zapade Kitaia," *Nezavisimaia gazeta* (3 August 1994); and Keith Martin, "China and Central Asia: Between Seduction and Suspicion," *RFE/RL Research Report* 3, no. 25 (24 June 1994): 26–36.

14. Vladimir Kuznechevsky, "Together Into the 21st Century," *Rossiiskaia gazeta* (30 June 1995), in *CDPSP* 47, no. 26 (26 July 1995): 25. Part of the decline was accounted for by the process of shifting from barter to cash and credit transactions. Russian-Chinese trade recovered somewhat in the first seven months of 1995, with figures up 3.9% above for the same period in 1994, at $2.74 billion. *OMRI Daily Digest* (3 October 1995).

15. Xinhua Economic News Service, 29 October 1999.

16. Interfax News Service (26 August 1999).

17. David Kerr, "Problems in Sino-Russian Economic Relations," *Europe-Asia Studies* 50 (1998): 1133–56.

18. Sergei Blagov, "Security: Muted Response to Russia's Call for Multi-Polar World," Inter Press Service (26 August 1999); AFP News Service (5 July 2000).

19. Personal interview, Vladivostok, 13 March 2000. Neela Banerjee, "Russia as a 'Land of Opportunity'," *Christian Science Monitor* (30 April 1999); Yelena Matveyeva, "Xenophobia Grips the Far East," *Moscow News*, no. 8 (24 February–2 March 1995): 14.

20. Valerii Venevtsev and Denis Demkin, "1500 ga russko-kitaiskikh problem," *Vladivostok* (25 January 1995): 6; Gennady Chufrin, "Border Drawn by Compromise," *Moscow News*, no. 8 (24 February–2 March 1995): 14; Oleg Kryuchek, "Referendum on Demarcation of Russian-Chinese Border Proposed," *Segodnia* (25 March 1995), in *CDPSP* 47, no. 12 (1995): 25.

21. These positions were clearly enunciated during a series of interviews conducted in February 1995 at the National Institute for Defense Studies, at the prime minister's office, and with Japanese scholars.

22. In late April 1994, Moscow and Tokyo agreed in principle to begin construction on two facilities to treat the radioactive waste from Russia's Pacific fleet. Radio Free Europe/Radio Liberty *Daily Report*, 3 May 1994.

23. *Izvestiia*, 17 February 1995, 3.

24. *Moskovskaia deklaratsiia ob ustanovlenii sozidatel'nogo partnerstva mezhdu Iaponei i Rossiskoi federatsiei* (13 November 1998).

25. Japan External Trade Organization (JETRO), White Paper 1998, available at www.jetro.go.jp/WHITEPAPER/Invest98/

26. Interfax (31 August 1999).

27. Data from the Japan External Trade Organization; and *Direction of Trade Statistics* (Washington, D.C.: IMF, June 1995), 166.

28. Direction of Trade Statistics (Washington, D.C.: International Monetary Fund, various issues).

29. The following section draws on Charles E. Ziegler, "Russo-Japanese Relations: A New Start for the Twenty-first Century?" *Problems of Post-Communism* 46 (May/June 1999): 15–25.

30. Mark Valencia, "Energy and Insecurity in Asia," *Survival* 39 (autumn 1997): 86.

31. Ibid., 88–89.

32. Keun-Wook Paik and Jae-Yong Choi, "Pipeline gas trade between Asian Russia, Northeast Asia gets fresh look," *Oil and Gas Journal*, 18 August 1997. Japan's energy infrastructure, however, is tailored to Middle East oil and faces greater obstacles in converting to natural gas than Korea.

33. ITAR-TASS, 29 January 1999.

34. Andrei Ivanov, "Kiriyenko Got Everything He Wanted in Japan—And Set Off for China," *Kommersant* (15 July 1998), in *CDPSP* 50 (12 August 1998): 19.

35. *Vladivostok News*, 1 June 1998 (http://vn.vladnews.ru/1998/iss168/text/sakh1.html)

36. *Japan's Assistance Programs for Russia*, Ministry of Foreign Affairs (Japan), May 1997.

37. Russel Working, "Sakhalin is a 'Giant Gas Pump on the Pacific Rim': So Why is it Taking so Long to Get Out the Petroleum?" *Vladivostok News*, 18 September 1998 (http://vn.vladnews.ru/1998/CURRENT/text/sakh1.html)

38. See V. Moiseev, "On the Korean Settlement," *International Affairs* (Moscow) 43 (1997): 65–72.

39. Interfax (28 May 1999).

40. *International Herald Tribune*, 22 May 1995, 4.

41. *Jane's Defence Weekly*, 13 May 1995, 3.

42. The Korean military, however, opposes acquisition of the subs, claiming they are unreliable as strategic weapons platforms. *Korea Times* (2 July 1999); United Press International (2 September 1999).

43. *Far Eastern Economic Review* (29 December 1994–5 January 1995): 14–15.

44. See Hyon-Sik Kim, "The Russian Security Interests in Northeast Asia," *Korean Journal of Defense Analysis* 6, no. 1 (summer 1994): 172.

45. *Korean Statistical Yearbook* (Seoul: National Statistical Office, 1993), 300–301; Korea Trade Association; and *Rossiiskie vesti* (7 February 1995), in *CDPSP* 47, no. 6 (8 March 1995): 29–30.

46. *The Korea Herald*, 4 January 1999.

47. Interfax (28 May 1999).

48. *The Korea Herald*, 29 March 1999.

49. Yevgeny Aleksandrov, "Immoral Position: Russia and Nuclear Security in Korea," *Pravda* (7 May 1993), in *CDPSP* 45, no. 18 (2 June 1993): 21–22.

50. Aleksandr Platkovskii, "Moskva khochet druzhit' c Pkhen'ianom, no na novykh printsipakh," *Izvestiia* (8 September 1995): 3.

51. Dean A. Wilkening, *How Much Ballistic Missile Defense is Too Much?*, Center for International Security and Cooperation, October 1998; Jim Wolf, "Going Ballistic," *Far Eastern Economic Review* (18 February 1999): 26–27.

52. See, for example, Hans J. Michelman and Panayotis Soldatos, eds., *Federalism and International Relations: The Role of Subnational Units* (Oxford: Clarendon Press, 1990).

53. See the excellent study by John J. Stephan, *The Russian Far East: A History* (Stanford: Stanford University Press, 1994).

54. *Izvestiia* (16 May 2000).

III
Europe

Resting on its Laurels:
The West Faces the East

STEPHEN BLANK

THE RECENT ACTIVITY OF THE NORTH ATLANTIC TREATY ORGANIZA-
tion (NATO) and the European Union (EU) suggests that NATO
enlargement has unleashed a process that will allow the West to
finally consolidate the victory of 1989 that ended the cold war.
Specifically NATO enlargement, the EU's decision to start accession talks with Central and East European states and actively take
up a Common Foreign and Security Policy (CFSP), and the campaign in Kosovo to resist ethnic cleansing are all major steps
toward realizing a truly democratic, integrated, and collective European security community. However, there are drawbacks or
costs, both visible and invisible, to these actions. First, many of
these commitments are still in an early, reversible stage or may be
distorted before fruition. Second, those actions enlarge the distance between a prospering, dynamic West, and a floundering
Russia thereby creating potential new sources of tension. Nor are
these achievements as yet consolidated in domestic, popular institutions either in Europe or the United States. Future progress cru-
cially depends on achieving that consolidation and on solving the
Russian problem.

The collapse of the Soviet bloc and the end of the cold war gave
the West the greatest political-military victory of modern times
with scarcely a shot and challenged the Western alliance to lead the
recasting of a legitimate and viable world order. What this world
order, or at least its European dimension, entails is to sustain the
ability of the new states, in and out of the former USSR, to function
as sovereign, economically viable, secure, and politically coherent
entities, to define a legitimate order that allows them to find an
equally legitimate scope for realizing their national interests, and,
most of all, move to overcome the division of Europe. The achievements cited above indicate how much has been done, but also how
much awaits further action.

Today much of the former Yugoslavia lies under Western military occupation, which will last for a long time. Yet one key to whether a lasting peace will endure in this region is the degree to which those areas now occupied can become states that truly follow liberal domestic and international policies. It is still unclear that any future Albania or Bosnia, let alone unoccupied Serbia will be democratized internally if they are no longer occupied or that Croatia too will find its way into a Western trajectory any time soon. If the West truly is serious about Balkan integration, it will have to expend significant economic, political, and military resources to achieve that goal. Although the EU now talks of a major plan to restore the area, when the extent of the bill and of long-term engagement to overcome the Balkans' structural deformations are revealed, they are unlikely to evoke an outpouring of enthusiasm from a Europe still reluctant to reform its economy or extend the EU eastwards.

Poland, Hungary, and the Czech Republic appear to have returned to the West inasmuch as they are now in NATO and are seriously pursuing membership in the EU. But only if the entire former Soviet bloc, including the formerly neutral but Leninist Yugoslavia, is integrated into European structures can Europe attain true peace and stability. This is not just due to the war in Yugoslavia but also because the European security organizations have made it clear that the security of areas like the Caucasus, hardly a peaceable kingdom, are now firmly part of the European security agenda.[1] Indeed, the wars in the former Yugoslavia tell us that without such integration the order that emerged in 1989–91 remains inherently unstable and can lurch back toward authoritarianism and war.

Therefore three tasks now confront the members of the Atlantic Alliance, integrating the Central European states, creating and consolidating a legitimate and durable peaceful Balkan order that permits progress toward integrating the Balkans with Europe, and facilitating a similar kind of order for the Baltic States and the Commonwealth of Independent States (CIS), including Russia, Belarus, Ukraine, and Transcaucasia. Apart from the steps outlined above, another encouraging factor is that some of the newly integrated or integrating members like Poland have taken the responsibility of exporting security to the Baltic states and Ukraine to stabilize those areas. Poland's support for a transparent border with Ukraine, even if it joins the EU and must support the latter's strict border rules contained in the Schengen agreements, demonstrates considerable foresight and maturity.[2] And Poland's policy also extends to the military sphere with support for mixed Polish-Lithuanian-Ukrainian battalions to serve in Kosovo and participation in the Danish-German-Polish corps of NATO.[3]

These trends have clearly been given new life by the U.S. led process of NATO enlargement which have regenerated the flattering impetus for European integration. Just four or five years ago such cautious optimism was unwarranted. As the late Col. S. Nelson Drew (who gave his life for European security in Yugoslavia) observed in 1994,

> Indeed, while many of NATO's new "partners" have expressed concern that the "Partnership" has not evolved far enough or fast enough, a convincing case can be made that the events of the past five years may have outstripped the capabilities of Trans-Atlantic and European security institutions—and the political will of their members—to adapt to them.[4]

Drew's concern was hardly his alone. Many Western observers expressed an increasingly dyspeptic view of European institutions' capability for constructive action vis-à-vis the Balkan, Central European, and Russian challenges. A leading U.S. analyst of Eastern Europe James Brown commented that the Organization for Security and Cooperation in Europe (OSCE) was moribund, useless, irrelevant, and unwieldy. He also observed that one good thing to come out of its Budapest meeting in 1994 that generated an international code of conduct for members and confirmed its work in mediating and preventing ethnic conflicts, was that the OSCE "will generate no more false hopes."[5] Catherine McArdle Kelleher darkly opined that the OSCE might be growing in scope only because it actually does little or nothing.[6]

The same bleak view applied to the EU/WEU (European Union/Western European Union) and the CFSP agreed upon at Maastricht by the EU in 1991 and that would take place through the WEU. At the WEU's 1995 Madrid summit, leaders congratulated themselves in the official communiqué about the CFSP's progress.[7] However, a WEU committee, led by Lord Finsberg, referred so scathingly to the WEU's failure to make progress on its agenda as to call its very utility into question.[8] In February 1996, the WEU's assembly concluded that NATO remains the sole effective provider of European security and that the WEU, in the absence of any real resolve on the part of states to create a pan-European collective security system, "is not at present able to establish a basis for a European defence policy."[9] While the WEU has not actually changed and NATO and the United States still effectively dominate the assets which the WEU or combined Joint Task Forces form NATO countries would have to command, the call for a joint Western European defense initiated by England and France in December 1998 and the deepening commitment to this process generated by the Kosovo campaign suggests that new trends will come into being.

Similarly, observers of the EU's expansion or widening process agreed at that time that the EU had made virtually no effort to overcome its agricultural or industrial barriers to European integration and dare not do so lest domestic interest groups take umbrage. Thus economic outreach to the East lagged and still lags.[10] The real test of whether European integration on a day-to-day basis will occur is the degree to which the accession talks with new members lead to a meaningful conclusion sooner rather than later. One hopeful sign here is Russia's support for the inclusion of the Baltic states in the EU. While this signifies Russia's incomprehension of how the EU functions to ensure European security, it also means that the Baltic states and perhaps in the distant future, Ukraine can be economically integrated into Europe without Russian protests.[11]

Thus the EU must pass the tests it has set for itself in the Balkans and northeastern Europe. Until now, clearly, the EU had not overcome its apparent somnolence, if not paralysis, regarding security issues. In the Greco-Turkish crisis of 1996, the EU was nowhere to be found. Certainly it did not act when those two states almost went to war for a rock in the Aegean even though both states are NATO members and Turkey aspires to EU membership. France blamed the lack of a response on the fact that Italy, the EU's then president, was undergoing a cabinet crisis and had no effective head of government.[12] This cheap shot only confirmed the EU's bankruptcy as a security provider at the time. A U.S. report of the EU's role in this crisis then noted,

> Meetings of European foreign ministers to thrash out common policies, participants say, have become hopelessly bogged down in arguments as trivial as the order of the agenda and where to hold the next meeting. The struggle to achieve "foreign policy by committee" has threatened to paralyze the Union when it expands to as many as two dozen members over the coming years.[13]

The real test is the willingness to expend the economic-political-military resources necessary to make a CFSP a real and vibrant force for European security. While the new rhetoric is encouraging, practice is what will be decisive. Our allies already are having difficulty coming to terms with the revolution in military affairs (RMA), and the complaints about interoperability and the excessive role in the NATO of the U.S. contribution underscore the practical difficulties involved in implementing a CFSP and building a robust defense capability.[14] Until Kosovo Europe has seemed reluctant to acknowledge that it must show political will that may include the use of force to build security. As Vuk Draskovic, former deputy prime minister of Serbia, observed, at Rambouillet a number of European diplomats were not playing as a team. Given the difficulties involved in sustaining the anti-Serbia coalition, it is hardly to be dismissed that future coalitions in Europe might not be possible.[15] The continuation of wars in Yugoslavia and the Transcaucasus since 1992, Russia's trampling of Moldova's integrity and sovereignty, the Chechnya war, Russia's regression to the language and aspirations of neo-imperial spheres of influence and a wholly nineteenth-century *Machtpolitik* outlook demonstrated the difficulties inherent in formulating and executing coherent policies to fully realize the promise of the end of the cold war.

On closer examination we may see some of the reasons for this inconclusive policy in the domestic structures of Western governments. After 1989 virtually every key Western state underwent stagnation or crisis leading to high inflation, long recessions, currency collapses, high unemployment, and protracted political crises. Whether it took the form of continuing scandals and political gridlock in Italy, the collapse of political parties and the agitation for Quebec's independence in Canada, France's 1995 strikes due to its inability to meet current economic challenges at home or abroad, or the annual budgetary gridlock in the United States since 1986, the result is the same. Almost every Western government of 1989 was overthrown by inward looking political blocs who are neither sufficiently aware of nor interested in Europe's needs or who cannot conduct a consistent policy responsive to those needs because they cannot secure domestic consensus. This applies equally to the United States where much of the political establishment seems to take pride in its ignorance of and indifference about European security, hardly a basis on which to claim continuing leadership of Europe. Since domestic politics are increasingly narrowly focused, international cooperation weakens. Thus George Schopflin could write in 1994 that,

> Not only is the structure of international organizations set up to cope with the problems of the Cold War ill-suited to deal with post-

communism, but Western Europe has found itself in a twofold dilemma. The end of the Cold War has placed the question of the distribution of power and the nature of democratic institutions on the domestic agenda of most if not all of these states, the fate of Italy being the most vivid illustration, while at the same time the security vacuum in Central and Eastern Europe has posed a question of strategy to which they have no answer precisely because their domestic politics are in a state of turmoil. The economic recession has simply made this situation worse, because investment capital that might have gone to central and eastern Europe is not available, even while domestic pressure groups impose restrictions from the post-Communist world.[16]

At the same time, the Western governments during 1989–91 were themselves far too conservative and muscle-bound to respond to the fast-moving challenges of the period. Only Washington championed German reunification; France and Great Britain resisted it and France even thought of obstructing it.[17] France, for example, seems to have had no clear policy for Central and Eastern Europe. On the one hand it has drawn closer to the United States in NATO. Yet on the other hand, along with Russia, it has opposed the United States in Iraq, and often opposed Washington in NATO for traditional Gaullist reasons. Only in December 1998 did it take a decisive step for a purely European voice, but it did so by uniting with Great Britain, hardly its traditional partner. Yet France remains deeply concerned with also tying Germany down to it, a policy that only ties France more to Germany while arguably impeding both states' ability to deal with European issues.[18] Indeed, an analysis of French foreign and defense policies since 1989 could lead one to suggest that containing Germany in a mutual embrace while ignoring Europe east of the Elbe is the true and only motive force behind French policy.

And when the successors of the regimes of 1989–91 came in they were even less able to make the case for Europe or inclined to. For example, Canada's defense policy, as stated in its 1995 white paper, stresses tailoring its armed forces to what domestic tolerances will allow, diminishes the formerly central role of NATO, and endorses a new multilateral orientation. This multilateralism should not be seen as a genuine commitment to truly multilateral or collective security but paradoxically as an assertion of a strategy dictated by the national interest, that is, a step toward a renationalized defense strategy.[19] While this strategy probably accords with domestic and fiscal constraints, it also has led to a self-centered and even potentially schizophrenic outlook. A penetrating analysis of the white paper observed that,

Canada views multilateralism as a means of continuing to participate actively in global affairs so as to increase the influence it might otherwise not exercise, including influence over the United States. It does want to see Washington take the lead on many issues but hopes to use multilateralism as a mechanism of restraining unilateral American actions and policies. Above all, Canada does not equate a commitment to multilateralism as requiring that it assume a greater share of the burden for defending Western interests around the globe.[20]

The scant utility of this approach for international or just European security readily emerges when one ponders the nature of multilateralism according to international relations theory. According to one analysis,

> Multilateralism tends to make security a nonexcludable good. This minimizes the hegemon's coercive power and its ability to extract payment for protection. It makes the sanctioning of free riders difficult (because domestic coalitions then feel exploited-SB) and threats of abandonment almost impossible. From a choice-theoretic perspective, multilateralism does not seem a convincing bargain or a determinate solution.[21]

In other words, Canada's stance and that of all others who similarly incline have made it harder for anyone to make a positive contribution to security. Former British Foreign Secretary Malcolm Rifkind worried at the time that the EU's foreign policy was failing because it is a policy of the lowest common denominator and hence useless as a means of advancing European security.[22] The mirage of multilateralism and the quest for it in the belief that the situation is now ripe for it and that this will bring European security closer, paradoxically made it harder to create either a *Machtordnung* or a *Friedensordnung* as Yugoslavia so tragically showed until 1995. As a result, NATO had to step in and graphically illustrate the impotence of other security providers there. The fact that NATO had to go to war again 1999 in Kosovo and Russia's travails show that the current order still remains inherently unstable and contains too many tendencies toward military resolution of crises.[23] The inability to progress beyond the status quo could spell either war or regression to some new form of blocs or spheres of influence policies in Europe as a last resort.

Certainly Russia prefers a great power concert over the heads of smaller powers and the division of Europe into spheres of influence. In that system it would have an equal status, according to its lights, or more accurately a "superequal" status. Dmitri Trenin of the Carnegie Endowment observes that Russia wants to be seated at the presidium table of all international issues.[24] Sergei Rogov, director of the USA and Canada Institute (ISKAN) went even further, urging that Russia regain its cold war status because "The Russian Federation is unwilling to consent to bear the geopolitical burden of the defeat of the Soviet Union in the cold war or to be reconciled with an unequal position in the new European order."[25] Therefore he argued that,

> First of all, Moscow should seek to preserve the special character of Russian-American relations. Washington should recognize the exceptional status of the Russian Federation in the formation of a new system of international relations, a role different from that which Germany, Japan, or China or any other center of power plays in the global arena.[26]

Moscow's complaints about NATO's disdain for its interests comes replete with a package of demands for a salve to its wounded psyche but also with a thoroughly antiquated demand for compensations and indemnities redolent of eighteenth-century diplomacy.[27] Consequently Russia's policies evoke suspicion even in well-disposed states like Finland. Thus the Finnish Institute of International Affairs recently reported that,

> In the realm of foreign and security policy, Russia is not committed to the principles of democratic peace and common values. Its chosen line of multipolarity implies that Russia is entitled to its own sphere of influence and the unilateral use of military force within it. Russia refuses to countenance any unipolar hegemonic aspirations, in particular it will not accept security arrangements in which the United States seems to have a leading role. As a solution, Russia proposes a Europe without dividing boundaries which will, however, require a buffer zone of militarily non-aligned countries between Russia and NATO. Russia's idea of Europe's new security architecture is therefore based on an equal partnership of great powers and supportive geopolitical solutions—not on common values accepted by all, nor on the right of every small state to define their own security policy. *The above summary of recent Russian developments is, in every aspect, practically in opposition to Finland's and the EU's fairly optimistic goals.* (emphasis author)[28]

Even some Russian analysts, for example, Tatiana Parkhalina of the NATO Documentation Center of the Academy of Sciences, insists that Russian elites must stop thinking about security in obsolete geopolitical contexts but rather address those issues from a contemporary economic-political framework as does the West.[29]

Until the war for Kosovo it seemed that the West had no ready answer for dealing with the crises of Central and Eastern Europe. Although we fully expressed the doctrines of liberalism and globalization discussed below, in practice the West seemed unsure of how to react to actual challenges to this doctrine in Yugoslavia or Chechnya where it did nothing. This led to a real absence of a coherent policy or moral-intellectual response to the challenges coming from east of the Elbe. As the prominent French analyst Nicole Gnesotto observed,

> The truth of the Yugoslav conflict is that our democracies are in such a state of conflict themselves that they are no longer capable of differentiating between the manageable and the unacceptable, even in the case of Serbia. Not that *Realpolitik* has not been a consideration in matters of war and peace—quite the contrary; but when in the name of strategic stability, some intend to negotiate, for each crisis, our principles in exchange for our interests—stability being more crucial than morals—is it not, *mutatis mutandis*, as a result of a confusion of values of the same order which previously led pacifists to proclaim "better red than dead"?—Apart from any moral considerations, should not the Western countries have in particular concluded, with a view to their own strategic interests, that a certain level of barbarity was in the long run incompatible with the security of a democratic Europe?—In the end what threatens the European order today is not so much the spectre of ethno-nationalism as the inability of the democracies to define the boundary between the legitimate and the unacceptable.[30]

The failures cited by Gnesotto apply equally to policy toward Russia. The crisis of 1998 where Russia's economy broke down revealed the bankruptcy of Western policy of calling Yeltsin's authoritarian improvisations reform. And there has been no willingness to admit to this failure or effort to find a new solution since then. Europe's moral-political failures before Kosovo were rooted in the breakdown of each state's internal political consensus. We can see the structural weaknesses affecting security policy at work in all the major Western states, but we can most profitably focus on the United States as an example even though each state has its own structural and peculiar reasons for the failure to devise coherent security policies. The United States, as the clear leader of the alliance, plays a disproportionate role in framing Western policy. If it cannot or will not act, neither will anyone else. Despite the apparent success of its policies in Kosovo the fact remains that it took place in the teeth of a clear congressional vote of no confidence in the administration.

The U.S. foreign policy consensus died in Vietnam. Since then, in virtually all crises abroad, we have experienced what former Assistant Secretary of State Richard Holbrooke, the architect of peace in Yugoslavia, calls the Vietmalia Syndrome. It is clear that important sectors of the elite (including the U.S. Army) view any extended foreign involvement with the utmost trepidation and want extensive assurances of prearranged success beforehand. Otherwise they may use their formidable power to prevent the deployment of U.S. resources or forces (and we do not only mean military deployment), obstruct the policy process to prevent any real action, or restrict the scope of presidential discretion.[31] In the aftermath of Vietnam, in 1975, Earl Ravenal observed that all future challenges will be seen as resembling Vietnam regardless of the realities of the case. And this perception will inhibit or constrain effective U.S. responses to these challenges.[32] Since Vietnam there has been an enormous proliferation of reporting, bureaucratic, investigative, and legislative requirements that constitute efforts to micromanage foreign policy. These obligations have frustrated presidents of both parties and contributed to major crises like the Iran-contra affair.

Because Congress is swayed more by short-term and partisan political calculation than by any vision of the national interest, few members will support policies that must deal with protracted and complex crises. As former Senator David Boren observed,

> With each new breakdown of bipartisan consensus and trust comes a new list of congressional restrictions on the executive branch. With new restrictions come new initiatives by the White House aimed at evading what are viewed as unwise limitations upon the prerogatives of the commander in chief. Executive evasions breed more congressional distrust and the cycle continues, paralleling the arms race in its destructive and irrational escalation.[33]

This process clearly emerged with regard to Bosnia and Kosovo. In Bosnia the Clinton administration had to commit troops first to get Congress to take responsible action and had to accept, as the price of the budgetary authorization, arming the Bosnian Muslims against the wishes of our allies and perhaps enhancing the risks to our forces there. In Kosovo, Clinton went to war without Congressional authorization and continued doing so in the face of a vote of no confidence by the Congress that refused to authorize the earlier commitment of troops. But what is worse in these cases is that Congress' desire to posture nationalistically and act timorously undermines the support for NATO expansion or intervention in Europe that it has simultaneously urged. Observers must constantly worry that if Congress is so unable to resolve itself on sending troops to a peace enforcement mission in Bosnia or Kosovo, what will it do to defend NATO members in a real crisis and will it pay the price of doing so?[34]

These structural constraints have led to a situation where absence of a post–cold war consensus on national interests and strategy compels presidents to engage in foreign policy adhocery and make periodic understandings with Congress or rather with new Congressional coalitions (as in the case of the North American Free Trade Agreement) on each issue. This process inherently diminishes presidential authority, power, and the consistency of policy.[35] This process derogates from a president's authority and from the credibility of U.S. commitments since broad coalitions are a prerequisite of success in the United States and policies that take time to mature are penalized, a psychology and political culture that are inimical to the requirements of successful strategies for international security.[36]

Today these factors make it harder for presidents to cope with their responsibilities for articulating and implementing policies with a broad strategic sweep that respond to novel conditions like the end of the cold war. One allied ambassador with considerable experience of dealing with Congress said in 1995–96, "These people don't seem to have a formed opinion of the outside world at all. It simply does not feature on their agenda."[37] If anything this trend has intensified since then. To the extent that a considered domestic, social, economic, or foreign policy becomes unattainable, the ensuing gridlock quickly weakens a state's ability to function abroad as France's 1995 strikes showed for it or Italy and Japan's domestic crises have shown for them.

A further cause for concern is the growing saliency of two related outlooks of U.S. constituencies and elites. The first stems from the traditional cognitive effort to separate war from politics and regard the military instrument as suitable only for operations, for example, MacArthur's "no substitute for victory." "For many Americans, U.S. foreign military involvement is designed not to project national power or to buy influence—but only to deal with threats and to oppose aggression, especially from nondemocratic states."[38] To this perhaps we should now add the phrase "or to avert humanitarian disasters" as an incipient Clinton doctrine seems to proclaim.[39] In a post-cold war world troops should logically come home and not be engaged in faraway indecisive peace operations where a clear national interest or overwhelming threat is not readily discernible. When this precept is coupled with the second belief that important constituencies and the politicians share, that the United States is somehow being economically victimized by its allies in Europe and Asia, the prognosis for coherent policy diminishes because its coalitional base is further fractured. Patrick Buchanan's campaign for the Republican party's presidential nomination in 1996 publicly exposed this fault line.

> This feeling sharpens burden-sharing disputes because it devalues the benefits Americans might receive from *any* new arrangement. It may not change since it reflects a deep–seated inclination to see international relations in terms of domestic values.[40]

The argument that we were spending too much on the war in Kosovo and that reconstruction is Europe's business grows out of this mood. But if reconstruction of the Balkans is the EU's business alone, will it then heed any subsequent expression of U.S. interests there, and what can make that expression a credible one?

Debilitating debates along these lines have characterized U.S. policies in administrations as diverse as Reagan and Clinton's. One can even trace the current gridlock and lack of strategic consensus back to the fights over Iran-contra, foreign and military aid, and SDI in the Reagan years.[41] Since the executive branch is not a place where long-range strategy is easily or effectively formulated given its present structure and responsibilities, it becomes almost impossible for a president to do much more than deal with short-term solutions. The upshot of this structural conundrum is that on every major issue of European security (or foreign policy) where Congress has a major voice, a new coalition must laboriously be formed with great delay, equivocation, and high risks of failure. Interested observers watching this spectacle must be concerned at the durability of the U.S. contribution to a new order in the Balkans. Any situation where a reliable consensus for long-term, steady, U.S. policies in Europe is missing when only the United States can lead Europe will invariably unnerve European politicians.

Indeed, it is not only the French argument that the United States will ultimately leave Europe or that Europe cannot leave its self-defense exclusively to the United States. By agreeing to joint European defense structures with France, British Prime Minister Tony Blair adopted the same argument. William Wallace has written that there no longer is a solid congressional or institutional basis for the U.S. commitment to European security and that U.S. leadership rests far too dangerously on the mutual suspicion of European states for each other, not on the vision coming out of Washington.[42] Hence it is not surprising that France, Germany, and Great Britain are acting jointly to reform European security structures so that they can act without waiting for Washington. While it is quite possible that this trend will only lessen our ability to lead on issues of European security, until Europe actually takes practical responsibility for its defense these moves do not visibly augment Europe's capacity to act autonomously.[43]

Furthermore, in both the Bush and Clinton administrations policy choices and personal idiosyncrasies have made it harder for the United States to exploit in strategic terms the victory of 1989–91. These policy decisions apply both to process as well as to content. George Bush's administration was singularly adept at making policy with a minimum of friction and at consolidating opportunities presented to it by the end of the cold war, namely German reunification, restructuring of NATO, and the Conventional Forces in Europe (CFE) treaty.[44] In all cases the Bush administration opted to keep Gorbachev in power because it was worried that any other regime would not be so compliant on those issues and that the chance to "lock in" those concessions might vanish. Similarly Soviet officials, virtually to a man, claimed that it was the Bush administration's proposals to recast NATO's military-political functions, doctrine, and nuclear policy in 1990 that allowed them to accept the terms of German reunification that eventually emerged.[45] Nonetheless this approach, though superbly managed, inevitably entailed serious costs. It was essentially a strategy for ending the cold war on American terms, not recasting a new order that included the former Warsaw Pact members or their successors in a viable new architecture. As Philip Zelikow and Condoleeza Rice, two architects and executants of American policy, wrote,

The United States intended to consolidate the democratic revolution in Europe, reduce Soviet military power in Eastern Europe, and eliminate the Soviet armed presence in Germany. American forces—though fewer in number—would remain. The harsh truth was that the American goal could be achieved only if the Soviet Union suffered a reversal of fortunes not unlike a catastrophic defeat in a war. The United States had decided to try to achieve the unification of Germany absolutely and unequivocally on Western terms. Yet American officials wanted the Soviets to accept this result and believe that they retained an appropriate, albeit diminished role in European affairs. They did not want

Moscow to nurture a lasting bitterness that would lead them someday to try and overthrow the European settlement.[46]

Yet the cost entailed for such a self-interested approach to the problem was to give the Soviets and now the Russians implicit hostages against the future which nobody had any interest or expectation in redeeming and to preserve a U.S. dominated security structure for a Europe that was no longer relevant to that structure. Although Moscow was implicitly guaranteed a place in a more peaceful Europe, nothing was made definite. Russian elites fabricated their own illusion that in a transformed, post–cold war Europe NATO would disappear. When this did not happen and NATO started enlarging, the shock of disillusionment soon gave way to cries of betrayal.[47] They actually believed what then German Foreign Minister Hans-Dietrich Genscher said during the negotiations over Germany's unification, "the alliances will increasingly become elements of cooperative security structures in which they can ultimately be absorbed."[48] Furthermore the fundamental conservatism of the U.S. government in 1989–92 meant that it was afraid up to the last moment to embrace or help manage the revolutionary change within Russia and the other Soviet republics even into 1992–93 when our policy was aptly summed up as Russia plus branch offices.[49] This policy lasted well into 1994 and the Clinton administration.[50] Indeed, the main concern was for stability, U.S. strategic superiority, and control over former Soviet nuclear weapons, a concern that in policymakers' minds obscured all else and thus delayed U.S. interest and ability to help shape the emerging Eurasian order.[51] When President Bush said the new enemy was instability, nobody asked how the West was to cope with the new instability because neither Bush nor his team had any answers or showed much energy in fighting instability. Even new programs, such as the Nunn-Lugar legislation on controlling those nuclear weapons, floundered around in the bureaucratic morass of Washington and Moscow with many people and bureaucracies getting airline tickets but little else.[52] As a result, today, it is beyond doubt that Russia and its armed forces do not exercise sufficient reasonable controls over their nuclear materials, possibly including weapons.[53]

The same problem affects U.S. policy toward the economic and political restructuring of the former Soviet bloc. The economic contribution has been laggard, insufficient, unimpressive, and often divorced from political restructuring.[54] As Western Europe and the United States did not open their markets to the CIS states sufficiently or invest enough in them since 1989, the new states' growth, though often impressive, has been stunted and purchased at the price of fracturing their internal democratic coalitions. And it appears that there was a net transfer of capital from Eastern Europe to the West, not vice versa. Such a situation can only inhibit reconstruction in Central and Eastern Europe.

The return of Communists in many states, especially in the former Soviet Union, represents a sense that democratic reform has not sufficiently caught on in the institutional sphere. This is particularly the case in Russia where the great danger lies not just in the election of anti-reform parliaments but in the collapse of a coherent, viable, democratic, and legitimate state or executive branch. The stagnation of genuine reform and the democratic impetus is the single greatest cause behind Russia's failure to overcome its crisis and is most saliently visible in the crisis of the state.

Indeed, for all its talk of promoting democracy, the Clinton administration's real efforts have not been particularly innovative or of sufficient scale to affect Russia's internal evolution. Or where they supported one trend, it turned out to be one that genuinely favored authoritarian corruption.[55] The administration's vacillating policies on Bosnia until 1995 and its unwillingness to admit that it is carrying out a strategy that seeks to limit Russia's coercive diplomacy of reintegration in the CIS and its "continental drift" on NATO enlargement all suggest a policy or policies that are ad hoc, reactive, and anything but coordinated and strategic.[56] In short, both administrations failed to heed Zbigniew Brzezinski's admonition to come up with a program for terminating the cold war that was symbolically compelling, politically substantive, and comprehensive across all the related issues.[57] So, absent grand strategy, we have endured a policy of drift and reaction, not mastery.

The upshot of this confused period in Western policy was a delay in launching the integration of Central Europe for which we are still paying. Two Balkan wars have been fought because we failed to take seriously what was happening there and sought to "insulate ourselves," as did our allies, against events there until it was clear that doing so compromised NATO's future and thus our vital interests in Europe.[58] In the Baltic region we now have a situation where the only issue that seems to be on the Baltic states' and Washington's agenda is NATO enlargement, precisely the one issue that makes further discussion impossible and precludes advances to meet more urgent threats and bring Northern Europe closer to Europe as a whole.[59]

Thus NATO enlargement and the processes it has spawned have begun the motor force and surrogates for the broader issue of European integration. Perhaps there was no other way insofar as the EU seems even now more interested in procrastination than in meaningful responses to contemporary security challenges. If not for NATO's move east, the EU probably would not have followed suit by 1999. So the progress listed above toward European integration is mainly due to NATO and Washington. But a European policy for the United States that believes "Eastern Europe's place in the world is [still] largely determined by the West's adversarial relationship with the Soviet Union" is insufficient.[60] That stance inadvertently appears to justify Moscow's deepest fears about Europe but provides little guidance or strategy for issues like the Baltic, Ukraine, and the Balkans.

Accordingly the risk exists that despite our rhetoric to the contrary European security remains divisible and that we do not really know how to promote Eastern European security. No security system can work if the West divides Europe a priori. Indeed, until Kosovo there was a widespread "pourquoi mourir pour Danzig?" outlook abroad. Willem van Eekelen, former secretary-general of the WEU, reflected that opinion when he wrote that it is no longer self-evident that European security is indivisible. "A common response will require far more joint preliminary analysis, consultation, and planning."[61] Such activity must precede, not react to, the crisis. Yet until now there was little sign of any action to act in concert before a crisis, as was the case in Iraq. Only a total breakdown of talks with Serbia and its decision to publicly thumb its nose at NATO produced a united effort but one that had more than a few visible fissures. As long as European security is divisible and so viewed, and policy is strictly reactive, Europe's response to crises will resemble the less than inspiring earlier Yugoslav example. And it is hardly clear how things in Kosovo or Bosnia will ultimately end since it seems clear that ethnic violence will dominate if NATO leaves now or any time in the next five to ten years. Especially if Serbia remains untransformed by post-1989 events, neither it nor Russia will contribute to a true Balkan security system. Where security is divisible, nobody will feel impelled to prevent conflict, discern, or feel an imminent threat.

Van Eekelen's views about security guarantees for Central and Eastern Europe were even more bleak because he did not expect (or seem to want) any before the year 2000. Furthermore, he preferred to evade and defer the issue while seemingly trying to perfect processes and procedures for multilateral coordination.

What kinds of guarantees would really be helpful in enhancing their perception of security? To whom should they be given and where do we draw the line? Such guarantees cannot be seen as directed against Russia, because it is no longer considered as an immediate threat and it no longer has borders with Central European countries. The problem then boils down to the question of the comparative relevance of security guarantees to our present major preoccupation with minority problems and regional instability. Only if there is consultation machinery with reciprocal rights and obligations, will it be possible to find an agreement on security guarantees.[62]

One would have thought that NATO and existing mechanisms suffice as forums for multilateral action even if Van Eekelen obviously was committed to expanding the WEU. Certainly, in Russia, for example, even some officers denied the need for new agencies and acknowledge NATO's real capabilities. They regarded NATO as,

> Effectively the sole organization capable of generalizing international peacekeeping experience gathered by other countries. Use of its structures enables it to operate anonymously and to avoid the risk of awakening in states that are parties to conflicts fears regarding an upsurge in expansionist sentiments in one influential member of the international community or another.[63]

NATO fulfills the requirement of impartiality and neutrality needed to be a peacemaker or peacekeeper and is so perceived abroad. But evidently some Western leaders have trouble grasping the implications of this fact or of acting upon it.

Van Eekelen's flight from making strategy and tough political decisions resembled Western policy beyond the Elbe. High-ranking Western officials acted and talked as if European security means Western, not Eastern, security.[64] Therefore since they could not agree on a common positive strategy abroad, their diplomacy remained ambivalent and they could only agree to a desire to insulate themselves as far as possible from the challenges emanating from Central and Eastern Europe. Insulation was a political and diplomatic strategy of the lowest common denominator like the EU's foreign policy. It was based on this fear of anybody acting and of the consequences of such action. Its premise ultimately became one of mutual paralysis until NATO finally acted. Indeed, the insulation strategy was set up precisely because no Western consensus existed.

> The commitment to attrition strategy in Bosnia is based upon a combination of factors, ranging from lack of agreement among the powers

about the end-state to be achieved in Bosnia-Herzegovina, the rest of Yugoslavia and the Balkans as a whole to divergent assessments of the military-political character of the struggle and the appropriate military-technical means to be applied.[65]

As Stanley Hoffmann pointed out with regard to the original Bosnian crisis, the international community sought to isolate the conflicts from broader European issues and pursue a limited policy of collective security against aggression.[66] The international community's "objective" was to limit the wars' brutality (or "shape" the Serbs' expected victory) and negotiate with all parties being treated as morally equivalent. That situation has now changed. Whether or not Europe understands this fact consciously, by enlarging NATO and going to war in Kosovo to defend moral standards, it has moved decisively toward acting on behalf of collective security and crisis management in Europe. This marks a considerable advance upon the hapless policies of 1991–95, but it entails long-term continuous and onerous responsibilities that may not be to each government's taste.

In other words, before 1995 leading Western policymakers failed to see that the insulation strategy itself ensures failure. If we remember that its operating premise was that the West could not agree about outcomes in Central and Eastern Europe or shape them constructively, its perpetuation reflected the West's ongoing abdication of political will to engage those regions seriously. By the same token NATO enlargement, even if this was not realized, meant a decisive break with that policy and the rhetorical espousal of Wilsonian liberalism as the basis for a liberalizing collective security community that would enforce morality as well as self-interest. Kosovo was the first test, but reshaping the Balkans as a whole is the real test in Central and Southeastern Europe.

But the European quandary does not end here because Russia and its relations with the CIS is now a legitimate security issue for Europe. For this reason the now truculent Wilsonian rhetoric emanating from Washington and Brussels about NATO and the U.S. future missions and roles in Europe and beyond could lead to a major crisis if not a disaster. For instance, the question of any future war between Russia and one of the CIS members poses the collective security issue before NATO in its starkest form. By all accounts NATO and those states are gravitating ever closer and their security is now a formal issue on NATO and the U.S.' agenda. U.S. interest goes far beyond oil and gas to encompass military-political integration of the CIS along with its economic integration to the West.[67]

But it is by no means clear that our allies are as vitally concerned to intervene in the Caucasus, for example. Any war in the CIS, which is fertile ground for conflict, might very well trigger at best only a similar attrition strategy as occurred in Bosnia with equally outrageous outcomes because the allies would be unable to establish a powerful consensus. However, if NATO were to intervene this might lead to a pan-European calamity for a number of reasons. On the one hand, it is not clear that if NATO were to involve itself in any future conflict there that it could sustain its cohesion. Precisely because NATO has now put its future relevance and coherence on the line in Kosovo and narrowly succeeded, it might feel obliged to do so again. This would ignore the fact that already in Kosovo the Norwegians want out and the Kosovo Liberation Army (KLA) will not accept the NATO objective of leaving the area under some nominal Yugoslav-Serbian autonomy. Protracted involvement in suppressing Kosovar nationalism is not what NATO should be doing now or in the future.

On the other hand, NATO's unity might not survive the expected Russian response to its enlargement into the CIS. Since Russian generals and political elites believe the single greatest danger emanating from Kosovo is NATO's propensity to act unilaterally and forcefully, any involvement there would raise the specter of a direct Russian response.[68] In such a war where Russia feels its vital interests and integrity are at risk, the tendencies of Russian military doctrine strongly point toward seeing what might start as a local, ethnic war as really a seamless web or unbroken escalation ladder all the way up to nuclear war where Russia would be obliged to launch first and preemptive strikes. Under current and forthcoming Russian strategy that means extended and expanded deterrence (rasshirennoe sderzhivanie) by nuclear means.[69] Since deterrence is first of all intended to obtain a political decision, that threat might engender just such a decision by key NATO allies to abstain thereby fragmenting NATO's unity and the effective conduct of military operations. As Kosovo showed, nobody is willing to risk any operations that might undermine allied cohesion at the lowest common denominator and coalition warfare necessarily impedes the kind of strategy we wish to pursue, even at the purely conventional level.

The absence of clear Western thinking about security structures and the pursuit of the will-o'-the-wisp of a European "security architecture" traumatized the Balkans during 1991–95, postponed the advent of true European integration, and overlooked pressing issues in Central and Eastern Europe. Clear thinking about that "architecture" would have shown that the West's will to use power to shape desirable outcomes in Europe and Yugoslavia specifically was the key to a solution anywhere. Political will is essential, not blueprints. Kosovo has now demonstrated the first step of that political will, but it will need to be exercised for a long time to come. Any effectively functioning collective security system *presupposes* a security regime, that is, widespread consensus on basic principles, the prior resolution of major problems, and a diminished role for military force.[70] In turn, creation of such a regime presupposes the political will to solve problems and create new norms or institutions for all of Europe. Since these prerequisites were absent in the CIS so we can expect similar outcomes to that of 1991–95 in a crisis there.

We must remember what are the implications of a divisible European security. Yugoslavia in 1991–95 and Chechnya illustrate that Western insulation of those wars and of East European problems from their own policies had become a key component of Western policy. The insulation strategy meant and accepted that European security is divisible and that the East remain outside any legitimate European system. Insulation separates states into those having security and those lacking it.[71] Naturally those lacking security will act on their own to get it, especially as they see themselves as victims of those who have cut them adrift. Or, those seeing the vacuum at the center will try and fill it, for example, by a renationalization of their security policies.[72] For example, Azerbaijan now openly talks of having NATO intervene in its war with Armenia, guard its pipelines, set up a base there and even contemplates a vast alliance against a Russian-led bloc.[73]

Thus insulation has fostered renationalization of European security agendas and a new form of the old division of Europe.[74] But once it ran into the competing logic of NATO enlargement its insufficiency became clear, and the logic of the latter process has taken root leaving some optimism for the future. Insulation failed precisely because it was implemented. In reflecting the lack of consensus and inaction in the West while Yugoslavia burned, it signaled others that they could pursue their own initiatives—Greek blockades of Macedonia, Italian efforts to renegotiate Italian minorities' rights in Croatia and Slovenia, Russian unilateral peacemaking, Chechnya, and threats to the Baltic and Central Europe if NATO expands. Implementing the insulation strategy only aggravated the conditions that had led to it, rendering it even more useless for conflict termination.

Renationalization of security policy, an outgrowth of that insulation strategy creates still other problems. It generates "an equal and opposite reaction," namely Central Europe's desire to expand NATO to rein in that process before Central and Eastern Europe explode. Even Russian analysts like Sergei Karaganov conceded that Yugoslavia's wars and the vacuum created thereby were a legitimate reason for expanding NATO.[75] But it also entailed Russia's drift away from partnership with the West toward a truculent if emasculated unilateralism. Every Russian political figure regards NATO's expansion as a mortal military-political threat to Russian interests that isolates Russia in and from Europe.

Russia opposes the current division of Europe and will react by further efforts to undo or revise the status quo—most likely first in the Caucasus, then Ukraine, and then the Balkans. These considerations vindicate the precept that the insulation strategy only works if Russia is stable and satisfied.[76] But since Russia is unstable and openly, vocally revisionist, insulation breaks down and Central Europe's, the Balkans', and Eastern Europe's problems must be dealt with in a concerted European-American forum and by a new strategy. For outsiders to influence outcomes there, they must learn from Kosovo. Namely they must sustain a military-political outcome over a long time, and not be hostage to Russian domestic politics. Yet this insight appeared to be lost on many in Europe. Michael Stuermer, director of the prestigious Stiftung Wissenschaft und Politik at Ebenhausen, wrote that Russia ought to be given a droit de regard over Central and Eastern Europe which would entail abridging Ukraine's and the Baltic states' prospects for integration with the EU, not to mention NATO.[77] And Stuermer is by no means alone in this call, just more candid.

The dead end into which insulation leads stems directly from its foundation concepts. Insulation is based on seeing Europe as what Richard Betts called a "post-Hobbesian pacific anarchy."[78] No major military or general threat to European security exists. Rather, possible or actual conflicts threaten small states while the absence of great power conflicts or threats reduces the importance of small states and their crises which apparently cannot effect rapid strategic changes in the balance of power and pose little threat to big powers who may safely ignore them. "Regional conflicts are now decoupled from the earlier linkage with superpower rivalry. Regional conflicts may be less critical but they may be freer to escalate to higher levels of violence."[79] More bluntly, European security is divisible.

This logic and policy of insulation clearly contradicts the view inherent in collective security that regional conflicts cannot be di-

vorced form the larger concept and that left unattended, will grow
into bigger conflagrations. That strategy worked only if Russia, too
large a factor to be ignored, is satisfied. "Russian satisfaction is a
prerequisite for the ability to insulate Western security from other
problems."[80] But Russia is neither stable nor satisfied. Furthermore, once Russia becomes a potential threat to European security
or an unpredictable factor, as it is now, due to Chechnya, its own
unreformed quality, and its efforts at unilateral peacemaking and
reintegration from above in the CIS, small states and their conflicts
are once again relevant.[81] This point seems to have finally regis-
tered in Washington. Undersecretary of State Strobe Talbott, the
administration's "point man" for Russian policy, wrote in 1996
that

> Russia is stepping up its call for economic and political integration
> among the former Soviet republics. In Eurasia, as in other parts of the
> world, we oppose coercion and intimidation of neighboring states. We
> will endorse regional cooperation only so long as it is truly and totally
> voluntary and only if it opens doors to the outside world.[82]

This recognition signifies U.S. awareness that it must resist Moscow's ambitions. In Transcaucasia and Central Asia the United
States has moved in 1995 in just that direction to block a Russian
sphere of influence, particularly with regard to control over energy supplies.[83] But declarations about energy policy, a tangible as
well as vital interest, are one thing, a strategy for meeting the challenges of European security is a much grander undertaking.

Moscow's 1994 diplomatic intervention in Yugoslavia displayed
its aim of using its presence to revise the post-1989 status quo that
had marginalized it in Central and Eastern Europe. This consideration should have led the West to rethink its policy. Moscow's opposition to NATO's expansion, preference that Europe should be
structured around two pillars organized under the OSCE and a
collective security system, one for NATO in its current boundaries
and another equal one for the CIS, and ambition to integrate this
system from Moscow for Russia's benefit, and have a free hand in
doing so should show Europe the dangers in Russian political
thinking and the fact that Russia's political class has fallen prey to
dangerous fantasies.[84]

Similarly, Russian revisionism and demands for equality demonstrate that Moscow still does not genuinely accept the status quo in
Europe. About this revisionism there can be no doubt. This revisionism has been openly expressed before Western audiences by

some of the highest ranking policymakers as well as by influential members of the policy analyst class in Moscow. For example, in 1996 Foreign Minister Yevgeny Primakov told the OSCE in 1996 that,

Today, the balance of forces resulting from the confrontation of the two blocs no longer exists, but the Helsinki agreements are not being fully applied. After the end of the Cold War certain countries in Europe—the Soviet Union, Czechoslovakia, and Yugoslavia—have disintegrated. A number of new states were formed in this space, but their borders are neither fixed nor guaranteed by the Helsinki agreements. Under the circumstances, there is a need for the establishment of a new system of security.[85]

As Russia also demands guarantees of its integrity against secessionist threats while the ministry of defense insists on retaining the old Soviet borders, Primakov confirmed what Alexei Arbatov called the duplicity of Russian border policy.[86] Nor is Primakov alone in this quest.

Andrei Kokoshin, former secretary of the Security Council and deputy defense minister, wrote in 1997 that,

Russia's security will be determined to a great extent by the process of the reintegration of the former Soviet Union. The social, cultural, geopolitical, and even historical prerequisites for the strengthening of this process already exist. Russian history bears witness to the fact that the changes in the geography of the state that occurred in the 1990s are not irreversible. If one looks at the space occupied by the Russian empire in the eighteenth and nineteenth centuries, and by the Soviet Union in the twentieth century, one can envisage the emergence there of a new, viable state-political entity.[87]

Alla Iaz'kova of Moscow State University and the Institute of World Economics and International Relations (IMEMO), openly says that Russia really would prefer a situation like that of 1945 and that the Russian elite intends to use the issue of Russians abroad as a means to destabilize Georgia, Moldova, the Baltic states, and possibly Ukraine.[88] She goes on to observe that,

After a series of nationalist demonstrations, both within the newly independent states and the Russian Federation, a consensus has emerged among a wide spectrum of Russian political organizations that Russian minorities in the Near Abroad must be protected. In this regard it is worth noting that a majority of Russians living in the new independent states appear to support some variant of the extremist agenda of Vladi-

mir Zhirinovsky. Many have backed secessionist efforts such as those in
Abkhazia and Transdniester as well as the armed conflict in Chechnya.
Despite this tendency toward extremism, Russia will continue to gear
its policies toward the new independent states on the basis of their
treatment of Russian minorities, though the means via which influence
will be exerted will differ depending on the situation.[89]

The linked fear of disintegration leads Russia's elite to make the
"defensive" demand for a sphere of influence along Russia's pe-
rimeter, that is, the Baltic and CIS states, to guard against further
disintegration of Russia proper.[90] And there are analysts who believe that border revisions among CIS states that carve them up
are feasible solutions to the problems of ethnic conflict that have
plagued them and Russia since 1992.[91]

Vasily Krivokhiza, first deputy director of Russia's Institute for
Strategic Studies, brings together much of what passes for establishment thinking by insisting on Primakov's concept of a multipolar world, global equality with Washington, defense of Russia's
integrity through reintegration, and regional engagement in a single whole that is shot through with old-fashioned and frankly imperialist notions of Russian security objectives. Krivokhiza writes
that,

> The more than thousand year experience of the Russian state and ele-
> mentary common sense demonstrate that geopolitical constants exist.
> One of these is the fact that stability inside Russia leads to her "aug-
> mentation" whereas instability leads to her neighbors' seizing [of] her
> territory, and even to centrifugal inclinations on the part of a number
> of her territories. This means that, in order to consolidate the CIS in
> one form or another, after having in parallel strengthened Russia, it is
> necessary in the first place to solve the problems inside Russia itself and
> to create international conditions that are favorable for the achieve-
> ment of these goals. This is why any kind of isolationism in our rela-
> tions with our close and distant neighbors is undesirable. But it is
> better to solve this task by means of the promotion of global or, at a
> minimum, of regional initiatives.[92]

The gap between these goals and Russian realities could be the
source of a major international crisis. There is no way that Russia's
armed forces can realize these goals even for the CIS under present conditions. Yet Russia now seeks to redouble its efforts to impose extended nuclear deterrence against any attack on CIS states,
even if nobody asked for it and despite the profoundly dangerous
risks for Russia. Its current nationwide military maneuvers are

premised as well on a NATO attack like Kosovo and based on not only restoring Russia's integrity, but also that of its neighbors as well![93]

Russia must extend this deterrence, not only because of its legitimate vital interest in CIS affairs, but also lest it too becomes a target of those attacks.[94] This reasoning applies even to small-scale conventional attacks for which a nuclear response is contraindicated.[95] Also on the basis of this logic Primakov advocated a global foreign policy because Russia is a great power without whom no major international problem can be solved, just as in Brezhnev's time.[96] As two high-ranking general staff officers argued in a 1997 study, even states lacking political and economic power can play major roles and be system forming poles in world politics' supposedly objectively emerging multipolar structure.[97] The fact that Russia has nothing to contribute to many issues other than obstruction seems to elude such analysts.

These policies are ruinous to Russia. They also destabilize its neighborhood making foreign intervention that much more likely. Foreign observers who see how Moscow tramples upon its neighbors' interests and acts like a neo-imperial hegemonic bully retain "an enemy image" of Russia. The Finnish report cited above exemplifies the point.

Russian unilateralism with regard to the CIS and its palpable disregard for these states' sovereignty is also visible in the September 1995 edict no. 940 signed by President Boris Yeltsin and urging the integration of these states around Russia in economics, politics, and defense, with regard only for how they contribute to Russia's interests.[98] This policy overtly contradicts Moscow's assertion that the OSCE should be Europe's premier peacemaking or security institution. We can also see Russia's double standard in operation in its efforts to keep Europe out of its regional conflicts or gain sanction for a free hand in regard to those conflicts.[99] Indeed, as Aleksandr Konovalov and Dmitri Evstatiev observed, Russia's intervention in regional ethnic conflicts will inevitably lead to resistance, probably of an armed nature. This is because

> [o]nly the involvement of international bodies in the process of discussion of the matter can provide the necessary objectivity for assessments. Russia cannot solely address the problem of ethnic minorities, since it is perceived by many others (especially the Baltic states and Ukraine) to be the main heir of the imperial past and the main source of totalitarian practice in inter-ethnic relations.[100]

Obviously if Russia blocks the OSCE and/or other agencies from acting where its vital interests are affected, Russia wins a free hand in those cases. In that case these organizations will become marginalized with dire consequences for European security. In that case we will revert to spheres of influence peacemaking, that is, a division of Europe into blocs and a renationalization of security agendas across Eurasia. Russia's inconsistency or double standard on peacemaking and European security issues helps explain the pervasive mistrust of Russia abroad. And its addiction to old thinking threatens to leave it even further behind a post-Kosovo Europe organized around the security principles that justified that conflict.

CONCLUSION

Kosovo shows that the West may be moving toward a more solidly conceived and executed vision of European integration based on collective values and security and working through NATO and a revamped and more effective EU. This cannot be said conclusively, but there are grounds for observing that something new is taking place, a movement to a new status quo after the decade of the "post-cold war era" that ended with Kosovo. Still there are serious domestic and international institutional obstacles to the effective realization of the dream of a Europe whole and free.

On the other hand, this move, coming as it did after a prolonged insulation strategy, breeds conflict with Russia that sees NATO as encroaching upon and threatening its vital interests. Moreover, it leads Russia to espouse with ever greater stridency concepts of international affairs that are wholly at variance with what appears to be taking shape as a Western consensus. Thus aligned to a strategic, political, and economic division of Europe, we may be redrawing an ideological line based on nationalism and concepts of world order. On both sides the tendency to unilateral action will grow. One can interpret NATO's campaign in Kosovo as exemplifying that unilateralism as does Russia. On the other hand, Russia has consistently sought a free hand throughout the CIS. Ultimately it seems therefore that in the foreseeable future the line from the Baltic to the Black Sea will be the real battleground of European political struggles and may even occasionally, if not more frequently, be the site of actual military conflicts, if not wars.

Europe and the United States must therefore understand what are the consequences of unwillingness to defend their own treaties and principles. If Russia and/or NATO can act unilaterally, everyone else will do so too and we will have a general renationalization of Europe's security agenda, something already in view thanks to Yugoslavia's wars. Second, we will have a new division of Europe into spheres of influence that both reflects and causes that renationalization process. That also means the reemergence of rival blocs that are perceived to threaten each other since they will coalesce around appropriate security institutions. Moscow, like the Soviet Union, will perceive any institution where it is not a member as a threat, especially if it is a military-political one.[101] Yet where it wants or has membership, Russia wants to write the rules to tie everyone else up and have a free hand in proclaiming the indivisibility of human rights and peace outside its bloc but not in the CIS.

This is obviously unacceptable to Europe and the United States. NATO, by dint of its ongoing enlargement, the cover it provides to the EU's parallel enlargement, and its intervention into Bosnia and now Kosovo, has embarked upon a course of action where stopping short is probably still more perilous than moving on to stabilize all of Europe including Russia (in Russia's case by depriving it of the means to challenge the status quo).

The same holds true for the United States, the moving spirit of NATO. As a recent favorable assessment of American hegemony and unipolarity commented,

> Doing too little is a greater danger than doing too much.—In many cases, U.S. involvement has been demand driven, as one would expect in a system with one clear leader. Rhetoric aside, U.S. engagement seems to most other elites to be necessary for the proper functioning of the system. In each region, cobbled-together security arrangements that require an American role seem preferable to the available alternatives. The more efficiently the United States performs this role, the more durable the system. If, on the other hand, the United States fails to translate its potential into the capabilities necessary to provide order, then great power struggles for power and security will reappear sooner. Local powers will then face incentives to provide security, sparking local counterbalancing and security competition. As the world becomes more dangerous, more second-tier states will enhance their military capabilities. In time the result could be an earlier structural shift to bi-or multipolarity and a quicker reemergence of conflict over the leadership of the international system.[102]

However, as the United States performs these actions to enhance order it uses and manifests power, thereby fueling the resentments against it and putting its self-proclaimed exceptionalism into greater and greater question as is now the case in China and Russia. Therefore future interventions must be handled with infinitely more finesse than were Bosnia or Kosovo lest they become inefficient interventions that do not advance the goals of ordered security. Absent that finesse, second-tier states like Moscow will confirm the admonitions uttered above. If we substitute the words "the Caucasus and Transcaucasus" for "Yugoslavia" and "Russia" for the "Soviets" or "Soviet Union" in the quote below, we see the unresolved contradiction or double standard at the heart of Russia's current policies and Moscow's current trend towards assuming old Soviet positions. Celeste Wallander and Jane Prokop note,

> First, the institutions the Soviet Union most opposed are those that may be most effective, and the one that the Soviets supported—the CSCE—has been least capable of responding to the [Yugoslav] conflict—furthermore, the source of the CSCE's ineffectiveness may be the very features the Soviets valued in it—comprehensiveness with respect both to membership and issues. Second, the very interdependence of security (military, economic, political, and so on) in Europe which lay behind Soviet calls for a "European space" contradicted the notion that the Yugoslav conflict was an "internal" matter. It was not merely a question of principle; armed conflict within that country might produce international conflict. *In order to have a consistent policy on interdependence and security in Europe, the Soviet Union would have had to open its domestic political affairs to international influence.*[103] (emphasis added)

Moscow claims both indivisibility of security and human rights under the supreme leadership of a collective security organization as it secures its own sphere of influence because collective security is the easiest form of international concord and organization to break. Under collective security it takes only one actor who cannot or will not respond to challenges to inhibit effective concerted action. But the divisibility of European security, if we let it become the status quo, returns us to the past of blocs, armed confrontation, spheres of influence, and so on. Lawrence Freedman rightly notes that Europe cannot tolerate many more cases of state-sponsored violence in the CIS.

> The tolerance of the European system to major upheavals in Russia and/or Ukraine should not be judged high. Even smaller-scale ructions can become dangerous if they start to threaten the equilibrium of a number of countries. If there is an underlying tendency towards instability, then the issue of intervention starts to be seen in a different light. The interest in the prevention of disorder takes on a higher value, because there can be less confidence that, left alone, most conflicts will peter out as the belligerents become exhausted.[104]

Yugoslavia and the conflicts in the CIS confirmed Freedman's insights and show that Europe now faces a challenge of the will. Kosovo and the twin processes of NATO and EU enlargement may be the answers to that test. Having established a peace process for Yugoslavia and having earlier asserted its collective prerogative through the CSCE, the West was able to compel Russia and the belligerents in Yugoslavia to formally (at least) accept Europe's extension of its security agenda and influence. However, Moscow's policy constitutes a standing challenge to Europe which still hesitates to accept the responsibilities of integration with the East. To the degree that Europe had already accepted this responsibility by including the area in the North Atlantic Cooperation Council and the Partnership for Peace, failure to meet Russia's challenge will mean that it has again failed to devise appropriate mechanisms for securing Europe. Integration of the CIS over time may provoke clashes with Russia, but failure to move forward will certainly breed conflict there. This may be a Hobson's choice but it is immanent in the logic embraced by the West in Kosovo. Therefore if Europe's East and South are denied security, neither will the West have it.

If European security, as defined by the OSCE's scope of activities, now includes Caucasia and Transcaucasia, the indivisibility of European security means just that. Conversely, failure to defend Europe's claims in those regions means the divisibility of European security and all the attendant consequences thereof. In the end the members of the Western alliance must continue to forge new and viable policies, strategies, and institutions to extend the security community that they created. Otherwise they will only be sitting on the laurels of the past as they fall deeper into the fear of acting. But resting on the laurels of past victories won by bayonets is fruitless. As Talleyrand pointed out to Napoleon, "you can do anything in the world with bayonets except sit on them."

NOTES

1. Stephen Blank, "Russia and Europe in the Caucasus," *European Security* 4, no. 4 (winter 1995): 622–45.
2. "Poland, Ukraine's Anchor to Europe," *Jamestown Foundation Prism*, 2 July 1999; *Radio Free Europe/Radio Liberty Newsline*, 24 June 1999; Warsaw, *Gazeta Wyborcza*, in Polish, 11 June 1999; *Foreign Broadcast Information Service, Eastern Europe* (henceforth *FBIS EEU*), 11 June 1999.
3. *Ibid.*
4. S. Nelson Drew, *NATO From Berlin to Bosnia: Trans-Atlantic Security in Transi-*

tion, McNair Paper, no. 35, National Defense University, Washington, D.C., 1995, p. 2.

5. J. F. Brown, "1994 Overview: Turmoil and Hope, East as Well as West," *Transition: The Year in Review: 1994, Part I*, 1995, p. 4.

6. Catherine McArdle Kelleher, "Cooperative Security in Europe: A New Order for the 1990s," Douglas T. Stuart and Stephen F. Szabo, eds., *Discord and Collaboration in a New Europe: Essays in Honor of Arnold Wolfers*, Paul H. Nitze, foreword, Washington, D.C., Foreign Policy Institute, Paul H. Nitze School of Advanced International Studies, Johns Hopkins University, 1994, p. 119.

7. Western European Union, *European Security: A Common Concept of the 27 WEU Countries*, WEU Council of Ministers, Madrid, 14 November 1995, paras. 127, 159–60.

8. Lord Finsberg, rapporteur, *WEU in the Atlantic Alliance*, WEU document 1487, 6 November 1995, passim.

9. Assembly of Western European Union, Extraordinary Session, Declaration, London, 22–23 February 1996.

10. See for example, "The EU Goes Cold on Enlargement," *The Economist* (28 October 1995): 57–58; Max Jakobson, "Ardent Europe-Builders Aren't Making Their Case to the People," *International Herald Tribune*, 13 December 1995, p. 8; Paris , *Le Monde*, in French, 8 December 1995, *Foreign Broadcast Information Service, Western Europe* (henceforth *FBIS WEU*), 95–239, 12 December 1995, p. 2; William Wallace, "European-Atlantic Security Institutions: Current State and Future Prospects," *The International Spectator* 29, no. 3 (July-September, 1994): p. 47.

11. Sherman Garnett, *Decisive Terrain: Russia and its Western Borderlands*, unpublished paper, 1997, p. 15.

12. William Drozdiak, "U.S. Role in Aegean Revives Doubts on EU," *Washington Post*, 7 February 1996, A17.

13. *Ibid*.

14. Charles Bremmer, "Conflict Exposed NATO's Military Flaws," *London Times*, 1 July 1999; J. A. C. Lewis, "Building a European Force," *Jane's Defence Weekly*, 23 June 1999, 22–23.

15. Rome, *La Repubblica, Internet Version*, in Italian, 14 March 1998, *Foreign Broadcast Information Service, Central Eurasia* (henceforth *FBIS SOV*), 15 March 1999. That reluctance persisted even late into the operation as it was clear that many allies attached all kinds of limiting conditions to its prosecution.

16. George Schopflin, "The Rise of Anti-Democratic Movements in Post-Communist Societies," Hugh Miall, ed., *Redefining Europe: New Patterns of Conflict and Cooperation* (London: Pinter Publishers, 1994), 143.

17. Philip Zelikow and Condoleeza Rice, *Germany Unified and Europe Transformed: A Study in Statecraft* (Cambridge, MA.: Harvard University Press, 1995).

18. On French policy see Philip Gordon, *A Certain Idea of France: French Security Policy and the Gaullist Legacy* (Princeton, N.J.: Princeton University Press, 1993).

19. Joel J. Sokolsky, *Canada: Getting it Right This Time: the 1994 Defence White Paper* (Carlisle Barracks, PA., Strategic Studies Institute, U.S. Army War College, 1995), 9.

20. Ibid., 23 Indeed the U.S. concept of multilateralism, as seen by Sokolsky, is no better; namely he claims that the United States invokes multilateralism as a "tool to be used when it can support the achievement of American interests, legitimize U.S. actions, and harmonize Western policies. Americans want to lead, on their own terms, and will be looking for followers."

21. Steve Weber, "Shaping the Postwar Balance of Power: Multilateralism in NATO," *International Organization* 46, no. 3, (summer 1992): 637.

22. Munich, *Suddeutsche Zeitung*, in German, 3–4 February 1996; *FBIS WEU*, 96–024, 5 February 1996, 11.

23. This point is in line with the Russian critique of Kosovo but it is still well taken—NATO's resort to force indicated a failure of policy and politics, not their success, and raised many troubling questions about the alliance's right to unilaterally attack a country over an internal problem while it is formally at peace with NATO.

24. Dmitry Trenin, "Transformation of Russian Foreign Policy: NATO Expansion Can Have Negative Consequences for the West," *Nezavisimaya Gazeta*, 5 February 1997.

25. Moscow, *Nezavisimaya Gazeta*, in Russian, 28 September 1996, *FBIS-SOV-96–211-S*, 28 September 1996.

26. Sergey M. Rogov, "Russia and NATO's Enlargement: The Search for a Compromise at the Helsinki Summit," Center for Naval Analyses, Alexandria, VA CIM 513/ May 1997, 10.

27. For a description of how this system worked, see Paul W. Schroeder, *The Transformation of European Politics, 1763–1848* (New York and Oxford: Clarendon Press, Oxford University Press, 1994), 5–11.

28. Finnish Institute of International Affairs, *Russia Beyond 2000: The Prospects for Russian Developments and Their Implications for Finland*, Helsinki, 1999, 1–2.

29. Tatiana Parkhalina, "Real'nye Rezul'taty i Mnimye Vygody," *Nezavisimaya Gazeta*, 4 June 1999, p. 3.

30. Nicole Gnesotto, *Lessons of Yugoslavia*, Chaillot Papers no. 14 (Paris: Institute for Security Studies of the Western European Union, 1994), 11.

31. Georgie Anne Geyer, "When Policy Is Driven by Desire," *Washington Times*, 25 February 1996, B-3.

32. Ravenal's observations are cited in Peter Rodman, *More Precious Than Peace: The Cold War and the Struggle for the Third World* (New York: Charles Scribner's Sons, 1994), 133.

33. *Ibid.* 425–26; for Boren's remarks, see also 134–37.

34. George Moffett, "Will US Fight Europe's Wars?" *Christian Science Monitor*, 5 December 1995, 1, 4.

35. Glenn P. Hastedt and Arnold J. Eksterowicz, "Presidential Leadership in the Post Cold War Era," *Presidential Studies Quarterly* 23, no. 3 (summer 1993): 448–52.

36. *Ibid.*

37. Michael Dobbs, "The Year-End Report From Foggy Bottom," *Washington Post Weekly*, 1–7 January 1996, 18.

38. Joseph Lepgold, "Does Europe Still Have a Place in U.S. Foreign Policy? A Domestic Politics Argument," in Stuart and Szabo, 188.

39. Stephen S. Rosenfeld, "Exultant Crusader," *Washington Post*, 2 July 1999, 27; Michael Kelly, "A Perfectly Clintonian Doctrine," *Washington Post*, 30 June 1999, 31; Marianne Lavelle, "The Clinton Doctrine," *U.S. News & World Report*, 28 June 1999, 9; Douglas Waller, "The Three Ifs of a Clinton Doctrine," *Time*, 28 June 1999, 35; Francine Kiefer, "Clinton 'Doctrine': Is it Substance or Spin?" *Christian Science Monitor*, 28 June 1999, 2.

40. Lepgold "Does Europe," 189.

41. George P. Shultz, *Turmoil and Triumph: My Years as Secretary of State*, New York: Charles Scribner's Sons, 1993, gives blow-by-blow accounts of these endless battles.

42. Wallace, "European-Atlantic Security," 49.

43. Frankfurt Am Main, *Frankfurter Allgemeine*, in German, 13 December 1995, *FBIS WEU*, 95–239, 13 December 1995, p. 9.

44. Zelikow and Rice, *Germany Unified*.

45. *Ibid.*, 252, 332.

46. *Ibid.*, 197.

47. *Ibid.*, 225 and this is only one of such statements by people like President Bush, his Secretary of State James Baker, NATO's Secretary-General Manfred Woerner, and so on.

48. This is the clear conclusion of the U.S. ambassador to Russia from 1987–91 Jack Matlock, Jack F. Matlock Jr., *Autopsy on An Empire: The American Ambassador's Account of the Collapse of the Soviet Union* (New York: Random House, 1995), 539, 591.

49. Michael Cox, "The Necessary Partnership? The Clinton Presidency and Post-Soviet Russia," *International Affairs* 70, no. 4 (1994): 647–48; Ilya Prizel, "The United States, Russia, and the New Democracies in Central Europe," Konrad Adenauer Stiftung, Sankt Augustin, Germany, 1995, pp. 9–19; Under Secretary of State Strobe Talbott, "Promoting Democracy and Prosperity in Central Asia," Address at the U.S.-Central Asia Business Conference, Washington, D.C., 3 May 1994, *U.S. Department of State Dispatch* 5, no. 19 (9 May 1994): 280.

50. Stephen J. Blank, *Russia, Ukraine and European Security* (Carlisle Barracks, PA: Strategic Studies Institute, U.S. Army War College, 1993), 3–4.

51. Heather Wilson, "Missed Opportunities," *The National Interest*, no. 34 (winter 1993–1994): 28–30.

52. The many reported cases of nuclear smuggling that have been verified in Europe and generally in the Western media as well as reports of deteriorating conditions at military installations confirm that there are insufficient controls over both fissile materials and weapons.

53. Thomas A. Baylis, *The West and Eastern Europe: Economic Statecraft and Political Change* (Westport, CT.: Praeger Publishers, 1994), 35, 166.

54. Janine R. Wedel, *Collision and Collusion: the Strange Case of Western Aid to Eastern Europe 1989–1998* (New York: St. Martin's Press, 1998).

55. Cox, "The Necessary Partnership," 645–52.

56. Bruce George and John Borawski, "Continental Drift," *European Security* 4, no. 1 (spring 1995): 1–25.

57. Zbigniew Brzezinski, "Ending the Cold War," Andrei G. Bochkarev and Don L. Mansfield, eds., *The United States and the USSR in a Changing World: Soviet and American Perspectives* (Boulder, CO: Westview Press, 1992), 52–54.

58. Baylis, *West and Eastern Europe*, 204–5.

59. Stephen Blank, "Nordic-Baltic Security in the Next Millennium: A Proposal," forthcoming.

60. Simon Serfaty, "All in the Family: The United States and Europe," *Current History*, November 1994, 354.

61. Willem Van Eekelen, "WEU's Role in the New European Security Environment," *International Defense Review, Defense '95*, March 1995, 23. He too argues there as well that economic and political security organizations are taking precedence over purely military institutions.

62. *Ibid.*, 26.

63. A. S. Skvortsov, N. P. Klokotov, N. I. Turko, "Ispol'zovanie Geopoliticheskikh Faktorov v Interesakh Resheniia Zadach Natsional'no-Gosudarstvennoi Bezopasnosti," *Voennaya Mysl'*, no. 2, March–April 1995, 22.

64. Dieter Mahncke, "Parameters of European Security," *Chaillot Papers*, no. 10 (Paris: Institute for Security Studies, Western European Union, 1993), 7.

65. Paul D'Anieri and Brian Schmiedeler, "European Security After the Cold War: The Policy of Insulationism?"*European Security* 2, no. 3 (Autumn 1993): 341–64, Jacob Kipp and LTC Timothy Thomas, USA, "International Ramifications of Yugoslavia's Serial Wars: The Challenge of Ethno-National Conflicts for a Post-Cold War European Order," *European Security* 1, no. 4 (winter 1992): 179–80.

66. Stanley Hoffmann, "What Will Satisfy Serbia's Nationalists?" *New York Times*, 4 December 1994, E19.

67. Stephen J. Blank, *U.S. Military Engagement with Transcaucasia and Central Asia* (Carlisle Barracks, PA: Strategic Studies Institute, U.S. Army War College, April 1999).

68. Based on author's conversations with Russian officials in Helsinki and Moscow, June, 1999.

69. Ibid.

70. Mahncke, "Parameters of European Security," 4–5.

71. D'Anieri and Schmiedeler, "European Security," 356–59.

72. Kipp and Thomas, "Internation Ramifications," 172, D'Anieri and Schmiedeler, "European Security," 354–59.

72. Moscow, *Segodnya*, in Russian, 26 August 1994, *Foreign Broadcast Information Service, FBIS Report* (henceforth *FBIS USR*), 94–099, 12 September 1994, 48–49.

73. Blank, *U.S. Military Engagement*.

74. D'Anieri and Schmiedeler, "European Security," 342.

75. Ibid.

76. Ibid.

77. Michael Stuermer, *NATO-Oeffnung: Transatlantischer Klaerungsbedarf*, Stiftung Wissenschaft und Politik, Ebenhausen, SWP-KAA 2933, November 1995, pp. 11–12.

78. D'Anieri and Schmiedeler, "European Security," 354.

79. Zbigniew Brzezinski, "The Consequences of the End of the Cold War for International Security, *Adelphi Papers*, no. 265 (winter 1991/1992): 4.

80. D'Anieri and Schmiedeler, "European Security," 342; Andrei Zagorskii, "Russia and the CIS," in Miall, 78.

81. D'Anieri and Schmiedeler, "European Security," 357–60.

82. Strobe Talbott, "Terms of Engagement," *New York Times*, 4 February 1996, E13.

83. "If We Clash It'll Be On The Caspian," *Current Digest of the Post-Soviet Press* (henceforth *CDPP*), 17, no. 21, (21 June 1995): 21.

84. This was apparent in the Russian presentations delivered at the XV Biennial Conference of the Heads of European International Affairs Research Institutes, Moscow, 24–26 January 1996 and has not much changed since.

85. Address by Y.M. Primakov to the OSCE Permanent Council, Vienna, 20 September 1996, p. 2, Transcript made available by the Embassy of the Russian Federation to the United States.

86. Moscow, *Mirovaya Ekonomika i Mezhdunarodnye Otnosheniya*, in Russian, July–September 1994, *Foreign Broadcast Information Service, Central Eurasia, FBIS Report*, 94–129, 29 November 1994, 48.

87. Andrei Kokoshin, *Reflections on Russia's Past, Present, and Future* (John F. Kennedy School of Government, Harvard University, Cambridge, MA.: *Strengthening Democratic Institutions Project*, 1998), 31.

88. Alla Iaz'kova, "The Emergence of Post-Cold War Russian Foreign Policy Priorities," in *The Yugoslav Conflict and its Implications for International Relations*, ed. Robert Craig Nation and Stefano Bianchini (Ravenna: Longo Editore, 1998), 112.

89. Ibid., 111.

90. Moscow, *Nezavisimaya Gazeta (NG Stsenarii-Supplement), in Russian,* 28 June 1996, *FBIS SOV* 96–128, 3 July 1996.

91. Edward Ozhiganov, "The Republic of Moldova: Transdniester and the 14th Army," in *Managing Conflict in the Former Soviet Union,* ed. Alexei Arbatov, Abram Chayes, Antonia Handler Chayes, and Lara Olson (Cambridge, MA.: MIT Press, 1997), 206–7.

92. Vasily Krivokhiza, *Russia's National Security Policy: Conceptions and Realities in Strengthening Democratic Institutions Project,* trans. Richard Weitz (John F. Kennedy School of Government, Harvard University, Cambridge, MA.: 1998), 32.

93. Moscow, *Segodnya,* in Russian, 30 April 1999, *FBIS SOV,* 30 April 1999.

94. Stephen Blank, "Proliferation and Counterproliferation in Russian Strategy," Paper presented to the JINSA-SSI Conference on Proliferation Strategies, Washington, D.C., 22 February 1999.

95. Ibid.

96. Trenin, e-mail letter from Darrell Hammer, Johnson's Russia List, 5 February 1997; e-mail transmission, J. Michael Waller, "Primakov's Imperial Line," *Perspective* 7, no. 3 (January–February 1997): 2–6; "Primakov, Setting a New, Tougher Foreign Policy," *Current Digest of the Post-Soviet Press* 49, no. 2 (12 February 1997): 4–7; Mohiaddin Mesbahi, "Russian Foreign Policy and Security in Central Asia and the Caucasus," *Central Asian Survey* 12, no. 2 (1993): 187 for Primakov's globalism and statement that history never nullifies geopolitical values.

97. V. K. Potemkin and Yu.V. Morozov, "Strategic Stability in the Twenty-First Century," *European Security* 6, no. 3 (autumn 1997): 43.

98. Moscow, *Rossiyskaya Gazeta,* in Russian, 23 September 1995, *Foreign Broadcast Information Service, Central Eurasia,* 95–188, 28 September 1995, 19–22.

99. Stephen Blank, "The OSCE, Russia, and Security in the Caucasus," *Helsinki Monitor* 6, no. 3 (1995): 70–71.

100. Alexander A. Konovalov and Dmitri Evstatiev, "The Problem of Ethnic Minority Rights Protection in the Newly Independent States," in *Minorities: The New Europe's Old Issue,* ed. Ian M. Cuthbertson and Jane Leibowitz, Joseph S. Nye Jr., foreword (New York: Institute for East-West Studies, 1993), 159–60.

101. Celeste A. Wallander and Jane Prokop, "Soviet Security Strategies Toward Europe: After the Wall With Their Backs up Against It," in *After the Cold War: International Institutions and State Strategies in Europe, 1981–1991,* ed. Robert O. Keohane, Joseph S. Nye, Stanley Hoffmann (Cambridge, MA.: Harvard University Press, 1993), 91–103.

102. William C. Wohlforth, "The Stability of a Unipolar World," *International Security* 24, no. 3 (summer 1999): 39.

103. Wallander and Prokop, "Soviet Security Strategies," 98.

104. Lawrence Freedman, ed., "Introduction," *Military Intervention in European Conflicts* (Oxford: Blackwell Publishers, 1994), 9.

The Logic of NATO Enlargement: Denationalization, Democratization, Defense of Human Rights, and Denuclearization

CHRISTOPHER JONES

IN THE LAST ANALYSIS NATO ENLARGEMENT IS THE USE OF MILITARY means to support a broader process of extending a transnational European civil society up to the state borders of Russia. During the cold war, NATO inadvertently encouraged among its members a partial denationalization of defense and a democratization of civil-military relations, including the acceptance of human rights standards for individuals and minority groups. NATO enlargement has already extended such norms to its three new members and has encouraged applicant-states to accept identical principles for national security systems. The logic of NATO enlargement in Central Europe has also provided the logic for NATO engagement in the former Yugoslavia: defense of the democratic rights of European citizens and minorities, even at great political and financial cost to NATO governments. This role was so unanticipated that NATO—and especially the United States—lacked the procedures necessary to match NATO's military means to its unprecedented political objectives. As Robert Hayden has argued, in pursuing its humanitarian objectives in Kosovo, the Clinton administration may have authorized some military actions indictable as war crimes.[1]

During the cold war, NATO encouraged a denuclearization of national defense except in the United States, the United Kingdom, and France. The unintended consequence of U.S. extended deterrence for Europe was preparing NATO members for their commitments to the Nuclear Non-Proliferation Treaty (NPT) of 1968. The ultimate logic of NATO enlargement is the further denuclearization of Alliance security policy in Europe, a development that Russia should welcome. Russia should recognize that NATO enlargement has already solved its principal European security problem since 1871—that of German military power. The recent revision of the Conventional Forces in Europe (CFE) treaty has reconfirmed this achievement by placing strict new limits on the size of national armed forces.[2] The new CFE treaty has also reconfirmed the denationalization of defense among NATO members.

NATO enlargement may also solve Russia's remaining strategic problems in Europe. One is the reciprocal NATO/Russia deployment of nuclear weapons. The second is the set of problems linking the rights of minorities such as those in the Baltic states with democratization of civil-military relations in the states that emerged from the vanished Soviet empire. In the end, Moscow needs to acknowledge that NATO has already become, as in the former Yugoslavia, its potential partner in preventing ethno-nationalist warfare in the zone of the Organization for Security and Cooperation in Europe (OSCE). Such wars threaten to tear apart the Russian Federation and draw Russia into ruinous ethnic conflicts with the successor states of the former USSR, like the bitter nationalist war now taking place in Chechnya. But, in the name of the ethno-statist ideology[3] that has emerged from the previous Soviet concept of socialist internationalism, Moscow may reject NATO's offer of partnership in the construction of a common home for Europe's multicultural democracies.

NATO IS NOT WHAT IT USED TO BE

The Helsinki Accords of 1975 were the symbol and substance of the transformation of NATO from a coalition based primarily on the national military interests of its motley membership to a coalition of transatlantic civil societies sharing common commitments to democracy and human rights, including the rights of ethnic and religious minorities.[4] The North Atlantic Treaty of 1949 was ambiguous about the relationship between the Alliance and democratic principles.

The preamble declared that the signatories sought "to safeguard the freedom, common heritage and civilization of their peoples, founded on the principles of democracy, individual liberty and the rule of law."[5] This was not a commitment to defend democracy but simply to defend the signatories. Not one of the treaty articles mentioned democracy as either a requirement for Alliance membership or a long-term goal for Alliance members. In November 1999, in response to protests over alleged U.S. support for the coup of the Greek colonels in 1967, President Clinton proclaimed, in Athens,

> When the junta took over in 1967 here the United States allowed its interests in prosecuting the Cold War to prevail over its interest—I should say, its obligation—to support democracy, which was, after all, the cause for which we fought the Cold War. It is important that we acknowledge that.[6]

It is equally important to acknowledge that "democracy" did not become NATO's unequivocal cause until the latter part of the cold war—specifically, during and after the 1975 Helsinki Conference. Article 10 of the 1949 North Atlantic Treaty provided for the admission of new members, but mentioned no requirements for membership. There was no provision requiring members to certify their records on human rights, on treatment of national minorities, or on democratic civilian control of national militaries, as did the 1995 and 1997 NATO requirements for new members. Article 6 of the 1949 Treaty called for the defense of Turkey. Turkey was not a signatory to the Treaty—and not a model of democracy at that time. Turkey was in fact "out of area." Still, Ankara received a security guarantee from the Alliance and joined NATO in 1952, along with Greece. (In 1950, Greece and Turkey had joined with Communist Yugoslavia to form the "Balkan Pact," an alliance directed against the USSR and implicitly backed by the United States).

In 1949, only a handful of the original NATO members could have met the criteria that NATO established in July 1997 for Poland, the Czech Republic, and Hungary in regard to democracy, human rights, and treatment of minorities.[7] In 1949, the United States still had Jim Crow laws on the books throughout the American South—and de facto segregation of Afro-Americans throughout the rest of the country, not to mention in the U.S. military itself, despite President Truman's efforts after 1948 to desegregate the U.S. military.[8]

Britain and France, America's key European military partners, were still repressing—sometimes with great brutality—anticolonial independence movements in Africa, the Mideast, and Asia. The original NATO treaty in fact required its members to defend the Algerian departments of France.[9] The Soviets were not altogether inaccurate in the 1950s when they denounced NATO as an imperialist alliance. With the exception of Spain, the USSR was the only European imperial power not invited to join NATO. And in fact the Soviets asked to join in 1954.[10] The Suez crisis of 1956 revealed to the United States, Britain, and France just how confused were their understandings of the role of the NATO alliance in maintaining European colonial empires. Spain, which also clung to its North African possessions, had a bilateral security treaty with the United States. Military cooperation between the United States and Spain was of critical importance to NATO's Mediterranean posture, as testified to by Spain's eventual accession to NATO.

Few if any of the founding fathers of NATO either intended or anticipated that NATO would cease being a coalition of distinct national forces. The French have yet to accept its transformation into an agency of partial denationalization. Throughout the NATO zone, partially denationalized militaries have accepted specialized roles within a more or less integrated multilateral coalition. With the exception of France, NATO states that could afford nuclear weapons, long-range delivery systems, and command and control systems necessary for these weapons have chosen instead to rely on U.S. systems. (Even France may have accepted from the United States critical technological assistance for its nuclear weapons systems.)[11]

National militaries have come under the control of parliamentary bodies dominated by middle classes committed to the values of civil society—especially human rights. These values, codified by the 1975 Helsinki accords and various documents of the European Union, are not those of nationalist *Realpolitik* of the 1871–1945 period or even of the 1949–67 period. They are the democratic values of what might be called the Brussels syndrome.

THE BRUSSELS SYNDROME

The Brussels syndrome at the end of the cold war was a self-perpetuating cycle in which ever-intensifying military-technological competition between the United States and USSR had perpetuated a partial denationalization of defense policy unanticipated by the founders of NATO, in large part because of the unexpected interaction of the military and economic coalitions of Western Europe formed during 1949–51.

'Hegemony on the Cheap.'

In this division of labor, the United States assumed responsibility for nuclear weapons and high-tech/ global power projection forces.

This was the practical consequence of article 5 of the North Atlantic Treaty: "an armed attack against one or more [members] in Europe or North America shall be considered an attack against them all." Article 5 had left open just what collective defense meant in practice. Over time, collective defense came to mean a division of labor that David Calleo called "hegemony on the cheap"—that is, reliance on U.S. nuclear weapons to offset Soviet conventional forces and also the Soviet nuclear threat.[12] This was extended deterrence. It meant that the Germans and other NATO members could renounce nuclear weapons in return for the American guarantee to pursue a policy of nuclear deterrence against both the conventional and nuclear forces of the USSR. The NATO division of labor on nuclear weapons evolved in part because of the unwillingness of either the Americans or the Europeans to provide the ninety-six divisions envisioned by the Lisbon force goals of 1952, or to meet the conventional requirements of flexible response, formally adopted as NATO doctrine in 1967.

The United States provided a nuclear guarantee to nonnuclear states and concentrated most of its military expenditures on the power-projection forces of the Navy and Air Force, although there was a serious and very expensive effort to develop a reinforcement capability for the Army forces in Europe and East Asia. The regional allies of the United States came to bear the responsibility for most conventional ground forces and increasingly expensive logistics systems. Thus collective defense turned into partially denationalized defense. The smaller NATO members eagerly embraced this division of labor, partly for economic reasons and partly because the NATO system effectively constrained Germany and other potential European powers. Public opinion in many NATO countries, particularly Germany, was generally against the acquisition of national nuclear weapons, even in the "Multilateral Force" variant considered by NATO in the late 1950s and early 1960s.[13] Sweden, a neutral, rejected the idea of becoming a declared nuclear weapons state. And the United States came to prefer bearing the costs of NATO's nuclear forces in order to retain exclusive command. Over time, however, Washington increasingly groused about "free riding" on U.S. defense budgets. The Europeans responded with complaints that the United States did not truly consult with them on alliance policy but merely informed them as to what Washington had decided would be NATO policy, particularly on nuclear issues.

The division of labor in military responsibilities often provoked misgivings in the larger states with economic-technological resources sufficient for independent national defense postures, including nuclear weapons. National military industries and their employees were often forced to surrender to U.S. defense contractors. European defense experts suffered recurrent nightmares that no U.S. president would ever in fact sacrifice Chicago for Hamburg. But no NATO member other than France was willing to assume the full costs of replacing the American nuclear guarantee. During the cold war, the United Kingdom mainly for financial reasons became increasingly dependent on U.S. systems to maintain its membership in the nuclear club.

From Warfare to Welfare

The dynamic of denationalization was reinforced by other unintended consequences of reliance on the U.S. nuclear guarantee. Calleo argues that when the colonial armies of Europe returned home from their former empires during the 1950s and early 1960s, European politicians found no reason to deploy these troops against the Warsaw Treaty Organization or to transfer expenditures for colonial forces to additional military expenditures for NATO.[14] Instead, according to Calleo, European politicians preferred to spend the "end-of-empire dividend" on European social-welfare entitlements—often double those of the United States. Thus, changing national budgetary priorities froze European defense ministries into a dependency relationship with the United States, even when Europe's economies could have sustained independent national military structures. Put another way, the U.S. warfare expenditures were indirect subsidies for European welfare systems.[15] Once these entitlements became part of the European social contract, no political leader outside of France was willing to threaten social expenditures by raising defense expenditures. And, in truth, France did not fully fund its "all horizons" security policy.

Foreign Trade and Alliance Cohesion

NATO promoted postwar economic recovery in Europe and in particular the explosive growth in foreign trade. This relationship has often been noted in the U.S. willingness to open its markets to the products of its military allies not only in Europe but East Asia. John Ruggie explains this in terms of a larger project of "embedded liberalism": the management of currency ratios of currencies by the Bretton Woods System (1944) and the International Monetary Fund; the Marshall Plan (1948–52) emphasis not only on national recovery but on intra-European trade; the systemic reduction of trade barriers by the General Agreement on Trade and Tariffs of 1947; the European Initiatives for the European Coal and Steel Community (ECSC, 1950); and finally the 1957 Treaty of Rome creating of the European Economic Community (EEC).[16]

But perhaps just as important to the initial development of intraeuropean trade and investment was the acceptance of the unwritten rule of the American alliance system: members can no longer go to war against their traditional enemies—France against Germany, Germany against the low countries, Korea against Japan, and so on. This condition, specifically mentioned in Robert Schuman's argument for the establishment of the ECSC, also applied to the Marshal Plan and then to NATO. (Admittedly, Greece and Turkey have frequently tried to violate this rule.)

In other words, membership in the U.S. alliance system meant that long-term investments either in export industries at home or direct foreign investment in neighboring European countries no longer ran the risks of disappearing into the maelstrom of great power military conflicts. This dynamic also applied to investment and trade with U.S. allies outside Europe. Eventually, the "unthinkability" of war among the European NATO allies came to rest mainly on the economic interdependence that developed under the auspices of the EEC/EC/EU. But this economic interdependence had developed in interaction with security interdependence. As for trade and investment with the socialist countries—COCOM (the Coordinating Commission for Multilateral Export Controls) simply ruled out large-scale economic ties with the East. During the cold war, military adversaries deliberately avoided economic interdependence.

From Freeriders to Subcontractors

The transformation of U.S. NATO allies from "freeriders" to European subcontractors for the "out-of-area" interests of the other U.S. allies was another element of the syndrome. All major U.S. allies—in East Asia, the Middle East, as well as Europe, came to have real stakes in distant regions where they could count on the regional alliances brokered by the United States to take care of their interests. And in their own regions their own defense expenditures in effect served the out-of-area interests of the distant members of the extended American alliance system, better described as the extended alliance of Atlantic and Pacific democracies.[17] Put another way, the Germans and Japanese found that the American alliance system was far cheaper than the cost of empire, with no loss in markets. The consequence was for NATO members to further solidify the structuring of national armed forces for regional missions and subregional missions, rather than the continental and overseas missions that even Belgium and Portugal had assigned to their armed forces during the early years of NATO.

Military Technology: from Spin-off to Spin-on

The efficiency of the NATO division of labor in defense expenditures contributed to alliance-wide economic developments that multiplied the economic and technological resources available to NATO militaries, including the United States. The dramatic economic expansion of the civilian economic bases of America's allies, especially in the Japanese case, had a number of unanticipated consequences of great military significance. One, noted by Robert Samuels, is that the Western defense ministries benefited enormously during the 1970s and 1980s by the shift of technological innovation from defense-unique industries to civilian-oriented "dual-use" industries.[18] Thus, NATO military industries benefited from the "spin-on" effect of the shift in major innovation to the civilian sector in Western economies.

By the end of the cold war, American superiority in military technology came to be based on the superiority of U.S. and Allied civilian R&D over Soviet military R&D and especially on Western superiority in sophisticated manufacturing, much of it performed by transnational corporations.[19] The Soviet experience demonstrated that a superpower without rich allies and the R&D facilities of transnational corporations could neither invent nor manufacture the civilian technologies required for advanced weapons in the 1980s, even if it had steadily made massive investments in defense plants, R&D facilities, and the training of world-class scientists.[20] At the beginning of the cold war, a USSR ravaged by World War II nonetheless had the industrial infrastructure necessary to develop nuclear weapons and to launch the first earth satellite. But Soviet military technology proved to be "spin-away": the advanced military technology developed by Soviet design bureaux almost never appeared in Soviet civilian products, with the exception of civilian aircraft and nuclear power plants.[21]

Low Defense Budgets

These NATO efficiencies in turn made possible historically low defense budgets as a proportion of GDP. Greater investments for

economic growth and technological innovation in the civilian economies further multiplied the economic and scientific resources
available to NATO. The "crisis of the middle powers" which Paul
Kennedy saw in the period from 1885 to 1945 disappeared[22]: medium-sized European economies no longer exhausted their economies in hopeless efforts to provide for their own security by their
own means. Kennedy claims that in 1937 France was spending 9.1
percent of national income on defense; Italy, 14.5; Germany, 23.5;
USSR, 26.4 and Japan, 28.2 [23] For the last decade of the cold war,
the European NATO states spent 3.6 percent of gross domestic
product on defense for the years 1980–84 and 3.3 percent for the
years 1985–89, according to official NATO figures.[24]

The USSR undoubtedly became a victim of Kennedy's "imperial
overstretch," but the United States did not. Compared to the defense budgets of NATO's first years, relative U.S. spending on defense during the cold war dropped after the highs of the early
Eisenhower era (around 10 percent of GNP for the period 1952–
1955).[25] According to official NATO figures, U.S. defense spending
as a percentage of GDP based on current prices was 6.4 for the
years 1970–74; 5.0 for the years 1975–79; 5.8 for the years
1980–84; 6.3 percent for the years 1985–89.[26] According to William Lee, defense spending for the USSR rose from 10–12% of
GDP in the late 1950s to 27 to 29 percent in the late 1980s.[27]

Added Values

The fusion of NATO and EU efficiencies produced a West European peace and prosperity which in turn sustained a social contract that placed political power in the democratic agencies of a
civil society thoroughly dominated by the middle classes. These
classes insisted upon standards of human rights that practitioners
of nineteenth-century *Realpolitik* would have regarded as socialist
utopianism. And all NATO politicians were required on pain of
electoral defeat to compete with each other in increasing or at least
maintaining the entitlements promised by the new social contract.
This was an enormous change—the end of the clear class divisions
that had characterized Europe since Roman times. Western
Europe was no longer the metropole of colonialism, nationalist
warfare, and recurrent pogroms against religious and ethnic minorities. By the mid 1970s, Europe offered the world several models of social-market economies advertised as considerably more
humane than the American system. The Brussels syndrome was
thus a process of continually adding not only value to the alliance

but adding democratic values as well. As noted by James Huntley and Brian Beedham, the Atlantic allies acquired—by historical stealth—an ideology of their own in the course of opposing the ideology of their military rival.[28] In Beedham's version: "The curious fate of the Atlantic democracies, which thought during their struggles with Hitler and Stalin that they were the anti-ideologists, is to discover now that they are in fact the guardians of what may be the last and best of the ideologies."[29]

Transformation of the Political Culture of the NATO Officer Corps

Perhaps the most discussed transformation, especially in the American case, has been that worked by what Eisenhower called the military-scientific complex and the military-industrial complex. C. Wright Mills was the first to point out that in the early cold war the senior levels of U.S. military were mimicking a civilian scientific/managerial "power elite." The course of economic and scientific development from 1945 placed a premium not only on scientific-technical knowledge for both civilian and military elites but on cosmopolitan managerial experiences and broad knowledge of foreign cultures. The career tracks of NATO officer corps probably may have placed even greater emphasis on familiarity with international affairs, foreign languages, and cultures. Probably no other Western career required so much recurrent schooling at ever-higher levels, usually in multinational settings.

All of the developments cited above had the effect of breaking previous linkages of national officer corps to conservative nationalist elites and the conservative nationalist values of nineteenth-century Europe and North America. Officer ranks were depleted of the sons of British peers, of Prussian Junkers, and of planters from the Old South. NATO officer ranks opened to the grandsons and even the granddaughters of the Afro-American slaves who had toiled for the founders of the Continental Army of 1776. The identification of the European militaries with spit-and-polish mentalities, authoritarian politics, blood-and-soil nationalism, the irredentism of territory and diaspora, religious conservatism, anti-Semitism, hostility to ethnic and religious minorities—all of these changed markedly. By the time of the Helsinki accords, NATO and the EC had together shifted the focus of European militaries to high-tech responsibilities inside a multinational coalition of democratic states united by shared values of human rights—including the rights of ethnic, religious minorities. The American military went through a similar but distinct internal transformation.[30]

Ideological Subversion of Enemy Regimes (Soft Power)

   Political democracy, economic wealth, social justice, and vibrant culture made NATO societies increasingly attractive to the citizens and soldiers of the enemy camp. The NATO/EU states became the "normal" countries by whose standards the citizens of East Central Europe came to judge their Communist rulers. Communist parties had expected their socioeconomic achievements to be judged by the standards of the Great Depression, not those of the Ku-Dam, West Berlin's glittering boulevard of consumerism, culture, and political self-expression. For East European critics of Communism, such as Vaclav Havel, the minimum acceptable socioeconomic norms were nothing less than the highest standards ever achieved in human history for per capita productivity, per capita consumption, and human freedom. If in fact U.S. defense budgets had subsidized the NATO social-market economies, such indirect expenditures on the soft power of the European democracies probably inflicted more damage on the Warsaw Pact (WP) than did the U.S. expenditures on military hardware.

The Brussels Syndrome After the Cold War: "Go East or Go Out of Business"

   After the political disintegration of the Warsaw Pact, the Council for Mutual Economic Assistance (CMEA), the USSR, Czechoslovakia, and Yugoslavia NATO discovered that it was morally impossible to confine the virtuous circle of the Brussels syndrome to Western Europe, though this was certainly the initial Alliance preference. [31] The ultimate rationale for NATO—and its annual budgets—was not safeguarding the careers of the NATO officer corps but managing genuine security threats. It took the disintegration of three Communist states and the savage ethno-nationalist wars in the former Yugoslavia for Brussels to understand that the security threat in Europe was not that of a single powerful state. It was not even that of a coalition of states, such as the Huntingtonian Union of Russia, Belarus, and Yugoslavia advocated by Alexander Lukashenko during the spring of 1999 or Yevgeny Primakov's even more unlikely coalition of Russia, India, and China.
   The military threat in Europe was the return of civil-military cultures on the pre-World War II or Soviet models, whether in Milosevic's Serbia, Meciar's Slovakia, or Yeltsin's Russia. If the Atlantic Alliance was to maintain its credibility as a provider of European security, NATO had to risk its credibility by responding in unprec-

edented ways to new security problems. To preserve the Brussels syndrome, the alliance had to extend it eastward. And to NATO's surprise, the Warsaw Pact had partially prepared its non-Soviet members for inclusion in the Atlantic Alliance.

THE WARSAW PACT WAS NEVER WHAT IT USED TO BE

The accidental historical role of the Warsaw Pact has been the partial preparation of former Soviet bloc allies, including East Germany, for membership in NATO by denationalizing security policies in the region. The primary legacy of the WP in Central and Eastern Europe was to deprive all its members but Russia and perhaps Ukraine of the military-industrial capabilities, national security bureaucracies, military-diplomatic training institutions, and the domestic political cultures to develop independent national defense postures and policies.

The WP thus left postcommunist elites of the former Soviet bloc, including the westernmost union republics of the USSR, in a situation of "path dependency" on coalition structures for credible national security policies. After Soviet troops withdrew from the region, the former WP states did not seek to "renationalize" security policy. They sought to join the surviving European military alliance system, albeit with frequent doubts and often something less than widespread public support. But despite occasional reconsiderations, members of both the Communist *nomenklatura* and the dissident intelligentsia appear to have accepted the basic supranational premises of the official "socialist internationalism" of the Soviet bloc[32]: there can be no effective "nationalist" solutions to the problems of military security, economic development, and technological innovation in contemporary Europe. Of course, the heirs of the Communist bloc rejected any restoration of their subordination to Moscow or any restoration of the domestic policies which Moscow once defined as "real socialism."

With parallel logic, the former WP states have asked for membership in the rival economic coalition of the CMEA. In applying to both NATO and the EU they have easily embraced the political requirement formerly demanded of WP/CMEA members: a political system based on common domestic norms. This included the accountability of each national regime to the ideological standards of the political center. The Moscow center had vested power in a *nomenklatura* that claimed to represent an international working class. Brussels was a decentralized center circuitously accountable to the ruling middle classes of Western Europe. The new members of NATO have also had to accept another familiar though probably unexpected norm: support of military intervention (in Yugoslavia) in the name of defending the core ideological values of the alliance. The "internationalism" of the Soviet bloc was thus unintended (and less than adequate) preparation for the multilateralism of the NATO/EU system, including its most recent manifestation in the Balkans.

Although the internal workings of the two cold war blocs were quite different, they both had the effect of partially denationalizing the external economic and security policies of their members and of requiring a shared set of domestic political values. There are, of course, significant "nationalist" challengers to the "Westernizers/ multilateralists" in the former Warsaw Pact states.[33] But so far the Westernizers have won the policy debates on security matters, even if these pro-NATO politicians have often disappointed Brussels in carrying out military reforms and meeting NATO's political, fiscal, administrative, and technological standards.[34]

The membership terms set by NATO in 1995 are almost devoid of "strategic" requirements in the cold war sense. The 1995 NATO study on enlargement identified the following requirements: democratic political institutions, civilian control of national militaries by elected officials, the rule of law through independent judicial systems, civil rights for individuals and minority groups, and resolution of outstanding problems of borders and diaspora.[35] The study did call for the development of military interoperability with NATO on multiple levels: national staffs, communications, logistics, weaponry, and so on. But the prerequisite for such military interoperability was a corresponding set of alliance standards for domestic politics.[36] From the perspective of European military history, the requirements of NATO enlargement and integration are extraordinary: they call for a continuation of the cold war "denationalization" of security culture.

After some brief experiments in regional multilateralism (the Pentagonal Group, the Visegrad Group) and neutralism (very briefly in both Slovakia and Bulgaria), all of the former Warsaw Pact states have filed applications to NATO, plus Estonia, Latvia, Lithuania, and Slovenia. Mark Kramer has recently argued that the decision of former Warsaw Pact states (except Russia) to remain nonnuclear military states is probably a function of their goal of achieving NATO membership. He also concludes that their nuclear policies (influenced by NATO) refute "realist" predictions that Europe would revert to its pre-cold war patterns for national security. That is: respond to an anarchic situation by maximizing the state's independent military capabilities, including the acquisition of weapons of mass destruction.[37] In pursuit of NATO membership, former WP states have also upheld the broader multilateral regimes of the Non-Proliferation Treaty and the arms control regimes associated with the OSCE. In other words, faced with the expense and uncertainties of becoming independent nuclear weapons states, the former members of the WP have opted for security dependence on an external coalition.

In contrast, none of the cold war European neutrals have filed applications for NATO membership (with the special exception of Slovenia, once part of neutral Yugoslavia). During the cold war Austria, Finland, Sweden, and Ireland developed their own "national" solutions to the problems of democratic civil-military relations, the problems of national minorities and diaspora, and the issue of nuclear weapons. So has Switzerland. To date, all five of these neutrals have found participation in NATO's Partnership for Peace a means of reconciling traditional policies of neutrality (that is, continued "nationalization" of defense) with ad-hoc cooperation with NATO on multilateral projects such as European peacekeeping. Perhaps their continued status as neutrals can be dismissed as freeriding on NATO. But none of the former WP states have chosen to be either free riders or neutrals, despite the proximity of the Austrian, Swiss, Finnish, and Swedish models.

For the foreseeable future, NATO does not need any of the former neutrals as new members. For them to join now would only confirm Russia's worst fears, particularly in the cases of Finland and Sweden. These states already have their own national variants on democratic civil-military relations, have renounced Weapons of Mass Destruction, and are secure in their belief that fellow members of the EU and the broader community of Atlantic democracies would not abandon them in the event of a military threat from Russia. Keeping the former neutrals out of NATO would highlight the poorly articulated but nonetheless operative rationale for NATO enlargement: expanding civil society eastward by subordinating national military establishments to Alliance standards on human rights and civil-military relations. The *quid pro quo* for the former Communist states willing to partially surrender their newly-gained national sovereignty is 1) a level of external security they could never achieve by purely national efforts,[38] and 2) the expectation of eventual membership in the European Union. In other words, the rationale for NATO enlargement in the former Warsaw Pact zone is to accept Brussels as the heir of Moscow.

THE WARSAW PACT'S PRINCIPAL STRATEGIC LEGACY: DENATIONALIZATION OF GERMAN SECURITY POLICY

Perhaps the important military-strategic legacy of the Warsaw Pact was its role in the denationalization of the National Peoples' Army of the German Democratic Republic and its contribution to the partial denationalization of the Bundeswehr of the Federal Republic of Germany (FRG).[39] Of course, the WP must share credit for this historical achievement with its adversarial collaborators: NATO and the leaders of the Federal Republic.

During the period from October 1989 to November 1990, Moscow and Brussels discovered a shared WP-NATO legacy of the partial denationalization of German security policy as demonstrated by their policies during the following sequence of events[40]:

1) The Soviet decision not to use armed force to reverse the collapse of Communist parties in the GDR and other WP states during October–November, 1989[41]; and Western pledges during 1989 and 1990 not to exploit the collapse of the GDR to improve the military position of NATO.[42]

2) Gorbachev's remarkably rapid acceptance in the spring of 1990 of German unification and the absorption of the National Peoples' Army into the Bundeswehr on the implicit understanding that the FRG would maintain its nonnuclear defensive military posture and actually reduce the armed forces of united Germany to a level below that maintained by the FRG during the cold war.[43]

3) Gorbachev's acceptance in July of 1990 of the membership of united Germany in NATO on the implicit understandings that NATO would maintain its commitment to the Helsinki settlement of 1975, that NATO states would sign the Conventional Forces in Europe Treaty in November 1990, and that the United States would observe the existing nuclear weapons treaties with the USSR and negotiate much lower levels of nuclear forces.[44]

4) The grudging tolerance by Gorbachev's successors of the first round of NATO enlargement. NATO membership for Poland, Hungary, and the Czech Republic had the effect of converting three of the FRG's eastern neighbors into NATO members and thus locking in the denationalization of the security policies of the states on the immediate borders to the east, north, and west. The first round of enlargement also evoked an equally grudging acceptance by the "realist

school" of Western commentators. But the Western critics of enlargement remain skeptical that NATO will have a "democratizing" and "denationalizing" effect on the new NATO members from the former WP. The argument here is that the "path dependency" of former WP members on coalition structures was in large part a consequence of the WP-NATO dynamics of denationalizing German security policy. The corollary is that their membership in NATO is in part a strategy of locking-in the denationalization of German security policy.

The primary integrative legacies of the Warsaw Pact for NATO are thus

1) The continued denationalization/denuclearization of German security policies in the post-1990 Federal Republic and the limitation of the military potential of unified Germany through reaffirmation of FRG membership in NATO.
2) The dual impact of NATO's first round of enlargement: a) preservation of the denationalized/denuclearized security postures of Poland, the Czech Republic, and Hungary; and b) the revalidation of German reliance on NATO to meet Berlin's immediate regional security needs in the East.
3) The possible preservation of denationalization/denuclearization of security postures in other Warsaw Pact states through further rounds of NATO enlargement.

ENLARGEMENT AND INTERVENTION

At the 23–24 April 1999 celebration in Washington of NATO's 50th anniversary, American and European leaders proclaimed their own "Brezhnev doctrine": a commitment to use armed force to defend and enforce the ideological values shared by the Atlantic democracies. The Allies defined these values as "democracy, human rights and the rule of law" in a statement justifying their decision of mid April to launch air attacks on Serbia.[45] NATO's objective was to force Yugoslavia's leader, Slobodan Milosevic, to halt his policy of "oppression, ethnic cleansing and violence" against the Kosovar Muslim population of Kosovo.[46]

The Milosevic state-building project for greater Serbia that began in 1987–89 has been that of "renationalizing" Yugoslavia's multiethnic federation by stratagems that were thoroughly "European" in their historical precedents.[47] But after the 1995 Bosnian-Serb massacres of hundreds of Bosnian Muslims at Srebrenica while UN soldiers looked away, NATO governments for the first time responded effectively to the threat posed by early twentieth-century European nationalism to postcommunist Europe. Led by the United States, NATO struck with high-tech air power, first in Bosnia in 1995 and in Serbia/Kosovo in 1999.

Deliberately or not, European, American, and Canadian leaders not only affirmed at their Washington meeting a "human rights" mission for NATO, but linked this mission to the process of further NATO enlargement and further cooperative engagement with Russia, Ukraine, and other states. Despite all the vagaries of NATO's air war[48] and the NATO-UN occupation of Kosovo, the logic linking Alliance policies on Kosovo with NATO engagement has been historical rather than haphazard.[49] The rationale for NATO's war in Kosovo and for NATO enlargement evolved from the "ideological" effect of the cold war on the two competing European military alliances. Particularly after the Helsinki agreements, each alliance had to develop a set of core ideological values for the reciprocal purposes of obligatory ideological polemics.[50] To be sure, future NATO actions in defense of human rights will be at times and places of NATO's own choosing, reflecting the misgivings of European and North American publics about such a radical transformation of their alliance. But NATO's cold war doctrines—massive retaliation and flexible response—always had their intra-alliance critics, perhaps for even better reasons.[51]

NATO's spontaneous declaration of war to defend the human rights of ethnic/religious minorities against the authoritarian-nationalist regime of Milosevic coincided with a series of carefully planned NATO declarations[52] covering NATO's past, its program for continued enlargement, its relationship with the West European Union and the European Union, its cooperation with members Partnership For Peace, its special programs for Russia and Ukraine, its intention to set in motion an economic reconstruction program for all of southeastern Europe, and its articulation of guidelines for a new "strategic concept." The "strategic concept" was short on concept and long on guidelines for organizing and deploying multinational configurations (Combined Joint Task Forces), with participation by non-NATO forces and cooperation with the Organization for Cooperation and Security in Europe, UN, and the International Criminal Tribunal for Yugoslavia (ICTY). Such configurations represent an implicit commitment on the part of participants to a denationalization of security policy.

The conceptual content of the April 1999 Strategic Concept remained open to further definition, reflecting the continuing internal debate over future missions. But the military victory in Kosovo may have resolved many of the intra-NATO political disputes, both about strategic concepts, further enlargement, and further cooperative engagement with Russia and Ukraine. After Kosovo, NATO's post-cold war mission is crystallizing as that of preserving the cold war partial denationalization of state security policies by expanding the membership and responsibilities of a multinational alliance now based on common democratic values and the emerging precedents of the ICTY. While putting in place the NATO-UN occupation forces for Kosovo's transition to an elected government, NATO and the EU called upon Serbs to abandon Milosevic and ultimately pursue membership in Brussel's military and economic structures—structures both transnational and democratic. One incentive for such a voluntary denationalization of security policy was the EU-US program for economic reconstruction of the entire region of southeastern Europe, including republics of the former Yugoslavia but excluding the zones controlled by Milosevic.[53] The other incentive had been the seventy-eight-day demonstration on Serbian soil of NATO's military power—or at least of U.S. air power.

En route to the 30–31 July 1999 Sarajevo meeting on Balkan reconstruction, Secretary of State Madeleine Albright stopped in Pristina, the capital of Kosovo. Reacting to the murder of fourteen Serbs a few days earlier, she warned, "You will not have the support of the world if you are intolerant and take the law into your own hands." Albright then declared, "If there is to be a true victory in Kosovo it cannot be a victory of Albanians over Serbs or NATO over Serbs. It must be a victory of those who believe in the rights of the individual over those who do not."[54] And implicitly, it must be a victory of the democratic/human rights values of a multinational coalition over the values of blood-and-soil nationalism in either its Serbian or Kosovar variant.

NATO's air attacks on Serbia had almost immediately provoked objections within the Alliance in regard both to the general idea of a "humanitarian" war and to the specific conduct of the American-led bombing campaign ("Madeleine's War").[55] Many argued that the hasty NATO decision to intervene in Yugoslavia in defense of an ethnoreligious minority constituted an assault on the conception of state sovereignty,[56] the most fundamental concept in the international system.

Pursuing this critical line in an essay entitled, "Of Crusades Old and New," the historian Walter McDougall asked, "Why should Americans enlist in the crusades preached by today's benevolent hegemonists? . . . [T]o enlarge our empire of freedom, to rekindle our idealism at home, to bolster the unity of the Western democracies and to give NATO a mission beyond self-defense?"[57] Other skeptics in Europe and America also warned about the open-ended implications of U.S. and NATO actions in Yugoslavia.[58]

Some critics objected that the NATO campaign in Kosovo jeopardized a much more important NATO interest in continued cooperation with Russia on policies related to weapons of mass destruction and European arms control[59]—not to mention the Chinese reaction to the accidental American bombing of Beijing's embassy in Belgrade.

Joseph Nye, one of the first to note the importance of "soft power" for U.S. foreign policy, wondered if the United States was not risking its claim to moral leadership by entangling itself in the ambiguities of Balkan politics.[60] For other European observers, the real lesson of Kosovo was just how far behind European militaries were in regard to U.S. capabilities for projecting power over great distances with great precision.[61] Even after the unexpected Milosevic acceptance of NATO's nonnegotiable demands on Kosovo, the German commentator Josef Joffe argued that NATO would never again undertake a mission like that in Kosovo.[62] In his view, the Kosovo war demonstrated that in a prolonged conflict over "human rights" NATO could neither accept nor inflict casualties without destroying its own unity.

Yet the opposite conclusion seems equally plausible. Key NATO leaders had demonstrated at real political risk to themselves that the Alliance could combine soft power, hard power, and staying power. One of the most eloquent justifications for NATO's policy in the former Yugoslavia came from a new member of NATO, Czech President Vaclav Havel.[63] He supported Alliance policy even though there was considerable criticism in Prague because of bitter memories of the WP invasion of Czechoslovakia. During a June visit to another NATO member, Havel told the Canadian Parliament:

This war gives human rights precedence over the rights of states. The Federal Republic of Yugoslavia has been attacked without a direct UN mandate for the Alliance's action. But the Alliance has not acted out of license, aggressiveness or disrespect for international law.

On the contrary: it has acted out of respect for the law—for the law that ranks higher than the protection of the sovereignty of states. It has acted out of respect for the rights of humanity, as they are articulated by our conscience as well as by other instruments of international law.[64]

But the critics of NATO's war in Kosovo may be correct in focusing on the tragic errors of the ill-planned bombing campaign. The haphazard tactics of the air war may have compromised NATO's human rights objectives.[65]

Victory in Kosovo led to the announcement of U.S. and EU programs that in effect sought to replicate in Southeast Europe the transforming sociopolitical experiences of Western Europe during the period from the announcement of the Marshall Plan to the creation of the EEC.[66] These highly ambitious, very expensive, and still unfunded projects recall the ambitious justifications for NATO enlargement offered by Secretary of State Albright.[67] In arguing for NATO enlargement, Albright had drawn fire for seeing unexplained connections between enlarging a military alliance designed for the cold war and supporting the development of democracy and market economies in East Central Europe. Alvin Rubinstein told a Congressional committee during the debate over admission of Poland, Hungary, and the Czech Republic: "If NATO membership is all it takes to transform nondemocratic societies and to ensure their future well-being, then why not extend this felicitous procedure to the countries of Central America, Central Africa and the Middle East? Experience teaches us otherwise: mere membership in a military alliance cannot remake a society's political culture."[68] The argument here is quite different: over the cold war NATO and the Warsaw Pact have reshaped the political security cultures of its members, in conjunction with other multilateral structures.

NATO's DEBT TO THE WARSAW PACT

NATO acquired an ideology of democracy and human rights in the course of creating and maintaining a system to rival that of the Soviet zone. Since the Madrid summit of 1997, NATO, consciously or not, has been exporting its pattern of civil-military relations to former WP members—virtually all of whom accept the logic of a coalition based on political values. Further evidence for such a conclusion emerged from the Washington, D.C., meeting on 16 July 1999 of the U.S.-Baltic Partnership Commission.

At this session Strobe Talbot, Deputy U.S. Secretary of State, told the Balts, "One of the principal lessons to come out of the Kosovo experience . . . is that security and stability of southern Europe will depend on exactly the kind of integration, institution building and democratization that are already so far advanced in northern Europe, specifically in the Baltic region." Talbot then took note of Russia's vehement objection to the membership of Estonia, Latvia, and Lithuania in NATO, but told reporters that membership for the three was "just short of inevitable . . . because of the extraordinary progress these three countries have made."[69]

The WP had referred to itself as "an alliance of a new type" precisely because it had been committed to the use of armed force in defense of its ideological formulas. The key formula justifying the "Brezhnev doctrine" of internal intervention was "joint defense of the gains of socialism against internal and external enemies."[70] In the name of values that were vital to maintaining its alliance system, Moscow had used the Warsaw Pact to violate prevailing Western conceptions of national sovereignty, first in Hungary and then in Czechoslovakia. NATO has now violated such conceptions of national sovereignty in Yugoslavia to defend the ideological principles that have become critical to the cohesion of the Atlantic alliance. Barely three weeks after joining NATO in early March of 1999, Hungary and the Czech Republic both endorsed NATO's own version of the Brezhnev doctrine.[71] To expropriate a phrase from the WP: joint defense of the gains of democracy against internal and external enemies.

NATO AND THE DENUCLEARIZATION OF EUROPEAN SECURITY

At a recent conference on "Nuclear Weapons in the Twenty-First Century," Jack Mendelsohn and Alexander Yereskovsky argued that there are multiple reasons for concluding that NATO enlargement would exacerbate tensions between Russia and NATO and considerably complicate maintaining arms control agreements in Europe for both conventional and nuclear weapons.[72] At a minimum, NATO enlargement "excludes" Russia from the club of European democracies. NATO enlargement not only draws lines that exclude Russia from "Europe," but lines that will exclude other states as well.

But by accepting such arguments, NATO would in effect cede to Russia and other former Communist states the right to define security concepts for Europe after the cold war. The postcommunist ideology of Russian security (and Serbian security) is that of statism: nation states accountable only to their domestic constituencies for the pursuit of nationalist goals. The new logic of NATO is that of upholding the mutual accountability of states to the broader European civil society made possible by the transformed multilateral structures that originated in the cold war. NATO states took the lead in drafting the OSCE statement of 19 November 1999, implicitly directed to the Russian war against Chechnya. The statement declared, "Participating states are accountable to their citizens and responsible to each other for their implementation of their OSCE commitments. We regard these commitments as our common achievement and therefore consider them to be matters of immediate and legitimate concern to all participating states."[73]

The current leaders of Russia and Serbia desire to return to a a pre-cold war Europe—the continent of Bismarck, Clemanceau, Lloyd George, Mussolini, Chamberlain, Hitler, Stalin—and de-Gaulle. In the last analysis, as demonstrated by John Mearsheimer,[74] the weapons of statist ideology are the weapons of mass destruction—above all, nuclear weapons.

At the conference noted above, several Canadian specialists on nuclear weapons policy—Senator Doug Roche, Ambassador Peggy Mason, and Bill Graham, chair of the House of Commons Standing Committee on Foreign Affairs[75]—have argued that NATO should move toward denuclearization of its security posture. Ambassador Enrique Moran-Moray, secretary-general of OPANAL (the Latin American-Caribbean organization for monitoring the region's nuclear non-proliferation treaty) has made a case for the stabilizing effects of nuclear-free zones on regional security.[76] Yerezkovsky, a former official of the Russian foreign ministry, has made specific proposals for removing U.S. nuclear weapons from NATO Europe and reconfiguring the European conventional balance to assuage Russian concerns about NATO's power projection capabilities.[77] Ambassador Thomas Graham of the United States (who played a key role in the 1995 renewal of the Nuclear Non-Proliferation Treaty) urged again that the United States and its allies adhere to the build-down provisions of the NPT in order to undercut the political prestige of nuclear weapons for states like India and Pakistan.[78] In addressing the question of why nuclear weapons confer prestige on states, Professor Jon Mercer identified the issue as that of redefining for a democratic community the terminology of WMD: the members of the nuclear club can just as well be described as hoodlums in the nuclear gang; Saddam Hussein as president of the Anthrax Club.[79]

NATO enlargement is perfectly compatible with all of the proposals above in regard to reducing or eliminating the role of nuclear weapons in European security postures and in diminishing the prestige value of nuclear weapons. In fact, enlargement may be the best instrument for achieving such goals. Paul Nitze has recently argued that the United States does not need nuclear weapons to achieve any of its security needs.[80] It has already renounced chemical and biological weapons. The same is true for NATO. According to several nuclear experts with long records of U.S. government service, U.S. high-tech weapons allow NATO to meet any conceivable military challenge without a disproportionate recourse to nuclear weapons. The only possible use for such weapons is that of "existential" deterrence against Russian nuclear forces. But the principal domestic justification for Russia's nuclear weapons in the European theater is NATO's own nuclear arsenal.

The initial impetus toward denationalization of security policy in NATO was reliance on American nuclear weapons for extended deterrence. The strategic rationale for these nuclear forces was to deter Soviet conventional forces. No such conventional threat now exists, not even from Russia.

To repeat: NATO's nuclear weapons were initially deployed to defend against a conventional threat. To repeat: there no longer is such a conventional danger. What Alliance nuclear forces now bestow on NATO members is a Russian nuclear threat.[81] In the past, Moscow's nuclear threat had also come to justify an existing American nuclear guarantee against Moscow's conventional forces.[82] The American nuclear guarantee had also had the collateral effect of driving the denationalization of security policy within NATO as states voluntarily renounced deployment of their own nuclear weapons. This development in turn helped propel processes of economic integration and the democratization of civil-military relations. That was the cold war.

Now that the Soviet conventional threat has disappeared, the best way to preserve the denationalization of the security within NATO originally driven by the U.S. guarantee of extended nuclear deterrence might well be an alliance-wide policy of extended denuclearization. Such a policy would reaffirm the dependence of each member on the coalition as a whole for the kind of military resources identified by Nitze. It would also open up the possibility for Russia to form a security community with NATO states, if Russia truly becomes part of the community of European democracies. An effective European security community is probably not possible as long as Russia, the United States, France, and Britain each insist on maintaining large national nuclear forces. Again: nuclear weapons are the weapons of statist ideologies.[83]

Nitze once observed that in the period from 1947 to 1953 the United States had actually pursued its own best interests when it had acted in the interests of a broader international community. According to Nitze, "The moment [beginning with the Eisenhower administration] we began to emphasize that our policy was directed primarily toward the pursuit of United States aims and interests, other nations were forced to look more closely to their own narrow interests."[84] The United States in 1999 may have options comparable to those Nitze saw in the period from 1947–53: the capacity to shape itself and its principal allies either in the image of Westphalian nation states or in the image of members of a broad, quasi-confederal, democratic community.[85] James Huntley has identified a potential community of democratic states located mainly around the shores of America's eastern, western, and southern oceans.[86] This democratic community possesses unsurpassed economic, technological, and cultural resources. It is bound together by common democratic principles, even if these principles are presently applied very differently from state to state. Nineteen of these states are now members of NATO. More are likely to apply, including at least one from Latin America.[87]

The dynamic of NATO enlargement now requires that the United States and NATO ask themselves again a very difficult question: do nuclear weapons belong in the arsenal of democracy? To answer this question, NATO's members must first ask themselves another question: what became of their cold war alliance? The answer offered here: NATO has evolved into an agency of democratization, denationalization, and the defense of human rights.

NOTES

1. Robert M. Haden, J.D., Ph.D, director, Center for Russian and East European Studies, University of Pittsburgh. Remarks of 6 December 1999, Woodrow Wilson International Center for Scholars.

2. Marc Lacey, "Summit in Turkey Places New Limits on Europe's Arms," *New York Times*, 20 November 1999, p. A-1; A-5.

3. Mikhail Alexeev, "Russia's 'Cold Peace' Consensus: Transcending the Presidential Elections," *Fletcher Forum* 21 (spring–summer 1997): 33–49 for a discussion of the shift from the Gorbachev paradigm of "internationalism" to the subsequent paradigm of state-centered nationalism. For an examination of the development of postcommunist Russian nationalism see Vera Tolz, "Conflicting 'Homeland Myths' and Nation-State Building in Postcommunist Russia," *Slavic Review* 57, no. 2 (summer 1998).

4. A number of observers have come to see the Helsinki accords as a turning

point in the nature of the Atlantic alliance and/or a turning point in the cold war, precisely because of the adoption of an "ideology" of human rights. The adoption appeared haphazard at the time, but historical in retrospect. Robert M. Gates, *From the Shadows: The Ultimate Insider's Story of Five Presidents and How They Won the Cold War* (New York: Simon and Schuster, 1996). See the chapters covering the Nixon and Carter administrations. See also James E. Goodby, *Europe Undivided: The New Logic of Peace in US-Russian Relations* (U.S. Institute of Peace, 1998), chap. 5.

5. See text of North Atlantic Treaty in <www.nat.int/docu/basictxt/treaty/htm>.

6. Marc Lacey, "Clinton Tries to Subdue Greeks' Anger at America," *New York Times*, 21 November 1999, p. A-6.

7. These descriptions of NATO civil-military relations can be found in the following extracts from chap. 1 "Purposes and Principles of NATO Enlargement" from the NATO document "Study on NATO Enlargement-September, 1995" in <NATODATA@cc1.kuleuven.ac.be>. Chapter 1 identifies the purposes of enlargement as "encouraging and supporting . . . civilian and democratic control over the military . . . fostering in new members of the alliance the patterns and habits of cooperation, consultation and consensus which characterize relations among current allies. . . . reinforcing the tendency toward integration and cooperation in Europe based on shared democratic values and thereby curbing the countervailing tendency toward disintegration along ethnic and territorial lines."

8. Richard M. Dalfiume, *Desegregation of the US Armed Forces: Fighting on Two Fronts* (Columbia: University of Missouri Press, 1969), chaps. 7, 8, 9.

9. "The North Atlantic Treaty", article 6: "For the purpose of Article 5, an armed attack on one or more of the Parties is deemed to include an armed attack:—on the territory of any of the Parties in Europe or North America, or on the Algerian Departments of France." This provision remained operative until 3 July 1962. See text of North Atlantic Treaty in <www.nat.int/docu/basictxt/treaty/htm>.

10. Anatoly Ivanovich Gribkov (former chief of staff, Warsaw Pact), *Sud'ba Varshavskogo Dogovora* (Moscow; Russkaia kniga, 1998), 16. The context of this statement is as follows, from p. 15:

At the Berlin meeting of foreign ministers of the USSR, USA, England and France, which took place from the 25th of January to 18 February, 1954, the Soviet government proposed the conclusion of a general European treaty on collective security. The goal of such a treaty—was a mutual renunciation of the use of force and of the threat of force., **to dissolve all existing alliances** (Gribkov's emphasis) and to resolve all contested questions by exclusively peaceful means. The proposal of the Soviet government was not adopted. (p.16) ". . . in the course of the Berlin meeting and afterward the ministers and state representatives of the Western countries broadly propagandized their thesis about the defensive character of the North Atlantic Pact. By this means they wanted to weaken the impact of the Soviet proposal for the establishment of a system of collective security in Europe.

In connection with this on 31 March 1954 the Soviet government proposed a diplomatic step: it sent a note (text of the note in the Appendix [pp.192–195 of the Gribkov book]) to the USA, England and France in which the USSR proposed that they consider the participation of the Soviet Union in the North Atlantic Pact, based on the assurances of its founders that this treaty has a defensive character. The Soviet government also declared that it did not see obstacles to the participation of the USA in the proposed treaty on collective security in Europe.

The official history of Soviet foreign policy edited by A. A. Gromyko and B. N. Ponomarev omits mention of the USSR's application to NATO or to the diplomatic note contained on pp. 192–95 of the Gribkov volume. See Gromyko and Ponomarev, eds., *Istoriia vneshnei politiki SSSR, 1945–1980* (Moscow: Nauka, 1981), chap. 22, esp. pp. 188–190. See also chap. 20 where this issue is omitted. Mikhail Alexeev, now a US-based scholar, remembers learning in a Soviet secondary school that the USSR applied to NATO.

11. Richard Ullman, "The Covert French Connection," *Foreign Policy* 75 (summer 1989).

12. David P. Calleo, *Beyond American Hegemony: The Future of the Western Alliance* (New York: Basic Books, 1987), 110–14.

13. See Marc Trachtenberg, *A Constructed Peace: The Making of the European Settlement, 1945–1963* (Princeton: Princeton University Press, 1999), chap. 5, "Eisenhower and Nuclear Sharing."

14. Calleo, *Beyond American Hegemony*, chap. 3.

15. *Ibid.*, 109–14.

16. John Ruggie, *Winning the Peace* (New York: Columbia University Press, 1996).

17. James R. Huntley, *Pax Democratica* (New York: St. Martins, 1998).

18. Richard J. Samuels, *Rich Nation, Strong Army: The Technological Transformation of Japan* (Ithaca: Cornell University Press, 1994), chap. 1.

19. John Deutch, Arnold Kanter, and Brent Scowcroft in "Saving NATO's Foundation, *Foreign Affairs* 78, no. 6 (November–December 1999) argue that plans for a European defense identity in military production could undermine the military-industrial-technological cooperation of the United States and its European allies.

20. Willian Odom, *The Collapse of the Soviet Military* (New Haven: Yale University Press, 1998), chap. 4.

21. Clifford Gaddy, *The Price of the Past: Russia's Struggle In the Legacy of a Militarized Economy* (Washington, D.C.: Brookings, 1996).

22. Paul Kennedy, *The Rise and Fall of the Great Powers* (New York: Random House, 1987). See chap. 6, "The Coming of a Bipolar World and the Crisis of the 'Middle Powers': Part Two, 1919–1942."

23. *Ibid.*, 296, 332.

24. "Documentation: Defense Expenditures of NATO Countries, 1975–1997," *NATO Review*, no. 1 (spring 1998): D-15, table 3.

25. John Lewis Gaddis, *Strategies of Containment* (New York: Oxford University Press), 359.

26. "Documentation . . ."

27. William T. Lee, *CIA Estimates of Soviet Military Expenditures* (Washington, DC: AEI Press, 1995), 161.

28. Huntley, *Pax Democratica*. Huntley has provided a historical overview of this process in the chapter entitled, "How the Democracies Saved Democracy."

29. Brian Beedham, "A Survey of the New Geopolitics: The Road to 2050," *The Economist* (31 July–6 August 1999): 13.

30. See Charles C. Moskos and John Sibley Butler, *All That We Can Be: Black Leadership and Racial Integration the Army Way* (New York: Basic Books, 1996).

31. See James A. Baker (with Thomas M. DeFrank), *The Politics of Diplomacy: Revolution, War and Peace, 1989–1992* (New York: G. P. Putnam's Sons 1995), 641.

And now, as this is being written (1995), the "humanitarian nightmare" in the heart of Europe continues. I do not believe it could have been prevented by any combination of political, diplomatic and economic pressures. In my opinion, the only way it might have been prevented or reversed would have been through the application of substantial military force early on, with all of the costs, particularly in lives, that that would have entailed—and, by everyone's reckoning, in that environment the casualties would have been staggering. President Bush's decision that our national interest did not require the United States of America to fight its fourth war in Europe in this century, with the loss of America's sons and daughters that would have ensured, was absolutely the right one. We cannot be, and should not be expected to be, the world's policemen, and the necessary support by the American people for the degree of force that would have been required in Bosnia could never have been built or maintained.

32. For an overview of "socialist internationalism" as a conceptual framework developed by Moscow to integrate and coordinate Warsaw Pact/CMEA policies in regard to security, economics, culture, and politics, see Teresa Rakowska Harmstone, *Warsaw Pact Integration* (Stanford: Hoover, 1989).

33. Sabrina Petra Ramet, *Whose Democracy: Nationalism, Religion and the Doctrine of Collective Rights in Post 1989 Eastern Europe* (Lantham, MD: Rowman and Littlefield, 1997); Ramet, ed., *The Radical Right in Central and Eastern Europe Since 1989* (University Park, PA: Penn State Press, 1999). See also Vladimir Tismaneanu, *Fantasies of Salvation: Democracy, Nationalism and Myth in Post-Communist Europe* (Princeton: Princeton University Press, 1998).

34. See Jeffry Simon, "Partnership for Peace: After the Washington Summit and Kosovo," *Strategic Forum*, no. 167, August 1999 (Institute for National Strategic Studies, National Defense University). See also Daniel M. Nelson, Thomas W. Szayna, "The Politics of NATO Enlargement in Poland, the Czech Republic, Hungary, Romania and Slovenia" (October 1997 conference paper) in <*www.nato.int/docu/review/articles*>.

35. These descriptions of NATO civil-military relations can be found in chap. 1 "Purposes and Principles of NATO Enlargement" from the NATO document "Study on NATO Enlargement—September, 1995" in <NATODA-TA@cc1.kuleuven.ac.be>. (See footnote 7 for relevant quotations from this text.)

36. Ibid.

37. Mark Kramer, "Neorealism, Nuclear Proliferation and East-Central European Strategies." *International Politics*, no. 35 (September 1998).

38. See Stephen Walt, *The Origins of Alliances* (Ithaca: Cornell University Press, 1987) for one way of understanding this process.

39. In *Europe Between the Superpowers* (New Haven: Yale University Press, 1979), Anton W. Deporte argued that NATO and the Warsaw Pact had for all practical purposes "solved" the German problem by incorporating West Germany and East Germany into the contending cold war alliances.

40. For a discussion of the shared interests on the German question during the negotiations of 1990, see S. F. Akhromeev, G. M. Kornienko, *Glazami marshala i diplomata* (Moscow: Mezhdunarodnye otnosheniia, 1992), 258–262. For an American discussion, see Philip Zelikow and Condoleezza Rice, *Germany Unified and Europe Transformed: A Study in Statecraft* (Cambridge; Harvard University Press, 1998), see introduction and chap. 6.

41. Dale R. Herspring, *Requiem for An Army: The Demise of the East German Military* (Rowman and Littleman, 1998).

42. Zelikow and Rice, *Germany Unified and Europe Transformed*.

43. Ibid.

44. Ibid.

45. "Statement on Kosovo Issued by the Heads of State and Government . . . meeting of the North Atlantic Council in Washington, D.C. 23rd and 24th April, 1999." <*www.nato.int/docu/pr/1999p99-062e.htm*>.

46. Ibid.

47. Gale Stokes, "Containing Nationalism: Solutions in the Balkans," *Problems of Post-Communism* 46, no. 4 (July–August, 1999). He writes on p. 9 "by forgetting the enormous costs that Europe sustained through the past two centuries of remapping state lines onto ethnic borders, analysts have misunderstood the wars of Yugoslav succession. They are not an aberrant Balkan phenomenon or the striking out of backward peoples involved in tribal warfare. They are the final working out of a hundred-year long European tradition of violence." For a further elaboration on this theme see in the same issue of *Problems of Post-Communism*, Robin A. Remington, "NATO Transformation and Miscalculation: Balkan Quicksand," 14–16.

48. Michael Ignatieff, "The Virtual Commander: How NATO Invented a New Kind of War," *The New Yorker*, 2 August 1999, 30–36.

49. James Robert Huntley, *Pax Democratica: A Strategy for the Twenty-First Century* (New York: St. Martin's 1998); see also Huntley, *Uniting the Democracies: Institutions of the Emerging Atlantic-Pacific System,* (New York: New York University Press, 1980). Huntley's *Pax Democratica* examines the past and possible trajectory of the overlapping institutional structures—military, economic, political, cultural and technological—that have consolidated a potential democratic community.

50. The preparations and presentations for the OSCE meetings in Belgrade (1980) and Madrid (1985) turned into such propaganda exercises for both alliances, each of which played to the neutral and nonaligned states at the OSCE events. For the military variations of these polemics see V. G. Kulikov (commander of the Warsaw Pact) ed., *Varshavskii dogovor- soiuz vo imia mira i sotsializma* (Moscow: Voenizdat, 1980) and the annual editions of *Soviet Military Power* published by the U.S. Department of Defense during the Reagan administration.

51. See Lawrence Freedman, *The Evolution of Nuclear Strategy* (New York: St. Martins, 1989). See conclusion, esp. 480–81.

52. See the following documents available at <*www.nato.int/docu/pr/1999p99 .htm*>, "The Alliance's Strategic Concept"; "Washington Summit Communique"; "Membership Action Plan"; "Chairman's Summary: Meeting of the North Atlantic Council at the level of Heads of State and Government with Countries in the Region of the Federal Republic of Yugoslavia."

53. Katharine Q. Seelye, "World Leaders Join in a Drive to Aid Balkans," *New York Times*, 31 July 1999, 1.

54. Jane Perlez, "Albright Tells Kosovars Not to Act Like Their Oppressors," *New York Times*, 30 July 1999, A3.

55. Ignatieff, "The Virtual Commander"; Joseph Nye, "The New National Interest," *Foreign Affairs* (July–August, 1999).

56. See reply by Thomas M. Franck, et al. in *Foreign Affairs* (June–July 1999) to Michael J. Glennon's "The New Internationalism," *Foreign Affairs* (May–June 1999).

57. Walter A. McDougall, "Of Crusades Old and New," *Orbis* (summer 1999).

58. Peter Rodman, "The Imperiled Alliance" and Edward Luttwak, "Letting Wars Burn," *Foreign Affairs* (July–August 1999).

59. Nye, "The New National Interest."

60. Ibid.

61. For coverage of a Pentagon study of the lessons of the Kosovo war, see Elizabeth Becker, "Military Leaders Tell Congress of NATO Errors in Kosovo," *New York Times*, 15 October 1999, p. A8. See also Vadim Solovyev, "RF Ministry of Defense Analyzes Results of Balkan Wars," *Nezavisimoye voyennoe obozrenye*, no. 25 (2–8 July 1999) in *Johnson's Russia List*, no. 3396, 17 July 1999.

62. Josef Joffe, "Three Unwritten Rules of the Serbian War," *New York Times*, 25 July 1999 "News of the Week in Review", p. 15. Joffe's three rules were 1) No casualties on the NATO side; 2) minimal casualties on the enemy side; 3) quick end to the war before Western support collapses. These three rules led him to the conclusion that "Kosovo will surely end up as the first and last 'good war' that NATO has ever fought."

63. Address by Vaclav Havel, president of the Czech Republic to the Senate and House of Commons of the Parliament of Canada", 29 April 1999. <www.hrad.cz/president/Havel/speeches/index_uk.html>.

64. Ibid.

65. Robert M. Haden (J.D., Ph.D), director, Center for Russian and East European Studies, University of Pittsburgh. Remarks of 6 December 1999, Woodrow Wilson International Center for Scholars. Ignatieff, "The Virtual Commander: How NATO Invented a New Kind of War" . . . ," *The New Yorker* (2 August 1999), 30–36.

66. Seelye, "World Leaders Join in a Drive to Aid Balkans."

67. "Enlarging NATO," U.S. Secretary of State Madeline Albright, *The Economist* (15 February 1997): 21–23.

68. An expanded version of Rubinstein's testimony is available as "The Unheard Case Against NATO Enlargement, *Problems of Post-Communism* (May–June 1997): 52.

69. Agence Francais de Presse, "US Says NATO Membership for Baltics Nearly Inevitable," *Johnson's Russia List* no. 3396, 17 July 1999.

70. A. A. Epishev, *Ideologicheskaia bor'ba po voennym voprosam* (Moscow: Voenizdat, 1974), 71–72: "the law of the necessity of the defense of socialism applies as long as imperialism exists, which is a constant threat to socialism. Moreover, as historical experience shows, this threat exists not only in the form of a direct attack on socialist countries, but in the form of the so-called 'peaceful counter-revolution.' " His volume provides the most detailed explanation of what the West called the "Brezhnev doctrine." Epishev was the head of the Main Political Administration of the Soviet Armed Forces.

71. Both Hungary and the Czech Republic signed "Statement on Kosovo Issued by the Heads of State and Government Participating In the Meeting of the North Atlantic Council in Washington, D.C. on 23rd and 24th April, 1999," available in <www.nato.int/docu/pr/1999p99–062e.htm>.

72. In press: proceedings from conference "Nuclear Weapons in the 21st Century," University of Washington, Seattle, 30 October 1999. (Lawyers Alliance for World Security/Committee for National Security, Washington, D.C.).

73. Marc Lacey, "Summit in Turkey. . . . Mild Statement on Chechnya . . . " *New York Times*, 20 November 1999, A-1; A-5.

74. John J. Mearsheimer, "The Case for a Ukrainian Nuclear Deterrent," *Foreign Affairs* 72, no. 3 (summer 1993).

75. In press: proceedings from conference "Nuclear Weapons in the Twenty-First Century."

76. Ibid.

77. Ibid.

78. Ibid.

79. Ibid.

80. Paul H. Nitze, "A Threat Mostly to Ourselves," *New York Times*, 28 October 1999, A25.

81. Barry Buzan and Eric Herring, *The Arms Dynamic in World Politics* (Boulder: Lynne Reinner, 1998), chaps. 1–6.

82. Ibid.

83. See Scott D. Sagan and Kenneth Waltz, *The Spread of Nuclear Weapons: A Debate* (New York: W.W. Norton, 1995); John J. Mearsheimer, "Back to the Future: Instability in Europe After the Cold War," *International Security* 15, no. 1 (summer 1990); Mearsheimer, "The Case for a Ukrainian Nuclear Deterrent," *Foreign Affairs* 72 (summer 1993): 61.

84. The quotation comes from Paul Nitze, "The Recovery of Ethics" (New York: Council on Religion and International Affairs, 1960). Quote from p. 34 of Huntley, *Pax Democratica*.

85. David C. Hendrickson, "In Our Own Image: The Sources of American Conduct in World Affairs," *The National Interest*, no. 50 (winter 1997/98). See also G. John Ikenberry, "Institutions, Strategic Restraint, and the Persistence of American Postwar Order," *International Security* 23, no. 3 (winter 1998/99).

86. See Huntley, *Pax Democratica*, esp. tables in the Appendix.

87. J. Samuel Fitch (University of Colorado), a specialist on Latin American militaries, reports that during the Menem adiministration, "Argentina sought membership in NATO, but neither the US nor NATO (especially Great Britain) was very enthusiastic about the proposal. The 'half a loaf' solution was a presidential declaration by Clinton that Argentina was a 'Non-NATO ally.' What that means in real terms is unclear." Personal communication to author.

IV

The Commonwealth of Independent States: The Near Abroad

Ukraine's Economic Dependence on Russia: Fuel, Credit, and Trade

Oles M. Smolansky

Ukraine's Dependence on Russia

UKRAINIAN-RUSSIAN ECONOMIC RELATIONS ARE CHARACTERIZED BY Kyiv's dependence on Moscow. Since 1991, this dependence has manifested itself in three distinct but interrelated ways: (1) Russia has been Ukraine's largest supplier of fuel (above all natural gas and petroleum, but also nuclear fuel needed for Ukraine's nuclear power stations); (2) Russia has been Ukraine's largest creditor; and (3) Russia has been Ukraine's largest trading partner.

Russia as Ukraine's Largest Supplier of Fuel

In the mid-1990s, when Ukraine's annual consumption of fuel stabilized at approximately 30 million tons of petroleum and 80 billion cubic meters (m^3) of natural gas, its domestic production fell to 4 million tons of oil and 18 billion m^3 of gas. This left Kyiv no choice but to import the rest. In line with the pattern established during the late Soviet period, Russia has been supplying approximately 90 percent of Ukraine's annual oil and more than 60 percent of its natural gas requirements. The remaining 15 to 20 percent of the gas imports have traditionally been delivered by Turkmenistan, and more recently, Uzbekistan.[1]

Kyiv addressed its dependency in a February 1995 decree, entitled "Ukraine's Oil and Gas Up to 2010." The nation's leaders concluded that Ukraine would still have to rely on its long-term suppliers, Russia and Turkmenistan, for natural gas. However, given the Russian Federation's dwindling petroleum reserves, Kyiv would be looking for other sources, preferably from the "Persian Gulf basin."[2] Ukraine became essentially dependent on one, rather than two, gas suppliers in early 1997, when the Russian gas monopoly Gazprom obtained a controlling bloc of shares in the joint Turkmenrosgas company.[3] This state of affairs did not last long, however. In mid-1997, Turkmenistan disbanded Turkmenrosgaz and discontinued gas deliveries to Ukraine because of the outstanding $200 million debt. Interestingly, Gazprom promptly offered to increase Russian deliveries by 20 billion m^3 a year—approximately the amount Turkmenrosgaz had traditionally supplied.[4]

Despite this discouraging turn of events, Kyiv clung to an optimistic, though unrealistic, point of view. Asked in early 1998 whether Ukraine could decrease its dependence on Russian energy resources, Prime Minister Valerii Pustovoitenko insisted that Kyiv should persevere in efforts to "develop our own oil and gas complex." He believed—naively—that this goal could be accomplished by attracting domestic and foreign capital for joint efforts to explore and exploit Ukraine's fuel reserves and by "diversifying energy sources." Instead of the Persian Gulf, however, Pustovoitenko now pinned his hopes on Azerbaijan.[5]

Russia as Ukraine's Largest Creditor

Since Ukraine has not been able to "pay as you go" for its Russian fuel deliveries, it is difficult to establish just how much Kyiv owes Moscow and for what. For example, in September 1996, Deputy Prime Minister Viktor Pynzenyk said that Ukraine's total foreign debt stood at $8.5 billion. Of this amount, Kyiv owed Moscow $5.5 billion, excluding interest and fines.[6] But in December, Prime Minister Pavlo Lazarenko announced that "Ukraine has paid off all its accumulated [natural] gas debts to Russia and Turkmenistan." Both were seemingly contradicted by Minister of Finance Ihor Mitiukov, who stated that, as of January 1997, Ukraine's total foreign debt had risen to $8.8 billion. Of this amount, Kyiv owed Russia and Turkmenistan over $4 billion for natural gas alone.[7]

Confusion prevailed in 1998 as well. In February, Gazprom Chairman Rem Viakhirev said that Ukraine's total natural gas indebtedness to Russia at the end of 1997 stood at $1.2 billion, a figure accepted by the Kremlin. Pustovoitenko disagreed. According to his calculations, Ukraine owed Gazprom $710 million.[8] Finally, in March 1998, representatives of Gazprom and Derzhnaftohazprom (Ukraine's state fuel monopoly) signed a protocol on Russian natural gas deliveries to Ukraine and on the schedule for repaying the gas debt. Both sides agreed that, as of 1 March 1998, Kyiv owed Gazprom $900 million and that money or goods to cover the gas debt would be handed over before the end of 1998.[9]

The novel element in Kyiv's position was the request to restructure the overall Ukrainian debt along the lines of the deal Russia had worked out with the members of the so-called Paris Club. (In 1996, this group of Western nations allowed Moscow to reschedule the Soviet/Russian debt over a 25-year period.) In other words, in 1997, Kyiv wanted the Kremlin to renegotiate the terms of the 1995 Ukrainian—Russian agreement which stipulated that the largest part of the debt was to be cleared in a ten-year period along equivalent twenty-five-year lines.[10] As of this writing, these efforts have not been successful.

Russia as Ukraine's Largest Trading Partner

After the collapse of the USSR in 1991, Ukraine emerged as Russia's most active trading partner within the Commonwealth of Independent States (CIS). In the first half of 1996, Belarus, Kazakhstan, and Ukraine accounted for 86.5 percent of Russia's trade volume with the CIS. Of the three, Ukraine's exports to Russia grew from 47 percent of the CIS total in the first half of 1994 to 52 percent in 1996, while its imports from Russia increased from 40 percent to 49 percent.[11] Their total trade turnover (i.e., exports and imports) in 1996 amounted to $17.7 billion, decreasing to $15.1 billion in 1997.[12] Notably, this was not a relationship between two relatively equal partners, as Kyiv was much more dependent on Moscow than vice versa. One important example of Ukraine's heavy commercial reliance on Russia was provided by the president of the Russian Union of Industrialists and Entrepreneurs: In 1996, "Ukraine's share in Russia's [overall] foreign trade turnover . . . [was] 13 percent, while the same indicator for Russia in Ukraine's foreign trade turnover . . . [was] 47 percent."[13]

In any event, economic relations between the two countries deteriorated sharply during the second half of 1996, leading President Leonid Kuchma to warn of an approaching "economic war." The uproar was precipitated by President Boris Yeltsin's August 1996 decree imposing a 20 percent value-added tax (VAT) on all goods imported from Ukraine. Clearly intended to demonstrate Moscow's displeasure with Kyiv's "uncooperative" stance on a number of issues (more below), the decree went into effect on 1 October. Bilateral trade declined significantly: in the first half of 1997, the volume of foreign trade between Ukraine and Russia dropped by 18 percent, while "the total export of commodities and services from Ukraine declined 27.5 percent." In early 1998, Kuchma noted that Russian trade restrictions had caused Ukraine to lose $3 billion.[14]

According to the Ukrainian media, Yeltsin's decree created an odd situation, as Moscow was now requiring Kyiv to pay taxes on both its imports from and exports to Russia. In contrast, in its trade with the other CIS members, Russia was levying a tax only on its exports. The Kremlin blamed Kyiv for this unusual state of affairs because in 1994 the latter had begun to levy a tax on imported goods. Its avowed purpose was "to stimulate domestic export-oriented producers." Ukraine countered by arguing that it had not singled out Russia for unfair treatment—the 1994 regulations applied to all of Kyiv's trading partners. Nor did Ukraine tax its exports. Nevertheless, for the time being, Moscow refused to budge, subjecting Kyiv to what amounted to double taxation.[15] Moreover, Moscow began to impose certain non-tariff restrictions on Ukrainian imports beyond the VAT. These included quotas and excise levies, among them a quota on Ukrainian sugar and an excise tax on Ukrainian alcohol—both major export items to the Russian Federation.[16]

In December 1996, in an apparent response to repeated Ukrainian requests for redress, Moscow lowered some of the excise taxes (including those on alcohol) and abolished the quota system. However, in their stead, Russia introduced the practice of "registering the barter contracts and [of] compulsory licensing of imported alcohol." It also retained the VAT and, as a result, in early 1997 "large amounts of goods" began accumulating along the Russian-Ukrainian border. Publicly, Kyiv found these measures difficult to understand, particularly as the trade differential between the two countries in 1996 equaled only $118 million on a turnover of more than $17 billion. But in 1997 Moscow's protectionist measures caused the trade imbalance between the two states to increase to $1.2 billion in Russia's favor.[17]

As economics became entangled with disputes over Crimea, the Black Sea Fleet, and other political issues, Yeltsin and Kuchma moved to defuse the heavily charged atmosphere. During an informal "tieless" summit held near Moscow in November 1997, the two presidents announced that the VAT on imports from the other's country was cancelled.[18] Although the official media of both states lauded this event as the "end of the trade war," many Ukrainian economists remained skeptical. For instance, Oleh Soskin, president of the Ukrainian Institute for the Transformation of Society, argued that the "primary challenge" to Ukrainian exports to Russia stemmed not from the VAT but from Russian customs and excise duties. He explained that the "VAT on sugar stands at only 10 percent, but customs and excise duties on sugar amount to 25 percent." Hence, he concluded, Russia would continue to collect a 25 percent tax on most Ukrainian exports, while Kyiv agreed to annul all taxes on the imported Russian goods.[19] An official in the Ukrainian Ministry of External Economic Relations confirmed that the trade between the two countries remained "asymmetrical": while Kyiv did not charge a VAT on Russian imports, Russia was levying a tax on its exports to Ukraine. This amounted to an annual loss of $680 million, an amount that "Ukrainian consumers are paying into the Russian budget."[20]

In February 1998, during Kuchma's state visit to Moscow, several documents were signed, including a treaty on economic cooperation between Russia and Ukraine for the period between 1998 and 2007. According to the Russian press, the agreement contained "concrete measures" designed to enhance economic cooperation and to foster commercial relations. Yeltsin believed that bilateral trade between the two states would double once the agreement was implemented. Kuchma went one step further, claiming that the program would "create favorable conditions for strategic partnership between Ukraine and Russia, since both sides realize the necessity of and the lack of alternatives to this path."[21] In reality, nothing has changed. Writing in July 1998, an astute observer noted that the anticipated expansion of bilateral trade relations remained confined to speeches and declarations.[22]

While trade and the availability of credit are important to Ukraine's continued independence, regular access to natural gas and petroleum is absolutely essential to its survival. For this reason, the supply of Russian (or Russian-controlled) fuel has been Moscow's main trump card in its manifold dealings with Kyiv. Both governments understand this basic fact of life and, while Russia has attempted to deprive Ukraine of opportunities to receive fuel from other sources, Kyiv has been trying just as hard to gain affordable access to other suppliers.

UKRAINE'S EFFORTS AT DIVERSIFICATION

In an attempt to circumvent Moscow's stranglehold on fuel supplies, Kyiv has been engaged in multilayered activity designed to stimulate its domestic production of oil and natural gas and to get Ukraine involved in major international projects, including explo-

ration, refining, and, above all, transportation of fuel from the producing countries to their European customers. With this in mind,
Kyiv launched joint ventures with a number of Western companies
to expedite the search and development of Ukraine's remaining
fuel deposits. Prior to 1997, Ukraine also signed agreements with
Iran, Azerbaijan, Uzbekistan, Iraq, Nigeria, and Libya to swap oil,
natural gas, and petroleum products for Ukranian agricultural
and industrial goods and technical expertise.[23] None of these
agreements have been implemented.

Ukraine has also endeavored to participate in the construction
and operation of parts of an international pipeline network intended to pump Middle Eastern and Caspian oil to Central and
Western Europe. To become a more attractive partner, Kyiv set out
to build a new oil terminal at Pivdennyi (near Odesa), capable of
processing 30 to 40 million tons of petroleum a year. Incoming oil
would then be shipped via a new pipeline to Brody, connecting
with the old Soviet "Druzhba" pipeline and, eventually, with ports
on the Baltic Sea. Although in May 1997 Kyiv claimed that Pivdennyi could already receive 12 million tons of petroleum a year,[24] neither the terminal nor the new pipeline are anywhere close to
completion. Work on both has proceeded slowly and sporadically.

Otherwise, during the 1990s, Kyiv concluded agreements to
participate in the construction of the Iran-Azerbaijan-Russia-
Ukraine-Europe oil and gas pipelines, the Turkmenistan-Iran-
Turkey-Europe gas pipelines, the Kuwait-Turkey oil pipeline, and
the Turkey-Ukraine oil pipeline.[25] None of these projects has advanced beyond the planning stage and the reason is not difficult
to discern. Neither Kyiv nor any of its potential partners possess
financial resources necessary to undertake projects of such magnitude and so far, with the exception of the Caspian oil (more below),
the West has been reluctant to underwrite the construction of new
pipelines.

Lacking funds, most of these projects have died a quiet death.
The only exception is the Turkish pipeline scheme, but it has
clearly been relegated to the back burner, because of Russia's pressure on Ukraine and the continued international oil embargo on
Iraq. (Before the imposition of sanctions, Iraq was Turkey's major
petroleum supplier.) In any event, the one project that is very
much alive today is the Azerbaijan-Georgia pipeline which might
be extended eastward across the Caspian Sea to Kazakhstan and
westward to the Mediterranean coast of Turkey.

Kyiv has lobbied hard for Ukraine's inclusion in the projected
Central Asia-Transcaucasus-Europe pipeline network. Initially, the

competition for the main pipeline involved Russia and Turkey and entailed a choice between the so-called northern and southern routes. The former used the existing Baku-Novorossiisk pipeline and the tankers carrying the Caspian oil to the Mediterranean via the Turkish Straits. The southern route envisaged the construction of a new pipeline from Baku, via Georgia and Turkey, to the Turkish Mediterranean port of Ceyhan. Another option was to pump petroleum via an old, Soviet-built pipeline (a new one was completed in 1998) to the Georgian Black Sea port of Supsa. Tankers would then carry the oil to the Turkish Black Sea port of Samsun and from there—via yet another projected pipeline—to Ceyhan. Neither the northern nor the southern route is problem-free. The former passes through Dagestan and Chechnya rendering it vulnerable to the political vicissitudes abounding in that region. Furthermore, the Turkish government has bowed to economic as well as ecological considerations and prohibited increasing the volume of tanker traffic through the narrow and congested Straits. The southern overland route requires the construction of a pipeline running through Turkey's inhospitable Kurdish region. Moreover, both southern route options entail high construction costs.

Ukraine has offered to ship at least some of the Caspian oil from Georgia to Odesa. From there, it would be pumped to the "Druzhba" pipeline, through which much of Russian petroleum is currently exported to Europe. Arguing for the western route, Kyiv made two points. First, one of the major disadvantages of the northern route was the inevitable blending of high-sulphur Russian petroleum with low-sulphur Caspian oil. This mixing would inevitably lower the quality of the exported oil. Second, the cost of the Ukrainian variant to transport the Caspian petroleum from Georgia to Central Europe via Ukraine was estimated at $1.3 billion, approximately twice the amount projected for the construction of the Azerbaijan-Georgia pipeline but almost half the projected cost of the Turkish overland pipeline, estimated at $2.5 billion. According to Kyiv's calculations, the use of the Ukrainian variant would cut the transportation costs of delivering Kazakh oil to Europe to between $33 and $37 per ton and Azeri oil to between $25 and $29 per ton. At the same time, Kyiv realized that the entire southern route plan—as well as its own western variant—were bound to encounter Moscow's opposition. Commenting on the subject, *Zerkalo nedeli* noted that the Russian press, reflecting the view of the government, had condemned the rapprochement between Azerbaijan, Georgia, and Ukraine because their cooperation was directed against Moscow.[26]

In retrospect, Russia's fears appear to have been overblown. Although on good terms with Kyiv, Baku initially appeared apprehensive about the economic implications of the Ukrainian proposal. The distances involved were longer than those of the Turkish project, the loading and unloading of tankers was cumbersome—and absent in the Turkish variant (absent, that is, until the oil reached Ceyhan), and the Russian Navy controlled the eastern portion of the Black Sea. As one Azeri official summed it up: the "Ukrainian route . . . [is] far from being the most promising one." In line with this position, Azerbaijan's President Heydar Aliev did not support Kuchma's proposal for a joint Ukrainian-Azeri-Georgian appeal for European financial backing of the Ukrainian project.

However, even if all of these problems could be solved and unfriendly attitudes could be changed, inquired *Zerkalo nedeli*, was it realistic to expect that the Ukrainian offer to transport the Caspian oil could be implemented any time soon? The answer was a resounding no, based on several factors. Ukraine had no tanker fleet to transport the petroleum, no terminal to unload it, and no pipeline to send it on its way to Central Europe. (One might add that there was also no hard currency to pay for the project).[27]

In early 1997, in spite of these problems, Kuchma came up with the idea of a "Transcaucasus Transport Corridor." Briefly, it would use existing rail lines that connect Baku with the Georgian ports of Poti or Supsa as well as ferries to transport approximately one million tons of "early" Azeri oil a year across the Black Sea to Odesa. Later, after the new pipeline between Baku and Supsa was completed in late 1998, Ukraine hoped to import about 7 million tons of the Caspian oil annually and sell most of it to Europe. In the meantime, Kyiv, as noted, expected to receive one million tons of petroleum a year and Baku as well as Tbilisi expressed their intention to cooperate with Ukraine in this respect.[28] As of this writing, little—if any—of the Azeri petroleum has found its way to Ukraine.

Given Ukraine's current annual petroleum imports of close to thirty million tons, how would the Transcaucasus Transport Corridor affect the country's chronic fuel shortage? It is true that one million tons is better than nothing, but how much difference does it actually make? According to Ukrainian sources, the major impact of the deal would be psychological: it would demonstrate Kyiv's "ability to escape dependence on Russian energy and . . . [would] make the market for the delivery of . . . [petroleum] to Ukraine more competitive, increasing volume, lowering prices, and improving terms of supply."[29] This optimism is understandable but reflects wishful thinking rather than reality.

As for the future, how realistic are the expectations that Caspian oil will be exported through Ukraine? As already indicated, not only will Russia insist on its share of the Azeri and Kazakh exports but, in the "friendly" camp, so too will Turkey. In other words, will Baku, pressured by Moscow as well as Ankara, remain solicitous of Kyiv's interests? Finally, and most important, where is Ukraine going to get the foreign exchange to pay for large quantities of oil (and, for that matter, gas)? Smaller amounts—say one million tons—could conceivably be bartered for agricultural and industrial goods, but hard currency for larger purchases is not likely to be available to Kyiv soon.

RUSSIAN REACTION

While Ukraine has pursued efforts designed to diminish its economic dependence on Russia, Moscow, for its part, has attempted to prevent Kyiv from achieving this goal. Three examples illustrate this point: fuel purchases, bilateral trade, and Pakistan's weapon purchases.

Diversification Efforts

Moscow has made no secret of its determined opposition to Kyiv's efforts to reduce its heavy dependence on Russian fuel. As early as 1995, *Kommersant-Daily*, commenting on the Ukrainian-Turkish pipeline construction project intended to transport Iraqi (or any other Persian Gulf) oil to the Turkish Black Sea port of Samsun, from where it would be shipped to Odesa and Central Europe, argued that for Ukraine to replace "Russian oil supplies with oil from Iraq and Iran" was uneconomical and "politically incorrect." Moreover, the project required building a new terminal near Odesa—a costly and ecologically untenable undertaking. Last but by no means least, *Kommersant-Daily* explained that if Ukraine became an "oil partner" of Turkey, Iraq, and Iran, this would "immediately change the strategic balance and weaken Russia's position in the Black Sea Fleet negotiations."[30] As usual, politics was closely intertwined with economics. *Nezavisimaia gazeta* stated bluntly that, if the Turkish pipeline was built, making Ukraine a "partner" of the Middle Eastern oil producers, Russia would lose a major customer, a customer to whom Moscow could "dictate

prices . . . [while using] Kyiv's dependency to achieve . . . [Russia's]
political aims." Moreover, Russia could also lose buyers or, at the
very least, face stiff competition in the fuel markets of Eastern and
Central Europe.[31] Although not associated with the government
and financed by different interest groups, on these particular issues the newspapers reflected the essence of the Kremlin's policy:
their views paralleled those contained in the government's official
Rossiiskaia gazeta.

Moscow's criticism of the Turkish pipeline project applies to the
Transcaucasus Transport Corridor as well. As correctly noted by
independent analyst Vitalii Portnikov

> Until recently, Russia's influence in the post-Soviet area was based on
> the dependence of these republics on its energy resources and on Mos-
> cow's capabilities in settling territorial conflicts. During the course of
> negotiations with Kyiv, when it was necessary to talk about the fleet,
> they recalled gas. During the course of negotiations with Baku, when
> it was necessary to talk about oil, they recalled Karabakh. The same
> with Tbilisi: the future of Abkhazia was predicated on the future of
> Russian military bases.

Portnikov believed that the Kremlin saw the prospect of major new
pipelines situated in Azerbaijan, Georgia, and Ukraine as "crip-
pling the entire structure." Baku and Tbilisi might no longer feel
compelled to consult with Moscow on the Nagorno-Karabakh and
Abkhazian crises, while Ukraine would attain a degree of unprecedented independence from Russia, creating a "totally new situation in the CIS." Interestingly, Portnikov noted that an example of
how to exert energy-related pressure had already been set. Announcing the decision to bypass Ukraine by building a new gas export pipeline through Belarus and Poland (the so-called Yamal
line), Gazprom chairman Rem Viakhirev "indicated in no uncertain terms" that Moscow would "start talking with Kyiv in a different language" after the project was completed.[32] To be sure, these
and other statements by high Russian functionaries were designed
at least in part to "soften up" Ukraine before bilateral negotiations
began on Gazprom's potential acquisition of various Ukrainian gas
transit and storage enterprises. In any case, such pronouncements
were threatening and no doubt had an impact on the thinking of
the Ukrainian leaders.

After several years of haggling, Kyiv and Moscow agreed to set
up a joint enterprise, Haztranzyt, intended to expand, improve,
and service the existing natural gas pipeline network in Ukraine,

designed to transport Russian natural gas to East and Central European customers. Long sought by Moscow, the deal had been blocked in the Ukrainian parliament because many lawmakers saw it as a Russian attempt to seize control of some of Ukraine's most profitable enterprises and facilities. In September 1996, the parliament relented, on condition that the Ukrainian government retain a 51 percent share in Haztranzyt, only to reverse itself later on the ground that Russian coownership of these facilities constituted an unacceptable threat to Ukraine's national security.[33]

This turn of events forced Gazprom to shift its position and to request ownership of some of Ukraine's most profitable gas-related properties as a means of settling Kyiv's debts. These included a set of export trunk pipelines as well as underground gas storage facilities. Gazprom's hopes to acquire these lucrative enterprises were raised in February 1998, when Presidents Kuchma and Yeltsin signed a Treaty on Economic Cooperation, 1998–2007, which, among other things, provided for "the involvement of Russian investors in the privatization of a number of Ukrainian enterprises." However, as it soon turned out, Kyiv was in no hurry to accommodate Gazprom. The Ukrainian delegation that went to Moscow in March 1998 to negotiate the outstanding problems with the Russian gas giant turned down Gazprom's request for both the trunk pipelines and the underground storage facilities.[34]

Russian pressure on Ukraine in connection with the fuel diversification projects, combined with Kyiv's meager financial resources, can be said to have produced the desired results. As of this writing, Ukraine has not received any fuel from sources outside the former Soviet Union. In fact, most of the imported petroleum and natural gas continues to be delivered by Russia itself, much of it on credit terms. And even the Transcaucasus Transport Corridor project, if it ever materializes, will be confined to the ex-Soviet economic space. However, Russia does not control the extraction, and is not likely to control the transportation, of much of the Azeri oil. As for the Corridor idea—the Transcaucasus railroad and the Black Sea ferries carrying approximately one million tons of oil a year—the scheme does not solve Ukraine's fuel problems and does not represent much of a threat to Russia's vital national interests. Nevertheless, Moscow can be expected to continue opposing it because it sets an unwelcome precedent which could one day develop into a major threat to Russian interests.

Levies

In 1996, as noted, Moscow introduced taxes and related devices designed to prevent Ukraine from increasing the volume of its exports to Russia. Although these measures were generally explained in terms of Kyiv's engagement in such unsavory practices as dumping (thus lowering the profits of the Russian producers), it was obvious to all concerned that Moscow's restrictions were intended to pressure Ukraine into joining the CIS Customs Union and to make Kyiv more responsive to tackling such politically charged issues as the Black Sea Fleet and the status of Sevastopol. It will be recalled that Ukraine has been the main opponent of the proposed Customs Union, seeing it as the first step to economic reintegration—under Russian control—of the former Soviet republics. In this instance, the pressure applied on Ukraine did not produce the desired results, as Kyiv refused to join the Customs Union. Moscow's efforts on behalf of the Black Sea Fleet, in contrast, were crowned with considerable success (see below), but fell short of satisfying the Russian nationalists.

The Tank Deal

The Ukraine-Pakistan tank deal offers another example of Moscow's pressure on Kyiv—in this instance, not to go through with the agreement to supply T-84 tanks to Pakistan. Concluded in 1996, the accord provided for the delivery of 320 tanks to Pakistan over four years at a value between $500 and $650 million. Since India traditionally maintained close relations with Moscow and since it remained a major purchaser of Russian military equipment, Russia's opposition was prompted, in part, by political considerations. However, since Russia also sees Ukraine as a potential rival in the international "arms bazaar," economic interests were involved as well.[35]

In early 1997, the Russian minister of foreign economic relations threatened to halt the shipment of Russian T-84 parts to Ukraine. The secretary of Ukraine's National Security and Defense Council warned that talk about unilateral cutoff of parts was a "double-edged sword." Other Ukrainian officials added that the necessary parts could be purchased in France, Slovakia, or Poland.[36] Whether this was ever done is not known. But in late summer 1997, the director of the Kharkiv-based tank works announced that Ukraine had acquired the capability of producing most of the T-84 components domestically and was therefore no longer dependent on the supply of the Russian-made parts.[37] As of this writing, several consignments of tanks have been delivered to Pakistan. Again, Russian pressure failed to produce the desired results.

Moscow's efforts to manipulate Kyiv have had mixed results, but the balance sheet seems to tilt in the Kremlin's favor. On the minus side of the ledger, the tank deal with Pakistan was concluded despite strong objections. Haztranzyt was set up on paper but has not been implemented, and efforts to induce Ukraine to join the CIS Customs Union backfired. But, on the plus side, different types of Russian discriminatory levies remain in effect, hampering Kyiv's ability to increase much-needed exports to its largest trading partner and, in so doing, to improve the performance of Ukraine's sputtering economy.

Moreover, on the key issue of oil shipments to and through Ukraine, Russia has been eminently successful. To repeat: the construction of the Turkish pipeline, designed to pump Middle Eastern oil to Ukraine; of the Pivdennyi oil terminal; and of a new pipeline from Odesa to Central Europe remain essentially frozen. To be sure, the Kremlin's pressure is not the only reason for Ukraine's foot dragging—political, economic, and especially financial considerations beyond Kyiv's (and, for that matter, Moscow's) control have been responsible as well. Nevertheless, the fact remains that Russia has exerted strong pressure and that Ukraine has apparently felt that it had no choice but to comply.

EVALUATION

In its relations with Ukraine, Russia holds—and has played—some important trump cards against Ukraine. Moscow has repeatedly tried to use Ukraine's heavy economic (fuel, commercial, and financial) dependency on Russia to compel Kyiv to comply with the Kremlin's wishes. Although, as already mentioned, the record is mixed, Moscow's ability to influence Ukraine has been significant. For one thing, although Kyiv has steadfastly refused to join the CIS Customs Union, Russia has utilized its position as Ukraine's major trading partner to pressure Kyiv to accept conditions for bilateral trade that the Ukrainian government regarded as harmful to the country's interests.

Moreover, Moscow has consistently rejected Kyiv's requests to renegotiate the 1995 debt-restructuring accord, thus subjecting Ukraine to additional—in this instance financial—pressure. Kyiv has responded by pleading for Western financial assistance; by proposing occasional deals, such as the sale to Russia of over twenty long-range bomber aircraft, inherited from the USSR; and, above all, by bartering for, instead of purchasing, Russian goods. Despite all of Kyiv's efforts, a sizeable debt remains unsettled and, if Moscow does not relent, it will have to be paid off by 2007. Whether Ukraine can successfully cope with this burden, given its enormous financial difficulties, remains to be seen.

Finally, and most significantly, the virtually absolute fuel dependence on Russia has placed Ukraine in a most unenviable position. Moscow can—and does—dictate the price of fuel, the credit terms, and the volume of deliveries. In the early post-Soviet period, Ukraine paid a price for imported petroleum that exceeded the rate charged on the international market. Kyiv also paid a higher price for Russian natural gas than did Moscow's Central European clients, including Poland. In addition, in August 1996, Moscow threatened to curtail the supply of fuel to the Ukrainian nuclear power plants, which are dependent on Russian deliveries, because of alleged nonpayment for supplies provided in 1996.[38] In early 1997, after Kuchma began pushing his Transcaucasus Transport Corridor scheme, Moscow's Federal Energy Commission advanced a plan for the construction of a new 250-km oil pipeline, connecting the central Russian city of Saratov with Novorossiisk. Its completion would enable Moscow to bypass Ukrainian territory and thus avoid transit fees. According to Ukrainian sources, the Federal Energy Commission's announcement was intended to discourage Kyiv from unilaterally raising fuel transit fees, as it occasionally—but unsuccessfully—had tried to do.[39] Russia is also constructing a major gas pipeline through Belarus and Poland which will bypass Ukraine. In short, by threatening to decrease (if not entirely suspend) fuel deliveries, manipulating prices, and refusing to compromise on transit tariffs, Moscow has kept Kyiv off balance and "persuaded" it to make concessions in a number of disputed issues, including the division of the Black Sea Fleet and the status of Sevastopol.

It is noteworthy that some Russian analysts wanted Moscow to use economic pressure to obtain political results. For example, in 1994 one of them argued that the acquisition, by means of a long-term lease, of the entire city of Sevastopol—rather than just parts of its harbor as suggested by Ukraine—could be achieved by issuing a threat to reduce drastically the supply of Russian natural gas. He noted that this method had been used in March 1994 and suggested that a new threat to curtail the delivery of gas and of nuclear fuel should suffice to bring Kyiv to its knees.[40] Moscow did not heed such extremist advice.

Whether Russia has done enough to bring about a change in Ukrainian economic and political policy is debatable. At the same time, however, it should be recognized that Kyiv holds some trump cards of its own and is therefore not totally helpless when subjected to Moscow's pressure. Despite its huge debt, Ukraine represents Russia's largest fuel export market. Its loss would severely affect Russia's economic well-being. Moreover, Russia currently relies on, and must therefore have access to Ukrainian transit facilities for the export of the bulk of its fuel and other freight to customers in Southern, Central, and Western Europe. In fact, commenting on the growing strains in bilateral relations in the wake of the introduction of the VAT in the fall of 1996, one Russian analyst warned that Moscow, too, could "suffer negative consequences." Expecting Kyiv to retaliate, he noted that Ukraine could raise transit tariffs on Russian oil and gas. Kyiv could also impose higher fees on Russian exports using Ukrainian rail lines or ports. To be sure, the analyst also believed that Russia could respond to these measures by raising the prices of petroleum and natural gas supplied to Ukraine and by lowering the volume of these supplies.[41] What he failed to mention was that some of the Russian fuel passing through Ukraine on its way to the European markets could be—and often is—diverted for use in Ukraine or for the sale abroad, causing some of Moscow's Central European customers to complain about the insufficient deliveries of Russian fuel. Moscow's complaints in Kyiv have usually fallen on deaf ears.

In any event, to let things go that far was clearly not in the interest of either party. This explains why, in spite of periodic bickering and occasional crises, the situation never really got out of hand. For the time being and for the foreseeable future, the two neighbors need each other to survive. While Ukraine represents Moscow's main fuel export market and an indispensable transit route for the export of Russian fuel and freight, it simply cannot function without the Russian oil and natural gas. In addition, in spite of the huge debt and other problems that have marred bilateral relations, Ukraine remains Russia's largest trading partner and the largest single market for Russian fuel exports. This state of affairs, as noted, is likely to continue for some time to come.

Another potentially important reason for the continuing cooperation between Ukraine and Russia in the fuel sector is what might be described as the mutually reinforcing nature of their energy trade. Specifically, despite the sharp drop in industrial output since 1990, Ukraine continues to import large quantities of Russian petroleum and natural gas. This enables some Ukrainian companies, created by the country's "fuel barons," to export sizeable quantities of Russian fuel to Central and West European customers. It stands to reason that the hard currency profits are divided among the Russian and Ukrainian elites engaged in the production and trading of fuel. Officially, the governments of the two states do not engage in or condone such practices, but it has been rumored that many highly placed officials connected with the fuel industry have benefited handsomely from their association. Nor is it a secret that the Russian and Ukrainian "fuel barons" have accumulated vast personal fortunes. As recently noted by the chairman of Naftohaz Ukrainy, "All the rich people in Ukraine owe their capital to Russian gas."[42] This elite interdependence may thus have been one of the important reasons the fuel trade between Russia and Ukraine has flourished since 1990 despite all the problems it created.[43]

The mutual recognition of interdependence, even if lopsided, combined with their respective internal weaknesses, has encouraged both Kyiv and Moscow to attempt to resolve some of their outstanding differences by political means. In the summer of 1997, presidents Kuchma and Yeltsin signed a Treaty of Friendship and Cooperation between the two states. According to its terms, Russia leased from Ukraine for a twenty-year period the more desirable parts of the Sevastopol harbor for use by the Russian Black Sea Fleet. This implied Russia's formal recognition that Crimea is an integral part of Ukraine. The treaty also put the seal on the division of the Black Sea Fleet. Nevertheless, while removing some important sources of tension, the treaty has not resolved all the outstanding problems. Russia continues to apply economic pressure to make Ukraine more compliant in the ongoing efforts to resolve the many differences dividing the two states.

The financial and economic crisis that gripped Russia in late summer and fall 1998 heavily affected Kyiv-Moscow relations. In one sense, Ukraine benefited from increased Russian interest in Ukrainian foodstuffs, and Moscow accepted more food as partial payment for fuel. At the same time, however, the Kremlin expressed no interest in Kuchma's proposal for the creation of a free-trade zone, seeing it as Kyiv's attempt to escape various taxes and fees that Moscow had imposed on Ukrainian exports to Russia. Otherwise, the collapse of the ruble negatively affected the value of the hryvna and greatly complicated the settlement of bilateral trade accounts. Most significantly, as Moscow moved to curtail imports (other than foodstuffs) from the Near Abroad, its decision was bound to hurt Ukraine, Russia's main trading partner in the post-Soviet space.

Conclusion

In commenting on the national security doctrine, adopted by the Supreme Council in January 1997, Secretary of the National Security Council Volodymyr Horbulin noted that the initiatives intended to protect Ukraine's interests had to be generated domestically. Among the major tasks facing Kyiv in this connection, he listed "reforming [Ukraine's] economy" and "decreasing, with Western assistance, our dependence on Russia in the matter of deliveries of [natural] gas and oil." Only then would relations between Kyiv and Moscow be put on "normal footing."[44] Horbulin was right on both counts: Ukraine's national security cannot be assured without a major overhaul of the country's economy and without decreasing Kyiv's economic dependence on Moscow. However, while the latter problem involves a relationship between two unequal partners and is, therefore, much more difficult for Kyiv to control, the Ukrainian government has had much more leeway—but little success—in tackling the problem of internal economic reform.

In any event, it should be obvious that the reality of Russian-Ukrainian relations has little in common with Kyiv's concept of national security. Therefore, the document should be seen as a statement of aspirations: it offers a list of objectives that, should they ever be reached, would enable Ukraine to establish itself as a truly independent state. In the meantime, Kyiv remains heavily dependent on Moscow in terms of fuel, trade, and credits with no chance of an early reversal of this, to the Ukrainian government deplorable, situation. Since fuel dependency and the resulting large debt are Ukraine's most vulnerable points, achieving fuel independence has long been one of Kyiv's most urgent foreign policy objectives. Indeed, as mentioned earlier, the Ukrainian government has gone to great lengths to arrange barter deals with several CIS and Middle Eastern fuel producers. For reasons presented above, these efforts have not produced the desired results.

If Ukraine is to end its fuel dependence on Russia, Kyiv will have to come up with money to pay for the imported fuel. If foreign exchange were to become available, oil and gas could be bought anywhere on the world market, including Russia, and more favorable terms of purchase could then be negotiated. This conclusion is easy to arrive at. The problem was and remains where and how money could be obtained. Before answering this question, it might be useful to recall that Ukraine's financial problems are not unique. Most of the members of the international community are faced with similar difficulties. Yet many of them have managed to generate sufficient revenues to pay for the imported fuel. Why not Ukraine?

The answer to this question is to be found not in Moscow, Baku, Ankara, or Washington, but in Kyiv. As Horbulin noted on another occasion, the main threats to Ukraine's security emanate not from external but from internal sources. Among the negative economic factors that are affecting domestic security, the secretary singled out "unpaid wages, pensions, and social benefits . . . [as well as] growing unemployment and 'the massive shadow economy, which breeds corruption and economic crime'." This state of affairs, he said, resulted from "the incompleteness and inconsistence" of reforms.[45] What Horbulin did not mention was that the lack of progress was also caused by the ongoing rivalry between the executive and legislative branches of government, a lack of imagination and initiative by the executive branch, the pronounced antireform sentiments of the left-wing majority in the parliament, the bloated, unwieldy, and generally corrupt bureaucracy which shows little respect for the law, and, last but not least, a punitive tax system. As a result, broad segments of the populace have become impoverished and the country's socioeconomic pyramid is characterized by an enormous gulf between the small upper layer of the super-rich and the poor masses, occupying its massive base.

Unless tackled and resolved, these problems are bound to destabilize Ukraine from within, exacerbating its dependence on Russia. In the end, Ukraine's very existence as an independent state is at stake. Yet, until 2000, there were no indications that official Kyiv was prepared to stop talking and start acting to remedy what has clearly developed into an untenable situation.

NOTES

This chapter appeared in *Problems of Post-Communism* 46, no. 2 (March/April 1999): 49–58. Reprinted with the permission of the publisher.

1. Oles Smolansky, "Ukraine and the Fuel Problem: Recent Developments," *The Ukrainian Quarterly* 52, no. 2–3 (summer-fall 1996): 143; and Kyiv Radio, 16 May 1997. Foreign Broadcast Information Service, *Daily Report: Central Eurasia* (hereinafter FBIS/SOV), 136, 16 May 1997.

2. Petro Shpak, director of the Institute of Geological Sciences of the National Academy of Sciences of Ukraine, *Uriadovyi kur'er* (Kyiv), 20 April 1995.

3. Interview with *Ukraina moloda* (Kyiv), 27 March 1997, as quoted in FBIS/SOV-97-068, 10 April 1997.

4. Larisa Ostrolutskaia, *Obshchaia gazeta* (Moscow), 11 September 1997, as quoted in FBIS/SOV-97-267, 25 September 1997.

5. Larisa Ostrolutskaia, *Obshchaia gazeta*, 29 January 1998. As quoted in FBIS/SOV-98-040, 11 February 1998.

6. Ivan Dmytrenko, *Narodna armiia* (Kyiv), 21 September 1996, as quoted in FBIS/UMA (Eurasia Military Affairs)-96-216S (21 September 1996) and *Nezavisimaia gazeta* (Moscow), 2 November 1996.

7. OMRI *Daily Digest* 2, no. 30 (12 February 1997) and Alla Eremenko, *Zerkalo nedeli* (Kyiv), 8 May 1997.

8. Moscow Radio, 12 February 1998, as quoted in FBIS/SOV-98-043, 12 February 1998, and 1 March 1998, as quoted in FBIS/SOV-98-060, 1 March 1998.

9. Moscow Radio, 7 March 1998, as quoted in FBIS/SOV-98-066, 7 March 1998.

10. Andrei Kapustin, *Nezavisimaia gazeta*, 22 February 1997, and Moscow Radio, 27 March 1997, as quoted in FBIS/SOV-97-086, 27 March 1997.

11. Evgenii Vasil'chuk, *Finansovye izvestiia* (Moscow), 26 September 1996.

12. Viktor Timoshenko, *Nezavisimaia gazeta*, 18 October 1997, and Konstantin Zvarych, *Zerkalo nedeli*, 7 March 1998.

13. *Trud* (Moscow), 24 May 1997, as quoted in FBIS/SOV-97-103, 31 May 1997.

14. Moscow Radio, 21 August 1997, as quoted in FBIS/SOV-97-233, 21 August 1997, and 1 March 1998, as quoted in FBIS/SOV-98-060, 1 March 1998.

15. Konstantin Zvarych, *Zerkalo nedeli*, 22 February 1997, and Dmytro Mossienko, *Eastern Economist*, 5 January 1998.

16. Aleksei Chichkin, *Rossiiskaia gazeta* (Moscow), 12 October 1996.

17. Material in this paragraph is based on Zvarych (see n. 12) and Moscow Radio, 6 February 1997, as quoted in FBIS/SOV-97-026, 10 February 1997.

18. The *New York Times*, 17 November 1997.

19. Al'bina Iushkevich, Anatolii Skychko, and Viktor Timoshenko, *Vseukrainskie vedomosti* (Kyiv), 13 January 1998, as quoted in FBIS/SOV-98-022, 23 January 1998.

20. Tat'iana Silina, *Kievskie vedomosti* (Kyiv), 5 March 1998, as quoted in FBIS/SOV-98-075, 17 March 1998.

21. Ekaterina Tesemnikova, Viktor Timoshenko, *Nezavisimaia gazeta*, 28 February 1998.

22. Ivan Rybalko, *Zerkalo nedeli*, 18 July 1998.

23. "Ukraine and the Fuel Problem" (n. 1), 160.

24. *Nezavisimaia gazeta*, 6 May 1997.

25. Above material is based on "Ukraine and the Fuel Problem" (n. 1), 165–66.

26. Mikhail Sokolovskii, *Zerkalo nedeli*, 22 March 1997. On the cost of the Turkish pipeline, see interview with the Ukrainian ambassador to Azerbaijan, *Uriadovyi kur'er*, 4 July 1998.

27. The material in the above paragraphs is based on Rostislav Khotin, *Zerkalo nedeli*, 29 March 1997.

28. Andrei Kapustin, *Nezavisimaia gazeta*, 21 February 1997, and Kyiv Radio, 3 March 1997, as quoted in FBIS/SOV-97-062, 3 March 1997.

29. Kyiv Radio, 3 March 1997, as quoted in FBIS/SOV-97-062, 3 March 1997.

30. Articles by A. Baneva and A. Volyntseva, *Kommersant-Daily* (Moscow), 14 and 29 April 1995.

31. Anatolii Martsinovskii, *Nezavisimaia gazeta*, 7 September 1996. For more details, see Vitalii Panov, *Rossiiskaia gazeta*, 28 September 1996.

32. Vitalii Portnikov, *Obshchaia gazeta*, 10 April 1997, as quoted in FBIS/SOV-97-100, 11 April 1997.

33. Moscow Radio, 19 March 1997, as quoted in FBIS/SOV-97-078, 19 March 1997, and Larisa Ostrolutskaia (n.4).

34. Ekaterina Vasil'chenko, *Rossiiskaia gazeta* (Biznes v Rossii Supplement), 7 March 1998, and Moscow Radio, 6 March 1998, as quoted in FBIS/SOV-98-065, 6 March 1998.

35. Boris Vinogradov, *Izvestiia* (Moscow), 20 July 1996.

36. *Nezavisimaia gazeta*, 27 February 1997, and Moscow Radio, 6 March 1997, as quoted in FBIS/UMA-97-065, 6 March 1997.

37. Andrei Korbut, *Nezavisimaia gazeta*, 4 September 1997.

38. Zakhar Zlyva, *Ukraina moloda*, 11 September 1996, as quoted in FBIS/SOV-96-181, 11 September 1996.

39. Moscow Radio, 27 February 1997, as quoted in FBIS/SOV-97-040, 27 February 1997.

40. Konstantin Levin, "Simferopol' Will Get Oil Only in Exchange for Sevastopol," *Kommersant-Daily*, 8 December 1994, as quoted in FBIS/SOV, 9 December 1994, 10.

41. Aleksei Chichkin, *Rossiiskaia gazeta*, 12 October 1996.

42. Viktor Timoshenko, *Nezavisimaia gazeta*, 16 October 1998.

43. The author is grateful to an anonymous reviewer for suggesting this hypothesis.

44. *Zerkalo nedeli*, 18 January 1997.

45. Moscow Radio, 30 December 1997, as quoted in FBIS/SOV-97-364, 30 December 1997.

V
Russia and the United States:
An Evolving Relationship

On Russian-American Relations

HENRY TROFIMENKO

THE UNANTICIPATED RESULTS OF THE WELL-INTENTIONED BUT DIS-
mally implemented *perestroika* in the Soviet Union and the follow-
up "reforms" in Russia were in effect equal to the country's defeat
in a war. As it appears, the damage caused to the country by those
developments has been much more severe than that inflicted upon
it by the German invasion.

The multinational country that stood firm against the Nazi
hordes all of a sudden disintegrated like Humpty Dumpty into fifteen separate pieces. The self-inflicted economic damage caused to
Russia alone during the last eight years of reform is several times
greater than the damage caused by the Nazi occupation of large
parts of its European territory and the hostilities. Come to think of
it: after five years of the Great Patriotic War (as the Russian part of
World War II is called in Russia), the gross domestic product
(GDP) of the USSR fell by 20 percent, while after the last eight
years of reform in Russia (1991–1998) the Russian GDP dropped
more than 50 percent! In fact, if one considers that, in their calculation of the GDP, Soviet statisticians excluded the cost of services
and that the share of services (essentially the speculative banking
operations) in the current calculations of the GDP equals 50 percent, then it follows that Russia's real GDP is now roughly a quarter
of that of 1990.[1]

The country's weight in the global balance of power dropped
dramatically. Russia—former core of one of the two superpowers—is now officially classified by the international financial institutions as a country with a transitional economy, in other words, a
developing country. Politically, it is virtually ignored by the leading world powers, notwithstanding occasional pep talk by their
leaders about the "importance of Russia" and Moscow's pro forma
inclusion in such international institutions as the G-7 group of industrial nations or the Asia-Pacific Economic Cooperation (APEC).

The decline of Russia as a major power has resulted in dramatic
shifts in the global correlation of forces. This process of readjust-

ments in the world power balance has not yet finished. It will go on until new global and regional coalitions of states—the main players in the world arena—are set. Then it will be possible to speak of the new global stability until it again will be challenged in a new trial of strengths. Because, regretfully, despite arousing rhetoric about a "new thinking," a "new world order," a "world without war and violence," the traditional "old thinking" still predominates in the world. Millennia-old methods of settling disputes and conflicts among nations, and often inside them, through bloodletting remain the same. Only the efficiency of the means for mass slaughter and selective destruction is perfected with every passing year as the NATO aggression against Yugoslavia in 1999 vividly demonstrated. War still remains the ultimate reasoning of kings and even of more democratic rulers, as the annually growing whopping figures for international arms production and military expenditures indicate. Not only the bloody methods of settling disputes, but the militaristic mentality that breeds war psychoses stays the same.

True, after the tectonic developments in the USSR, the world community took a long breath and fancied that maybe the world really became safe for democracy, and nations, forgetting past grievances and quarrels, will finally unite in brotherly embrace in the world community of free and happy peoples. If not all the nations, then at least the leading ones, claiming to be the most developed and civilized. That hope looked like a realistic one after the disappearance not simply of the evil empire, but the last empire on earth as such—the great Russian empire of czars and later commissars; after the steady advancement of the West European nations on the way toward ever more comprehensive economic and political union; after the liquidation of apartheid in South Africa—one of the most divided countries on earth.

In the situation of the post–cold war euphoria, of the multitude of positive steps made on the world arena first by the USSR's leader Gorbachev and then by Russia's Yeltsin, steps of fundamental nature, most convincingly proving to the world that the country has really broken with its imperialist past, the claims of some unreformed American cold war warriors about the brilliant victory of the United States in the cold war with Russia looked like laughable residue of the antiquated "old thinking," unbecoming in the new friendly, benign, peaceful international environment. Such an evaluation was confirmed by the rapid development of understanding and cooperation between the new USSR/Russia and the United States. One can name several pivotal points in time, landmarks on the road of continuing improvement in the relationship between the two countries.

LANDMARKS ON THE ROAD TO PARTNERSHIP

November 1985—a ground-breaking meeting in Geneva between the initiator of the *perestroika*, future Nobel Peace Prize laureate and the *Time* magazine Man of the Decade Mikhail Gorbachev and the seemingly incorrigible cold war warrior, U.S. President Ronald Reagan.

"Our meeting beside the glowing hearth went on for an hour and a half, and when it was over, I couldn't help but think something fundamental had changed in the relationship between our countries," writes President Reagan about his first meeting with Gorbachev. "I knew I hadn't changed. If anything, the world was changing, and it was changing for the better. The world was approaching the threshold of a new day."[2]

December 1987—In Washington, D.C., Mikhail Gorbachev and Ronald Reagan sign the treaty between the USA and the USSR on the elimination of their Intermediate-Range and Shorter-Range Missiles (INF Treaty), which envisaged destruction of these two whole classes of nuclear weapons in the arsenals of the two countries.

"The Treaty on the complete elimination of the Soviet and American missiles of intermediate and shorter range—I am convinced—will become a historic date in the chronicle of a constant striving of people from the earliest times toward world without wars," said Gorbachev, speaking at the White House. "I know: apropos signing of the Treaty on the IRM-SRM certain politicians and journalists are already pondering: who has won? I reject the way the question is put. This is an anachronism of the old thinking."[3]

It was not simple for Gorbachev to hammer out the treaty. His appointee—Defense Minister Yazov—had to apply some hand wringing to quite a few important generals who were aghast at the inclusion into the treaty of a brand-new Soviet "Oka" (SS-23) missile, which did not exactly reach the 500 kilometer range, relevant to the treaty. However, not to displease the United States, the missile was sacrificed.

The INF Treaty opened up a series of seminal steps on the road of real arms reductions, embodied later in the START-1 and START-2 treaties, the bilateral Soviet-American treaty on the dras-

tic reduction of chemical weapons, the multilateral treaties on reduction of conventional forces in Europe, complete elimination of
chemical weapons, and the open skies treaty. All those agreements
greatly contributed to the demilitarization of international politics
and improved atmosphere worldwide. They were accompanied by
the unilateral initiatives of the leaders of both countries designed,
among other things, to accelerate the disarmament process and to
severely curtail tactical nuclear weapons.

The Washington summit of 1987 also opened up the solution of
one of the most painful problems souring relations between the
United States and the Soviet Union—that of the Soviet intervention in Afghanistan. Gorbachev announced in the U.S. capital that
Moscow made a political decision to withdraw its troops from Afghanistan within a year. The realization of that decision by February 1989 greatly contributed to better understanding between
Moscow and Washington.

Autumn 1989—peaceful anticommunist democratic revolutions
in the East European satellites of the Soviet Union with acquies-
cence and encouragement on the part of Moscow. They culminated in the symbolic event—the opening, in November 1989, of
the Berlin Wall that for many years embodied the seemingly irreconcilable political, economic, and spiritual divide between the East
and the West and the dead set confrontation between the "two systems."

September 1990—the meeting between President Bush and
President Gorbachev in Helsinki, where Gorbachev committed
himself and his country to support the coalition headed by the
United States against Iraq—an old time friend and client of the
Soviet Union. Proving its new value system, Moscow denounced
the aggressor, in spite of its political sympathies for Baghdad and
the existence of the bilateral treaty of friendship and cooperation.
By this act, the long-standing Soviet concept of the Third World as
the third mainstream of the world revolutionary process,[4] an ally
in fighting "Western imperialism," was thrown overboard.

This decision was supported by the Soviet masses. What they
were resolutely against, however, was the idea of direct participation by the Soviet troops or volunteers in the anticipated military
action in the desert. Such an idea was actively promoted by Russian democrats who were trying to prove to the world and first of
all to the United States government that they were willing to go
"the whole hog" in their devotion to democracy and justice worldwide. Coming immediately in the wake of the Afghan tragedy that
resulted in thousands of Russian soldiers killed in action, such an

eagerness on the part of democrats to support with lives of Russian boys the triumph of a "just cause" in the sands of the Arabian peninsula was met by universal condemnation on the part of rank and file people. In a popular parlance, this condemnation was expressed as the denunciation of (foreign minister) "Shevardnadze's capitulation to Americans."

That was the time when the forces of nationalist Russian opposition to the political line of the "democratic government" started to organize and to consolidate using to the hilt the democrats' pressure for Russian military participation in the forthcoming war in the desert to discredit them. Those activities greatly contributed to the growth of nationalist sentiments across the Union and finally, to the latter's demise.

August 1991—the triumph of the Russian democratic forces over the conservative "forces of evil," who allegedly wanted to restore the old Stalinist system. This victory laid the ground for the liquidation of the Soviet Union, the formation of the loosely organized Commonwealth of Independent States (CIS), and a new drastic improvement in relations between Moscow and Washington that, after some initial hesitation, loudly welcomed the victory of Yeltsin and his supporters.

The emergence in December 1991 of independent Russia as the legal successor to the USSR resulted in further positive developments in relations between Moscow and Washington, the latter publicly rejoicing over the disappearance of its mighty chief opponent and global troublemaker.

The new, unquestionably cordial relationship between the two countries was underscored by the hearty welcome given to Russia's President Yeltsin during his June 1991 visit to the United States. The American newspapers blazed with headlines emphasizing the "eternal alliance" between the two countries: "Summit Sealed a New Friendship," "Russia is Given Most-Favored Status," "Space-Race Rivals Agree to Fly Joint Missions," "Yeltsin Speaks, and Congressional Wall Tumbles."

Summing up the most essential result of the summit, the *New York Times* in an editorial called extraordinary the deal hammered out by the two presidents with regard to strategic weapons. "It promises the longest step yet away from fear and toward real security. Russian President Yeltsin has made the boldest concessions, as Congress acknowledged yesterday with its tumultuous reception for him. He gives up nuclear parity, reducing Russia's arsenal to 3,000 warheads, while letting the U.S. retain 3,500. And he will deactivate and soon eliminate his most fearsome weapons. Presuming that both sides carry it to conclusion, this agreement closes the book on the past."[5]

As if to underscore new complete understanding between the two capitals, the Russian Ministry of Foreign Affairs accepted the guidance and advice of Washington on all important foreign policy matters. Russian foreign policy in fact became Americanized, denationalized. If famous Soviet Foreign Minister Andrei Gromyko had got the nickname Mr. Nyet (Mr. No) in international circles, new Russian Foreign Minister Andrei Kozyrev got the nickname Mr. Da (Yes Man). In the demonstration of an absolute loyalty to Washington it was asserted that Russia does not have any foreign policy interests that would differ from those of its Western partners. This alleged total coincidence of the national interests of Russia with those of the United States brought forth the idea of strategic partnership—a notion at one time often used in speeches both in Moscow and in Washington.[6]

Such sheepish behavior of the Russian foreign office (which evidently reflected the inclinations and preferences of the Russian president) produced rather unfavorable reaction from public circles in Russia and contributed to further consolidation of nationalist opposition to the Kremlin's foreign policy. Those sentiments found reflection in the critical attitudes of a large number of Russian parliamentarians toward official foreign policy line.

A new landmark event was the disbandment by President Yeltsin of the Russian Supreme Soviet with tank gunfire on Bloody Sunday, 3 October 1993. That action got a de facto approval from President Clinton, which consolidated the understanding between the two presidents and brought it to an apex of mutual trust.[7]

THE END OF EUPHORIA

The new Russian parliament, the Federal Assembly, whose lower house—the Duma—was popularly elected in December 1993[8] on the basis of the newly, albeit hastily, written Russian constitution, that gives the president almost dictatorial powers, got the majority of openly nationalistic parties: liberal democrats, Communists, and agrarians. Under the influence of heavy criticism of Russia's international behavior from representatives of those parties, Russian foreign policy started to grope for a more independent course. The first vivid manifestation of such a change were specific actions of Russian diplomacy in the Bosnian war in the spring of 1994. Moscow—in contrast to its Western partners that empathized with

Bosnia—started to unequivocally side with the Serbian cause and finally made the NATO countries take Moscow's new position into account.

Although this Russian intervention actually helped NATO out of the corner it painted itself into by its decision to bomb Serbian positions (because no NATO country was actually happy with such a compromise decision of the alliance's leadership), the sudden break of the Russian diplomacy out of its Western shackles was a shock to many in the Foggy Bottom and elsewhere.

Later on, Russia's foreign office started to formulate its own line in the Middle East and in Asia. Russia was trying to return to the Middle East at least as an alternative weapons supplier and, to a certain extent, as a counterweight to the United States, as Russia's active diplomacy with Iran, Iraq, Syria, Sudan, as well as some Persian Gulf states, indicates. In Asia, Russia was developing strong ties with China, strengthening its cooperation with India and the Republic of Korea, while attempting to restore close links with North Korea that were curtailed earlier to please the United States.[9] But, at the same time, Russia supported peacekeeping and peacemaking steps and initiatives of the United States and the West European countries designed to enhance stability in various quarters of the globe.

The shift in foreign policy was directly connected with the change in the management of the Russian Ministry of Foreign Affairs. By the beginning of 1996, Kozyrev lost the respect of the Russian public. In view of the approaching presidential elections, Boris Yeltsin, who in public opinion polls had almost the same rating as the other presidential candidate, Gennady Ziuganov (head of Russia's Communist party), needed to boost his image as a defender of Russian values and interests. For this reason, in early 1996, Yeltsin replaced Kozyrev with Yevgeny Primakov, who had an established reputation of an old "Middle East hand." (Before his appointment as foreign minister, Primakov served as director of Russia's Foreign Intelligence Service.)

However, as it turned out, the changes in the orientation and conduct of Russian foreign policy, introduced in the latter 1990s under the growing pressure of Russian public opinion, were mostly of style rather than substance. Yevgeny Primakov and Igor Ivanov, who replaced Primakov in September 1998 when the latter was appointed prime minister, regularly made tough policy pronouncements. The intent was to impress on the Russian public the idea that the country's foreign policy was independent and could not be manipulated by foreign states or statesmen. A typical example was provided by Mr. Ivanov during Secretary of State Madeleine Albright's January 1999 visit to Moscow: "If we are creating a market economy, this does not mean that our foreign policy ought to be marketable as well. . . . We are not putting our national interests on sale."[10]

This is sheer demagogy intended for domestic consumption. In reality, the national interests of Russia have been subordinated to Uncle Sam in exchange for economic donations and other kinds of "support." Up to this day, regular instructions, and sometimes rude pressure, from Washington determine the course of Moscow's foreign policy! This is all the more regretable because Washington's instructions often contradict the basic national interests of Russia. That is why even the many genuinely pro-Western factions of the Russian political elite could not help noticing that Moscow's obedient following the U.S. leadership and the multitude of concessions Russia made to the West did not bring any real dividends to Russia.

After Moscow—since the time of Gorbachev—started making concessions not only to common sense (or, to use Gorbachev's language, to universal human values), but, in large measure, also to the particular American preferences in world politics by satisfying all the requests and demands of her new Big Democratic Brother, it asked for almost nothing in return. For instance, when, in 1990, Moscow consented to the unification of Germany with NATO incorporating the new eastern part of the Federal Republic of Germany (FRG), the sole tiny concession Moscow bargained for and got from its new Western friends was the promise that foreign troops and nuclear weapons would not be deployed in this 200-mile-wide chunk of the former German Democratic Republic (GDR) territory. It never dawned even upon the most astute Soviet international analysts and advisers to the Politburo to suggest that Moscow insist on including into the two plus four treaty a clause that would preclude NATO from further eastward expansion. The author does not have the slightest doubt that at the time of composing that treaty its Western signatories would have graciously satisfied that request, considering the value of the prize they were getting.

But there was no need for such "trivial" stipulations that would have marred the grand celebration of the end of the cold war and of the awful, disgusting Soviet Communism. It was a natural presumption of almost everybody in Russia during this festival of love and joy that thankful and noble West would grandly reward the new USSR/Russia. And not only with huge financial donations to help it execute an unbelievable socioeconomic transformation from its totalitarian past to a new social system based, like in the adorable West, on private enterprise, democracy, and unhampered economic activities of free individuals. It was believed that the West would do its utmost to help the country politically and spiritually—accelerate its entry as an equal into the world community of free and prosperous nations.

Such great expectations, however, for a number of reasons, now evident to everybody, have not materialized. The anticipated ocean of lavish economic aid—akin to the Marshall plan, to the tune of $30 to $40 billion a year, as was often mentioned at various summits and high-level conferences, in reality boiled down to an economic enslavement of Russia by Western financial institutions through their credits and loans (that in great measure landed in the pockets of a multitude of important scoundrels and swindlers, including the members of the ruling class.)[11]

The U.S. government manipulates the Russian economy through the International Monetary Fund (IMF) in which Washington maintains a dominant position. In the 1990s, the Russian government became critically dependent on IMF credits and donations from other foreign sources, resembling a narcotics user's dependence on drugs. At the time of this writing, Russian debt to the IMF amounts to $16 billion. The last IMF credit to the tune of $4.5 billion, which the Fund started to disburse in late summer 1999, will actually be kept by the IMF as part of the Russian debt payment! In March 1999, Russia's total debt to foreign creditors, including debts on loans to the former Soviet Union, amounted to $155 billion.[12] Almost every year, the beggarly Russian government that has to use nearly one third of the country's budget expenditures on repayment of those loans and interest negotiates with the Western lenders the restructuring of the continuously growing indebtedness.[13]

Such total dependence on donations from abroad (including huge loans from the World Bank, the FRG, Japan, and other countries) deprives Russia of any maneuverability and flexibility in both its domestic and foreign policies. As for the domestic economy, during the 1990s, Russia has become a de facto colony of the United States: its economic policy is designed in Washington. Russian state budget has to be approved by the IMF before the Duma can vote it into a law. And the Fund prescribes very rigid economic parameters, though their implementation has led to the continued decline of Russian industry and agriculture. All of this has exacerbated Russia's severe socioeconomic crisis. As one observer put it:

"The basic problems of the Russian economy . . . [in the late 1990s] are well known: decline in production, budget deficits, state debt, unemployment, inflation, sliding rouble exchange rate, lack of investments, high interest rates on bank credits and, generally, substantial decline in the living standards of the population." To be sure, Russia faced similar problems in 1991. But, by the end of the decade, these problems "acquired catastrophic acuteness. By not solving even a single problem, the reforms led the country to the final bankruptcy."[14] Under these circumstances, it is ridiculous for a country, whose government officials constantly camp on the doorstep of various Washington offices hat in hand in search for more credits, to speak of an independent foreign policy.

Due to the country's total dependence on the IMF, its representatives visit any Russian institution or enterprise at will and reprimand its management for "improper" business practices or "undesirable" trade connections. The U.S. government seems to have control over everything in Russia, starting with the decisions on how many foreign students can study at Russian colleges and ending with the control over the storage of Russian nuclear weapons. One of Russia's recent prime ministers (who are frequently replaced on the president's whim) went so far as to suggest that the country's military-industrial complex can be saved only with the help of American credits.

The language used by the Russian officials and by the sycophantic press has become so impregnated with English words and terms that sometimes even a college-educated Russian has difficulty understanding the meaning of what is said or written. Just look at the shop signs in English or Anglicized Russian on the main street of St. Petersburg—Russia's second-largest city—and you will immediately feel that you are either in the United States or, more to the point, in some former British colony.

It is not surprising that, in such circumstances, any decision Washington demands of the Kremlin or any Russian policy change it suggests is invariably implemented by the slavish and totally corrupt camarilla that presently rules Russia. No wonder that, in the spring of 1999, during NATO's incessant bombing of Yugoslavia, which is regarded by most Russians as a sister-republic, it was Russia, in the person of the president's special representative—the notorious Chernomyrdin—that sold out the country to NATO. By hook and crook, he forced the Yugoslav president to agree to such humiliating conditions (including the occupation by the NATO forces of the Yugoslav province of Kosovo) that their acceptance by Belgrade surprised even the leaders of some NATO countries. It never dawned on that gas industry tycoon that, in the process, he sold out the dignity of Russia as well.

Because the feeling that their country has been turned into a U.S. colonial adjunct (whose main function is to supply raw materials to the West) is now universal in Russia, one can readily imagine what kind of an attitude a rank-and-file Russian has with regard to the so-called reforms and their main proponent—the United States.[15]

THE REALITY OF POWER POLITICS

The fact is that, despite Gorbachev's highfalutin discourses about the new thinking and a nonviolent world and despite Yeltsin's emotional appeals for strategic partnership with the United States, the world so far has not changed much spiritually or politically in comparison with what it used to be 50 or 100 years ago. Only the correlation of forces did change, and with it, the global power balance. And the most notable change is the fact that there are no two superpowers as was the case only ten years ago. There is now on the global scene only one superpower—the United States, and there is a pitiful, beggarly giant—Russia, which would not be of much interest to the U.S. authorities save for the fact that it is still the keeper of thousands of deliverable strategic nuclear warheads, which can reach American territory. In the new atmosphere of "partnership" those warheads are supposedly not targeted upon the American, or, for that matter, anybody else's cities, but this is hardly possible to verify.

It finally dawned upon experts on Russia, if not upon politicians, that all those claims of American cold warriors about the victory of the United States in the cold war were not just empty rhetoric, a stupid residue of the "old thinking," but cool evaluations by persons accustomed to reasoning in the *Realpolitik* terms, that is in the terms of geopolitics and the balances of power.

The initial American impression in the 1970s that there was a draw in the cold war between the two superpowers moved Washington to sign the Helsinki Final Act that legalized that draw and left intact the postwar European power balance, hammered out by the leaders of the Big Three in Yalta. But the picture of Russia lying prone in the 1990s proved the earlier American perceptions to be wrong. Cold-blooded review of the real, not imagined, situation pushed the U.S. powers that be to claim its lawful spoils. And the prize, as it appears, is, at a minimum, the whole Eastern (now Central) Europe and, probably, even bigger.

Politics is politics: it is the struggle for power and influence and not a charity performance. Moscow's assertions about some "measured balance" or a "balance of interests" as the only acceptable ground for the settlement of international disputes seem to the American adepts of *Realpolitik* a sheer nonsense of uneducated simpletons because interests that are not supported by utilizable power mean nothing in geopolitics.

It doesn't matter much for the Washington leadership that the region in question is already out of Russia's domain. That is, of course, welcome from the point of view of the U.S. strategists. But until it firmly joins the American-dominated institutions, it is still considered a "no-man's land" or a "power vacuum" to use the proper geopoliticians' cliche. So the forceful striving to incorporate into NATO—for starters—Poland, Hungary, and the Czech Republic is not the result of some inhuman greed of some crazy American politicians, but a normal readjustment in the balance of power according to the real weights of the present participants in the "European concert" of nations, the United States included. As simple as that.

"American leadership is our first principle and a central lesson of this century," educated former U.S. Secretary of State Warren Christopher those who were hard to grasp "the self-evident truth." "By leading—whether through an alliance like NATO, a coalition of nations, or the United Nations—we can augment our power and leverage our resources . . . [T]he Iron Curtain must not be replaced with a veil of indifference" (Sic.-H.T.). That is why NATO's "mission endures even though the Cold War has receded into the past. . . . Under American leadership . . . , the Alliance began a steady, deliberate and transparent process that will lead to NATO's expansion. . . . It will help ensure that no part of Europe will revert to a zone of great power competition or a sphere of influence."[16] In other words, there will be no divisions in Europe into spheres of influence and no "great power competition" because the whole region will irreversibly become the sphere of influence of the United States, the world's sole remaining superpower.

In the summer of 1999, Poland, Hungary, and the Czech Republic were officially admitted to NATO. That happened at the alliance's summit in Washington, D.C., which was devoted to the organization's fiftieth anniversary. The summit also mapped further steps for NATO's eastward expansion. Among the new candidates for membership, special attention was paid to the three newly independent Baltic republics, whose territory is strategically located along the northwest corner of Russia, as well as to Ukraine that, in July 1997, signed a special partnership charter with NATO. In a Declaration of the Heads of State and Government participating in the NATO-Ukraine Commission summit in Washington on 24 April 1999, "the President of Ukraine reaffirmed his country's determination . . . to pursue its goal of integration in European and transatlantic structures."[17] (It is noteworthy that the Ukrainian president participated in the festivities in spite of the fact that another European Slavic country—Yugoslavia—was at that very time barbarously bombed into the Middle Ages by the NATO air forces.) Thus, one more infamous page in the history of the Russian ruling clan's betrayal of the country's national interests was turned. The fact of the matter is that Ukraine would have never dared to join the openly anti-Russian bloc, had it not been for Moscow's own policies: it was the Kremlin itself that gave the green light for NATO's unhindered eastward expansion.

To be sure, NATO, as the winner in the cold war, would have tried to expand eastward ignoring the expected Russian opposition in any case, though many U.S. experts, including Henry Kissinger, initially considered the securing of a neutral status for the former communist states of Eastern Europe as the maximum gain possible. At the same time, it is clear that the American leaders never expected that Russia itself would help them in this project and, even more significantly, would legally sanction such expansion. Actually, the very idea of the east with which such an enterprise could have been effected must have dawned upon the White House only after the American experts became convinced that the new Russian leaders were but American lackeys, totally dependent on Washington's favors, and after President Yeltsin, during his August 1993 visit to Warsaw, publicly endorsed Poland's desire to join NATO.

Initially, the U.S. Republican leadership was very cautious in engaging Russia in attempts to cooperate with NATO. Russia was first lured to join the North Atlantic Cooperation Council (NACC), a politico-military organization created in December 1991 specially for the purpose of involving former adversaries into cooperation with NATO. Later, Russia joined its follow-up—the Partnership for Peace (PfP) organized in 1994. It soon dawned even upon the dumbest of Russian political analysts and foreign policy experts that membership in those two institutions was offered to Russia as a sop or a carrot in order to ease Moscow's swallowing of the "new

European security architecture," as the American plan to expand NATO eastward was euphemistically called. One might even say that both NACC and PfP were specifically created for that purpose.[18]

The United States gained Russia's official sanction for NATO's expansion after President Yeltsin on 27 May 1997, in Paris, signed the so-called Founding Act, concocted by then Foreign Minister Yevgeny Primakov, Secretary of State Madeleine Albright, and NATO Secretary-General Javier Solana. The act is a hollow document, compiled essentially from texts, borrowed from the UN charter and various NATO documents (particularly those that support and clarify the bloc's expansionist policy). It firmly ties Russia to NATO, thus limiting its foreign policy choices, but it does not constrain the United States one jot! By signing this act, the Russian president personally dumped the Helsinki Final Act and thus opened the way for the destruction of the legal basis on which the whole system of international relations in Europe as well as continental peace were based.

Mrs. Albright cynically presented to the public this act (that also created a proforma Russia-NATO Joint Permanent Council, where Russia is occasionally and selectively informed about the forthcoming NATO moves) as a "pacifier" for Russia.[19] The fact that the act is not worth the paper it is printed on was vividly demonstrated in the spring of 1999, when NATO unleashed its air attacks on peaceful Yugoslavia—close ally of Russia—without ever consulting Moscow. (Actually, many international experts agree that the U.S. "humanitarian intervention" in Yugoslavia was meant to be a "lesson for Russia," similar to the "message" which Hitler, in the spring of 1941, sent to Russia when Germany barbarously bombed and then occupied Yugoslavia.) In any event, the Founding Act unquestionably gave freedom of action to the leaders of the newly independent countries (NIC)—the former republics of the USSR—to seek closer ties with NATO, often at the expense of the vital security interests of Russia.[20]

To solidify the spoils of victory in the cold war and to tilt the present balance of forces in Europe still more in favor of the United States and its allies is, at present, one of Washington's most important foreign policy goals. But this task is only one of the many in the broader scheme of American aspirations on the global arena. There can be no doubt that the United States is striving for world hegemony. Such aspirations are clearly stated in President Clinton's many statements regarding the necessity of Washington's world leadership as well as in a number of official documents published by the U.S. government and the U.S.-dominated Atlantic Alliance.[21] These aspirations are also confirmed by the practical actions of American diplomacy and by Washington's military actions, such as its unilateral decisions to bomb Afghanistan, Sudan, and Yugoslavia. They are also exemplified by many extraterritorial laws, adopted by the U.S. Congress in the past few years, that are intended to regulate relations between foreign countries and third parties; by dozens of economic sanctions applied in the past decade by the United States to foreign countries, including Russia; and by unceremonious meddling of American diplomatic representatives in purely internal affairs of other countries. This drive for world hegemony is confirmed as well by the contempt that the U.S. leadership has shown toward the UN (including the nonpayment of dues) and its Security Council. Washington has constantly evaded the latter by unilaterally embarking on its international "peace missions," among them the 1991 military intervention in Panama and the more recent air campaign, waged against the sovereign, nonaligned Yugoslavia.

The most recent demonstration of the American imperial contempt toward the rest of the world community occurred in October 1999, when the U.S. Senate refused to ratify—and then killed—the Comprehensive Nuclear Test Ban Treaty on the ground that it allegedly impinges upon the sovereignty of the United States. In its pursuit of hegemony, Washington relies essentially on the nonmilitary instruments of suasion and coercion which are applied against the background of substantial presence of the U.S. military power worldwide.

The concrete short-term aim of the U.S. government is to make the United States the dominant power on the Eurasian continent. This goal is a post–cold war upgrade of its traditional determination not to allow any single power to dominate Eurasia. In order to achieve it (and, according to classic geopolitics, this would be tantamount to achieving global domination), the United States needs first of all to establish command over Russia (which it now has almost achieved). For this purpose, Washington also needs to turn the adjacent belt of independent states—from Turkey to Mongolia—into a zone of unquestionable U.S. influence. And finally, if not command over China, the United States also requires some kind of a deal with Beijing that would secure at least 15 to 20 years of relative peace. According to the calculations of American statesmen and experts, this peaceful period would enable the country to ensure the perpetuation of "soft" global domination through America's economic and financial preponderance, supremacy in communications, command of modern information technology, organizational prowess, and leadership in modern science and technology.

It is impossible to develop in a short chapter detailed support of the above theses. But they are quite sufficiently explained and justified in the writings of prominent U.S. politicians and foreign policy experts, as well as in the documents of the departments of State and Defense. The important point in the context of this discussion is that these goals determine Washington's policy of support of the servile Kremlin administration, the policy of engagement with China, and the firm backing of Japan and of the Republic of Korea—the reliable U.S. allies in the Asia-Pacific region. They also explain the U.S. desire to strengthen relations with India and the ASEAN countries.

The particulars of Washington's present policy toward Russia are the following: theoretically, it is irrelevant for the United States whether, in the long run, Russia remains a unified country or whether it disintegrates into a number of fiefdoms. Nor does Washington care whether the latter are governed democratically or by some strongman. American economic and political domination over a group of allegedly independent states on the territory of former Russia would be as overwhelming as is the case today with present Russia and the other NICs. The only snag is that Russia continues to possess a powerful nuclear arsenal. Until the United States solves the problem of denuclearization of Russia (either through acquiring total control over its nuclear arsenal, diminishing its nuclear stock to an "acceptable minimum" by means of arms control agreements, or neutralizing these weapons in some other way), Washington will retain an interest in preserving Russia as a unified state under a firm control of the central—but pro-American—government. The United States cannot allow a situation to develop where some provincial rulers might "privatize" strategic nuclear missiles located on the territory under their control, as notorious Russian general—and now governor—Lebed' once proposed to do in his Krasnoyarsk region. From Washington's point of view, this would be a nightmare, explaining why it has been very lenient toward Boris Yeltsin and his clique: they will not permit such a situation to arise. This has been the psychological underpinning of the Clinton administration's support of the Russian "reformers."

Nevertheless, gradually—beginning with the Russian financial default in August 1998—the White House and its advisers began to realize that Yeltsin and his team of cronies had neglected the job entrusted to them by Washington (and, for that matter, by the people of Russia): to keep the country safe, sound, and a single entity. The Americans suddenly discovered that Russia is nearing collapse, largely because the only job the Kremlin rulers do well is to fill their pockets with money which they steal from Russia's destitute masses. These rulers have become so engrossed in stealing state (i.e., the people's) property and money that they have had no time for anything else.[22]

More than that: to make it handier to plunder the state coffers, President Yeltsin actually wrecked the top management of the attorney general's office. The dozens of billions of rubles that were acquired dishonestly were easily converted into dollars. By means of various intricate schemes, these funds were then deposited in foreign banks and offshore "safe havens" or were used to purchase properties abroad. That is why, on the eve of the new parliamentary and presidential elections in Russia in 1999–2000, Washington gave a go-ahead to (or deliberately did not interfere with) the U.S. press muckraking campaign aimed at uncovering unprecedented in the newer European history sweep of corruption in Russia's government circles, including a merger with the money-laundering operations of the Russian gangster underworld![23]

Prompted by the appropriate advice of the G-7 finance ministers, the IMF, in September 1999, decided to suspend the disbursement of financial aid to Russia until permanent independent foreign oversight of the gold and foreign currency reserves of the Central Bank of Russia was established. (The Russian government accepted that condition thus *de facto* confirming the correctness of press accusations that it vehemently denied publicly.) This was—so far—the ultimate humiliation of Russia, but definitely there are more such experiences in store, unless some noncolonial government is formed in Moscow as a result of the forthcoming parliamentary and presidential elections in Russia. However, such an outcome seems doubtful, because Washington's grip on the upper strata of Russian society is very tight. The American leaders, for their part, hoped that by means of such revelations they were helping their more honest protégés in Russia (who surely do not lack the necessary financial support) to win the governance of the country. (What kind of a ruling team Russia will have will become known after the publication of this chapter.) In a way, the sacrifice of Yeltsin and his team can be considered a preemptive move by the Clinton administration on the eve of new presidential elections in the United States to avoid the blame that it had "lost Russia."

The Western leaders, remarks Sergei Markov, director of the Moscow Institute for Political Research, "talk straight to the Russian elite: 'If it is true that the power in Russia does not belong to the Russian mafia, prove it by putting the mafiosi behind bars. If you want . . . to do business with civilized people, begin by establishing a civilized order in your own house. Make it so that the laws work in your own country, that honest people can do business, that the stolen money can be found, and that the thieves are in prison and not in the government.' "[24]

The U.S. authorities hope to tie Russia more strongly to NATO and its peacekeeping operations in order to have more control over the Russian military. Simultaneously, they want to sow the seeds of mistrust between Russia and China in order to prevent cooperation between them in opposition to the U.S. drive for global domination.

The United States, having designated the Transcaucasus region as a sphere of its vital interests, is doing everything in its power to decrease Russian presence in that area. By various means, it tries to undercut Russia's relations with oil-rich Azerbaijan. The U.S. government is also playing an intricate game in Georgia, where it is trying to push President Shevardnadze farther away from Moscow. Given all this, it is incomprehensible why the Kremlin applied for American help and cooperation in tracking down the Chechen terrorist leaders who, in the autumn of 1999, undertook a massive armed invasion of the Dagestan republic of Russia. Ostensibly, they are also responsible for blowing up dwelling complexes in a number of Russian cities. There are only two plausible explanations for Moscow's initiative: either the Russian officials were ordered to do so by Washington (which is eager to examine the activities of the terrorists "from the other side"), or the Kremlin was trying to pacify the FBI and other U.S. law enforcement agencies that have been deeply involved in the investigation of Russian money laundering. There is no doubt that the United States is opposing terrorism, but it is very doubtful that Washington would really help Russia in its fight against the insurgencies and secessionist movements in northern Caucasus. It seems that the ultimate goal of the United States is to gradually squeeze Russia out of that strategically very important region.[25] A larger, but related, U.S. goal is not to permit Russia to restore in the present CIS space the level of cohesion that existed in the former Soviet Union.

However, as noted earlier, America's biggest worry is Russia's nuclear arsenal over which, many in Washington seem to believe, the government is losing proper control. In this respect, the

United States does give Russia every possible assistance to safe-guard nuclear as well as chemical weapons through the Nunn-Lugar program of "cooperative threat reduction." While being deeply involved in these activities, the U.S. military is trying to obtain some control over the Russian nuclear weapons. Specifically, it seems in this respect that Washington's most urgent task is to diminish the Russian nuclear arsenal as much as possible. For this reason, it has persistently pressed Moscow to ratify the START-2 Treaty, which the Russian Duma has so far refused to do. This task has become more difficult since the U.S. decision to "punish" Yugoslavia. Still, during the 1998 summit in Moscow, President Clinton persuaded the senile Yeltsin to agree to the liquidation of fifty tons of weapons-grade plutonium (allegedly on a reciprocal basis).[26]

This liquidation will decrease Russia's capacity to produce nuclear weapons (its main means of defense in the absence of a strong army) and will cost the country hundreds of millions of dollars that would have been better used if invested in some constructive economic projects. The American government is also very eager to impose on Russia a new START-3 treaty. The latter would further diminish the nuclear arsenals of both countries by 30 to 40 percent thus reducing the Russian strategic nuclear arsenal to the level that the American military might grudgingly consider "acceptable." In this connection, it is important to remember that the United States will soon deploy a countrywide ballistic missile defense system, based on the latest American technology. (This system, by the way, can be easily augmented by U.S. deployment of the so-called Theater Ballistic Missile Defense [BMD] in Poland or the Baltic states for the sole purpose of destroying Russia's remaining strategic missiles either by means of a preventive strike or—in the improbable case of a Russian missile attack on the United States—during their boost phase, when the missiles are especially vulnerable.)

In order to obtain legal sanction for the decision to deploy such a system, the U.S. administration insists on the Kremlin's approval of the "necessary corrections" to the 1972 Moscow-Washington Anti-Ballistic Missile (ABM) Treaty. It will be recalled that the latter explicitly forbids the deployment by the signatories of countrywide ABM defense systems. Nevertheless, high American officials visiting Moscow have been twisting the arms of the Russian military and parliamentarians to make them agree to "appropriate changes" in the treaty. Such changes will in fact destroy the treaty as a meaningful contract while preserving it as a "document," permitting the United States to do the very thing the treaty was made to preclude.[27] It is doubtful that the Duma will approve of these changes even if the government does.

The United States is also interested in keeping Russia as a business partner but prefers to keep it in the role of the supplier of oil and raw materials. However, some private American companies are ready to improve cooperation with the handicapped Russian military-industrial complex in order to obtain for next to nothing some unique Russian technologies in such areas as aviation, missile construction, machine building, and space exploration. This has been happening on a large scale.[28]

At the same time, the interests of American farmers dictate that Russia remains the net importer of agricultural products for as long as possible and does not become a competitive supplier of such goods. In this respect they do not have to worry. The ogre of Russian *Agroprom*—the remnant from the old Stalinist days which continues running the still essentially collectivized Russian agriculture—will take care that it remains ruined and nonreformed, because such state of things gives a lot of income and influence to the old Party *nomenclatura* that commands the *Agroprom*.

FOREIGN POLICY OPTIONS FOR RUSSIA

The United States would not have been that bold nowadays in pressing for the expansion of NATO and for Russian concessions were Russia in a better shape economically and politically. Many Russians did realize the true situation a while ago. At the end of 1993, Andrei Novikov, a Russian political scientist, wrote: "It is necessary to recognize that the phenomenon that occurred was not just the defeat of Communism, but the national defeat of Russia, a mighty geopolitical collapse, the loss of national consciousness, which is bordering on national nonexistence."[29] It was a strong, but exact, formulation which is now daily recalled in Russia. An ever wider circle of Russian intellectuals perceive the U.S. policy toward Russia as aiming to undercut their country, to prevent it from rising from its knees. The fact that Russia was placed in such a position was due, in a large measure, to the activities of the so-called reformers who, in reality, are American agents of influence in high government circles of Russia.

Assessing the recent White House document on the U.S. National Security Strategy, the Center for Politico-Military Research of the Russian Academy of Military-Political Science came to the following conclusion: "The operational level of threats to the national interests of Russia from the United States . . . consists of the system of measures and actions of military-political, economic, financial, and other nature, carried out by Washington with the aim of 'forcing out' the Russian Federation from the positions it holds in the world, of discrediting and discriminating against Moscow in the international arena, and of preventing the revival of Russia and its transformation into a new 'power center,' potentially dangerous to the national (global) interests of the United States."[30]

Nikolai Ryzhkov, a prominent Russian politician, former chairman of the Council of Ministers of the USSR, and now a member of the Duma, adds that Russia in recent years "essentially became the object of informational and cultural aggression on the part of the United States. It is the Americans, through their stooges in our country, who determine the policies of the Russian TV. There is occurring a dilution of traditional values, imposition on the people of the 'American way of life'. . . . Formally standing against Islamic fundamentalism, the Americans in point of fact direct the extremists against their rivals—first of all against Russia and increasingly also against Europe, creating a certain Islamic 'green belt' of instability in the south of Eurasia."[31]

Such a realization signified not just the end of the "period of romanticism" in American-Russian relations, as Blair Ruble, the director of the Kennan Institute in Washington, D.C., has put it. It meant that the transference to a geopolitical competition in relations between the United States and Russia was inevitable. It is a competition essentially devoid of ideological basis, but tinted anew on both sides with past images and beliefs, infused almost with mother's milk. It is patently clear that, although some limited strategic partnership between Russia and the United States is quite possible (it even existed in the 1970s when the USSR and the United States became partners in controlling the strategic arms race), the divergence of many national interests of each country would make it difficult for them to pursue similar courses on many foreign policy matters. At the same time, it is clear that though the differences in the objective national interests of the two countries presuppose occasional misunderstandings and even some conflicts, all of them can be quietly resolved in a peaceful international environment. The two sides will reach a dead end in their relations only if they continue on their present course of action.

To avoid that, the United States ought to stop treating Russia as its vassal, constantly discriminating against it in trade relations, prying into every aspect of Russian life with its advice and "corrections." To begin with, Washington should stop thinking that the small coterie of its lackeys in the top echelons of the Russian government and a small number of Russian *nouveau riches* of cosmopolitan persuasion as well as young fans of American heavy metal music will turn Russia into a U.S. domain. They are not a strong enough force to do so in the face of dozens of millions of patriotic Russian people, proud of their country's past achievements and glory and united by the essentially collectivist psychology. These people are constantly striving for fairness and justice, and equate fairness with truth and happiness. They survived the more than 200 years-long Mongolian yoke and effected a mighty rebirth of their country. Even the ruthless Bolsheviks, during the seventy years of their permanent revolution, failed to crush the spiritual strength of the Russian people or to radically change their customs, mores, and ways of doing things. Much less so can Americans succeed in imposing the American way of life upon this essentially Slavonic civilization, especially in a situation when the transoceanic *dirigisme* of Russian politics and economics evokes most passionate condemnation and rejection on the part of the absolute majority of the Russian citizens.

As far as Russia is concerned, the most immediate task it must perform in order to snap out of the rut leading to a catastrophe is to stop following American advice and guidance. The continuation of a denationalized policy is fraught with a real danger of an explosion of the people's wrath. The Russian government should clearly formulate its short- and long-term goals and priorities geared to pursue the genuine national interests of Russia. Among the most urgent tasks of this kind are the insurance of unity and independence of the country, the guarantee of its security, the restoration of the national economic base, and the radical improvement in the material well-being of the population. Even the U.S. experts advise the Russian "elite" to stop stealing the people's wealth. The country that is so rich in raw materials, energy, water resources, forests, and arable land and populated by industrious people can support itself without foreign donations. As the calculations of authoritative Russian economists show, while Russia in the past several years borrowed money to the tune of $60 to $70 billion (interest payments included), it transferred to the West, virtually as a gift, about $300 billion.

It is also high time for the Russian leadership (which, as many in Russia hope, will be "refurbished" after the elections) to realize that present-day Russia, even if it restores its sovereignty, will be no match for the United States in the observable future. Such realization presupposes that all the illusions of grandeur, of leading the world to new heights of wisdom, of catching up with the United States, should be abandoned, and that the most absurd of all the international games played in the second half of the twentieth century—the game of U.S.–Russian competition in accumulating strategic nuclear weaponry, which ruined the mighty USSR—should be stopped, at least on the part of Russia.

It is clear that Russia will not launch its missiles against the United States. Nor can one imagine that the United States, which will undoubtedly retain some influence on the weaker Russia (and there are many leverages to make that influence work), will be mad enough to impose upon its geopolitical rival total obedience by subjecting to a nuclear attack a country that has its own nuclear weapons arsenal. But, it is also important to understand that such a Russian arsenal should in no way be a copy of the American one or a mirror image of its quantity and quality. This arsenal ought to contain what the Russian strategists, not obsessed with some ideological fervor, consider to be sufficient for ensuring the country's safety and security. This issue should be considered and decided on its own merits and not on the basis of some consensus with American experts or advisers. For the United States is still keeping Russia on the hook of the so-called strategic parity, which no longer exists, while at the same time trying to strip it down to the bare nuclear feet.

Russia does not need parity with the United States in nuclear weapons which are actually unusable in a war. What it needs to feel safe and free from American pressure is the assured ability to drop but several nuclear devices on a maximum of three U.S. cities. Washington's awareness of such a Russian capability will forever exclude the possibility of such an action on the part of any U.S. president. Russian specialists do know how many strategic nuclear weapons and in what kind of a deployment they need for such a defensive purpose. And once Russia stops playing the American game, all the previous bilateral agreements between the USSR/ Russia and the United States, regarding the levels of nuclear armaments, should be made null and void. Conversely, Russia and the United States might mutually pledge that for a certain period of time they will not exceed the levels of offensive strategic arms, stipulated by the START-1 Treaty. If the United States wants to build a countrywide ABM system or a world-wide BDM system, or even some universewide defense system, let it be its own business. Maybe, if Washington really proceeds to build some such systems, the time frame for Russia to catch up with the United States in the quality of life for its citizens would be drastically shortened.

All future agreements on the weapons of mass destruction (WMD) or some other types of deadly weaponry, as determined by the UN majority, should be negotiated and concluded only on a global basis, such as the presently existing treaties on banning chemical and bacteriological weapons, antipersonnel land mines, and all nuclear weapons tests. All should include a stipulation that, if, after three years from the day of the signing of the agreement, it is not ratified by some leading powers (named in the special protocol, like is done in the current treaty on banning nuclear weapons testing), it would be considered invalid.

In the process of restructuring the approach to super-deadly arms, the UN might also review the future ways of ensuring nonproliferation of such weaponry and adopting the most effective ones. This seems advisable because the present approach, which seems to be preferred by the United States, namely the bombing of a suspected proliferator into oblivion, is not only inhuman and immoral but actually enhances the striving of many countries clandestinely to obtain and deploy some WMD gadgetry. The cases of Israel, India, Pakistan, and Iraq vividly demonstrate this.

As the overwhelming majority of honest Russian politicians, business people, and journalists see it, the only one way to preserve lasting peace on earth is through the strengthening of the UN and its institutions. The alternative way, which is actually followed by Washington, is to "strengthen peace" by increasing omnipresence of the United States and its chief instrument for "humanitarian operations"—NATO, a military bloc which was created as the main instrument for waging the cold war against the Soviet Union. Actually, as Washington's actions on the world arena clearly demonstrate, it is trying to replace the UN with NATO, retaining the former as a policy instrument, which is used occasionally, especially for dealing with the poor countries of the Third World. The United States prefers for Russia to stay with NATO (but not inside it), so it is said on the West European side of the Eurasian continent, thus helping to bring the American order to the eastern part of the continent. Those tactics won't work, however hard the United States might try, and the leading American political scientists understand that.[32]

But the joy of the moment, the feeling of an emerging American global hegemony, obstructs the vision of the current U.S. leadership. Most of them seem to have fallen into the state of euphoria in which the famous harebrained "new thinker" of the world, Mr. Gorbachev, was a few years ago. Everything seems to be achievable and permissible because "the United States is on the right path" and because its course is supported by the American economic and military might. That impression is surely illusory. Faced with the new U.S. arrogance of power, the East will unite to stop the onslaught by what might be rightly called American imperialism in order to return the world to traditional multinational politics and individual national pursuits of happiness. And that "East," in all probability, will begin from the western tip of Europe, NATO shackles notwithstanding, because no country in the present world, not even the smallest, is happy to exist under the rule of some "unquestioned master."

NOTES

1. See *Rossiiskii statisticheskii ezhegodnik* [Russian Statistical Yearbook] (Moscow: Goskomstat Rossii, 1994), 252; *Itogi*, 17 December 1996, 14; *Nezavisimaia Gazeta-Politekonomiia*, no.6 (April 1999): 15. After the demise of the Soviet Union, Russia inherited about 60 percent of the economic potential of the USSR.

2. Ronald Reagan, *An American Life* (New York: Pocket Books, 1990), 15.

3. M. S. Gorbachev, *Izbrannye rechi i stat'i* [Selected Speeches and Articles] (Moscow: Politizdat, 1988), 493, 495.

4. "History knows quite a few unions among states, built on the basis of temporary coincidence of interests, on accidental diplomatic combinations. But the bonds of the socialist commonwealth with young national states, with the national liberation movement are based on a different foundation. They rest upon the community of basic interests. . . . We have a common enemy—imperialism, common aim—to do away for good with colonial and imperialist oppression. . . ." N. S. Khrushchev, *Problemy natsional'no-osvoboditel'noi bor'by* [Problems of National Liberation Struggle] (Moscow: Politizdat, 1963), 24.

5. *New York Times*, 18 June 1992, A18.

6. Initially the idea of such a partnership was evoked by President Clinton on the eve of his meeting with President Yeltsin in Vancouver in April 1993. Speaking before the American Society of Newspaper Editors, President Clinton said: "The interests of all Americans lie with efforts that enhance our security and our prosperity. That's why our interests lie with Russian reform and with Russian reformers led by Boris Yeltsin. . . . I believe it is essential that we act prudently but urgently to do all we can to strike a strategic alliance with Russian reform." *New York Times*, 2 April 1993, A6.

7. Explaining the American government's reaction to the Russian tanks' fusillade of the parliament (the Russian White House, as it was called), Mr. Strobe Talbott, at that time a special adviser to the secretary of state on the New Independent States, told U.S. congressmen two days later that President Yeltsin had two options: "one, quick and dirty, to rush in like gangbusters with guns blazing; the other, a slow, phased, piecemeal retaking of the building, giving those inside the maximum chance to surrender. Even though the loss of life was still substantial, we find it significant—and **heartening**—that President Yeltsin opted for No. 2." (Emphasis mine—H.T. *U.S. Department of State Dispatch*, 18 October 1993, 722.) It evidently took a lot of imagination and dissembling on the part of Mr. Talbott to call the tank attack on the parliament building full of civilians—deputies as well

as service personnel—"a slow, phased . . . retaking of the building." Can we imagine such an action taking place in the United States?

8. The first Duma was elected for the term of two years. The next Duma was elected in 1995 for a four-year term. The last Duma elections took place in December 1999. The upper house of the Federal Assembly—the Council of the Federation—is composed of the governors of Russia's regions and national republics as well as of chairmen of the regional and republican assemblies. All of them are popularly elected in their respective regions or republics.

9. Sensing the trend of the times, even Kozyrev, by the end of 1994, began to change his image from "Mr. Yes" to "Mr. Tough." In 1995, he repeatedly invoked the threat of a possible use of Russian military forces. In this connection, *Izvestiia* put him into the group of "power ministers," that is, those directly responsible for the use of force, such as ministers of defense, security, and internal affairs. But all of his "strong statements" were designed for internal consumption only and he continued to behave as an errand boy of the U.S. State Department. In this capacity, he enjoyed the support of President Yeltsin.

10. Quoted in *Figury i litsa* ("Personalities and Faces," a Saturday supplement to *Nezavisimaia gazeta*), no. 6 (March 1999): 10.

11. Recently, the existence of such practice was confirmed by the investigations of Russian money laundering through Western banks, detailed in many articles in *New York Times* and other Western newspapers, and by the hearings on the Russian money laundering, conducted by the U.S. House of Representatives in September 1999.

12. The data supplied by the chairman of Russia's Accounting Office, H. Karmokov, *Nezavisimaia gazeta*, May 1999, 4.

13. Such a restructuring is tantamount to shifting the responsibility for repayment to future Russian governments. And while being in deep financial crisis, Russia ventured to take upon itself the repayment of yet another ancient debt. One of the most incompetent prime ministers of the past 300 years, Viktor Chernomyrdin, agreed to repay the debt which the czarist government incurred to France during World War I and which the Russian revolutionary government in 1918 declared to have been paid in full by the blood of the Russian soldiers who died in the war.

14. Economist Sergei Semenishchev, vice-president of *New Economic Perspective* (a foundation). *Nezavisimaia gazeta—Politekonomiia*, no.6 (April 1999): 15.

15. "As the 1990s unfolded, 'reform' and 'market' went from being part of the vocabulary of triumph and hope to being, in the ears of many Russians, almost four-letter words. The noun kapitalizm came increasingly to be modified with the adjective dikii (savage). Accordingly, 'the West' went from being an object of emulation to a target of resentment," acknowledges one of the influential U.S. observers of the Russian scene. Deputy Secretary Strobe Talbott Address at Stanford University, 6 November 1998. *U.S. Department of State Press Release*.

16. Warren Christopher, "America's Leadership, America's Opportunity," *Foreign Policy* (spring 1995): 8–9, 18–19.

17. *NATO Press Release* (http://www.nato.int.docu/pr/1999/p,99–068e.htm).

18. The NATO document on the subject of the organization's enlargement actually confirmed that impression. The important role of PfP, says the document, is, inter alia, to "serve as a means to strengthen relations with partner countries which may be unlikely to join the Alliance early or at all"; "further development of the NATO-Russia relationship . . . should take place in rough parallel with NATO's own enlargement." *Study on NATO Enlargement* (September 1995): 3, 9–10.

19. For more details, see my *Russian National Interests and the Current Crisis in Russia* (Brookfield, MA: Aldershot, 1999): 158–67.

20. Now some of these states allow the United States to establish military bases on their territories and offer big chunks of their land to military training grounds for NATO troops.

21. See, for instance, *A National Security Strategy for a New Century,* a White House document released in October 1998, the *Annual Report of the U.S. Department of Defense to Congress* for 1999. The Alliance's *Strategic Concept,* approved by the heads of state and government participating in the meeting of the North Atlantic Council in Washington, D.C., on 23–24 April 1999. For example, the White House National Security Strategy Report states plainly: "at this moment in history, the United States is called upon to lead—to organize the forces of freedom and progress; to channel the unruly energies of the global economy into positive avenues; and to advance our prosperity, reinforce our democratic ideals and values, and enhance our security. . . . Our strategic approach recognizes that we must lead abroad if we are to be secure at home. . . . We must be prepared and willing to use all appropriate instruments of national power to influence the actions of other states and non-state actors" (iv, 1). Is this not a powerful statement of a global domination goal?

22. When, at the end of 1998, commenting on Dr. Dimitri Simes' article on Russia in *The National Interest,* I stated that the basic mistake most foreign experts on Russia make is not to see that Russia is now ruled by "robbers, embezzlers, and crooks," he reproached me in his reply for looking at Russia only in "black and white" terms. I hope that the recent exposures in the world press of the criminal financial activities of the top Russian rulers, including Boris Yeltsin, opened the eyes of America's "Russia hands" on the sweep of the Russian *kleptokratiia* and *bandokratiia* in the high echelons of the government. See *The National Interest,* no. 55 (spring 1999): 118–19.

23. The meaning of the scandal that happened in the West under the label "Secret Bank Deposits of the President" is dual. First, this is a formal pretext not only for prosecution but for a grandiose *political court trial,* whose outcome is predetermined, of the regime and its central personage. Second, this is a signal that the West has abandoned Yeltsin: it will not only deny him political asylum (should he ever want one), but will also guarantee his extradition. Aleksandr Sevastianov, "Stavka na vozmezdie" (Reliance on Retribution), *Nezavisimaia gazeta,* 29 September 1999, 8.

24. Sergei Markov, "Rossiiskaia elita takovoi poka ne iavliaetsia" [The Russian Elite is Not Yet An Elite], *Nezavisimaia gazeta,* 19 September 1999, 3.

25. "The West will exert colossal political pressure on Russia in order not to allow a restoration of the Russian control over the North Caucasus. The final crushing defeat of 'independent Ichkeria' will create the danger of collapse of the anti-Russian regimes in Azerbaijan and Georgia, and will also sharply increase the probability of a failure of the Baku-Ceyhan oil-pipeline construction project, which, according to the designs of the architects of the 'new world order,' ought to become the 'pivot' of the U.S. military pressure in the Caucasus," wrote two left-wing analysts, Aleksandr Borodai and Aleksandr Rudakov. *Zavtra,* no. 39 (September–October 1999): 3.

26. This came on top of an earlier agreement to sell the United States a large amount of plutonium at a much reduced price. And all this is happening at a time when steel, fertilizers, and other commodities exported by Russia are being pushed out of the U.S. market with the active help of the Clinton administration.

27. The treaty has already been sufficiently diluted by the Yeltsin-Clinton agreement, reached at the March 1997 summit, which, in fact, abolished the differentiation between strategic and tactical antimissiles.

28. As early as the beginning of 1992, leaders of the U.S. antimissile "Star Wars" program worked out a plan to take advantage of the collapse of the Soviet Union by acquiring some of its most advanced technologies and hiring about a thousand of its scientists and engineers. "This," wrote *Aviation Week and Space Technology* "could be a post-cold-war equivalent of Operation Paper Clip after World War Two, when Americans recruited leaders of the pioneering German V-2 rocket project." The "Star Wars" program also drew up a shopping list of Soviet-developed technologies in more than fifty areas vital to aerospace research. *Aviation Week and Space Technology*, 15 September 1992, p.8.

29. *Literaturnaia gazeta*, 15 December 1993, 6.

30. "Manifest Panamerikanizma. Real'naia strategiia SSHA po otnosheniiu k Rossii znachitel'no otlichaetsia ot deklariruemoi" [The Manifesto of Pan-Americanism. The Real Strategy of the USA Towards Russia Is Significantly Different from the Declared One], *Nezavisimoe voennoe obozrenie*, no.22 (1999): 4.

31. Nikolai Ryzhkov, "Konfrontatsiia ili dialog?" [Confrontation or Dialogue?], *Nezavisimaia gazeta*, 28 September 1999, 8.

32. To see that, it is enough to browse through the March/April 1999 issue of *Foreign Affairs*. All the articles in the issue not only question, but unequivocally repudiate the possibility of a unipolar world, managed by the United States. The leading U.S. researcher of the phenomenon of globalism, Professor Samuel Huntington, says: "First, it would behoove Americans to stop acting and talking as if this were a unipolar world. It is not. To deal with any major global issue, the United States needs the cooperation of a least some major powers. Unilateral sanctions and interventions are recipes for foreign policy disasters. Second, American leaders should abandon the benign-hegemon illusion that a natural congruity exists between their interests and values and those of the rest of the world. It does not. . . . Most of the world, as Mandela said, does not want the United States to be its policeman." Samuel P. Huntington, "The Lonely Superpower," *Foreign Affairs* (March/April 1999): 47–49.

"Blurred Focus"
U.S. Policy Toward Russia in the Yeltsin Era

Harvey Sicherman

THE END OF THE COLD WAR LEFT THE UNITED STATES AS THE SOLE superpower, and its former adversary, the Soviet Union, existed no longer. Overnight Moscow became the ruler of a shrunken realm, its dimensions more comparable to the Russia of the early seventeenth century than the expanding power of recent history. But the Russian Federation still retained a formidable nuclear arsenal and large armed forces. It also contained raw materials, markets, skilled workers, and industrial resources important, if not crucial, to the economies of surrounding states.

The recession of Russian power also presented the United States with fundamental challenges, albeit of a more welcome nature than it had faced for five decades. By 1992, George Bush's late cold war call for a Europe "whole and free" appeared tantilizingly close to realization. Russia's sudden lurch away from Communism and empire freed Europe of the fear of war after the bloodiest century in its history; and Moscow's new profession of interest in economic and political reform offered the prospect of free market democracies encompassing the entire continent.

This giddy prospect was soon tempered by a series of hard questions about U.S. policy and U.S.-Russian relations. Should Moscow's withdrawal from Central Europe be accompanied by Washington's retirement from Central Europe, specifically a lessening of its commitment to NATO? Was the perennial question of whether Russia was truly a "Western power" now to be answered by including or excluding Moscow from the postwar European security arrangement? What weight should the new Russia play in U.S. policy: defeated superpower or new partner, or perhaps both? And how could the United States and its allies assist the promising Yeltsin government along the painful road of remaking Russia?

A president of the United States could not answer these questions with the cold calculations of detached statesmanship. The very end of the cold war had abruptly thrust domestic issues to the fore. There was no immediate threat from abroad and the biggest villain on the horizon, Saddam's Iraq, had been laid low in the triumphant Gulf War. International aid was hostage to budget deficits and competing claims. There would be no Marshall Plan, no memorable schemes for a U.S.-led transformation of Russia. Still, two presidents, one Republican and one Democrat, did provide answers of sorts, and these might well be summarized in advance of the complex tale that unfolded over the course of a decade.

The terms of German unification made clear that the United States would remain a major European power anchored in NATO. This reflected the underlying consensus transmitted from the World War II generation that the Europeans alone could not contain the potential danger of a united Germany. Hence, NATO's purpose had been not only to keep Russia "out" but the Germans "down," that is, harmless. There would be no voluntary American retirement to match the Russian retreat. Moreover, the uncertain course of Russian reform early on not only reaffirmed America's role in Europe, but enlarged it. The newly freed central European states haplessly located between Germany and Russia sought refuge in NATO and by 1996, the United States was prepared to allow them in. "Western Europe" thus expanded eastward, eliminating the neutral zone Moscow had hoped to see, in exchange for which the Russians received what President Clinton called "a voice, but not a veto" in NATO's decisions.

Alongside this ambiguous answer came the Balkan crises in two installments. During these episodes, Russia acted as a power less significant for the help it might render than the harm it might cause. Despite an aura of cooperation, Moscow retained a security conception quite at odds with its putative Western partners.

On the symbolic level, the United States continued to treat Russia as if it were its principal partner. President Clinton held nineteen meetings with Boris Yeltsin, not Jiang Zemin. Russia even took symbolic precedence over America's Western allies. It was Moscow, not London, that Clinton chose as the spot to mark the fiftieth anniversary of the end of World War II.

By the end of the decade, however, it had become clear that Russia was not, and was not likely to become, the great stable anchor of U.S. hopes. The crash of the Russian economy in 1998, signifying the failure of the U.S.-supported international reform effort, was accompanied by Moscow's fresh war against Chechnya. A whole series of fractious points disturbed the relationship. Ameri-

can disappointment and even anger with Russia was fully recipro-
cated as Moscow attempted to join with Beijing in an anti-
American alliance that gave diplomatic expression to Russia's
resentments.

On the American side, this gloomy state of affairs was due less
to presidential distraction, as some have argued, than to a more
elementary problem.[1] Clinton and his team *were* focused on Russia
from the start, but their focus was the "democratic partner" of
their hopes embodied by Boris Yeltsin, not the reality. At each
stage, whether in Chechnya, Bosnia, or Kosovo, in arms control
and arms sales, in economic reform and the lack thereof, Moscow
simply did not play the role assigned to it by Washington. Nor did
Yeltsin live up to expectations. Instead, it was schizophrenia, Russian style: a dizzying mix of old-new and new-old, acts of promise
and peril. So the focus blurred as Washington, squinting for the
democratic partner, found its lens increasingly out of touch with
reality. This led inevitably to a recalibration that took its most evident form in a revised lexicon: by 1995, Russia was no longer to be
a "democratic partner" but a "pragmatic partner."[2] This concept,
too, came under heavy pressure in the course of the Kosovo, financial, and Chechnya crises. Thus, as Clinton's presidency
wound down (and Yeltsin's ended), U.S. policy toward Russia remained ambiguous, stranded somewhere between the expired
threat and the unborn ally, leaving to new leadership the difficult
task of defining the relationship.

THE END OF THE SOVIET UNION

The strange death of the Soviet Union in December 1991 left
Americans in a joyous but perplexed mood. To everyone's as-
tonishment, the state founded by Lenin and built by Stalin went
quietly to its grave after a violent life of seventy-four years. A full-
scale debate broke out in Washington over such questions as why
the Soviet empire fell, what role the United States had played in
bringing it about, and whether the peaceful end of Communism
meant that the Russians wanted Western democratic values, not
just a more efficient economy.[3] Upon the answers to these questions also hinged another judgment: whether the new Russia
would become an ally or partner of the West, thus fulfilling America's objective of a Europe whole and free, or resume its pre-Soviet
position of a semi-Western (or semi-Asiatic) country, part of an in-

ternational balance of power but not really part of that vague but
reassuring common concept, the "West."

Bill Clinton, following George Bush, was ready to endorse Russia as a potential ally, but this view had less to do with an analysis
of Russia than of American politics. To put it simply: the end of the
USSR had made it safe to elect a Democrat to the presidency. The
threat from abroad had truly disappeared and the defeat of Saddam Hussein seemed to ratify an unchallenged American supremacy. George Bush's spectacular foreign policy successes rendered
Bill Clinton's international inexperience irrelevant to the campaign. The new president was free to focus on domestic issues.

Russia, however, was not far from Clinton's mind. A forgotten
preelection incident illustrated his willingness to embrace both Yeltsin and Russia. By early 1992, a shaky Boris Yeltsin was appealing
to the Bush administration for a concrete sign of support; that is,
financial assistance. Bush subscribed fully to the argument that a
free-market economy would buttress a democratic and peaceful
Russia. He preferred, however, to let the main burden of economic
rehabilitation be directed by the multilateral International Monetary Fund (IMF) and that America's European partners (such as
Germany) provide most direct assistance not only because this reduced the cost to the United States, but also because it provided a
kind of political cover. In particular, the IMF's advice was "expert"
and presumably apolitical, free of foreign policy criteria, and based
purely on economic judgments. This might insulate reform from
the inevitable political stresses both in Moscow itself and its former
Western adversaries as Russia suffered the strain of reform.

Strapped by recession and budget deficits, Bush struggled to
find a domestic focus for his reelection campaign, while avoiding
additional foreign commitments. He did not encourage a bipartisan group of senators who sought to offer Russia serious American
assistance. Then on 9 March, former President Nixon, frustrated
by White House inaction, wrote publicly of the administration's
"pathetically inadequate response" to the high stakes game of Russia's future: "we are playing as if it's a penny-ante game."[4] As word
came that Bill Clinton would also announce his support for more
aid, Bush hastily decided to beat him to the punch, announcing his
own aid package on 1 April 1992, an hour before Clinton's speech.
Secretary of State Baker, whose policy planning staff had been urging such a move since January, was left to follow up three weeks
later with a more detailed plan. Thus, Clinton had been willing to
argue for increased foreign aid—even more unpopular now that
the Soviet threat had lapsed—despite his emphasis on domestic

need.[5] He had done so, certain of bipartisan support, amplified by Richard Nixon's publicly critical stand. This was not to be the last such interplay between Clinton and Nixon on Russia.

CLINTON AND RUSSIA

The new president had thus staked support for Russia as part of his campaign. Although Clinton had visited Eastern Europe and the Soviet Union while abroad at Oxford during the late 1960s, he was no expert. Otherwise, Clinton's controversial record on the Vietnam draft and his apprenticeship in Senator Fulbright's office put him on the side of those suspicious of America's "arrogance of power" and readiness to use force in the name of anti-Sovietism. Moreover, his chief foreign policy appointees had served during the Carter administration, remembered for its critique of the "inordinate fear of Communism" and its disastrous handling of the Iran hostage crisis. This background left the new team anxious to prove that it could manage foreign policy effectively, especially with Russia.

The new president promised to focus on the economy "like a laser," leaving much of foreign policy to Secretary of State Warren Christopher. Following Clinton's lead, Christopher put the advancement of American economic interests at the head of the list.[6] Russia, however was an exception from the start. Strobe Talbott, a *Time* magazine correspondent, an old Clinton friend, and reputed Russophile, was appointed ambassador-at-large to the Russian-sponsored Commonwealth of Independent States (CIS) that consisted of Russia itself and all the former republics except for the Baltics and Georgia. Given Clinton's preference for discussion with friends over organized bureaucratic procedures—what Colin Powell called "graduate seminar bull sessions"—this was a significant signal.[7]

Another signal was Clinton's agreement to an early meeting with Yeltsin and even before that, his public consultations in March with former President Richard Nixon apparently designed to protect his right flank as he embraced an increased aid package for Russia.[8] Nixon was not the only senior statesman urging this policy. George Kennan, famous for enunciating the Containment Doctrine, added his prestigious view that Russia was ripe if not entirely ready for a Western embrace. Kennan saw the Russians attempting three revolutions at once: from dictatorship to democracy; from empire to federation; and from Communism to capitalism. West-

ern support and encouragement would be necessary (if not sufficient) to bring the Russians forward in each case.[9]

When Clinton met Yeltsin for the first time on 4 April 1993 at
Vancouver he was therefore intellectually and politically prepared
to "up the ante." Alongside a renewed commitment to the international economic effort overseen by the IMF, Clinton offered fresh
rhetoric—a proclamation of a "new democratic partnership"—and
a $1.6 billion aid package. Yeltsin, burnishing his democratic cre-
dentials, had just been reelected himself to his post as president of
postcommunist Russia. The election, the aid, and the U.S. en-
dorsement were used to help the Russian leader in his increasingly
difficult struggle with the Communist-dominated parliament, a
holdover from the Soviet era.

ARCHITECTS AND ARCHITECTURE

The Clinton administration's wholesale embrace of Yeltsin affected the developing debate in the United States and Europe over
post–cold war security arrangements. As the Warsaw Pact joined
the Soviet Union in the "trash-heap of history," the newly independent and former Communist states in Central and Eastern Europe began to look for "anchors." Moving the metaphor from sea
to land, the Western powers replied with "architecture": increasingly elaborate diplomacy that built upon existing institutions,
such as the Council for Security and Cooperation in Europe
(CSCE) and even NATO, which in 1991 had invited its former
enemy to join the newly conceived North Atlantic Cooperation
Council.

By early 1993, however, the uncertain course of Russian domestic reform and what appeared to be a revival of an aggressive foreign policy had disillusioned some of the earlier advocates of all
inclusive security arrangements. Moscow threatened the Baltic
states over treatment of Russians there; in Moldavia and in Central
Asia, the Russians used violence to reassert their influence; and opposition to the START (Strategic Arms Reduction Treaty) and CFE
(Conventional Forces in Europe) treaties was mounting in the
Communist-dominated Duma.[10] Chancellor Kohl's Germany, the
earliest beneficiary at the end of the cold war and the biggest single
investor in Russia's rehabilitation, foresaw trouble.[11] Meanwhile,
the democratic reforms in Poland and Hungary had lost support
steadily to the former Communist parties as economic change dis-
tressed their citizens.[12]

In the face of these events, the existing architecture began to look very flimsy. The CSCE to which virtually all of Europe belonged had been described by former Secretary of State Baker as "the conscience of the continent." It could not offer security assurances. That left the European Union, the vehicle of Western European economic integration; it was long on security resolutions but short on substance, and its main contribution could be economic. But the Union was itself torn by the debate over "deepening or expanding." The Franco-German partnership at its heart faced its own strains after German reunification. The resolve at Maastricht, in December 1991, to complete monetary union in 1999 made early expansion impossible. The only other supranational European institution was the Western European Union, a refugee from the failed European Army experiment of the 1950s. It lacked military forces and political gravitas.

By default, NATO stood alone as the most effective surviving security institution. But NATO was "cold war," deployed to defend Western Europe and led by the United States. What could it do for Central and Eastern Europe? If its role was to prevent a new Russian threat, then how could Russia be incorporated? And if Russia were not incorporated, would that not isolate Moscow, encourage the antiwesterners, and store up great trouble for the future?

The newly emancipated democracies in Warsaw, Budapest, and Prague argued for NATO expansion on historical and geopolitical grounds. The Middle Europeans had been the victims, first of German Nazism and then of Russian Communism. A situation in which the Germans were timid and the Russians weak struck them as highly unnatural. Only one international organization had dealt successfully with the Germans and the Russians: NATO. And so, as the Russian reform seemed to falter, their arguments for joining NATO became more persuasive.

Strobe Talbott and others in the administration, however, saw Russian reform and Yeltsin himself to be the crucial determination of Central Europe's security prospects. Talbott argued successfully through much of 1993 that by embracing Yeltsin, Clinton had chosen the strategic pivot of his policy toward Europe; NATO expansion could only harm Yeltsin while threatening to become a self-fulfilling prophecy by arousing Russian nationalism.[13] This argument also enjoyed the Pentagon's support. Secretary of Defense William Perry saw the arms control treaties as far more important to U.S. national security than the extension of guarantees to indefensible states so near to Russia.[14] By summer 1993, then, the Russia "first" policy—Russia as America's democratic partner—was firmly established. Moscow was to be the coarchitect of a "Europe whole and free" because the unity and freedom of the continent seemed to depend so heavily upon the future of Yeltsin's reform.

THE NEW-OLD RUSSIA

In September 1993, Yeltsin and the Communist-dominated Parliament (the Supreme Soviet) finally came to blows. Led by Ruslan Khasbulatov (speaker of the Parliament) and Alexander Rutskoi (Yeltsin's vice president in the election of March 1993), the anti-Yeltsin parties attempted a coup. Aided by part of the military, Yeltsin ordered the bombardment and seizure of the Duma's seat, the "White House," and then arrested its leaders. A total of 187 lives were lost.

Yeltsin then offered a new constitution, this time giving the president enormous powers, and called for fresh elections to ratify both the constitution and his leadership. These actions brought great controversy in Russia and abroad. Until September, the Russians had managed to overthrow a brutal regime with little bloodshed; now many of the leaders of that overthrow (Rutskoi stood with Yeltsin in defying the 1991 coup) had attacked each other. But President Clinton had no doubts. He supported Yeltsin fully and publicly as the only legitimate elected leader of the country.

In December, anticipating a massive victory for the democratic and reform parties, Vice-President Gore and a large delegation came to Moscow to celebrate. Then the votes were tallied. There was some question as to whether the 50 percent threshold to ratify the constitution had been reached, but there was no question about the parliamentary results.[15] The Lower House, the Duma, would be dominated by a "Red-Brown" coalition. Communists and fellow travelers made up the largest bloc followed by Zhirinovsky's Liberal Democratic Party, shockingly antiwestern, antidemocratic, and anti-Semitic. Yeltsin himself produced the most alarming statistic: a full 30 percent of the military had voted for Zhirinovsky.[16]

The election results also seemed to ratify another troubling development. In November 1993, the Russian security establishment had produced a new military doctrine profoundly disturbing to those who read it.[17] It emphasized nuclear weapons, argued for a smaller conventional force but still competitive with NATO, and declared Russia's security borders to be the same as the old Soviet Union. Military intervention beyond Russia's borders was justified to help Russians living abroad. Indeed, the doctrine proposed a sphere of interest—the "Near Abroad"—that looked remarkably like the old Soviet insistence that neighbors accommodate themselves to Moscow's security demands.

Yeltsin's own views on these matters were obscure. He had already begun to levitate above parties and factions, speaking of democracy but not supporting the democratic parties, acting as head of the government but above the bureaucratic machine. Superb in a crisis and a veteran infighter, government itself was not his strength. He was idle or absent for long periods, widely believed to be suffering from a debilitating alcoholism.

The democrats and reformers had clearly been rejected by a considerable portion of the people and Yeltsin, very much the populist, drew his conclusions. In mid-January he recruited an old time "Communist industrialist," Victor Chernomyrdin, head of the oil-gas monopoly Gazprom, to serve as prime minister, forcing out many of the reformers. The remaining symbol of wholesale cooperation with the West, Foreign Minister Andrei Kozyrev, suddenly became more assertive on the Balkans, the Middle East, and NATO, although never assertive enough for the Duma. That body also delivered a telling signal to Yeltsin when on 23 February 1994, the failed coup makers of September were granted amnesty and released.

PARTNERSHIP FOR PEACE AND LOSS OF CONSENSUS

These events shocked the United States and its allies, raising the possibilities that the Russian experiment had failed. Yet there seemed little choice; there was no alternative to Yeltsin and limited leverage on all other matters. The return of nuclear weapons from Ukraine and Kazakhstan to Russia, which the United States advocated in order to bring them under the arms control regime established by START-1, was at its most delicate stage. Enough also remained of the economic reform so that the Western aid packages (at this point mostly German) would not be cut off.

Under the pressure of these events, Washington began to modify its policy. In Europe, the Germans supported the increasingly anxious requests by the Poles, Hungarians, Czechs, and others that they be allowed to join NATO.[18] Early in 1994, Clinton journeyed to Brussels where on 10 January he secured NATO approval for a new "Partnership for Peace" (PfP). This more fraternal language replaced Bush's North Atlantic Cooperation Council. Like its predecessor it was a program of greater military cooperation, an outreach of sorts to "forge new security relationships." The NATO Summit also expressed the Alliance's readiness to consider expansion.

This appeared to fit well with the Clinton administration's proclaimed grand design: the "enlargement" of the circle of "market democracies" primarily through economics.[19] But NATO was not an economic alliance, and its enlargement was based on a geopolitical rationale that might antagonize the bigger prize of a democratic, free-market Russia. Attempting to tread this line, Secretary of State Christopher explained to Yeltsin himself in October 1993—a bare fortnight after the battle with the Duma—that the process initiated by the Partnership for Peace (PfP) would be very gradual and very transparent. Yeltsin told Christopher that the PfP was an "act of genius," but as Christopher later wrote, the Russian leader liked it because he thought the PfP would delay NATO expansion indefinitely, a conclusion not hard to reach given Clinton's own ambiguity.[20]

Clinton himself ratified Christopher's approach when he declared on 9 January that NATO needed to deter "the dream of empire" but should not "draw a new line between East and West that could create a self-fulfilling prophecy of future confrontation." He took this position to Prague on 11–12 January where, surrounded by a vast media crowd, he crossed the historic Charles Bridge together with Czech President Vaclav Havel to symbolize the new era. Clinton also met separately with the leaders of the so-called Visegrad Group, the presidents and prime ministers of Poland, the Czech Republic, Slovakia, and Hungary. Sharply divided by interests and personalities, they nonetheless delivered a singular message: they had to join NATO if democracy, prosperity, and security in the region was to survive. Clinton was impressed. He said publicly that the issue was no longer "whether but when" NATO was to be expanded.[21]

Then, on 13 January Clinton and Yeltsin issued a joint U.S.–Russian declaration in Moscow describing the PfP as an "important element of an emerging new European Security Architecture."[22] This summit was topped off when Yeltsin, Clinton, and Ukrainian President Leonid Kravchuk agreed to dismantle Ukraine's nuclear arsenal.

Clinton's various tactics seemed to give all parties something while leaving a disquieting ambiguity. Was PfP truly a corridor or antechamber leading to membership for everyone including Russia? Was Russian approval a sign that Clinton had given Yeltsin a veto on the membership issue? Where were the Russians going anyway?

The new policy did not hold up well under congressional scrutiny. Clinton, like Bush before him, had benefited from congressional support for engagement with Russia that if anything was more enthusiastic than the president himself. In 1991, senators Nunn and Lugar authored an imaginative program to "buyout" the accumulated Russian weapons-grade plutonium.[23] Congress also endorsed various initiatives, especially those that encouraged private investment in Russia. Clinton, further protected on his flanks by Nixon, had proceeded without much objection to *increase* foreign assistance to Russia at a time when the foreign aid and defense budgets were being drastically cut.[24]

By the winter of 1993–94, however, this consensus suddenly fractured under the weight of events in Russia and increasing complaints—including Polish and Ukrainian ethnic lobbies—that the U.S. policy was feeding Moscow's revived ambitions. Yeltsin's appointment of Chernomyrdin as prime minister in early January 1994, forcing the exodus of most of the economic reformers, set the stage in Washington for congressional irritation to boil over. When Strobe Talbott himself was nominated to be deputy secretary of state, he was assailed strongly by Senator Lugar and others for a "Russia first" approach that, in view of recent trends, seemed to invite a revived Russian sphere of influence. Talbott was confirmed to his post on 24 February 1994 by a vote of 66–31 (all 31 were Republicans), a significant vote of opposition to such a high ranking appointee.[25]

Despite President Clinton's reassurances to the Visegrad Group that NATO was indeed open to new members, the course of events in 1994 strengthened those who saw PfP itself to be, as Senator Lugar put it, a "program for postponement."[26] The PfP did not seem to go much further than Bush's North Atlantic Cooperation Council in practical terms, nor did it seem to discriminate realistically about membership qualifications: (Romania, the least reformed of the former Soviet satellites was the first to join.) Moreover, membership was open to all sorts of states, including Sweden, for example (non-NATO EU) and the Central Asian quartet, whose relationship to Europe was tangential. Indeed, it was not until August 1994, when newly appointed Assistant Secretary of State Richard Holbrooke galvanized the state and Pentagon bureaucracies, that the president's decision to support NATO expansion was actually given the necessary procedural shape.[27]

Amidst this confusion, the Russians soon made clear both their real objective and their objections to PfP. Newly appointed Defense Minister Pavel Grachev visited NATO in May 1994 to deliver a disconcerting message. Russia had only a modest interest in joining the PfP. Instead, Grachev explained Moscow's real objective: to gain a determining say in NATO's decision-making or failing that to paralyze the alliance under the somnolent CSCE.[28] In short, the Russians still regarded NATO as an adversary. Or, to put it in geopolitical terms, Moscow wanted a retraction of American power symbolized by NATO to compensate for its own retraction from Central Europe, or if not, at least no expansion of American power through a NATO move eastward.

Grachev may have been disturbing, but at least he was consistent. The rest of the Russian government, however, swung between conciliation and confrontation. Foreign Minister Andrei Kozyrev sought to allay some fears by agreeing to join PfP in principle, but the official ratification of a specific PfP arrangement with Russia was left to Yeltsin himself. On 11 December 1994, however, Yeltsin astounded the United States by refusing to join the Partnership. In a public tantrum he also described NATO expansion as a threat to Russia, declaring that it would bring a "cold peace" and a redivided continent.[29] The Russians would sign on to the PfP in May 1995, but did nothing with it.

ALTERNATIVE ARCHITECTURE: THE CONTACT GROUP

This apparent deadend was overshadowed by the rapidly deteriorating Bosnian crisis which provided its own commentary on Europe's "security architecture." Initially, the Balkan crisis had been largely handled by the Western powers, Russia contributing only a token unit to the UN force that policed the cease-fire between Serbs and Croatians in Croatia's Krajina region. While this unit became infamous for corruption and Serb sympathy, the Yeltsin government steered clear of the Balkans despite its nationalist critics.

The threat of massive Western intervention in Bosnia and the newly aggressive Duma prodded more activity from Moscow. The UN had been discredited by weakness in the face of blatant Serb intimidation, "ethnic cleansing," and deliberate attacks on civilians. By spring 1994, the United States tried another tack. Borrowing a device used by the State Department in Southern Africa in the early 1980s, the United States proposed a "contact group" of the major states. The United States, Russia, France, Britain, and Germany would establish a new diplomacy to fix the Bosnian problem. This looked like a revival of the "Concert of the Great Powers," who had imposed a solution on the Balkans under Bismark's mediation at the Congress of Berlin in 1878. The Contact Group was formally announced on 24 April 1994, shortly after the Gorazde cease-fire.[30]

The Contact Group operated on an implicit assumption that the great powers could deliver the small powers. Russia's role was obvious: to pursuade their historic "wards," the Serbs, on whose behalf they had made war in 1914, to behave. At first the Contact Group seemed a political master stroke for Yeltsin. The PfP and all the blather about NATO was theory; the Bosnia crisis was real. As he turned toward his nationalist critics in the Duma, he could show that Russia was now a critical factor in the Balkans. This appealed on another level, too. Russian geopoliticians, clearly in charge of the new security doctrine, were well aware that Yugoslavia had been an "American account" during the cold war, Marshal Tito's peculiar neutrality denying the Soviets an Adriatic port and direct access to Greece. Now Russia would have a hand that could actually enlarge its influence compared to the Soviet era.

After painful negotiation, the Contact Group did concoct a new plan in late July, which, under Russian pressure, offered the Serbs an improvement over earlier offers. Still it was not enough. The Serbs rejected the terms.

Russian Foreign Minister Kozyrev loudly denounced the Serb recalcitrance, but he could not, or would not, deliver their compliance. When his partners began to threaten the Serbs, Kozyrev dissented, denouncing the use of force.[31] The Contact Group was paralyzed.

Finally, in spring and summer 1995, a series of Serb atrocities beginning in the UN "safe zone" at Serbrenica forced Washington's hand. Clinton was suddenly caught between the demands of newly elected French President Chirac to "get tough or get out" and a veto-proof congressional demand to lift the embargo, led by Senate majority leader Bob Dole. A successful surprise offensive by the Croats in August, supplemented by U.S. supported NATO bombing, brought the Serbs to negotiation. Orchestrated by Assistant Secretary of State Richard Holbrooke, the parties were duly assembled at a Dayton Ohio Air Force Base. A new NATO force with a large American component was to be inserted to "implement" Dayton, or at least select parts of it.

But where was Russia? These developments turned the Contact Group into a dangerous fiasco for Yeltsin, who appeared irrelevant. Clinton and his diplomats, however, were anxious to use

Russia's earlier condemnation of Serb behavior to good effect. The Russians were therefore to be included in the Implementation Force (IFOR) in order to isolate the Serbs completely and to avoid the isolation of Russia itself from the action.

But how to do it? The Russians would not serve under NATO. Many in Washington, full of misgivings about the plan, saw potential disaster in putting a Russian force friendly to the Serbs adjacent to American forces.

Both 1994 and 1995 had been bad years for U.S.–Russian relations, but Clinton and Yeltsin, each for his own reasons, were determined to reach an understanding that rebuffed their critics. Thus it was at FDR's estate, Hyde Park, chosen deliberately to symbolize U.S.–Russian cooperation, that on 23 October 1995 they were able to announce both "profound understanding" and a practical arrangement for Bosnia. Russian dignity allowed for subservience to a U.S. officer but not a NATO one. A token Russian force would join IFOR. Its commander would coordinate with the American officer who headed IFOR, wearing his "U.S. hat," not his NATO hat. And so, on 21 December 1995 a Russian brigade arrived at the critical Posavina Corridor connecting the Serb areas of Bosnia with Serbia, where it sat placidly until the Kosovo crisis four years later, when one of its units made a dramatic dash to secure the Pristina airport ahead of NATO.

These last minute maneuvers prevented a Russian defection from the American plan and put a cooperative face on U.S.–Russian relations, something of benefit to both Clinton and Yeltsin as they faced arduous reelection campaigns in 1996. But this facade could not alter the overall conclusion. In a brief time, perhaps three months, the ghost of the nineteenth-century Concert of Great Powers had been summoned, only to prove a figment of historical imagination. It had not worked because (in the American view) the Russians would not or could not deliver the Serbs. Was this because a Serb defeat was not in Russia's interests in which case Moscow had been duplicitous with the Contact Group? Or was Moscow's influence in Belgrade no more than misleading legend? If this were true then Russian claims to Great Powerdom were empty. In any event, Washington had redefined its expectation. On 4 May 1995, Secretary of State Christopher referred to Russia as "a pragmatic partner"—the Pentagon's preferred locution—rather than a democratic partner, the new lexicon indicating a more limited harmony.

"BUILDING DOWN": ARMS CONTROL AND PROLIFERATION

The pyrotechnics of the Balkans and NATO expansion over-shadowed another and highly significant activity left over from the cold war: arms control. Both the United States and the Soviet Union had agreed upon a massive program to reduce both their nuclear (START-1 and 2) and conventional arsenals (Conventional Forces in Europe, CFE). While Russia agreed to take on the Soviet role, the geopolitical basis for both processes had been altered significantly. Overnight Ukraine, Belarus, and Kazakstan became major nuclear powers. On the conventional side, Russian forces were withdrawn from German territory and the Baltics.

Two very special problems also arose from the Moscow government's shaky administrative control and its acute need for money: (1) potential proliferation of nuclear weapons and (2) arms sales to U.S. adversaries, such as Iran. American fears of a rogue state equipped with nuclear missiles, arising in part from these problems, also renewed pressure on the Clinton administration to build a missile defense system, reopening the debate over the twenty-five-year-old Anti-Ballistic Missile (ABM) treaty.

The U.S. policy put a high premium on the so-called "build down" provisions of the START treaties and control of nuclear weapons materials. To aid this process, the Nunn-Lugar Act set up several financial incentives, including support for Russian nuclear scientists, the purchase of plutonium, and aid for the dismantling of the nuclear weapons. These efforts brought very uneven results.

It would be best to start at the "top." By the late 1980s, both countries possessed 10,000 to 12,000 warheads. START-1 began the process of reducing the launchers to about 6,000 a piece (the warheads themselves were exempt) but START-2 offers the most dramatic change. If carried out, it would limit each side to 3,000 to 3,500 deployed warheads and, most importantly, would also ban the MIRVed ICBMs, considered the most destabilizing part of the arsenals. START-2 also promised large savings ($5 billion over seven years for the United States) in maintenance and operation.

The treaty, while the product of a late cold war military balance, offered advantages for both sides including mutual reductions in the advantages held by both sides (the Russian MIRVed SS-18s, the American bombers, and submarines). It would establish the force levels comparable to what the Soviet Union possessed in 1976 and the United States in 1962.[32] The overall objective was to improve the ability of both deterrent forces to survive first strikes with devastating retaliatory forces—the so-called MAD (Mutually Assured Destruction) deterrence. A key element in this mix was the prohibition against large-scale missile defenses as codified in the ABM treaty.

Although signed in January 1993, the U.S. Senate did not ratify the treaty until January 1996. The Duma delayed even longer, finally approving on April 14, 2000, after years of Russian complaints about "unfairness." One concerned the cost of restructuring Moscow's MIRVed missiles to single warheads and the building of new missiles to sustain equality. Another was that U.S. systems, such as bombers, could be rapidly reconverted from conventional to nuclear while Russia had much less flexibility to "upload" because so much of its force was concentrated in multiple warhead launch vehicles.[33] Finally, the Russians fear that America plans to deploy a missile defense, ostensibly against rogue states, that would put them at a terminal disadvantage.

Washington and Moscow have argued repeatedly over the ABM issue. The Russians, while retaining far more extensive air defense systems than the United States, have stressed ever since the Reagan Star Wars initiative that their "build-down" depends on the United States not "building-up" a serious antimissile system. But the Clinton administration, while still enamored of the MAD theory, has come under increasing pressure to deploy some sort of defense. Experience with the Iraqi Scuds in the Gulf War and fears about missiles in the hands of states such as Iran and North Korea have strengthened military and congressional advocates for ABMS. A long and delicate negotiation on how to define theater versus strategic defenses resulted in a January 1996 agreement to test and deploy lower-velocity systems—which the Russians refused to sign.[34]

At this juncture, the Clinton administration set out to rescue the entire edifice of U.S.–Russian arms control which appeared to be slipping into the ABM morass while levels of arms were still at the very high START-1 levels. At the Helsinki Summit (20–21 March 1997), Clinton and Yeltsin agreed to delay the START-2 levels by a year (2002 vs. 2001) so that U.S.–Russia equality would continue. A START-3 negotiation would also commence upon the Duma ratification of START 2, its objective to reduce nuclear levels even lower, to 2,000–2,500 warheads. START-3 would also dismantle warheads for the first time, not only launchers as had been the case with START-1 and 2. Finally, the United States and Russia agreed on a "demarcation line" for missile defense that will allow current U.S. programs to proceed. Despite obvious administration reluctance, these changes—START-2 and ABM—will require Senate approval.[35]

Proliferation

The United States has had a frustrating experience overall on the proliferation issue. On one side of the ledger, Washington persuaded the new nuclear powers created by the Soviet demise—Ukraine, Belarus and Kazakhstan—to dismantle or return their weapons to Moscow's control in return for either financial aid or political reassurances. This was a time-consuming business complicated by domestic political strife and anti-Russian sentiments in each state but ultimately successful. On the other side of the ledger, Nunn-Lugar, the purchase of plutonium, and the safeguarding of sites have gone much less happily. The Russians were not prepared to use much of Nunn-Lugar; the inventory accounting of the plutonium also raised suspicion whether it originated from the nuclear arsenal or was simply reactor fuel. A partly hidden struggle continues against criminal and bureaucratic elements on securing existing weapons.[36]

Even more vexing to the United States has been Russia's arms and reactor sales. Whether to Iran, to China, or even to Greek Cyprus, Moscow has replayed, on a smaller scale, the old Soviet habit of buying influence with weapons; unlike the Soviets, hard cash is required. Especially in the case of the reactor sales to Iran, the United States has exerted pressure at the highest levels to prevent the transaction. Washington's leverage, however, has been undercut by its own solution to the North Korean proliferation problem: its proposed sale of similar reactors to Pyongyang because they produce less plutonium than the current machines.

Finally, Washington has countenanced a nearly continuous Russian violation of the CFE treaty on conventional arms since late 1995 when it came into full legal force. Moscow's Central Asian policy and its war in Chechnya are the main reasons why the 1990 treaty has never been kept. Another is the cost: Russia is reluctant to bear the high cost of destroying weapons, redeploying, and demobilizing forces who have neither housing nor employment. This, like the arms sale to Iran, proved a highly volatile negotiation because the flank powers, such as Turkey, feared adjustment would be made at the expense of their local balance.

In late May 1996, the CFE treaty was "adjusted" in a way that did indeed allow the Russians current levels of arms, extending by four years Moscow's deadline to reduce forces further and then not by much. Geographical limits were also changed to give the Russians more flexibility, and new compliance measures were added including inspectors. The treaty was thus upheld by conceding to Moscow the importance of its interests in Central Asia.

ENERGY AND POLITICS IN THE "NEAR ABROAD"

The Soviet Union had been an Asian empire, not only a European one, and its demise suddenly produced five countries (Kazakhstan, Turkmenistan, Uzbekistan, Tajikistan, and Kyrgyzstan) quite unprepared for sovereign independence. Many were rich in natural resources, especially oil and gas, much of it underdeveloped and with no ready outlet to market. Several, especially Kazakhstan, had large Russian populations suddenly demoted from overdog status. Their rulers were by and large the old Communist era appointees, accustomed to relying on Moscow for direction and survival.

Moscow's new security doctrine of the "Near Abroad," reinforced by the state dominated powerful oil and gas enterprises, reflected renewed interest in the fate of these states. The Russians feared Iranian or Turkish inspired Muslim insurrection to the south and burgeoning Chinese economic influence to the east. The region's natural resources were an enormous treasure house for a Russian economy increasingly dependent on raw materials, hard cash, and foreign investment. Within two years, Moscow had reestablished a considerable measure of influence over the new states, especially Kazakhstan, Turkmenistan (economic pressure), Georgia (help for rebels), Azerbaijan (military help for Armenia), and Tajikistan (combat units). The result was not the old Soviet empire but rather "the reassertion of Russian hegemony."[37] This took the form of the Tashkent Agreement on Collective Security (signed by four of the five Central Asian states) and forward deployment of military resources on a scale that strained weakened Russian capabilities.[38] Moreover, as noted earlier, Moscow was willing to violate the CFE treaty in order to subdue its Chechnyan province, located on the main oil and gas transmission routes through the Caucasus.

These efforts ran counter to formal American interest in the independence of Central Asia. The United States could not do much to alter these circumstances.

Any ideas that these states might somehow become truly independent simply did not reckon with the reality of weak governments, ethnic conflict, demographic change, and uncertain identities.[39] Finally, U.S. containment of Iran mandated opposition to any pipelines running through that country, thus eliminating one potential route for energy exports free of Russian control. Instead, the United States emphasized the potential economic development of the region and the importance of "stability."

In 1996, the Clinton administration began a rather more ambitious policy in Central Asia based on these lines. Its apparent purpose was to facilitate the emergence of the new states from the Russian sphere through economic development of oil and gas, and closer ties to Turkey. The most notable transaction was the American effort to broker a deal that would allow for the export of Azerbaijani oil. Turkey's original arrangement with the government of Azerbaijan—reached without the agreement of Lukoil, the Russian monopoly—was canceled after a Russian-supported coup.[40] A new agreement reached in September 1994 allowed an $8 billion consortium to develop the fields in the Caspian. The Azerbaijan International Operating Company (AIOC) was created to run it, and Lukoil promptly bought a 10 percent stake even as the Russian Foreign Ministry insisted that Moscow's permission was needed to extract anything from the Caspian "Lake."

Eventually, a complex arrangement was reached that called for "early oil" to be exported through the Baku-Novorossiisk pipeline while other oil would flow through a new Baku-Ceyhan line.[41] In November 1999, the arrangement was fully sealed at a gala ceremony in Istanbul and hailed as "historic" by the president of Georgia, Eduard Schevardnadze. But this remains to be financed. Meanwhile, overall U.S. policy lacks the resources and stable local states to replace the Russian hegemony. Nor is there widespread agreement that anything about the region is a U.S. vital interest.[42]

Reprise: NATO Expansion

In 1996, despite war in Chechnya and widespread discontent over corruption and economic decline, Boris Yeltsin raised himself once more from physical and political decrepitude to win reelection. Mobilizing a relatively small turnout against a "return to Communism," he only slightly exceeded his Communist opponent on the first round, winning the second on 3 July 1996 by 54 percent to 40 percent, partly through the cooption of the other popular candidate, the charismatic but politically inexperienced General Alexander Lebed. Yeltsin then spent the next six months recovering physically, his other achievement being the skillful use of Lebed to gain a peace in Chechnya, followed soon thereafter by Lebed's dismissal.

Bill Clinton, too, faced reelection in 1996, but his was to be a much easier passage than Yeltsin's as he triumphed easily over Senator Dole although falling short of a plurality thanks to Ross Perot's Independent Party. Foreign policy played a very small part in the elections.

Clinton's new secretary of state, Madeleine Albright, was far more familiar with Central and Eastern Europe, including Russia, than Warren Christopher. The Czech-born Albright, however, retained Christopher's emphasis on "pragmatism" which was soon to be put to severe tests on both the NATO issue and the Balkans. The second terms of Yeltsin and Clinton were thus subjected to a repetition of problems already encountered but at a higher level of strain. Indeed, no sooner had Yeltsin been reelected than in July 1996, at U.S. urging, NATO announced its readiness to accept the Czech Republic, Hungary, and Poland as full members of NATO.

Moscow's strategy to counter what many Russians considered to be an aggressive expansion into their former sphere of influence took several forms. Even before the final stage of NATO expansion, the Russians were attempting to assemble an anti-American coalition in Asia, chiefly through China. Shortly after accepting a Clinton summit visit that confirmed publicly Washington's desire to see him reelected, Yeltsin traveled to Shanghai where on 25 April 1996, he and the president of the Peoples Republic of China (PRC) signed a broad set of agreements. These included relaxation of border tensions, ambitious trade objectives, and security arrangements with Kazakhstan, Kyrgyzstan, and Tajikistan. Moscow took Beijing's side in the spring military tensions over Taiwan. The joint communiqué's denunciation of "hegemonism, power politics, and repeated imposition of pressures" sounded like an old Soviet playbook.

One could dispute whether Russia's interests in Asia were menaced more by American "hegemony" or China's growing economic influence over the thinly populated Russian East. Nonetheless, the political signal was of a peace with the 1994–96 change in Moscow's attitudes. After reviewing the leading schools of thought in Russia on national security, one analyst concluded: "Telltale signs of revisionism abound. . . . Intellectually Russia appears ready for a revisionism that will be hard to accommodate should its relative powers increase."[43] A widespread consensus of disillusion with the United States views Washington's policy as designed to keep Russia weak the better to prolong American sole superpowerdom.[44]

In this context, the imminent expansion of NATO aggravated Russian resentment. For Washington, expansion was a mix of international and domestic motives, but the accusation that the entire decision was a byproduct of Clinton's reelection campaign is surely misplaced. Basically, that decision had been made in 1993–94 and the arguments for and against it circulated for at least two years before the formal expansion date.[45] By early 1997, the State Department and the White House were busily campaigning to ease its passage through the Senate.

Administration spokesmen, including the secretary of state, were at pains to depict expansion as not directed at Russia. The president was prepared to go some distance to persuade Yeltsin to come along. This was bound to be tricky, especially because Yeltsin himself had denounced NATO while various analysts representing a broad spectrum of Moscow viewpoints decried expansion as a violation of trust if not of promises dating to German unification.[46] Clinton, for his part, would not describe expansion as a hedge against a renewed Russian attempt to dominate Central Europe for fear of offending Moscow, but he could not accede to Russian objections lest he confirm just such a sphere.

The Helsinki Summit of 19–20 March 1997 therefore represented less a meeting of minds than, as Churchill once said of Versailles, a "collision of embarrassed demagogues." Clinton and Yeltsin merely confirmed their determination to soldier on with useful illusions. The Americans wanted Russian assent to NATO expansion the better to prevent a divisive battle in the Senate; the Russians wanted American assent to a Russian role in affecting NATO decisions. Inevitably the unequal relations between the sole superpower and the fading former superpower determined the outcome and Yeltsin, like Gorbachev before him, bargained for the best knowing that in the end he could not stop NATO expansion. The result was the "NATO-Russia Founding Act" that created a Permanent Joint Council to be chaired by the NATO secretary general and joined by a Russian diplomat and a national ambassador from the NATO members. The council was to operate by consensus. Clinton called this a "voice but not a veto" for Russia, while Yeltsin declared that in the absence of consensus, "action" would not be taken.

On the military level, NATO agreed to restrictions similar to those that governed NATO's first expansion, that is, the incorporation of East Germany. The alliance saw no need to deploy nuclear weapons or to station large permanent forces, but ruled out neither and evaded the Russian demand that would have prohibited the use and building of infrastructure for rapid reinforcement.

The "Founding Act" diplomacy did not formally dispel Russian opposition, but it surely offered a figleaf of sorts to cover the obvious conflict between Washington and Moscow. It may also have eased Senate passage. Despite the opposition of many prominent foreign policy experts including Kennan, who argued that expansion would guarantee a hostile Russia (repeating the errors made after World War I with Germany), the Senate voted overwhelmingly 80 to 19 on 30 April 1998 to approve NATO expansion. The administration assured the opponents that the cost would not be high and that the Russians were resigned to it. Simultaneously, proponents were told that the Founding Act and its military provisos would not give Moscow a veto over NATO's defense obligations to new members.

THE RUSSIAN BUST

Beneath and alongside the hectic course of U.S. and Russian diplomacy there lay a significant assumption, namely that democratic and free market reform would produce a more prosperous Russia ready to join the international economy. As noted earlier, both the Bush and Clinton administrations saw an international assistance plan led by the IMF as the best way to guide Russia through its painful transformation while minimizing political resentments. Arguably this policy lacked sufficient resources, but even more so it suffered from a profound—at times willful— misreading of the Russian reality.

The twisting course of the Russian economic policies have baffled many analysts, but the results over the past decade speak for themselves. A vast inflation in 1992–95 wiped out the so-called ruble overhang—the mattress money—that cushioned the population. The state-dominated economy was ruthlessly exploited by a class of former Communist-era managers and a new group of entrepreneurs who, among them, divided up the declining GDP: they were "rent seekers" rather than "profit seekers" in Anders Aslund's terminology.[47] By the time of Yeltsin's reelection the old managers and new "oligarchs" had also bought extensive political protection.

Thus, a precipitously declining GDP and a growing impoverishment of the population contrasted with the fabulous wealth of a small group at the top. Russia was deindustrializing and decapitalizing in the macro, relying on raw materials for foreign exchange while its government drew increasingly on short-term foreign loans to finance itself as tax revenues fell. "Privatization" of the remaining large enterprises through auctions became a way for the big banks to acquire assets cheaply in exchange for lending the government monies they never expected to be repaid. The numerous private companies mostly at retail level that sprang up in the early 90s were soon subjected to a rapacious bureaucracy that doubled in size, adding 1 to 2 million since 1992. Meanwhile a botched monetary reform that essentially devalued the assets of existing industrial enterprises made it difficult, if not impossible, to establish equity values, essential for bank-lending and productive foreign investment.[48] In the absence of a banking system and in the presence of a confiscatory tax and licensing regimen, Russian businesses resorted to barter. The demonetizing of the economy also meant that the IMF's preferred instrument of reform—the Russian Central Bank—had less and less impact on real transactions.

While this was going on, the IMF, supported by the United States and other Western powers, proceeded about its business with remarkable calm. Preaching privatization, tight money, and macrostabilization, the IMF interpreted such actions as cuts in subsidies, an end to the lucrative alcohol and tobacco monopoly assigned to the National Sport Foundation, and the abolition of the ruble zone for the former Soviet republics as substantial progress on the road to reform. In spring 1996, the IMF concluded a three-year Extended Fund Facility in order to extend and solidify Russia's economic transformation. That this occurred in the midst of Yeltsin's desperate campaign against the Communists certainly strengthened the view of those in Moscow and abroad who saw the IMF as just another political operation largely influenced by the United States.

The IMF credits allowed a major influx of foreign investment into stocks and bonds, particularly government (about half of the rise from $2.5 billion to $6.2 billion—in one year!) In September 1997, Russia's ruble convertibility and slowing inflation were advertised as signs of stabilization. Chernomyrdin told a bankers' conference that "Objectively, Russia stands on the threshold of economic growth," and among the foreign economists, even seasoned observers agreed with him.[49] No doubt, these assuring developments persuaded even so cautious a statesman as Warren Christopher to write in his memoirs, published in May 1998, that American persistence and the "partnership" policy was finally paying off in Russian economic recovery.[50]

In early summer, however, several dramatic events revealed the true state of affairs. Yeltsin sacked Chernomyrdin whom he suspected of collusion at his expense with the oligarch Berezovsky; Berezovsky, in turn, had been hurt by the IMF's insistence on an "open" auction of state oil company assets. The new prime minister, Kiriyenko, was a young unknown; it required all of Yeltsin's guile and bluster to get him confirmed. Meanwhile, the oligarchs were clearly unprepared to finance the government in the absence of the auction incentive.

Then the international oil market collapsed because of competitive overproduction. As oil prices hovered in the $10 to $12 range versus $23 to $25 the year before, Russia's hard currency earnings suffered drastic reduction. Compounding the problem was the Asian financial crisis which had begun a year earlier with successive devaluations across East Asia. Nervous portfolio investors began casting anxious eyes at economies with corrupt governments, sinking foreign exchange reserves and weak records of domestic reform. Yeltsin's Russia qualified on all those counts. Moreover, by the summer of 1998, foreigners held more than a third of a rapidly escalating government debt. The Central Bank, partly to uphold the new convertible ruble-dollar rate in the face of mounting deficits, raised rates to 100 percent.

As the ruble suddenly sank in the spring the IMF hastily concocted a support package despite warnings that the Russians might devalue anyway after a number of vulnerable investors—including some of the oligarchs—had bailed. In any event, Russia did devalue and did default in August. The oligarchs, owing dollars and holding ruble assets, were badly damaged. But so were foreign investors. (The Soros Fund reportedly lost $2 billion.)[51]

The Russian collapse also shook the IMF to its roots and with it, the U.S. Treasury whose Deputy Lawrence Summers had worked closely with Strobe Talbott in promoting the IMF-led reform process. A further shock came unexpectedly when in September, the international investors' "flight to quality" led to rising bond prices across the board, ruining a leading so-called derivative "hedge fund"—Long-Term Capital of New York—whose investment formula depended on a mix of rising and falling bond prices. The Federal Reserve Board "jaw-boned" Long-Term Capital's investors, including leading Wall Street firms, to bail it out before panic engulfed the stock market. Chairman Greenspan followed that up by making clear that his fight against inflation would now become a battle against deflation; he lowered interest rates, bolstering the market.[52] These moves averted a serious international crisis with overtones of the 1929 crash.

It was too close for comfort. Clearly the United States, the IMF, and even some international investors had badly misread the Russian situation.

Following the Russian collapse and the appointment of the veteran KGB agent turned diplomat Yevgeny Primakov, other unsavory aspects of Moscow's financial operation emerged. Chubais, the most prominent of the reformers who had been appointed in the early summer as a deputy prime minister to reassure the West, said outright that the Russians had cheated the IMF.[53] Soon various scandals surfaced: an offshore banking operation that secretly managed a large chunk of Russia's reserves; money laundering at a New York bank; charges of bribery that reached Yeltsin's immediate family; and evidence of corruption by Chernomyrdin that Vice President Gore had angrily dismissed when warned by the CIA.[54] Clinton himself called Yeltsin to hear his denial of the charges about his family.

Following these troubles, the Russian economy staged a modest recovery, despite the absence of foreign capital, to the surprise and delight of many analysts.[55] This reflected a grim fact: the financial bust hardly affected a Russian economy running largely on self-financing industry—barter—that demonetized years earlier. Meanwhile, the end of imports for lack of hard currency created a market for local goods. More recently, the resurgence of oil prices has bolstered Russia's foreign exchange reserves. The Russian government also renegotiated its onerous $32 billion Soviet-era private sector debt and wants a similar deal on sovereign debt, although this would harm relations with Germany, holder of roughly half of the $42 billion owed.[56] Russia is clearly preparing to reenter international capital markets, but these rearrangements will have to be accompanied by major legal, accounting, and administrative changes to attract private investment beyond the oil sector.

For the United States, the Russian "bust" exploded illusions that should never have been cherished, especially after 1996. Washington's policy of using the "technical and neutral" IMF had not only failed to produce reform, it tarnished the Fund's reputation while not protecting the United States against the political recriminations that followed the Russian corruption scandals.[57] Still, neither Bush nor Clinton had ever put a commanding sum of their money on the table and until 1996–97, neither had private investors. Over the 1992–98 period, the United States invested $5.45 billion, some

$4.48 in reform and humanitarian projects and the rest for the Nunn-Lugar program known as "Threat Reduction."[58] This included purchases of weapons grade plutonium. The IMF itself lent $15.6 billion, and its current lending plans are merely rollovers allowing the Russians to remain out of default on repayment. Six more billion came from the World Bank and a few billion more from the European Bank for Reconstruction and Development. Moscow itself admits that foreign investment was under $10 billion, meager compared to the $30 plus billion placed in China over a comparable period.[59]

Some have argued, as Nixon did in 1992–93, that larger sums could have "bought" reform.[60] If so, then the cause of reform was lost in the same time frame that produced the "red-brown" Duma, itself an enduring obstacle to change. The "halfway house" that Yeltsin built went far to discredit both free markets and democracy because it became a redistributionist free-for-all among a small group of former Soviet officials and quick-witted entrepreneurs who bought political protection en route, "while others were restrained by a weak but large and intrusive state" where the bureaucracy actually grew even beyond the excesses of the Soviet era.[61] Thus in the eyes of many Russians, the United States and indeed the Western powers became accomplices to the impoverishment and decline of the country under Yeltsin.

Kosovo

While the Russian financial bust was exploding assumptions about Moscow's free market reforms, the Balkans crisis once again intruded on U.S.–Russia relations—this time to reinforce the suspicions of both parties. For the United States (and NATO) Kosovo illustrated once more that Moscow's role varied between marginal and the mischievous with an occasional constructive act under duress. For Russia, the Western attack on Yugoslavia meant that the American superpower had begun a dangerous crusade to remake states according to its own arrogant criteria.

The episode certainly demonstrated that Russia could not use the newly established Founding Act with its Permanent Joint Council to affect NATO's decisions. Shortly after its creation, for example, Moscow sought a joint discussion on the subject of NATO's New Strategic Concept which sanctioned NATO's "out of area" activities exemplified by the Bosnia mission. When NATO finally agreed to talk, it became clear that the Russians would have no say.[62] A fortnight before NATO's attack on Yugoslavia, the Russian chief of staff used a meeting of the Council to warn against the use of force. Both the air campaign and the subsequent adoption by NATO of the Strategic Concept led Russia to suspend its participation in the Council. Yeltsin's fig leaf had been shredded.

As for Kosovo itself, the situation was at once very complex and very simple. President Bush had warned Serb President Milosevic against fomenting ethnic violence in the largely Albanian province that also had been the Serb historic heartland. For seven years, Kosovo's peace depended on the passive resistance of local Albanian leaders while neighboring Albania and Macedonia controlled the borders against an insurgency. But in 1997, following the collapse of the Albanian state in a corruption scandal, arms suddenly became abundant. An Albanian resistance began to assassinate Serb police and in February 1998, Milosevic employed such brutal methods that the Contact Group reimposed international sanctions against Belgrade that had been dropped after the Bosnia agreement.

Secretary of State Albright vowed that the lessons from Bosnia had been learned, but apparently not well enough. It took until late August to get a UN call for a ceasefire and then a NATO agreement to use force against Yugoslavia if it did not stop tactics that were driving hundreds of thousands of Kosovars from their homes. Once more Richard Holbrooke entered the fray; Slobodan Milosevic agreed to a reduction of forces and a corps of international monitors. Taking advantage of NATO's obvious reluctance, the Serbs began a campaign to force the Kosovars out en masse leading to a massacre on 29 January 1999. The United States then convened a conference in Rambouillet, France, designed to create an autonomous Kosovo pacified by the presence of 28,000 NATO peacekeepers. Only after it became clear that the Serbs would not sign did the Kosovars—the pacifist party and the Kosovo Liberation Army (KLA), fighting the Serbs for an independent Kosovo which would presage a Greater Albania—accede to U.S. wishes. On 18 March the Serbs refused. Meanwhile, the Serb military had begun systematically to force the Albanians across the borders.

Yeltsin's then prime minister, the veteran diplomat Yevgeny Primakov, had been en route to Washington in pursuit of a fresh IMF loan, but he returned to Moscow in symbolic opposition to the NATO air campaign which began on 24 March. Evidently, Washington and its allies expected that several days of light bombing would turn Milosevic around; he, in turn, expected NATO to cave once it was clear that he would resist. As a consequence of these

miscalculations, NATO quickly revised its plans, shifting its targets
from Kosovo to the civilian infrastructure of Serbia and embarking
upon a military buildup that in its latter stages suggested an imminent ground invasion. Meanwhile, the Serb forces in Kosovo succeeded in forcing more than a million Kosovars from their homes
and executed some 10,000 in a terror campaign. The KLA holed
up in the mountains.

NATO's actions aroused great latent hostility in Russia against
the Alliance and the United States including angry public demonstrations. After breaking off PfP contacts and expelling NATO representatives, Moscow deployed a naval reconnaissance force to the
Mediterranean where presumably it could offer valuable intelligence to the ineffective Yugoslav air defenses. NATO planes, after
losing a stealth fighter, conducted high altitude strikes that mini-
mized losses at some cost to accuracy.

In this ominous atmosphere, NATO held its fiftieth anniversary
celebration in Washington on 24 April. The Russians declined to
attend as a guest. But Clinton, determined to repeat the winning
tactics in Bosnia, sought Russian involvement to obtain a UN Security Council resolution approving an international security
force. Primakov's first attempt to use this as leverage in Belgrade
failed when he could not produce a halt to the bombing as a pre-
condition for negotiations. Primakov then shifted toward NATO,
demanding an end to "ethnic cleansing and separation."

The Russian and Serb positions coincided on the need to put the
issue into the UN and to have that body control an international
force. On 6 May the United States led NATO into a joint declaration of principles for peace, to be submitted to the UN Security
Council. This did indeed give Russia a veto over the terms of
agreement, but it only mattered if NATO was prepared to ease its
military pressure, which it was not. Finally on 3 June, as NATO
began active preparations to deploy large ground forces, Milosevic
agreed to a ceasefire. This was clinched on 9 June when Russian
Foreign Minister Ivanov agreed to vote for an international force
immediately after the bombing stopped. As in Bosnia, the Russians
had been the bearer of the bad news to Milosevic that further
armed resistance was futile.

As the complex sequence of agreement signing, Serb withdrawal, verification, bombing suspension, Security Council vote,
and deployment of the international security force unwound,
there was a final dramatic moment. Contrary to the agreements
governing the Bosnia force, a Russian armed column suddenly de-
camped on 11 June and raced toward Pristina airport. There had

been no arrangement for Russian troops in Kosovo yet and General Wesley Clark, supreme commander of NATO, saw this as an aggressive attempt to preempt NATO's plans at a strategic location.

Questions have been raised whether and why the Russian troops were actually commanded to enter Kosovo. (One story is that they wanted to retrieve some advanced avionics on Yugoslav fighters stationed in underground bunkers.) Whatever glitch existed in Moscow's chain of command, however, was dwarfed by a full-scale crisis in NATO itself. General Clark's orders to block the airport were refused by his British subordinate General Sir Michael Jackson, who appealed to London for support. In Washington, the argument against a potential armed clash with the Russians found a ready ear; NATO did not move.[63] But on 25 June, when the Russians sought to reinforce the two hundred isolated soldiers at Pristina, Hungary, Bulgaria, and Romania denied the use of their airspace. A day later, this crisis was resolved when a joint NATO–Russian schedule eventually allowed 3,600 Russian troops to be deployed. NATO insisted, however, that no Russian zone be carved out that might partition Kosovo.

In October 1999, the Kosovo experience was reflected in a new Russian strategic doctrine superseding the much more benign 1997 revision which had posited domestic strife and disturbances in the Near Abroad as the main threats. Instead, the Russians listed a large number of dangers clearly associated with NATO or the U.S., such as armed intervention into domestic affairs, use of force without a UN mandate, and undermining of international arms control agreements. Nuclear weapons were once again hoisted up to the front-line of defenses.[64] Little was heard of partnership with the West.

Conclusion

On 31 December 1999, a sometimes tearful Boris Yeltsin announced his resignation as president of Russia. He begged forgiveness for his failures and confessed that he had believed, mistakenly, that "we could overcome everything in one spurt."[65] Calling for "new politicians, new faces," Yeltsin then appointed his prime minister of six months, Vladimir Putin, in his place.

Shortly thereafter, Bill Clinton used a brief essay on the departing Russian leader to summarize the achievements of the Yeltsin era. Among these were regular elections, thousands of nongovernmental organizations, and some 900,000 private businesses. Clinton also took the occasion to acknowledge that "the partnership we established has been subject to plenty of strains." He warned against the "growing tendency . . . to cast doubt on whether Russia and the U.S. do indeed have common interests outweighing our differences." And as evidence of those common interests, he listed the successes of partnership, among them 5,000 nuclear weapons dismantled, the withdrawal of Russian troops from the Baltics, and "a positive role" in the Balkans.[66]

As this narrative demonstrates, Clinton's list was largely achieved in his first term, and Russia's role in the Balkans was controversial at best. The doubt about common interests derived not only from the lack of achievement from 1996 onwards, but also the failure of economic reform. Gloom about Russia's future permeated the views of foreign observers, and even Strobe Talbott expressed pessimism about the country's direction.

American disillusion with Russia derived first and foremost from a faulty focus: Russia as the United States wanted it to be rather than what it was, in reality.

Washington had reached this pass on a bipartisan route. Bush had proclaimed the benefit of a democratic Russia but lacked the political confidence and the imagination to create a new security structure or a dramatic economic embrace that might have given Washington real leverage, especially on the critical issues of economic reform. Clinton took over the idea of using the IMF as the major international tool of reform and especially after 1996, shared that agency's misunderstanding of what was really happening to the Russian economy. The Balkan experiences, and the frustrations on various arms control and regional policies, had drained Clinton's policy of support in the Congress long before the crash of 1998 or the Kosovo war of 1999.

In retrospect, one can select several milestones over the Yeltsin era that eventually disfigured the U.S. approach:

(1) Political Change (1992–94): These years, which began with Yeltsin's ascendancy and ended with the red-brown Duma, set the subsequent pattern to a remarkable extent. Events in Russia and Russian actions abroad dethroned the "Russia first" school in Washington and put NATO expansion forward as a hedge against a reversion to Russian imperialism.

(2) Economic Reform (1996): To secure Yeltsin's reelection, the United States was willing to push the IMF into extending loans that were obviously influenced by politics rather than

economics. This contributed to the bubble that burst after the Asian financial panic. In its wake the United States appeared the dupe of Russian corruption, the string-puller for the IMF, and the partner of a discredited Yeltsin, whose legacy was an impoverished Russia.

(3) Kosovo (1999): Coming after the earlier failed experiment of the Contact Group and the equally questionable Founding Act mechanism that accompanied NATO expansion, Washington shifted erratically between disregard and deference in its dealings with Moscow. The Russian dash for Pristina airport threatened a clash with NATO, echoing 1914, which was averted only by a crisis in the Alliance's chain of command, perhaps illustrating Marx's observation that history repeats itself, once as tragedy and then as farce.

What the U.S. administration and many analysts missed was Russia's reemergence from the debris of the Soviet Union as a great power almost on the pre-1914 model. Its leaders had a well-defined sense of geographic "space," including a preferred protective glacis of neutral or accommodating states, a desire to retain control of natural resources and an acute fear of the instabilities unleashed by the lapse of Soviet power. While Russia today faces no threat of invasion or attack, its geopoliticians concluded by 1993–94 that the country faced long-term dangers—a German dominated Europe to the West, an Islamic menace from Central Asia, and a Chinese challenge from the East. These troubles were not very different from those that had beset the late Brezhnev era. Gorbachev's new thinking and then Yeltsin's early embrace of the West had both been designed to eliminate tensions with the United States in expectation of a rescuing partnership which would not diminish Moscow's international influence over its own self-defined vital interests. Both approaches have failed and the Russian state has now been thrown back on its own resources. This is more or less the essence of what Vladimir Putin had to say in a millennium message issued almost at the same time as Yeltsin's resignation.[67]

It remains unclear whether U.S. policymakers are prepared to deal with Russia as great power. In a larger sense, much of American foreign policy since 1914 has been designed to get beyond the balance of power world that still constitutes Russian thinking. It does not help that Washington's actions so often appear to be the prerogative of a sole superpower rather than the idealistic or humanitarian objectives imputed to them by American leaders. Faced by this morass of misunderstandings and dashed expectations, Secretary of State Albright invoked Tolstoy's observation that "the strongest of all warriors are these two—time and patience."[68] Unfortunately, statesmen in Washington and Moscow do not have the luxury of either. The Balkans, Iraq, proliferation, missile defense, the Caucasus, and economic reform are all points of friction passed down from the Clinton and Yeltsin presidencies. Some will demand decisions sooner rather than later. But in each case, the United States will do better if its leaders see Russia in the clear focus of reality, neither determined adversary nor natural ally, but a power of great potential finding its own way.

NOTES

I wish to thank Mark Kohut for research assistance on this essay.

1. For this argument see Stephen Sestanovich, "The Collapsing Partnership: Why the U.S. Has No Russia Policy," in *Eagle Adrift: American Foreign Policy at The End of The Century*, ed. by Robert J. Lieber (New York: Longman), 1996.

2. Warren Christopher, White House Press Briefing, 4 May 1995.

3. See for example, *The National Interest*, special issue, "The Strange Death of Soviet Communism," (spring 1993).

4. See *New York Times*, OpEd 9 March 1992.

5. Buzz Bissinger in his *Say A Prayer For the City* relates how, after the riots in Los Angeles later that year, a group of Democratic big city mayors tried to use the federal government's support for Russian aid as leverage to loosen White House resistance to additional urban spending.

6. See Christopher's Confirmation Testimony in Warren Christopher, *In the Stream of History: Shaping Foreign Policy for a New Era* (Stanford, CA.: Stanford University Press, 1998), 27.

7. See Woodward, *The Agenda* (New York: Simon & Schuster, 1994) and *The Choice* (New York: Simon and Schuster, 1996). See also Colin Powell with Joseph E. Persico, *My American Journal* (New York: Ballantine Books, 1996) 560, 572.

8. This was not entirely Clinton's doing. Nixon had let it be known that he could be critical publicly of Clinton, as he had done with Bush. The former president sought to persuade the new president of a "historic chance to do something;" presidential engagement was the only way to assure effective U.S. action. See Monica Crowley, *Nixon Off the Record* (Random House, 1996).

9. George F. Kennan, "Communism in Russian History," *Foreign Affairs* 69, no. 5 (winter 90/91): 177–78.

10. See Carl Bildt, "The Baltic Litmus Test," *Foreign Affairs* (September/October 1994). Olcott Martha Brill, "Central Asia's Post-Empire Politics," *Orbis* (spring 1992). Lockwood Dunbar, "Bush, Yeltsin sign START II; Senate Approval Expected," *Arms Control Today* (January/February 1993).

11. See Thomas Kielinger and Max Otte, "Germany: The Pressured Power," *Foreign Policy*, Number 91 (summer 1993): 52.

12. On 19 September 1993 Poland's Democratic Left Alliance (the former

Communists) won 171 out of 460 seats in the lower Parliament with 20.4% of the vote. *Foreign Affairs Agenda 1994*, 224.

13. A good journalistic account of Talbott and his views may be found in Michael Dobbs, "Mission to Moscow," *Washington Post*, National Edition, 10–16 June 1996.

14. Secretary of Defense William Perry's speech at George Washington University, 14 March 1994, *Defense Issues*, "Forge Realistic, Pragmatic Relations With Russia."

15. 58.4% voted to ratify the Constitution. FBIS-Sov-93–242, 20 December 1993, "Voter Turnout 54.8%," 3.

16. FBIS-Sov-93–244, 22 December 1993, "Yeltsin Holds News Conference on Vote Results," 5. It was rumored that Zhirinovsky enjoyed a majority of the votes cast by units guarding Moscow.

17. *Washington Post*, 4 November 1993.

18. See Victor Gray, "Germany: The "Reluctant Power" Turns East," *Parameters* (autumn 1994).

19. See speech given by Anthony Lake at Johns Hopkins, 1993.

20. See Christopher, *In the Stream of History*, 93–94. See also James Goldgeier, "NATO Enlargement: Anatomy of a Decision," *Washington Quarterly* (winter 1998): 100.

21. See *International Herald Tribune*, 13 January 1994.

22. FBIS-Sov-94–010, 14 January 1994, "Yeltsin Backs Partnership for Peace," 15.

23. Allan E. Goodman, ed. "The Nunn-Lugar Initiative-Cooperative Demilitarization of the Former Soviet Union," *The Diplomatic Record*, Westview Press 1995.

24. On 23 September 1993 the U.S. Senate passed a bill that included $2.5 billion in aid to Russia.

25. *Facts on File*, 24 February 1994, p.124G1. Reportedly this vote also dealt a heavy blow to Talbott's ambition to succeed the much criticized Warren Christopher as secretary of state.

26. Nick Williams, "Partnership for Peace: Permanent Fixture or Declining Asset," *Survival* 38, no.1 (spring 1996): 99.

27. Goldgeier, "NATO Enlargement," 100.

28. *International Herald Tribune*, 8 June 1994.

29. *Washington Post*, 12 December 1993.

30. *New York Times*, 26 April 1994.

31. *New York Times*, 15 December 1994.

32. See Jack Mendelson, "START II and Beyond," *Arms Control Today* (October 1996): 3.

33. Ibid., 4.

34. See *New York Times*, 31 October 1996. For a discussion of Russian objections see *Arms Control Today*, July 1996.

35. Clinton agreed to submit the changes for Senate approval as part of the negotiation over the Chemical Arms Treaty in May 1997. See *New York Times*, 25 April 1997. *Washington Post*, 26 April 1997. But the Chemical Treaty was defeated by the Senate on 13 October 1999, and neither of the arms control treaties have been resubmitted.

36. *New York Times*, 29 January 1996.

37. Herbert J. Ellison and Bruce Acker, *The New Russia and Asia: 1991–1995*, The National Bureau of Asian Research, June 1996, vol. 7, no. 1, p. 33.

38. See Sherman W. Garnett, "Russia and Its Borderlands: A Geography of Violence," *Parameters* (spring 1997).

39. Domestic lobbies, in this case Armenian, assured that the United States would not take up the Turkish supported cause of Azerbaijan, sentencing that state to isolation and Russian domination. See S. Fredrick Starr, "Power Failure in the Caspian," *The National Interest*, no. 47 (spring 1997): 25. Martha Brill Olcott "Central Asia's New States: Independence and Regional Security," USIP Press, 1996.

40. Ibid.

41. See Gareth M. Winnow, "Turkey's Role in Caspian Pipeline Politics," *Jane's Intelligence Review*, February 1997.

42. See Anatol Lieven, "The (Not So) Great Game," *The National Interest* (winter 1999/2000) for this argument.

43. See William Wohlforth, "Redefining Security: Russia's Intellectual Adjustment to Decline," *Harvard International Review* (winter 1996–97): 60.

44. Ibid. See also Alexei K. Pushkov, "Don't Isolate Russia," *The National Interest* (spring 1997): 58–62.

45. Goldgeier, "NATO Enlargement," 100.

46. See Harvey Sicherman, "NATO, Germany and Pragmatism's Finest Hour," *Orbis* (fall 1997), that reviews the evidence for and against the "promise."

47. Anders Aslund, "Why has Russia's Economic Transformation Been So Arduous," a paper presented at the World Bank's Annual Bank Conference on Development Economies, Washington, D.C., 28–30 April 1999.

48. Steve Moody, "Decapitalizing Russian Capitalism," *Orbis* (winter 1996).

49. See *Financial Times*, 2 September 1997. Anders Aslund was quoted saying, "The economy is looking fine, it is stabilizing. The question is, is it beginning to grow, and I think it is." He predicted a "very gradual improvement."

50. Warren Christopher, *In the Stream of History: Shaping Foreign Policy For a New Era* (Stanford: Stanford University Press, 1998).

51. See *Financial Times*, 27 August 1998.

52. See *Wall Street Journal*, 17 November 1998 for a good account of the Fed's activities.

53. Chubais's interview with the Russian newspaper *Kommersant*, 8 September 1998 set off a controversy when the *Los Angeles Times* Moscow Bureau Chief Richard C. Paddock translated the word "kinuli" as "conned," apparently slang for a deceitful act, although this was contested by others including Chubais. In clarifying the matter, Chubais issued an "open letter" to offer a better translation: "we cheated them out of $20 billion." For a critique of the IMF, see Jeffrey D. Sachs, "Calling the IMF to Account," *New York Times*, 8 September 1999.

54. See *Washington Post*, 27 August 1999, and *New York Times*, 23 November 1998. Sean O'Neill's "Leon Fuerth: Tutoring Prince Albert" in *World Policy Journal* (winter 1999/2000): 61–62, offers a good summary of Gore's experience with the Joint Commission including the corruption issue. Other articles include David Ignatiev, "Russian Crapshoot," *Washington Post*, 1 September 1999, and Fritz Ermarth, "A Scandal, Then a Charade," *New York Times*, 12 September 1999.

55. See Michael McFaul, *Foreign Policy* (winter 1999–2000).

56. The new argument reduced the private debt by one-third, rolling over the balance into 30-year Eurobonds with a seven year grace period—the so-called London Club of commercial creditors believing that it was better to get two-thirds rather than nothing. See *Financial Times*, 12–13 February 2000.

57. Some of these became American scandals including a highly publicized

Harvard project that involved Chubais. For one version see See Janine R. Wedel, "Tainted Transactions," *The National Interest* no. 59, spring 2000 and the indignant reacting of Sachs, Aslund and others in *The National Interest* no. 60, summer 2000.

58. Figures from McFaul, *Foreign Policy*.

59. See an article written by Putin found on the Kremlin's website (http://www.pravitelstvo.gov.ru/english/statVP_engl_1.html).

60. Aslund, "Russia's Economic Transformation."

61. Ibid., 14.

62. See Foreign Minister Igor Ivanov's statement, quoted in Oksana Autmenko, "Russia, NATO, and European Security After Kosovo," *Survival* (winter 1999–2000): 130.

63. See *Washington Post*, 10 September 1999.

64. A good account of this doctrine is to be found in Autmenko, "Russia, NATO."

65. Full English text reprinted in *Washington Post*, 1 January 2000.

66. Bill Clinton, "Remembering Yeltsin," *Time*, 155, no. 1 (1 January 2000).

67. Putin, see note 59. For more on Putin, see Graham Humes, "Vladimir Vladimirovich Putin in 1994: A Personal Recollection," *E-Notes* (13 January 2000), and see Harvey Sicherman, "Yeltsin's Legacy and Putin's Plans," *E-Notes* (18 January 2000).

68. See address by Secretary of State Madeleine K. Albright on U.S.-Russian relations at the Carnegie Endowment for International Peace, Washington, D.C. on 16 September 1999 as released by the office of the spokesman, U.S. Department of State. This sober defense of U.S. policy, like Russia, "a work in progress," did not deter Albright from endorsing Putin in February 2000 as a leader of democratic reform, an enthusiasm not shared by Russia's own democratic parties.

Conclusion: Lessons From a System in Transition

THE CONTRIBUTORS TO THIS VOLUME HAVE NOT BEEN ABLE TO "cover the globe" completely (like a certain well-known paint manufacturer), but they have examined the recent history of much of its real estate. What, then, are the lessons to be learned from their case studies?

THE BACKDROP: AN INTELLIGENCE FAILURE

Goodman's recounting of the failure of the American intelligence apparatus to anticipate, even in the penultimate moment, the incipient disintegration of the Eastern bloc and the subsequent collapse of the "Evil Empire" provides an interesting and instructive backdrop to the regional/national case studies that follow. It demonstrates how a narrow, ideologically driven worldview can cloud our vision, obscuring in some cases our ability to see what is taking place right before our eyes.

In this instance, Goodman details the chain of events by which the American intelligence process became so politicized during the 1980s that the results of much U.S. intelligence-gathering activity were not only rendered useless but, indeed, became counterproductive vis-à-vis helping American foreign policy adapt to the changing world system.

Unfortunately, and perhaps even more importantly, the author suggests that some of the same habits of mind continue to hold sway within key sectors of the U.S. intelligence community to this very day; that is, rather than admit the errors of the recent past and learn from them, the Central Intelligence Agency (CIA) has made a concerted effort to cover its earlier failures by selectively declassifying its more accurate estimates from the previous decade.

In the meantime, this tradition of demonizing perceived enemies and overestimating their abilities has undoubtedly had a negative impact on Washington's episodic efforts to deal with an

344

international scene that has been changing so rapidly that it sometimes seems chaotic. At the very least it has caused the United States to miss opportunities to improve relationships with a number of countries around the world.

One inference to be drawn from Goodman's analysis is that our intelligence processes were traditionally set up to focus primarily upon a single major enemy and, thus, its practitioners have had difficulty in adapting to a world where our adversaries are fragmented and dispersed. For example, the current relentless search for "ties" between various terrorist organizations and the attempt to find a centralized leadership for "international terrorism" (Usama bin Laden seems to be the current leading candidate) may well be a symptom of that mindset.

While terrorist factions with grievances against a number of governments in countries around the world may well seek out similarly situated groups from other countries for support and training, it is quite clear that their various causes are distinct. Thus, it is highly unlikely that they will readily "take orders" from some central authority in another part of the world. Moreover, they are unlikely to be willing to give up their cause simply because a blow is struck against other terrorist groups that may have been providing them with assistance. Finally, Western countries are likely targets for such groups primarily to the extent that they are seen as assisting in the perpetuation of the grievances which motivate these groups.

The various regions that encompass much of the Third World are the locus of many of the inequities and resulting complaints against which most terrorist organizations are arrayed. Of course, many of the governments of various Third World nations also define themselves as having legitimate grievances against the Western developed countries. Indeed, these regions comprising the Third World are interestingly diverse, especially in terms of the impact that the end of the cold war has had upon them and, thus, in the complexity that they present to the foreign policy analysts and planners of the great powers.

THE THIRD WORLD

In his analysis of Latin America, Raymond Duncan (chapter 2) acknowledges that some of the major developments in the 1990s were underway before the end of the cold war, but he contends that this milestone has significantly accelerated those trends. Before Gorbachev, the Kremlin's policy in Latin America (outside of Cuba) appears to have been one of exacerbating security problems for the United States in its own backyard on an opportunistic basis. In other words, even in Moscow, the region was regarded principally as an American sphere of influence.

He explains a number of major realities that need to be understood before one can assess the impact of the collapse of the Soviet Union on Latin America. First, Yeltsin's policy in that part of the world was essentially a continuation of that begun under Gorbachev's "New Thinking." Second, the major trends of expanding democracy, increasing economic interdependence with the United States, growing foreign investment, and the decline of leftist movements in the region predate the disintegration of the USSR. Finally, with the exception of Cuba, the Soviet investment in Latin America was not as great as many Western analysts claimed and/or feared. (The success of Castro's Communist revolution in 1959 was for the Kremlin a *fait accompli*, one that Soviet leaders could not but hail and support given the tenor of the times, but it was not their actions that brought it about.)

Even given these realities, Duncan contends that the collapse of the Soviet Union has had significant consequences for Latin America. For one thing, the impact on Cuba has been profound. It became essentially devalued as a model in the eyes of its neighbors. More importantly, the end of the perceived Communist threat in the rest of the hemisphere has accelerated the trend toward a complex, multidimensional agenda in U.S.–Latin American relations. This, in turn, has led to an enhancement of the trend away from military regimes and toward more democratic political systems; indeed, Latin American militaries have now begun to search for new roles. Finally, these developments have further emboldened private investors and enhanced the movement toward market economies, and this has led to better relations with the United States.

By the middle of the 1990s, as it became clear to the Kremlin that American "good will" was producing few tangible benefits for Russia, a renewed interest in reasserting Russia's great power status even in far-flung areas like Latin America emerged in Moscow. As a result, the Kremlin made some efforts to reestablish links with Cuba, but the resources to prop up the Castro regime on a traditional client basis were simply unavailable. There were also attempts to enhance Russian political and economic relations with such countries as Brazil, Argentina, and Colombia. However, despite its great power aspirations, for the foreseeable future Russia will almost surely have to accept the geopolitical reality that Latin America is an American sphere of influence.

The end result is that Washington's priorities in Latin America have shifted to direct concern with strengthening bilateral relations with its various neighbors to the south since it is no longer preoccupied with countering the "Communist threat to the region." Unfortunately, the old mindset, which often led to counterproductive and sometimes contradictory policy decisions, has survived. For example, the current rage for stamping out the supply sources for the drug trade shows signs of occasionally inducing the same sort of policy irrationality. On the other side of the coin, absent some tangible threat to direct American interests, there is a longstanding tendency in Washington to relegate Latin American concerns to the margins of American foreign policy.

In any case, basic problems remain. The Big-Brother-to-the-North concern is a long standing one; it far predates the birth of the Soviet Union. However, in Duncan's view, the new atmosphere appears to provide the opportunity for real progress in U.S.–Latin American relations and for the promotion of indigenous regional development, democracy, and political stability. Russia is unlikely to play a major role in any case. The prime external actor is and will continue to be the United States.

The cold war made many parts of Sub-Saharan Africa a *de facto* surrogate battleground, creating a disaster for many of Africa's people. However, it also kept Africa "on the map," and the end of superpower competition, according to Marina Ottaway in chapter 3, has led to the threat of the region being "marginalized." Now, few of the region's countries, mostly in the Horn of Africa (also discussed briefly by Stephen Page in a later chapter), can still hope to play "the security card" with the United States, and that only to the extent that they are seen in Washington as dependable allies in the confrontation between the United States and Islamic fundamentalist movements and governments.

The colonial and postcolonial eras have involved widespread exploitation of Africa's people and resources, as well as disruption of its social fabric by both outsiders and indigenous "leaders." These processes have only served to deepen internal rivalries and regional conflicts even though they were often controlled (i.e., suppressed) for extended periods by totalitarian rule.

The collapse of the USSR and the demise of the accompanying myth that authoritarian rule was the fast track to development (and thus was justified in the long-range interests of the people) has undermined the rationale by which many African regimes

have claimed legitimacy. The result, however, has often been turmoil and disintegration exacerbated by traditional ethnic and
tribal hostilities.

In Ottaway's opinion, the only hope for improving the status of
most African nations in the new millennium is economic growth
and development. Unfortunately, several factors including widespread political instability, the region's underdeveloped infrastructure (including its undereducated population), endemic
corruption (some African countries are virtual kleptocracies[1]), and
government policies hostile to private development all combine to
make that process exceptionally difficult.

The only long-term prospect for most African nations to avoid
marginalization (and thus chronic status as "have nots") is integration into the international economy on a sustainable basis. That
will, in Ottaway's view, ultimately depend upon domestic policies
and internal stability. Thus, there is a compelling need to devise a
regional order that can be enforced from within Africa to replace
the old colonial and cold war systems. Moreover, most African nations begin from a position of enormous competitive disadvantage,
and so their prospects for any near-term improvement in status
look very dim. Put differently, the African states will need to do
substantial boot-strapping, but the traditional means to effect such
processes are controlled by the very nations which have concluded
that they are no longer very interested in Africa. In sum, Sub-
Saharan Africa faces the daunting challenge of creating truly African solutions to its problems.

The essence of Henri Barkey's argument in chapter 4 is that
during the cold war period most Middle Eastern regimes manipulated the superpower competition for their own benefit, using one
side or the other (sometimes switching sides, especially with
changes in governments) to supply weapons and to provide political and economic support. The very threat of alliance shifting was
also a continuing source of leverage. Barkey contends that the collapse of the USSR and the end of the cold war have served "to accelerate certain regional trends and add an additional dynamic to
domestic and regional change within the area."

He points out that the end of the USSR has introduced three
global changes not specific to but importantly affecting the Middle
East. These include an increased emphasis on economic issues, the
erosion of an important source of legitimation for authoritarian
rule in the Third World, and the unleashing of new waves of ethnic
politics in many localities around the world. In response to these
changes, most Middle Eastern nations are struggling to find ways

to open up their economies without creating such enormous social change as to tear the fabric of their societies. In many of these nations there is strong, tradition-based resistance to privatization, and as they compete for the resources of international investors this resistance constitutes a source of risk which sends many investors elsewhere. Without substantial economic reform, these same countries seem destined to be left behind as the global economy evolves, and that, in turn, will likely exacerbate domestic political problems.

Consequently, what Barkey sees is forces that will continue to impel a "pluralistic imperative" in the region. The "new realism" that appears to be infusing current efforts to effect a viable settlement of the Arab-Israeli conflict is probably partially a result of that development. However, any stable, durable settlement of that long-run conflict will produce expectations of a "peace dividend," setting off a chain of circumstances likely to force regimes to confront their very real internal problems, especially their rising population pressures.

With the breakup of the USSR, the geopolitical map of the Middle East was inevitably transformed; a key component of that transformation is the fact that the former Soviet Central Asian republics, with their predominantly Muslim populations, began to reach out to their neighbors to the south and west to establish both cultural and economic ties. Thus, one can now characterize the map of the Middle East as having been redrawn, with the result that Russia is situated farther from the region than was true of the USSR; it is certainly no longer a contiguous state. However, the Kremlin has significant residual economic interests in the region (most notably in Iraq). It would also like to forestall penetration of the markets of the former Central Asian republics with their huge energy potentials by Middle Eastern as well as Western countries.

Indeed, the fact of a large Muslim population not only in the Commonwealth of Independent States (CIS) but in specific enclaves within the Russian Federation makes for some tricky ethnic politics. The current second round of conflict in Chechnya shows just how difficult Moscow's relations with Russia's indigenous Muslim populations can be. In addition to the direct human and material costs of the war in Chechnya, the attempt to impose a military solution inevitably complicates the Kremlin's relations with the former Soviet Central Asian republics and with the Muslim countries of the Middle East. However, the Kremlin leaders clearly feel that they cannot allow full play to the secessionist impulses of the

Chechen rebels, for there are too many other potential Chechnyas waiting in the wings within the Russian Federation.

Interestingly, the collapse of the Soviet Union has had one other significant ethnic effect within the region. That is, Jewish emigration from Russia into Israel has accelerated to such a point that Israel now has a very substantial Russian minority, some of whose members retain ties to Russia. This factor cannot be ignored in Israeli domestic politics.

In conclusion, Barkey characterizes the region as continuing a period of uncertainty, and he sees most current political leaders as having shown scant "vision" for dealing with this changed world. One possible outcome is an attempt to return to "patriarchal tradition." The extent to which such an outcome would bring long-term benefit to the region and its inhabitants is, of course, open to speculation.

In another part of the Middle East, the collapse of the old order has also required the states of the Red Sea and Persian Gulf regions to recalculate their national interests, and their resources for dealing both with their neighbors and the larger world. According to Stephen Page in chapter 5, this has produced quite different outcomes in the two regions. Specifically, the collapse of the USSR (and, indeed, Gorbachev's "New Thinking" which preceded that collapse) robbed the Red Sea area of its former strategic importance. It, like most of the rest of Africa, has essentially been left to its own devices.

All of the Red Sea countries (Ethiopia, Eritrea, Yemen, Somalia, Djibouti, and Sudan), are afflicted by internal strife and most by conflicts with their neighbors. As a result, the external powers now see the area as a potential quagmire. For example, the American-backed UN mission in Somalia in the early 1990s began as a humanitarian mission, and it was enjoying some success while it was confined to that objective. It was only when it took on an ill-defined political/military security component that it turned into a disaster. However, it has become the region's object lesson in the minds of great power policymakers.

The Persian Gulf, in contrast, has enjoyed a very different fate because the Western powers define themselves as having important interests there. The West is dependent on the region's oil, and, if anything, the collapse of the USSR has emboldened some of the regional powers. For example, Saddam Hussein appeared to believe at the time of his 1990 invasion of Kuwait that no effective coalition would be mounted against him.

The smaller states (the monarchies) have "bought" those aspects of modernity that they want and have managed thus far to stave off (by coopting or coercing potential dissidents) those aspects of modernism that threaten "traditional rule" but maintenance of such a status quo appears to be an enduring struggle. Having had the Western/Arab coalition extend itself to reestablish the sovereignty of Kuwait, the ruling family was forced to resuscitate its constitution (suspended in 1976) and to hold parliamentary elections. However, in late 1999, that body denied the extension of suffrage to women.

In the meantime, the old threats of "godless modernity" and "godless Communism" have been replaced by that of Islamic fundamentalism. The clerical leaders of this movement resent the modern tastes/habits of the ruling families and their pro-Western orientation, and the old appeals to the masses' distrust of secular threats will not work against the fundamentalists; indeed, the latter occupy the moral high ground.

The Soviet Union never had much clout in the Gulf region except in Iraq (and even that tended to be overestimated in the West), and whatever currency it had in most of the Gulf went up in smoke as a result of its invasion of Afghanistan. However, the USSR actually gained some stature in the monarchies by publicly supporting the alliance during the Gulf War.

In the post–cold war world, this region is both more and less important to the West. It is more important economically because the Western nations are increasingly dependent on the region's oil. It is less important strategically because of the collapse of the other superpower and the evaporation of the attendant threat. Unfortunately, the lack of that superpower tension has removed what was once an implicit constraint on now increasing internal instability in the region.

Economically, Russia needs to sell arms, for its weapons industry has long been the most functional and competitive sector of its economy. The West has in fact tried to prevent the sale of some Russian equipment and arms (e.g., submarines and nuclear reactors) to Iran under the rubric of preventing a destabilization of the regional balance of power. However, as Russian foreign policy has become more assertive and independent in the latter part of the 1990s, it has stepped up attempts to increase arms sales to Iran.

For its part, Tehran has been willing to buy from the Russians because the West would not sell such items to the Islamic Republic while making high tech material available to the Arab states of the Gulf (excluding Iraq). Even so, the Western market share of the region's arms trade has increased. The opposite is true of Moscow, and many members of the Russian elite see this as yet another Western ploy for grinding down their once proud country and another instance of Western greed.

Russia's attempts at strengthening its relations with Iran are complicated by the longer term problem of its obvious desire for the readmission of Iraq into the good graces of the international community. Moscow's ties to Baghdad were among its strongest in the Third World in the two decades prior to the Gulf War. While it joined the coalition calling for Iraq's withdrawal from Kuwait, it has subsequently emerged as an advocate for its former Iraqi friends. In addition to their traditionally strong ties, Russia, as the legatee of the USSR, is still owed well over $6 billion and would like to see Iraq regain its prewar status as a functioning economy from which it could recover that debt and with which it could foster renewed trade.

American policy in the Persian Gulf seems best described by the phrase "dual containment" of Iran and Iraq, both of which have been labeled "backlash" states by U.S. policymakers. This policy only works to the extent that other vendor countries can be persuaded to treat the two as pariah nations, and it has not worked very well in the case of Iran. Some Russians see this dual containment policy as an American attempt to get rid of the current rulers of both of these states in the hope of replacing them with leaders more amenable to Washington's views and more receptive to the reentry of U.S. business interests. Indeed, there has in recent years been some moderation in the tone of the Iranian leadership.

Clearly many U.S. and Russian interests in the Gulf are not complementary, and the United States as "top dog" has made few if any concessions to Russian views/interests in recent years. Predictably, as noted, this breeds resentment in Moscow and always invites the eternal dialectic of international affairs—success breeds failure. That is, by being but a bystander in the game during this period of instability, the Russians could be long-term winners in the event of major internal upheavals in the countries of the Gulf.

In South Asia, Shirin Tahir-Kheli (chapter 6) examines the tangled web of evolving relationships between and among the two major regional powers (India and Pakistan) and the two superpowers, as well as China, during the period following the 1947 British withdrawal from the subcontinent. Predictably, since the early period of independence for India and Pakistan and the initial flaring of their rivalry coincided with the dawning of the cold war, the two were inevitably drawn into that larger struggle. Sometimes they were seen as pawns of the superpowers, with India linked nominally to the USSR and Pakistan to the United States (and China), but more often they behaved as independent actors attempting to leverage their own interests as they defined them through cooperation with or resistance to one or another of these external powers. For example, in the late 1970s and through much of the 1980s, the Soviet invasion of Afghanistan led to an improvement in Washington's relations with Pakistan because the latter was used as a major supply and training center for the anti-Communist *Mujahidin* who fought in Afghanistan.

Moscow's withdrawal from Afghanistan, followed by the collapse of the Soviet regime, forced the regional powers to review their respective policies. Because its nations lived "in the shadow of the cold war," the entire fabric of international relations in South Asia was shaped by the East-West struggle, and both India and Pakistan enjoyed substantial benefits as a result.

Among the changes induced by the end of the East-West struggle has been a major reorientation in India's policies, or more precisely, the normalization of its relations with both China and the United States. This trend was facilitated by the changes taking place inside India. The introduction of major economic reforms pointed to the desirability of improved relations with the West. Washington, in particular, was receptive to overtures from New Delhi, and, by the mid-1990s, the United States had emerged as India's major foreign trading partner.

Pakistan, on the other hand, turned northward. In the early post–cold war period, Islamabad expected continued support from Washington, but, with the demise of the USSR, the United States virtually lost interest in the region's struggles and Pakistan's role in them. Other factors complicating the relationship were America's growing preoccupation with its own economic affairs and Washington's disapproval of Pakistan's nuclear program. This led ultimately to the termination of U.S. assistance in 1990.

In addition to religious and cultural affinity and geographic proximity, Pakistan's interest in Afghanistan and the former Soviet republics in Central Asia has also been driven by its desire to gain direct access to the area's vast fuel deposits, particularly Turkmen gas. The former Central Asian republics appear eager to export their fuel directly, bypassing Russia. However, the main stumbling block remains the highly unsettled situation in Afghanistan through which Turkmen gas would have to flow to reach Pakistan. In other words, there is continuing internal strife in Afghanistan, despite the apparently decided advantage enjoyed by the Taliban movement since their capture of Kabul (and most of the countryside) and their installation as the ruling regime. This makes the arrangement of any long-term agreement vis-à-vis the transport of Central Asian fuel through Afghanistan highly problematic.

Moreover, the use of Pakistan as the conduit for arms into Afghanistan beginning after the Soviet invasion has left as its legacy what Tahir-Kheli calls the "Kalashnikov culture." That is, along with the guns transiting Pakistan into Afghanistan came a reverse trail of drugs destined for the American market. The violent criminal culture thus created continues to make life difficult for ordinary Pakistanis. In sum, most of the nations of the region have already begun the process of conducting their foreign policies based upon their own resources. They will have to continue doing that rather than relying on the assumption that great powers will seek to influence them by trying to win their "friendship."

One issue does seem guaranteed to recapture world attention for the area, at least temporarily—the spread of nuclear weapons. The explosion by India of an underground nuclear device in May 1998 and Pakistan's rapid response with the test of a comparable device was front page news around the world. Given the long-run acrimony between the two nations, especially over Kashmir, the major powers rushed to damp down the crisis. As the December 1999 hijacking of an Indian airliner and charges that its perpetrators were based in Pakistan clearly show, this conflict has a way of bubbling to the surface in unpredictable fashion. It makes the continuing great power concern about nuclear proliferation in South Asia seem well-founded indeed.

Charles Ziegler in chapter 7 contends that Moscow's relations with the states of East Asia have been influenced by a complex set of factors (strategic, political, and economic), both foreign and domestic. The disintegration of the USSR, along with the resulting changed American attitude toward the region, has dramatically altered the entire framework of international relations in East Asia.

During the cold war, the Soviet government was predominately interested in security issues in the Far East. That is, the Kremlin was primarily preoccupied with fending off what it perceived to be security threats from both the United States and China. Gorbachev attempted to mitigate these and other problems by improving relations with both Washington and Beijing. This had the latent effect of diminishing the importance to Moscow of relations with such regional allies as North Korea and Vietnam. Since the collapse of the Soviet Union, the balance of power and interests has shifted even more dramatically. Russia is now seen as a virtual nonthreat to the West, unable to get its own house in order. As a consequence, American security concerns in East Asia have been enormously reduced, and China, with its immense population and rapidly expanding economy, is the newly emerging great power of consequence.

While the close alliance of the 1950s between China and the Soviet Union seems unlikely to be regained, Moscow and Beijing have common interests and views on a number of issues, most importantly their opposition to American dominance in international political and economic affairs (especially the United States' preeminence in arms sales). Thus, there is a growing convergence in many of their foreign policy positions. As a result of these facts, China is likely to remain of paramount concern in Russia's Asian policy for the foreseeable future.

Japan, given its tremendous economic power, is still an entity to be reckoned with, but its relative importance has also declined as other Asian economies have flourished and its own looming domestic problems have begun to surface. Moreover, its relations with Russia are scarred by territorial disputes of such a nature that any attempt to settle them on a basis satisfactory to Tokyo will run headlong into a stone wall of Russian domestic opposition.

Recently, there has been some improvement of relations between Russia and Japan on the local level in the Far East. Moreover, there is general awareness that both could benefit from enhanced exploitation of Russia's far eastern fuel reserves. Joint ventures in this arena have already begun.

Even in the Gorbachev era, the USSR's relations with North Korea had deteriorated, a decline that has become even more pronounced in the post-Soviet period. Indeed, the Yeltsin government has spent considerable effort on improving its relations with South Korea and on urging that the whole of Korea become a nuclear-free zone, policies the Kremlin knew would not be greeted warmly in Pyongyang. While Russia has in recent years tried to maintain some of its ties to North Korea, when matters of significance dictate, the Kremlin does not hesitate to offend its former allies. Clearly, the Kremlin seeks to have good relations with both Koreas, but for the near term, South Korea is the more valuable trading partner.

One potentially threatening development from the Russian perspective is the current American proposal to create a Theater Missile Defense (TMD) system in South Korea, Japan, and Taiwan. If such a system became operational, its deployment would completely upset the current regional balance of power in East Asia. Not too surprisingly, then, the proposal has been met with Russian insistence that it would violate the 1972 Anti-Ballistic Missile Treaty and would provoke a regional arms race. Washington's wish to re-negotiate the 1972 ABM Treaty is tacit acknowledgment that the Russian interpretation on that point is correct.

Three main conclusions arise from Ziegler's examination of Russia's relations with East Asia. First, following an interval of "relative neglect," both during earlier periods of Soviet authority and immediately following the upheaval attendant to the collapse of the USSR, Moscow has now begun to mount a more activist policy toward the region, one aimed at improving relations with all its major countries. This has resulted primarily from the government's response to domestic sentiment among those who advocate a policy designed to pursue Russia's "national interests," although there is no firm agreement about what those interests are as they pertain to East Asia. Clearly, however, the consensus is that Russia must reclaim its status as a great power.

Second, the general pattern of Moscow's former neglect of the Eastern region has led to a tradition of "subnational foreign policies" in which local authorities maintained their own close ties with neighboring states. The interests of these localities and the central government often do not coincide, and whose interests will prevail in such situations is by no means always clear. In any case, this state of affairs inevitably complicates Moscow's relations with its neighbors in East Asia.

Finally, Russia and the United States no longer confront each other as rival superpowers in Northeast Asia, but a range of unsettled issues, especially in America's relations with China and Japan, as well as the changing security environment in the region, suggests a period of volatility in the international affairs of the region is likely for the near term.

EUROPE

In the third section of this anthology, two analysts have examined the impact of the end of the cold war on the international relations of Europe, West and East. What unfolds is yet another story of opportunities and challenges.

Stephen Blank in chapter 8 examines recent developments and he argues that the European Union (EU) and the United States were initially ill-prepared to deal with the transformations wrought by the collapse of the Soviet Union, and thus their policies in the early 1990s were "inconclusive."

Blank sees three challenges as having emerged for the West if the promises of the end of the cold war are to be realized: (1) integrating the Central European states (e.g., Poland, Hungary, and others) into the West; (2) establishing a legitimate and durable peace in the Balkans, so that the Balkan states too can eventually be integrated with Europe; and (3) creating a similar order for the Baltic states, as well as Russia, Belarus, Ukraine, and Transcaucasia.

He is mostly critical of early efforts in this domain. In his view, the component states of the EU were so absorbed with their own domestic political agendas in the first half of the past decade that it was unrealistic to expect the EU to integrate fully additional states from among its former adversaries to the East. However, in 1997, NATO did authorize an expansion to include the Czech Republic, Hungary, and Poland.

This decision, predictably, was not warmly received in Moscow. In an attempt to ease Russia's growing misgivings, the West made some minor political and economic concessions to Yeltsin. Among these were limited membership in G-7 (a consultative group of the world's leading industrial nations) and creation of a Russia–NATO political council. From Moscow's perspective, these concessions and the laggard, limited economic aid provided to Russia have been far too little too late.

More recent events have begun to show the West's dawning realization of the "indivisibility of European security." Most important among them, according to Blank, has been NATO's decisive response to the crisis in Kosovo. He argues that unless this newer approach is pursued vigorously, there is still the risk of a renationalization of Europe and a new division of Europe into "spheres of influence" and rival blocs, along with the attendant likelihood of armed conflict which such a situation entails.

The West has yet to devise a coherent set of policies for preventing and/or dealing with crises like that in Kosovo or more generally the collective security of an enlarged Europe. Moreover, it is not clear that there is the will to create and pursue such policies on a sustained basis. In Blank's view, the easy road of inaction in response to any attempts to breach the principle of Europe's indivisibility will only breed future problems for all concerned.

Christopher Jones shares Blank's view concerning the indivisibility of Europe. In chapter 9, he argues that the enlargement of NATO actually solves what historically has been Russia's primary security problem—its concern with German military power. He believes that the logic of the situation should also allay Russian concerns about strategic nuclear defense. That is, he makes a visionary argument for the denuclearization of Europe (indeed for world-wide progressive, reciprocal nuclear disarmament), showing how it is justified and how it would benefit both Russia and the West. Regrettably, his is a scholar's rational analysis, and he suggests no mechanism for setting the process in motion.

Jones presents a sophisticated analysis of how the "division of labor" created by NATO produced a variety of important residual economic and technological benefits to its member states (the United States included) that were never available to the USSR and its Warsaw Pact allies. What evolved is a process that he calls "the Brussels Syndrome," which he defines as "a self-perpetuating cycle in which ever-intensifying military-technological competition between the US and USSR . . . perpetuated a partial denationalization of defense policy unanticipated by the founders of NATO" (p. 230).

What this division of labor produced was a West European reliance on the American nuclear deterrent to neutralize the perceived Soviet threat while the European allies bore the major responsibility for conventional forces. This form of collective security became a form of denationalized defense. The cooperative habits built in the military arena in due course spread into economic policy as well. The cost savings provided by this arrangement allowed the Western European democracies to create expansive social welfare entitlement programs and transformed most Western democracies into middle-class–dominated civil societies.

Most important of all, an implicit understanding was generated that using military means to settle disputes between and among member nations was a threat to the survival of the Western alliance and thus was unthinkable. (Greece and Turkey have sometimes trampled this principle, but they have been roundly denounced for doing so.) Indeed, NATO transformed the political culture of the officer corps of its constituent states so that they are no longer linked to the conservative nationalistic traditions of the past. In sum, while NATO began as a military alliance, the sweeping socio-economic benefits which accrued to its member nations helped to promulgate to the rest of the world an ideology of democratic politics and market economics.

Jones shows that for the Eastern bloc countries membership in the Warsaw Pact, while it did not produce most of the kinds of benefits that enured to members of NATO, did have the effect of denationalizing security policy in the bloc and thus has partially prepared the former Soviet allies for membership in NATO. The two defense organizations were organized in a very different fashion. The former Soviet satellites were deprived by the Soviet system of the standard total set of military capabilities (i.e., they lacked the relevant support bureaucracies, military training institutions, and national defense policy planning apparatuses), while the Western allies engaged in a voluntary division of labor. However, both systems have taught their ruling elites that there are no viable separate solutions to military security and economic development problems.

The status of Europe, West and East, is thus still largely unsettled, and that inevitably poses enormous challenges to the leaders of all European countries. However, the view from the Kremlin is further complicated by an issue even closer to home, namely the evolving status of the former Soviet republics in the Near Abroad.

THE NEAR ABROAD

Most seasoned observers of Russian foreign policy would agree that the issue of the Near Abroad now holds primacy in the minds of Kremlin policymakers. That is, Moscow has apparently concluded that if Russia is to reassert its status as a great power, it must first reestablish its influence in the former Soviet space whose component parts gained nominal independence with the dissolution of the USSR. The creation of the CIS in December 1991 was the opening gambit in the effort to reintegrate the former Soviet republics (minus the Baltic states) under Russian leadership.

From Moscow's perspective, this effort, unfortunately, has not been totally successful. That is, an organization has been established, its bureaucratic infrastructure has been created, countless meetings have been held, and hundreds of resolutions have been passed, but the tangible benefits to Moscow have been meager at best. Most of the former republics, with the exception of Belarus, having tasted the fruits of independence, appear determined not to revert to their former positions of complete subordination. This movement for self-determination has been led by Ukraine, despite the fact that its ties to Moscow are ancient and close.

Even before the Bolshevik era, Ukraine was among the most "russified" of the areas in the Russian Empire, and, during the Soviet period, the Kremlin made sure that it continued to be bound to Moscow by deep and complex ties of interdependence. Even so, there was always a strong nationalist strain within some segments of the Ukrainian population. In the euphoria which followed the downfall of the old Soviet regime, a wave of nationalist sentiment swept through the country. However, the celebratory sentiment died rapidly as the economic situation deteriorated and the realization dawned that Ukraine could not readily replace all the old ties of economic interdependence with Moscow in a market driven world.

As Oles Smolansky explains in chapter 10, Moscow held too many "trump cards" for Ukraine to simply cut its cord to Moscow. Indeed, the most striking feature of relations between post-Soviet Russia and Ukraine is Kyiv's economic dependence on Russia. This manifests itself in the following ways: (1) Russia is by far Ukraine's largest supplier of fuel (oil and natural gas); (2) Russia is Ukraine's largest creditor; and (3) Russia is generally Ukraine's largest trading partner, even apart from the fuel trade.

Not surprisingly, Moscow has tried repeatedly to use Ukraine's economic dependence to compel Kyiv to comply with the Kremlin's wishes in a variety of policy matters. Although Russia's apparent leverage is enormous, the Kremlin's overall record of successfully influencing Ukrainian policy is, at best, mixed. Thus, Russia succeeded in imposing on Ukraine trade conditions that Kyiv regards as harmful to its interests and rejected Ukraine's requests to renegotiate their 1995 debt-restructuring agreement. Moscow has also dictated the price and volume of fuel it has exported to Ukraine.

At the same time, the Kremlin has not been able to persuade Ukraine to bow to its wishes in a number of political/economic issues (e.g., the status of Crimea, Ukraine's 1996 deal to sell tanks to Pakistan, the breakup and disposition of the Black Sea Fleet, and so on). This relative independence by Ukraine has been due to the fact that Kyiv has a few trump cards of its own. That is, Ukraine is Russia's largest fuel export market, a market Moscow appears determined to keep. Moreover, Russian fuel exports to European markets (and a major source of its hard currency) rely mainly on the pipeline network situated in Ukraine. (Transit through Ukraine is characteristic of much of Russia's export freight.) In fact, Russian and Ukrainian "fuel barons" now cooperate closely in the lucrative export trade with Europe.

In sum, Russia and Ukraine are like two spouses trapped in a bad marriage. Each controls resources that are crucial to their desired lifestyle, and so divorce is unthinkable for either the more or less powerful partner. While the relationship between Moscow and Kyiv is especially important to both, it is in many ways emblematic of the relations between the Kremlin and many of its former subordinate republics. The old Soviet system was deliberately constructed to make the peripheral areas dependent on the center, but as the Ukrainian case shows, the leverage which that ought to create for Moscow is often difficult to actualize.

RUSSIA AND THE UNITED STATES: AN EVOLVING RELATIONSHIP

The last two chapters by Henry Trofimenko and Harvey Sicherman examine, albeit from different viewpoints, the impact of the collapse of the Soviet Union on the relationship between the current and former superpowers. Both agree that the relationship has undergone a sweeping change—Russia has been relegated to the status of a secondary power designated by the world's leading financial analysts as having a "transitional" (i.e., developing) economy, while the United States has reached the pinnacle of its military and political power and is now essentially unchallenged in its capacity to project its might beyond its national borders. Both analysts agree that it was developments in the Soviet Union that precipitated the change, but their respective views on the desirability of the results of those changes understandably diverge.

Initially, according to Trofimenko, the early post-Soviet relationship between Gorbachev and Yeltsin's Russia and the United States was close, harmonious, and productive, but in his view the Russians made almost all the concessions that produced this harmony. However, by 1993, clouds appeared on the political horizon as Russian leaders began voicing their displeasure with the evolving shape of the Moscow-Washington relationship.

This change in the Kremlin's attitude and policy toward the West resulted from (1) nationalist pressures, exerted by the Communist and ultranationalist groupings in and outside of the Russian parliament; and (2) the unhelpful, arrogant behavior of the United States and its allies toward Russia. Specifically, according to Trofimenko, Moscow received almost none of the anticipated benefits from its pro-Western orientation (e.g., no significant financial/economic assistance, no admission to "respectable" Western political or economic organizations). Moreover, Washington added insult to injury by espousing the cause of NATO expansion which Trofimenko sees (in a view widely shared by Russians) as an attempt by the United States to fill the power vacuum in Eastern Europe. In fact, he describes the key American goal in this fashion: "There can be no doubt that the United States is striving for *world hegemony*" (p. 294, emphasis added). To achieve its objectives,

Trofimenko concludes, the United States is trying to keep Russia supine, a posture that most Russians inevitably resent.

While once it seemed that the West was interested in preserving Russia and fostering democracy there, Trofimenko claims that now it cares only about controlling Russia's nuclear arsenal. Western leaders once thought they could count on the Yeltsin-led government to accomplish that task, but the latter focused almost exclusively on the aggrandizement of its own material position and cared nothing for the Russian people.

This concern over the Russian nuclear force is the primary source of the current American insistence on modifying the 1972 ABM treaty (originally instigated by Washington). The changes being sought would allow continued development by the United States of its "Star Wars" defense system. If successful, such a system would dramatically alter the strategic balance of power in the world, once again to the detriment of Russia. This American pressure, along with the recent expansion of NATO, has stiffened the Duma's resistance to the ratification of the START-II treaty. Indeed, it continues to make it more difficult in terms of Russia's domestic politics to achieve the kinds of internal reforms that the West still claims it would like to see enacted.

Trofimenko implies that most Western analysts have failed to understand something very important about the nature of the Russian people. To wit, the majority of Russia's large population are well-educated, industrious citizens of what was once a modern nation, but they are also the legatees of a proud Slavonic civilization whose total transformation they will resist as they have resisted a succession of other tyrannies through many generations.

Trofimenko expresses the hope that eventually Washington will come to understand that helping Russia achieve internal stability and the status which it desires within a democratic and free Europe will be in everyone's self-interest. In sum, he warns that policies designed to push Russia out of Europe and/or denigrate its status as a great power will force the Kremlin to turn eastward toward Asia, and that could be counterproductive for all in the long run.

Sicherman implicitly agrees that it was initiatives by Moscow that brought about the end to the cold war. However, he assigns the blame for the later negative developments in the Washington-Moscow relationship to both Russian and American leaders. In his view, Bush and Clinton's Russia policies, while well-intentioned, have been based on a flawed understanding of the situation. The problem, as he sees it, was that official Washington focused not on Russian reality but on "the democratic partner of . . . [its] hopes"—

Yeltsin." Specifically, on almost every issue (e.g., Chechnya, Central Asia, Bosnia, arms control and arms sales, or economic reform), things did not work out as hoped because "Moscow simply did not play the role assigned to it."

This realization forced the Clinton administration to recalibrate its approach, leading, among other things, to the decision to expand NATO. Of course, the assumption that Moscow should simply "play the role assigned to it" by Washington would likely be cited by Russian analysts like Trofimenko as just the sort of American attitude which has led to the decline in the Moscow-Washington relationship.

The decision by the United States to press for the expansion of NATO to include some of the former Soviet satellites rests in Sicherman's view on the need to "hedge" against a renewed Russian attempt to reassert its dominance over Central Europe, a policy motive that Clinton has been loathe to acknowledge directly. As Sicherman sees it, today's Russia is still beset by enormous economic problems, including inflation, bureaucratic excess, widespread corruption, and "demonetization" (i.e., it has become essentially dependent internally on a barter economy). It is, however, still a large and powerful country, one which has emerged from the ashes of the Soviet Union as a great power almost on a pre–World War I model. Until and unless the West is prepared to deal with Russia as a great power, "neither determined adversary nor natural ally," Western leaders will continue making policy from a position of "blurred vision."

LESSONS FOR INTERESTING TIMES

The cold war is over and there is little nostalgia for its incipient nuclear terror. However, there is no doubt that the adversarial system which it bred gave a sense of predictability to international affairs that is now gone, and this fact has inordinately complicated the lives of those who must make international policy. The period of transition from the cold war is now only a decade old, but there are some useful lessons to be learned from intensive analyses of the impact of these sweeping changes in various parts of the world.

These events have profoundly altered the way that leaders of most developing countries must look at the world. Smaller nations have long used the rivalries of great powers as leverage for the pursuit of their own goals; however, when those larger rivalries fade or shift, lesser powers must find new approaches to securing

their national interests. Indeed, in some instances a reassessment
of those interests, especially as concerns their relative priority, is in
order. Other things being equal, the leaders of those nations who
first grasp the realities of the new situation are likely to benefit
most from the change.

Unfortunately, other things rarely are equal. Thus, those Third
World nations whose leaders used the cold war as their primary
source of leverage to extract from the industrial nations (especially
the superpower rivals) technical, military, and economic aid are
now essentially out of luck. According to our case analysts, this includes many of the states of Sub-Saharan Africa, the Red Sea region, and South Asia.

The cold war, because its conflict dynamic encouraged the superpowers and their allies to funnel huge amounts of modern
arms into many such less fortunate nations, actually led to the ex-
acerbation of existing local rivalries and created new ones. Parenthetically, much of this weaponry was paid for by the governments
of the producer nations whose own defense industries consequently came to comprise an even more significant sector of their
own economies. Markets do not, as many economists still tell their
students, respond to *needs*; they respond to needs coupled with *resources*. Thus, the decline of this arms market (i.e., its inability to
arrange payment) has had a near-term negative effect on some of
those same producer economies.

It is difficult to see what aspects of the "new world order" are of
immediate benefit to such developing countries, save the reduced
likelihood of their territory being used as a battleground on which
to stage modern warfare. Indeed, in such countries, a sweeping re-
appraisal of the priority that has traditionally been assigned to internal rivalries and those with neighboring states is a likely
prerequisite to improving their standing in the global community.
That is, they can ill-afford to squander meager resources on such
conflicts. In this regard, it appears that those areas of the world
which were essentially *not* heavily embroiled in the cold war, like
much of Latin America, actually face a less traumatic transition in
this new era.

Three other Third World regions are likely to remain in the international spotlight, each for distinctive reasons. The Persian Gulf
area sits atop the largest proven and readily extractable oil deposits
in the world, and the entire global economy as we currently know
it depends upon the continuing, dependable flow of that oil. Most
scholars readily acknowledge that the ability to mount a rapid and
effective coalition to defeat Saddam Hussein in 1990–91, despite

the political rhetoric by Western politicians about the need to defend Kuwait's right to survive as an independent state, was actually based on the widely shared recognition by politicians in all the coalition states (and beyond) of that oil dependence.

The whole of the Middle East with its legendary image as the crossroads of the world (at least of the Eastern Hemisphere) and its long tradition of conflicting cultures is unlikely to fade into obscurity any time soon. While chances for a resolution of the Arab-Israeli dispute look more promising than ever, a settlement is not yet an accomplished fact. Thus, the dispute continues to be a potential problem, and the conflict there remains as an incipient threat to the vital flow of petroleum to the West, essentially ensuring that the rest of the world will continue to care about what happens in the Middle East. Even should a viable long-term solution to the regional conflict be found, the electorates in many Western countries for reasons of culture and religion will continue to exhibit a lively interest in the region's affairs.

Similarly, East Asia with its mushrooming market economies will continue to be a significant area in world affairs even though some of its countries are still burdened by residual baggage from the cold war (e.g., North Korea and Vietnam) and/or the constraints of their leftist ideologies (e.g., China and Cambodia). There is now a great deal less public commentary about the twenty-first century becoming the Pacific century than there was even ten years ago, but the mere presence of Japan, China, and the Four Tigers guarantee the area's importance in the political economy of the evolving world, despite the recent regional economic downturn. Should Russia get its economic and political house in order, it too could become an important player on the Asian scene, only enhancing the area's stature. The political future of China is at best uncertain, but a nation which comprises about twenty percent of the world's population will inevitably be a major force in world affairs for a long time to come.

Both of our case analysts of Europe call for the continuing integration of Europe, implying that European security (both military and economic) rests upon such unity. The earlier unity achieved in NATO (and the yielding of some of the control over national armed forces attendant thereto) rested upon the widely shared perception of a threat to the very survival of the nations involved. Similarly, the substantial progress made toward economic union also rests on a widely shared understanding that it is larger political-economic units which generally have the most clout in a global market.

Whether the more diffuse challenges of the post-Soviet world will constitute sufficient motivation for countries used to dealing with each other historically as cultural, political, economic, and/or military competitors to cooperate at a level that will require them to redefine the very nature of the principle of national sovereignty is still an open question. It will no doubt call for a quality of vision and leadership, an ability to think long term, that is generally in short supply among politicians who must stand periodically for re-election.

Daunting though these prospects are in Western Europe, they pale in comparison to the magnitude of the equivalent task in Central and Eastern Europe. For there, most of the nations involved are just emerging from a long period during which their national sovereignty was trampled with regularity and during which their economic well-being was also commonly subordinated to external entities and principles over which they had no control. There is *de facto* a yearning, a kind of "pent-up demand," for expressions of national sovereignty in many of these countries that is readily understandable in light of their status during the last half century.

The only incentive that makes sense to the average voter in these countries to justify making the sacrifices necessary to facilitate integration with the rest of Europe is the promise of a standard of living comparable to that enjoyed by their Western neighbors, but the stresses and strains involved in the transformation from state-controlled to market economies have actually led to a substantial decline in the living standards of many segments of their citizenry. The personal freedom to complain openly about the government's policies when one is worried about the ability to feed one's children and/or care for one's aging parents seems to many people a questionable trade-off. The patience of this populace may not survive the transition without huge infusions of Western aid, assistance which the West has thus far seen as "too expensive" or "too risky" to extend.

Nowhere is this dilemma more keenly felt than in the CIS itself, both among the Russians themselves and among the nationalities that had been marginalized and subordinated under Soviet rule, with its overt policy of russification. The initial euphoria of nationhood in many of the former republics gave way quickly, however, to a dawning realization that the same old crowd seemed to control the levers of power and to exercise them for their own personal gain without interference from Moscow (and therefore without external restraint). Thus, the looting of the resources of many of these new nations has proceeded apace, and whatever material gain was to be had by the removal of the Soviet yoke has mostly disappeared into private bank accounts. Moreover, it has become apparent that the old Soviet system was designed to make the various republics economically interdependent with each other as well as dependent upon Moscow. Thus, the putative political independence of the republics did not result in the ability to go it alone.

Except for those emersed in the party and state apparatus, most ordinary Russians greeted the end of the Communist era and the resulting emergence of greater personal liberty with expected enthusiasm. Unfortunately, they then were forced to watch helplessly as their country fell into disarray, declining from its status as one of the world's two superpowers to that of a developing nation. To exacerbate the problem, the new Russia has been left to deal with the restiveness of several long repressed nationalities within its own borders. This occurred in a context where there is no historical precedent for democratic resolution of factional differences. The results in such places as Chechnya have been predictably disastrous.

The hoped for trade-off of an improving standard of living has only been realized by a minuscule segment of the population, with most of the newly rich becoming the object of private scorn by much of the public, viewed as "crooks," either figuratively or literally. The early Russian experience with capitalism has brought out some of the worst excesses of that system, with few of the restraints that have evolved in the industrial West to soften its harshest features. If ways cannot be found to mitigate these negative consequences for the ordinary people who comprise its citizenry, then the political future of Russia sems uncertain indeed.

While the impulse in the West to savor its "triumph" in the cold war is understandable, now that several years have passed, it is time to turn from celebration to the hard work of assuring that the victory was not an empty one. The world has changed, but having long focused our ingenuity so successfully on the technology of destruction, we must acknowledge that the world is still a dangerous place, one where deeply held hatreds abound.

In response, we can adopt a latter-day version of a garrison mentality and "circle the wagons," further dividing the world into "friends and foes," trying to arrange the balance of forces so that "the winners" are selected exclusively from among those within the charmed circle and "the losers" are contained. Or, we can attempt to create a new international framework in which our former adversaries have a vital stake, one which guarantees that their self-interests lie with participating in the cooperative endeavor to foster a secure, liveable future for all nations. For those needing a historical referent to recommend this later course of action, they need look no further than the dramatically different consequences of the varying treatments accorded the vanquished by the victors following the two world wars.

NOTE

1. The term *kleptocracy* means, in essence, an authority system in which it is the norm that people at each level of power will extort (i.e., steal) substantial amounts from the people immediately below them in the hierarchy, often to cover partially the costs of what is being taken from them by their superiors.

Contributors

HENRI J. BARKEY is the Bernard L. and Bertha F. Cohen Professor of International Relations at Lehigh University. He served on the State Department's Policy Planning Staff from 1998 to 2000 and is the author (with Graham Fuller) of *Turkey's Kurdish Question* and of *The State and the Industrialization Crisis in Turkey*. Professor Barkey has also edited *The Reluctant Neighbor: Turkey's Role in the Middle East* and *The Politics of Economic Reform in the Middle East*, and has published numerous articles in professional journals.

STEPHEN J. BLANK is Professor of Russian National Security Studies at the Strategic Studies Institute of the U.S. Army War College. He has published over 150 articles on Soviet/Russian military and foreign policies, and is the editor of *Imperial Decline: Russia's Changing Role in Asia*. Dr. Blank is also the author of *The Sorcerer as Apprentice: Stalin's Commissariat of Nationalities* and the co-editor of *The Soviet Military and the Future*.

W. RAYMOND DUNCAN is Distinguished Teaching Professor of Political Science at SUNY College at Brockport. He has written extensively on Soviet-Third World relations, with special attention to the Soviet-Cuban relationship and its cold war impact on the Caribbean Basin and Central America. Professor Duncan has traveled throughout Latin America, most recently Cuba, Central America, and Mexico. He previously worked with the National Intelligence Council in Washington, D.C. and taught at the Naval War College in Newport, Rhode Island.

MELVIN A. GOODMAN, Soviet analyst at the Central Intelligence Agency from 1966 to 1986, is Professor of International Security at the National War College and Senior Fellow at the Center for International Policy in Washington, D.C. He is also Adjunct Professor at American University and Johns Hopkins University. He is co-author of *The Wars of Eduard Shevardnadze*, contributor to *National Insecurity: U.S. Intelligence After the Cold War*, editor of *The Cold*

369

War: Lessons Learned, and co-author of *The Phantom Defense: The Case Against National Missile Defense*.

CHRISTOPHER JONES is Associate Professor at the Jackson School of International Affairs at the University of Washington. He is the author of *Soviet Influence in Eastern Europe: Political Autonomy and the Warsaw Pact* and co-author of a 3-volume study for the Canadian Department of National Defense, *The Warsaw Pact: The Question of Cohesion*. His work on NATO enlargement includes "Brussels as the Heir of Moscow," in the July–August 1998 issue of *Problems of Post-Communism*.

MARINA OTTAWAY is Senior Associate and Co-Director of the Democracy Project at the Carnegie Endowment for International Peace. She is also Adjunct Professor of African Studies at the School of Advanced International Studies, Johns Hopkins University. She has carried out research in Africa for many years and has taught at universities in Ethiopia, Zambia, Egypt, and South Africa. Having written extensively on South Africa and the Horn, Dr. Ottaway's current focus is upon problems of democratic transformation in Africa. She is the author of *Democracy and Ethnic Nationalism: African and Eastern European Experiences* and the editor of *Democracy in Africa: The Hard Road Ahead*. Dr. Ottaway has just completed a book, *Africa's New Leaders: Democracy or State Reconstruction?*

STEPHEN PAGE is the author of *The Soviet Union and the Yemens: Influence in Asymmetrical Relationships*. In the post-Soviet period he has written widely on Russian foreign policy in Central Asia. Currently, he is Head of the Department of Political Studies, Queen's University, Kingston, Ontario, Canada.

HARVEY SICHERMAN is president of the Foreign Policy Research Institute in Philadelphia. He worked as special assistant to Secretary of State Alexander M. Haig, Jr. (1981–82) and consultant to Secretary of State George P. Shultz (1988), and served on Secretary of State James A. Baker's Policy Planning Staff (1990–91). Dr. Sicherman has written numerous books and articles on U.S. foreign policy.

BETTIE MORETZ SMOLANSKY, Professor of Sociology at Moravian College, is currently serving as the College's Dean for Academic Affairs. She has collaborated with Oles Smolansky on *The USSR and Iraq: The Soviet Quest for Influence* and on a number of articles and chapters on international affairs. She has also published articles on a variety of topics in her discipline and on pedagogical issues in college teaching.

OLES M. SMOLANSKY is University Distinguished Professor of International Relations at Lehigh University. He is the author of *The Soviet Union and the Arab East Under Khrushchev* and, with Bettie M. Smolansky, of *The USSR and Iraq*. He also co-edited *Russia and America: From Rivalry to Reconciliation* and *Regional Power Rivalries in the New Eurasia: Russia, Turkey, and Iran*.

SHIRIN R. TAHIR-KHELI is Research Professor and Director, South Asia Program at Johns Hopkins University School of Advanced International Studies. Prior to her current assignment, she has held a number of high-level posts in the U.S. government. Dr. Tahir-Kheli left Washington in 1993 to become a Fellow at Princeton University's Center of International Studies and co-chaired a Council on Foreign Relations Study Group on India and Pakistan. She is the author of *India, Pakistan, and the United States: Breaking With the Past*.

HENRY TROFIMENKO is Professor at the Russian Diplomatic Academy of the Russian Academy of Sciences, a Senior Analyst at Moscow's Institute for the Study of the U.S.A. and Canada, and the author of *U.S. Military Doctrine* and *USSR-US: A Half Century of Peaceful Coexistence*.

CHARLES E. ZIEGLER is a Professor and Chair of the Department of Political Science at the University of Louisville. He is the author of *The History of Russia, Foreign Policy and East Asia,* and *Environmental Policy in the USSR,* and many articles and book chapters on Russian politics and foreign policy. He has been a Fulbright scholar in Korea, an International Affairs Fellow with the Council on Foreign Relations, and a national Fellow at the Hoover Institution. Ziegler is also Executive Director of the Louisville Committee on Foreign Relations.

Index

Mujahidin, the: and Gorbachev, 157; and Pakistan, 163

Multilateralism, 63, 198–99, 208–9, 239–40, 246, 248; treaties, 284

"Multilateral Force" variant, 231

Muslim Brotherhood: and political instability in the Middle East, 120

Muslim states/population/fundamentalism: in the Middle East, 110, 111, 115; in Pakistan, 151, 164; and the invasion of Afghanistan, 159; in Kashmir, 164; in China, 173–74; in Central Asia, 175; in Bosnia, 202–3, 243; in Kosovo, 242; and Russian fear of, 326

Mutual and balanced force reductions (MBFR), 36

Mutual Defense Agreement (between India and the Soviet Union), 151

Mutually Assured Destruction (MAD) deterrence: 324

NAFTA: and Latin America, 48, 51, 63, 64, 67, 69, 71; and Chile, 122

Najibullah (Afghanistan's Communist leader): and the Soviet Union, 157

Nationalism/nationalists: and Soviet support for in Latin America, 51–52; in Africa, 81, 89, 90, 91; in the Middle East, 106, 109, 119; in the Persian Gulf, 133, 137, 141, 145; and the Red Sea region, 145; in Russia, 165–66, 168, 170, 171, 176, 180–81, 183, 185–86; in China, 172, 174, 184–86; as cause of instability in Europe, 201; in U.S. during crisis in Kosovo, 202–3, 211; demonstrations of in Russia, 215–16; in European consensus in the post-cold war era, 218; and warfare in the zone of the OSCE, 228; as the cause of warfare in Western Europe, 235–36; and conservative elites/values, 236–37; of European militaries, 236–67; and "socialist internationalism," 238; threat to in Europe, 243; as foe of human rights, 244; and statism, 248–49; and the Black Sea Fleet, 270; and Russian opposition to democracy, 285; and Russian opposition to Russia's sheepish foreign

policy, 286; and support for the newly elected Federal Assembly in Russia, 286–87; and NATO enlargement, 315–16; and criticism of Yeltsin during Balkan crisis, 320–21

National Missile Defense (NMD) shield: and U.S. security in Northeast Asia, 185

National Party, the: in Africa, 84, 90

National People's Army: denationalization of, 241–42

National Security and Defense Council (of Ukraine), 270, 275

National Security Council (NSC) (U.S.), 34, 36, 39

National Sport Foundation, 331

NATO (North Atlantic Treaty Organization): and the CIA, 36; and Africa, 79–80, 82; and opposition to its attacks on Yugoslavia, 173; and membership of Poland, Hungary, and the Czech Republic, 194–95; and European security, 195–96, 208–11, 237; and the U.S.'s excessive role in, 197; and France's ties with the U.S. in, 198; diminished role of, 198; and intervention in Yugoslavia, 199; and intervention in Kosovo, 16, 199, 218, 334; and Russia's disdain for, 200; and suspicion of its policies, 200; and the U.S. Congress, 102–3; and the Bush administration, 205; and Russian involvement in, 206, 304; and war in the Balkans, 207; and multilateralism, 209; as a peacekeeper/peacemaker, 209, 304; and insulation strategy, 209–10; and intervention in Azerbaijan-Armenian war, 212; and Ukraine and Baltic states' integration into, 213; as model for Russian military maneuvers, 216–17; and European integration, 218; and unilateralism, 218–19; and the Helsinki Accords, 228–30; original treaty of, 229–30; and the Brussels Syndrome, 230–50; and division of labor, 231–32; and promotion of foreign trade, 232–33; and European "free riders," 233–34; and military technology, 234; and low defense budgets, 234–35; advantage of fu-